CIMA

PRACTICE & REVISION KIT

STRATEGIC
PAPER E3
ENTERPRISE STRATEGY

Our Kit has a **brand new look** for CIMA's new 2010 syllabus.

In this Kit we:

- Discuss the **best strategies** for revising and taking your E3 exam
- Show you how to be well prepared for the **2010 exams**
- Give you **lots of great guidance** on tackling questions
- Demonstrate how you can **build your own exams**
- Provide you with **two** mock exams

FOR EXAMS IN 2010

First edition January 2010

ISBN 9780 7517 7520 4

British Library Cataloguing-in-Publication Data
A catalogue record for this book
is available from the British Library

Published by

BPP Learning Media Ltd
BPP House, Aldine Place
London W12 8AA

www.bpp.com/learningmedia

Printed in the United Kingdom

> Your learning materials, published by BPP Learning Media Ltd, are printed on paper sourced from sustainable, managed forests.

All our rights reserved. No part of this publication may be reproduced, stored in a retrieval system or transmitted, in any form or by any means, electronic, mechanical, photocopying, recording or otherwise, without the prior written permission of BPP Learning Media Ltd.

We are grateful to the Chartered Institute of Management Accountants for permission to reproduce past examination questions. The answers to past examination questions have been prepared by BPP Learning Media Ltd.

©
BPP Learning Media Ltd
2010

A note about copyright

Dear Customer

What does the little © mean and why does it matter?

Your market-leading BPP books, course materials and e-learning materials do not write and update themselves. People write them: on their own behalf or as employees of an organisation that invests in this activity. Copyright law protects their livelihoods. It does so by creating rights over the use of the content.

Breach of copyright is a form of theft – as well as being a criminal offence in some jurisdictions, it is potentially a serious breach of professional ethics.

With current technology, things might seem a bit hazy but, basically, without the express permission of BPP Learning Media:

- Photocopying our materials is a breach of copyright
- Scanning, ripcasting or conversion of our digital materials into different file formats, uploading them to facebook or emailing them to your friends is a breach of copyright

You can, of course, sell your books, in the form in which you have bought them – once you have finished with them. (Is this fair to your fellow students? We update for a reason.) But the e-products are sold on a single user licence basis: we do not supply 'unlock' codes to people who have bought them second-hand.

And what about outside the UK? BPP Learning Media strives to make our materials available at prices students can afford by local printing arrangements, pricing policies and partnerships which are clearly listed on our website. A tiny minority ignore this and indulge in criminal activity by illegally photocopying our material or supporting organisations that do. If they act illegally and unethically in one area, can you really trust them?

Contents

	Page
Finding questions and using the Practice and Revision Kit	
Question index	iv
Topic index	vi
Using your BPP Learning Media Practice and Revision Kit	viii
Passing E3	
Revising E3	ix
Passing the E3 exam	x
The exam paper	xiii
What the examiner means	xiv
Planning your question practice	
BPP's question plan	xv
Build your own exams	xx
Questions and answers	
Questions	3
Answers	71

Exam practice

Mock exam 1
- Questions — 269
- Plan of attack — 283
- Answers — 285

Mock exam 2
- Questions — 299
- Plan of attack — 313
- Answers — 315

Mathematical tables — 333

Review form & free prize draw

Stop press
Because of publishing deadlines, BPP Learning Media has been unable to include CIMA's pilot paper for the 2010 syllabus in this Kit. BPP Learning Media will be posting its solutions to pilot papers online before the May 2010 exams. Please see http://www.bpp.com/learningmedia/news-and-events/cima2010.asp for details.

Question index

The headings in this checklist/index indicate the main topics of questions, but questions often cover several different topics.

Questions set under the old syllabus's *Management Accounting – Business Strategy (MABS) exam* are included because their style and content are similar to those that appear in the Paper E3 exam.

	Marks	Time allocation Mins	Page number Question	Page number Answer
Strategic models				
1 Industry analysis (MABS, 5/05)	25	45	3	71
2 Qualispecs	25	45	3	73
3 Automobile components (MABS, 11/07)	25	45	4	77
Parts A & B: Strategic development and strategic options				
4 Digwell explorations	25	45	5	80
5 CTC – Strategic objectives (MABS, 11/06)	25	45	5	84
6 EEE – Stakeholder analysis (MABS, 11/06)	25	45	6	87
7 Island stakeholders (MABS, 5/07)	25	45	7	89
8 Genetically modified plants (MABS, 5/09)	25	45	7	93
9 Tobacco planning (MABS, 11/05)	25	45	8	96
10 Timber company (MABS, 11/07)	25	45	8	98
11 FFF – Competitor analysis (MABS, 11/06, adapted)	25	45	9	102
12 Water charity (MABS, 5/08)	25	45	10	104
13 Scenario planning (MABS, 5/07)	25	45	10	108
14 GC	25	45	11	112
15 Value activities (MABS, 5/06)	25	45	12	114
16 Benchmarking in a charity (MABS, 5/05)	25	45	12	117
17 Product portfolio (MABS, 5/06)	25	45	13	120
18 Chemical manufacturer (MABS, 11/06)	25	45	14	124
19 Competitor benchmarking	25	45	14	126
20 Printing company (MABS, 5/09)	25	45	15	129
21 Conglomerate value (MABS, 5/08)	25	45	15	131
22 Telecommunications joint venture (MABS, 5/09)	25	45	17	135
23 Plastics manufacturer (MABS, 11/07)	25	45	17	138
24 Biotechnology company (MABS, 5/08)	25	45	18	142
25 Internet strategy (MABS, Pilot paper)	25	45	19	149
26 Sole supplier (MABS, 11/05)	25	45	19	152
27 IT outsourcing (MABS, 5/05)	25	45	20	155
28 Supplying and outsourcing (MABS, 5/07)	25	45	20	158

Introduction

	Marks	Time allocation Mins	Page number Question	Answer
Part C: Change Management				
29 Contact Services	25	45	22	162
30 Brian Jolson	25	45	23	165
31 Heritage Trust	25	45	23	168
32 Goldcorn	25	45	25	172
33 ChemiCo	25	45	26	175
34 ProfTech	25	45	27	178
Part D: Implementation of Strategic Plans				
35 Operating theatre (MABS, 5/06)	25	45	28	182
36 Transfer prices	25	45	28	184
37 Royal Botanical (MABS, Pilot paper)	25	45	29	186
38 Management styles (MABS, 11/07)	25	45	29	189
39 Performance measurement (MABS, 5/07)	25	45	30	192
40 International acquisition (MABS, 5/08)	25	45	30	195
41 Computer company (MABS, 11/08)	25	45	31	199
42 Global environmental charity (MABS, 5/09)	25	45	32	203
Practice scenarios				
43 Pipeco (MABS, 5/05)	50	90	33	205
44 Island transport (MABS, 11/05)	50	90	34	209
45 Specialist cars (MABS, 5/06)	50	90	36	214
46 AAA (MABS, 11/06)	50	90	38	218
47 AFR (MABS, 5/07)	50	90	40	224
48 Food manufacturer (MABS, 11/07)	50	90	41	230
49 Machine components (MABS, 5/08)	50	90	43	234
50 Training College (MABS, 11/08)	50	90	45	239
51 European Bank (MABS, 5/09)	50	90	48	245
Section A Case studies				
52 ReuseR	50	90	50	249
53 Domusco	50	90	55	254
54 Zubinos	50	90	61	260

Mock exam 1
Questions 55-58

Mock exam 2
Questions 59-62

Planning your question practice
Our guidance from page xv shows you how to organise your question practice, either by attempting questions from each syllabus area or by building your own exams – tackling questions as a series of practice exams.

Topic index

Listed below are the key Paper E3 syllabus topics and the numbers of the questions in this Kit covering those topics.

If you need to concentrate your practice and revision on certain topics or if you want to attempt all available questions that refer to a particular subject you will find this index useful.

Note: Case Study questions tend to cover a wide range of topics. However, parts of these questions have been listed when they deal with a specific topic.

Syllabus topic	Question numbers
Balanced scorecard	37, 41, 42, 46(a)
Benchmarking	16, 19, 52(d)
Business process re-engineering	35
Change and communication	32
Change and context	29, 30
Change and culture	31, 38
Change management styles	30, 34
Competitive advantage of nations	3
Competitive strategies	Mock exam 2 (Qn 1(c))
Competitor analysis	11
Corporate appraisal (SWOT)	2
Corporate social responsibility (CSR)	8, 10, 17 (c), 53(c)
Customer account profitability	48
Data mining, data warehousing	Mock Exam 2 (Qn 2)
Disposals and divestment	21
E-business and e-commerce	25, 49, 54(d)
Environmental analysis	1, 12, 13 (a)
Ethics and social responsibility	4, 10
Force field analysis	34(a)
Franchises	54
Gap analysis	48 (a)
Implementing change	32, 33, 34, 38, 52(c)
Information systems	26 (b), 35
Industry lifecycle	20
IS strategy	Mock Exam 1 (Qn 2)
IT strategy	27
Joint ventures	22, Mock Exam 1 (Qn 1)
Knowledge management	46 (c)
Leading change	31
Management styles	38
Mission statement	20, 54 (a)
Nature of change	Mock Exam 1 (Qn 1)
Organisational culture	31
Outsourcing	27, 28 (b)
Performance measurement	37, 39, 40, 53(a)
Portfolio analysis, product portfolio	14, 17, 47, 50
Process innovation	35
Product life cycle	17
Relationship marketing	43(c), 51, Mock Exam 2 (Qn 2)
Resistance to change	31, 32, 34, 42, Mock Exam 2 (Qn 3)

Syllabus topic	Question numbers
Scenario planning	13 (b)
Stage models of change	Mock Exam 2 (Qn 4)
Stakeholders	4, 6, 7, 8, 33(a), Mock Exam 1 (Qn 4), Mock Exam 2 (Qn 1)
Strategic allegiances	33(b)
Strategic information	3 (b), 40
Strategic objectives	5
Strategic options	10, 18, 21, 23, 24
Strategic planning	5, 9, Mock Exam 1 (Qn 2)
Supply chain management	26 (a), 28
Transfer prices	36
Triggers for change	Mock Exam 2 (Qn 4)
Value chain	15, Mock Exam 2 (Qn 3)

Using your BPP Learning Media Practice and Revision Kit

Tackling revision and the exam

You can significantly improve your chances of passing by tackling revision and the exam in the right ways. Our advice is based on feedback from CIMA. We focus on Paper E3; we discuss revising the syllabus, what to do (and what not to do) in the exam, how to approach different types of question and ways of obtaining easy marks.

Selecting questions

We provide signposts to help you plan your revision.

- A full **question index**
- A **topic index**, listing all the questions that cover key topics, so that you can locate the questions that provide practice on these topics, and see the different ways in which they might be examined
- **BPP's question plan**, highlighting the most important questions
- **Build your own exams**, showing you how you can practise questions in a series of exams

Making the most of question practice

We realise that you need more than questions and model answers to get the most from your question practice.

- Our **Top tips** provide essential advice on tackling questions and presenting answers
- We show you how you can pick up **Easy marks** on questions, as picking up all readily available marks can make the difference between passing and failing
- We include **marking guides** to show you what the examiner rewards
- We summarise **Examiner's comments** to show you how students coped with the questions
- We refer to the **BPP 2009 Study Text** for detailed coverage of the topics covered in each question

Attempting mock exams

There are two mock exams that provide practice at coping with the pressures of the exam day. We strongly recommend that you attempt them under exam conditions, because they reflect the question styles and syllabus coverage of the exam. To help you get the most out of doing these exams, we provide guidance on how you should have approached the whole exam.

Our other products

BPP Learning Media also offers these products for practising and revising the E3 exam:

Passcards	Summarising what you should know in visual, easy to remember, form
Success CDs	Covering the vital elements of the E3 syllabus in less than 90 minutes and also containing exam hints to help you fine tune your strategy
i-Pass	Providing computer-based testing in a variety of formats, ideal for self-assessment
Interactive Passcards	Allowing you to learn actively with a clear visual format summarising what you must know

You can purchase these products by visiting www.bpp.com/mybpp

Revising E3

The E3 exam

This will be a time-pressured exam that combines a relatively small amount of calculations with more wide-ranging discussions of aspects of business strategy. It is very important that you have a good understanding of the process of designing and implementing strategy as a whole, that you can appreciate the strategic issues being identified in a question.

Topics to revise

You need to be comfortable with **all areas of the syllabus** as questions, particularly compulsory Question 1, will often span a number of syllabus areas. Question spotting will absolutely **not work** on this paper. It is better to go into the exam knowing a reasonable amount about most of the syllabus rather than concentrating on a few topics.

Interaction with the competitive environment

- Strategies are developed in a context, so it is important to understand how an organisation's external environment and its stakeholders affect strategy development.
- Make sure you also understand the different approaches organisations can take to strategic planning: in particular, appreciating the differences between the rational planning model and more emergent strategies.
- Information systems (IS) and information technology (IT) can have a significant impact on an organisation and its competitive position.

Evaluating strategic position and strategic choices

- Alongside external factors and context, the internal resources and capabilities of an organisation also shape its strategic options
- You need to be prepared to identifying different strategic options, making use of key models such as Ansoff's matrix or Porter's generic strategies
- You may need to evaluate the appropriateness of different strategic options for an organisation
- You need to have a good general understanding of the process of strategy formulation

Change management

- Implementing a strategy is likely to involve tools and techniques associated with change management, and you may need to evaluate the tools, techniques and strategies an organisation is using to manage a change process
- You may also need to recommend how change can be managed successfully to support an organisation's strategy

Implementation of strategic plans and performance evaluation

- Performance measurement is very important for an organisation to be able to evaluate the performance implications of a given strategy, and whether it is delivering the benefits an organisation hoped it would.
- Performance measures can be both financial and non-financial
- An organisation may need to improve its knowledge management strategies or its information systems to provide the information it needs to monitor performance effectively.

Question practice

Question practice under timed conditions is essential, so that you get used to the pressures of answering exam questions in **limited time**. In your practice, you need to get used not only to applying your knowledge to the specific context given by the scenario, but also to allocating your time between the different requirements in each question. It's particularly important to do questions from both sections of the paper in full to see how the numerical and written elements balance in longer questions.

Question practice is also important so that you get used to **applying your knowledge** to the problems given in question scenarios. You need to make sure your answers are directly relevant to the scenario, rather than describing theories and models more generally. Practising questions is an invaluable way of acquiring this skill.

Passing the E3 exam

Avoiding weaknesses

You will enhance your chances significantly if you ensure you avoid these mistakes:

- Little or no time spent studying the preseen material ahead of the exam
- Failure to read the question and the question requirements
- Failure to pick up key points from the scenario, eg size of organisation, history and culture of organisation, objectives and goals of organisation
- Failure to apply knowledge to the specific circumstances of the scenario
- Failure to make realistic recommendations or practical suggestions
- Time management – spending excessive time on strong areas or too long on areas you struggle with
- Poor English, structure and presentation

To help you avoid these weaknesses, it is important you get into good habits early on. Five such good habits are:

- **Plan your answer carefully**, making sure you identify ALL the requirements of the question
- **Identify the key verbs** (evaluate, discuss etc) used in the question, and make sure your answer fulfils the requirements of the verbs. (A list of the verbs CIMA use in their exams is included at page xiv.)
- Make sure the points you make are **relevant to the question**; for example, do they help explain what a company should do, why it should do it, or how it could do it? Examiners' comments from exams under the old syllabus reveal a frustration at candidates' apparent inability to answer the question set. To score well in this exam, you have to produce an answer which is relevant to the question actually set.
- Only use **theory** if you are **specifically asked** to; do not waste time writing all you know about a theory when you have not been asked to do so.
- Mostly importantly of all, **tailor your answer specifically to the question** and the organisation described in the scenario. Make sure you are giving **practical advice** which is appropriate for that organisation, not just general business advice. One way to help with this is to regularly refer to the name of the organisation in the scenario, or its key personnel, in your answer.

Using the preseen material

Although you should do some research on the preseen material for the Section A case study in advance of the exam, the focus for your answer should come from the **unseen** material.

If the research you have done based on the preseen material is not relevant when you see the unseen material, don't worry.

The main mark-scoring points will come from the **unseen** material. As a result, the main focus of your attention when planning and writing your answer should be on the unseen material. Only include material from the preseen – or from your research on it – if it is **specifically relevant** to the unseen material and the question requirements set.

Using the reading time

We recommend that you spend the first part of the reading time choosing the Section B questions you will do, on the basis of your knowledge of syllabus areas tested and whether you can fulfil **all** the question requirements. We suggest that you should note on the paper any ideas that come to you about these questions.

However, don't spend the reading time going through and analysing the Section B question requirements in detail; leave that until the three hours writing time. Instead you should be looking to spend as much of the reading time as possible looking at the **Section A scenario**, and in particular identifying the significance of the additional information you have been given in the **unseen material**.

Whilst you're reading the paper, remember to keep thinking about strategic issues for every scenario that you read.

Choosing which questions to answer first

Spending most of your reading time on the Section A scenario will mean that you can get underway with planning and writing your answer to the Section A question as soon as the three hours start. It will give you more actual writing time during the one and a half hours you should allocate to it, and it's writing time that you'll need.

During the second half of the exam, you can put Section A aside and concentrate on the two Section B questions you've chosen.

However, our recommendations are not inflexible. If you really think the Section A question looks a lot harder than the Section B questions you've chosen, then do those first, but **DON'T run over time on them.** You must leave yourself an hour and a half to tackle the Section A question. When you come back to it, having had initial thoughts during the reading time, you should be able to generate more ideas and find the question is not as bad as it looks.

Numerical analysis and computation

Although the majority of the marks available in E3 will be for discussion and analysis, the exam is likely to offer some marks for the analysis of numerical data, and for performing calculations. It is unlikely that the calculations themselves will be particularly complex, but it will be very important that you understand the significance of the numerical data and use it to **support the strategic arguments** in your answer.

Knowledge and application

You will need to bring two different professional attributes to this exam to score well.

The first, simpler one, is **technical knowledge**. You need to be familiar with the key models and theories used at all stages of the strategic process. However, the emphasis here is on 'key': you will not be expected to discuss obscure academic ideas in detail.

The second attribute is the ability to **apply these basic ideas**. As a general principle, there are likely to be only a few marks available for knowledge itself. The emphasis in strategic level exams is on using knowledge to analyse and resolve practical problems. When analysing a problem, you need to decide which **models** and **ideas** offer help in solving it, explain how they do so, and then make **practical suggestions** for future action.

This second requirement (application) is far more difficult to master than the first (knowledge). You cannot acquire the ability to apply ideas simply by reading or even by learning things by heart. Most people find that they must practise the skills of problem analysis and application by tackling example questions.

Remember that any strategies you recommend must be suitable and feasible for the organisation, and must be acceptable to shareholders, managers and other key stakeholders.

Depth of explanation

Remember that depth of discussion is also important. Discussing a point will often involve writing a paragraph containing 2-3 sentences not simply giving a list of ideas.. Each paragraph should:

- Make a point
- Explain the point in sufficient detail as required by the action verb
- Relate the point to the scenario and demonstrate why it is important to the organisation in the scenario.

As a general guideline, a well-explained point can be worth up to 2 marks.

However, simply **identifying** a relevant point is only likely to score ½ mark or 1 mark. To score all the marks available you will have to **discuss, explain** or **evaluate** the point as required by the action verb in the question requirement.

Remember that the marking schemes for discussion questions will be fairly general, and you will gain credit for all relevant points. Good discussion focused on the question scenario, with evaluation of pros and cons supported by examples, will score well.

Gaining the easy marks

Unsurprisingly perhaps for a strategic level paper, it is not possible to say where there will definitely be easy marks. There will be a small number of marks available for purely technical knowledge, so you should aim to get these. There may also be some relatively easy marks for doing some numerical calculations and providing sensible analysis based on those calculations.

However, in the main, you are likely to gain the majority of the relatively easier marks, (or to avoid losing easy marks) through following certain basic techniques:

- Setting out answers clearly and professionally, and writing short, punchy paragraphs

- Clearly labelling the points you make in discussions so that the marker can identify them all rather than getting lost in the detail

- Providing answers in the form requested, (eg producing a report if a report is asked for); using the correct level of details for the question verb used; and giving recommendations if required

The exam paper

Format of the paper

		Number of marks
Section A:	A maximum of 4 compulsory questions, totalling 50 marks, all relating to a preseen study and further new unseen case material	50
Section B:	2 out of 3 questions, 25 marks each	50
		100

Time allowed: 3 hours, plus 20 minutes reading time

All three syllabus subjects at strategic level (E3, P3 and F3) must be studied concurrently. The *preseen* case study material for the Section A question is the same for the three subjects.

CIMA guidance

CIMA has indicated that credit will be given for focusing on the right principles and making practical evaluations and recommendations in a variety of different business scenarios, including manufacturing, retailing and service organisations, and including both the public and private sectors of the economy.

A likely weakness of answers is excessive focus on details. Plausible alternative answers could be given to many strategic questions, so model answers should not be regarded as all-inclusive.

Preseen

CIMA has indicated that they do not want students spending excessive amounts of time doing research based on the preseen material. The exam questions will be specific, and so there will be few marks earned from general background research.

Marks will be earned by answering the specific questions set, which will draw heavily on material provided in the unseen case study.

Numerical content

The paper is likely to have about a 10-15% numerical content, and questions may also require candidates to analyse and interpret numerical data.

Breadth of question coverage

Questions in *both* sections of the paper may cover more than one syllabus area. This feature, coupled with the very limited amount of choice you have in which questions to answer in this exam, suggests it will be very unwise to try to question spot for E3.

Knowledge from other syllabuses

Candidates should also use their knowledge from other Strategic level papers. One aim of this paper is to prepare candidates for the TOPCIMA case study.

Pilot paper

CIMA have provided a specimen exam paper for the exam, and you can view this on their website: www.cimaglobal.com.

What the examiner means

The table below has been prepared by CIMA to help you interpret exam questions.

Learning objective	Verbs used	Definition	Examples in the Kit
1 Knowledge			
What you are expected to know	• List	• Make a list of	
	• State	• Express, fully or clearly, the details of/facts of	
	• Define	• Give the exact meaning of	
2 Comprehension			
What you are expected to understand	• Describe	• Communicate the key features of	1
	• Distinguish	• Highlight the differences between	
	• Explain	• Make clear or intelligible/state the meaning or purpose of	23 (b)
	• Identify	• Recognise, establish or select after consideration	4 (b)
	• Illustrate	• Use an example to describe or explain something	
3 Application			
How you are expected to apply your knowledge	• Apply	• Put to practical use	
	• Calculate/compute	• Ascertain or reckon mathematically	48 (c)
	• Demonstrate	• Prove the certainty or exhibit by practical means	
	• Prepare	• Make or get ready for use	37 (a)
	• Reconcile	• Make or prove consistent/compatible	
	• Solve	• Find an answer to	
	• Tabulate	• Arrange in a table	
4 Analysis			
How you are expected to analyse the detail of what you have learned	• Analyse	• Examine in detail the structure of	6 (b)
	• Categorise	• Place into a defined class or division	
	• Compare and contrast	• Show the similarities and/or differences between	
	• Construct	• Build up or complete	
	• Discuss	• Examine in detail by argument	7
	• Interpret	• Translate into intelligible or familiar terms	
	• Prioritise	• Place in order of priority or sequence for action	
	• Produce	• Create or bring into existence	5 (b)
5 Evaluation			
How you are expected to use your learning to evaluate, make decisions or recommendations	• Advise	• Counsel, inform or notify	5 (c)
	• Evaluate	• Appraise or assess the value of	13
	• Recommend	• Propose a course of action	9

Planning your question practice

We have already stressed that question practice should be right at the centre of your revision. Whilst you will spend some time looking at your notes and the Paper E3 Passcards, you should spend the majority of your revision time practising questions.

We recommend two ways in which you can practise questions.

- Use **BPP Learning Media's question plan** to work systematically through the syllabus and attempt key and other questions on a section-by-section basis
- **Build your own exams** – attempt the questions as a series of practice exams

These ways are suggestions and simply following them is no guarantee of success. You or your college may prefer an alternative but equally valid approach.

BPP's question plan

The plan below requires you to devote a **minimum of 30 hours** to revision of Paper E3. Any time you can spend over and above this should only increase your chances of success.

Review your notes and the chapter summaries in the Paper E3 **Passcards** for each section of the syllabus.

Answer the key questions for that section. These questions have boxes round the question number in the table below and you should answer them in full. Even if you are short of time you must attempt these questions if you want to pass the exam. You should complete your answers without referring to our solutions.

Attempt the other questions in that section. For some questions we have suggested that you prepare **answer plans or do the calculations** rather than full solutions. Planning an answer means that you should spend about 20% of the time allowance for the questions brainstorming the question and drawing up a list of points to be included in the answer.

Attempt Mock exams 1 and 2 under strict exam conditions.

Syllabus section	2009 Passcards chapters	Questions in this Kit	Comments	Done ☑
Strategic models (b/f management level E2)		2	Answer in full. Corporate appraisal (SWOT analysis) is a key aspect of business strategy. The important point to note in (a) is that simply listing factors will not score well. You must note the second part of the requirement; to 'discuss' the key strategic challenges facing the company.	☐
		3	Prepare an answer plan for this question (from the MABS, November 2007 exam). You should identify from the scenario that Porter's diamond is the relevant theory for (a), and this is brought forward knowledge from E2. However, you need to make sure the location factors you discuss relate directly to the company in question. Part (b) is a very practical question; commercial awareness is important here (and in E3 as a whole).	☐
Strategic development & strategic options	1-8	5	Answer in full. A key part of answering this question well is to make sure your answer is tailored directly to the company given in the scenario. General discussions around objectives (part a) and strategic planning (part c) will score poorly.	☐
		6	Answer in full. Stakeholder analysis has historically been a popular exam topic. However, simply producing Mendelow's matrix is not the way to approach stakeholder questions at strategic level. Notice again the importance of context in part (b), and the links between (b) and (c). You need to make sure your recommendation in (c) is consistent with your analysis in (b).	☐
		7	Prepare an answer plan. This question is another one about stakeholders, but it is tricky because you must avoid duplicating ideas between (a) and (b), whilst making sure your answer relates to the scenario. This means that careful planning is required.	☐
		8	Prepare an answer plan. This question combines ideas about stakeholders and corporate social responsibility. Make sure you address the specific groups and issues identified in the question.	☐
		10	Answer in full. This question addresses the topical issue of corporate social responsibility. However, note this is a business strategy exam so you need to balance sustainability and CSR issues with an organisation's objective of delivering value for its owners.	☐
		12	Answer in full. Environmental analysis is another core aspect of strategy development. However, once again, note you are not asked to describe theories or models but to explain how an organisation would benefit from doing an environmental analysis. As always, make sure your answer is specifically related to the organisation (a charity) described in the scenario.	☐
		13	Prepare an answer plan for part (b) only. Scenario planning is an important strategic technique you need to be familiar with. This is quite a factual question, so it will demonstrate whether or not you know the stages involved in scenario planning.	☐

Syllabus section	2009 Passcards chapters	Questions in this Kit	Comments	Done ☑
		15	Answer in full. This is a good question about the value chain. Remember you get marks by applying your knowledge to the scenario rather than simply describing the value chain. Also, make sure your answer to part (b) follows from your answer to part (a).	☐
		16	Answer in full. This question tests your knowledge of benchmarking, and also your ability to apply it to a specific scenario.	☐
		18	Answer in full. Notice the way the three parts of this question inter-relate: (a) identify the threats the company faces; (b) suggest possible ways the company may respond to them; (c) recommend the best way to respond. Make sure your arguments are consistent throughout the three parts.	☐
		21	Answer in full. This is another question where the action verb is 'evaluate', so you need to provide a balanced argument as to whether the assertions made are valid or not. Part (c) is important – looking at the strategic options for disposals (as opposed to the Ansoff matrix and options for growth which students often seem more familiar with).	☐
		22	Answer in full. This question tests your knowledge of joint ventures, and the risks of expanding through a joint venture. However, make sure you understand the requirement for part (b) very carefully: you are asked to discuss the benefits for country C rather then the joint venture companies.	☐
		23	Prepare an answer plan. This question, from the MABS, November 2007 exam, follows a relatively familiar pattern. Part (a(i)) asks you to discuss the difficulties a company is facing, then (a(ii)) asks you to identify, and evaluate strategies to deal with them, before finally recommending the most appropriate.	☐
		24	Answer in full. This question is based around the 'suitability, acceptability, feasibility' framework used for evaluating strategic options. As always, make sure you think about the specific context of the scenario and who the key stakeholders are.	☐
		26	Prepare an answer plan. This is a good example of a question which is essentially practical rather than theoretical. To score well, you need to read the requirements carefully, apply the action verbs correctly (eg evaluate), and relate your answers to the scenario.	☐
		28	Prepare an answer plan for this question. Many organisations face decisions about whether to outsource or supply in house so the requirement here (to assess the advantages or disadvantages of these decisions) is looking at a very realistic problem. Make sure your answer includes a balance of advantages and disadvantages, and you explain why the proposals could be good or bad for the company.	☐

Syllabus section	2009 Passcards chapters	Questions in this Kit	Comments	Done ☑
Change management	9 - 10	30	Answer in full. Pat (a) of this question looks at the context of change management, while part (b) looks more specifically at styles of change management.	☐
		31	Prepare an answer plan. Part (a) is a test of knowledge, but parts (b) and (c) need to be related to the scenario.	☐
		32	Answer in full. This question looks at a number of different aspects of change management: types of change (part (a)), communicating change (part (b)), and resistance to change (part (c)).	☐
		33	Answer in full. This question combines a number of strategic ideas: stakeholders, strategic alliances and change implementation. Make sure your answers to all the parts relate specifically to the scenario and don't become a generic discussion.	☐
		34	Answer in full. Part (a) requires you to apply an important change management model. Parts (b) and (c) are quite practical – why is change being resisted, but how can that resistance be overcome so that change can be implemented successfully?	☐
Implementation of strategic plans	11 – 13	35	Prepare an answer plan, but review the solution thoroughly if you are unhappy with this question. When this question was tested under the old syllabus (MABS, 5/06) it was answered very badly, so make sure you are comfortable with these topics.	☐
		38	Answer in full. This question looks at management styles and change management. Make sure you pay attention to the scenario, in particular noting who is being affected by the changes.	☐
		39	Answer in full. This question tests your ability to apply your knowledge of performance measurement to a scenario. Make sure your answer is practical and tailored to the organisation in the scenario.	☐
		40	Answer in full. This question addresses the difficulties of performance measurement in international divisions following an acquisition; so you need to be aware of the limitations of measurement techniques (ROI; RI) as well as their uses for a company.	☐
		41	The balanced scorecard is an important performance measurement tool. Make sure the measures you recommend in part (b) are specifically relevant to DD rather then being general measures.	☐
		42	Answer in full. This is another question dealing with the balances scorecard (part (a)), but coupling it with change management issues (parts (b) and (c)).	☐

Syllabus section	2009 Passcards chapters	Questions in this Kit	Comments	Done ☑
Preseen and unseen case studies		52	Answer in full.	☐
		53	Answer in full.	☐
		54	Answer in full.	☐
			Questions 52 – 54 mirror the format of the actual Section A questions in the E3 exam, so they are essential practice for this paper.	

Build your own exams

Having revised your notes and the BPP Passcards, you can attempt the questions in the Kit as a series of practice exams, making them up yourself or using the mock exams that we have listed below.

	Practice exams		
Section A			
1	52	53	54
Section B			
2	10	21	8
3	24	33	15
4	41	42	38

Whichever practice exams you use, you must also attempt **Mock exams 1 and 2** at the end of your revision.

QUESTIONS

Questions   3

STRATEGIC MODELS

Questions 1-3 cover key strategic models which are assumed knowledge brought forward from E2.

1 Industry analysis (*MABS*, 5/05)   45 mins

2XA is an established light engineering manufacturer operating in a single country within the European Union (EU). With 300 employees, the majority of whom are employed in the manufacturing processes, the company is run like a large family business. 2XA supplies components to specialist car manufacturers and manufacturers of light aircraft, all of which are small companies. 2XA has had the same customers for a number of years and there are many personal friendships between the senior management of 2XA and those who own or manage those customer companies.

Since most of 2XA's sales are a result of repeat business it does not actively market its products. What marketing it currently does consists of an occasional advert in trade magazines and attendance at trade fairs where the Sales Director, and a few office staff, offer light refreshments to their existing customers and anyone who stops at their stand.

In the past two years 2XA has started to lose customers to more aggressive suppliers from neighbouring countries, which have entered 2XA's home market. The board of directors is concerned at the loss of business and is not sure why it has happened. It has decided that it is time to become more proactive in its approach to the market and feels the need to know more about both the competitive environment and the competitors themselves.

Required

As the Management Accountant you have been asked to:

(a) Explain what is meant by industry analysis using any models you consider appropriate.   **(5 marks)**

(b) Describe the information that 2XA might include in such an analysis.   **(10 marks)**

(c) Advise the directors as to the possible sources of the information which 2XA could use in performing an industry analysis.   **(10 marks)**

(Total = 25 marks)

2 Qualispecs   45 mins

Qualispecs has a reputation for quality, traditional products. It has a group of optician shops, both rented and owned, from which it sells its spectacles. Recently, it has suffered intense competition and eroding customer loyalty, but a new chief executive has joined from one of its major rivals *Fastglass*.

Fastglass is capturing *Qualispecs*' market through partnership with a high-street shopping group. These shops install mini-labs in which prescriptions for spectacles are dispensed within an hour. Some competitors have successfully experimented with designer frames and sunglasses. Others have reduced costs through new computer-aided production methods.

Qualispecs has continued to operate as it always has, letting the product 'speak for itself' and failing to utilise advances in technology. Although production costs remain high, *Qualispecs* is financially secure and has large cash reserves. Fortunately, the country's most popular sports star recently received a prestigious international award wearing a pair of *Qualispecs*' spectacles.

The new Chief Executive has established as a priority the need for improved financial performance. Following a review she discovers that:

(i)   targets are set centrally and shops report monthly. Site profitability varies enormously, and fixed costs are high in shopping malls

(ii) shops exercise no control over job roles, working conditions, and pay rates

(iii) individual staff pay is increased annually according to a pre-determined pay scale

Everyone also receives a small one-off payment based on group financial performance.

Market analysts predict a slowdown in the national economy but feel that consumer spending will continue to increase, particularly among 18-30 year olds.

Required

(a) Produce a corporate appraisal of Qualispecs, taking account of internal and external factors, and discuss the key strategic challenges facing the company. **(16 marks)**

(b) Corporate appraisal offers a 'snapshot' of the present. In order to focus on the future, there is a need to develop realistic policies and programmes. Recommend, with reasons, strategies from your appraisal that would enable Qualispecs to build on its past success. **(9 marks)**

(Total = 25 marks)

3 Automobile components (*MABS*, 11/07) — 45 mins

G supplies electronic components to the automobile industry by exporting from the home country in which it is currently based. The company has recently set up a research facility in the home country to develop hydrogen fuel cells. The concept of hydrogen fuel cells has attracted a great deal of interest from the environmental lobby since it offers the prospect of very environmentally friendly vehicles. The market for these vehicles is in the development stage and there have been relatively few sales so far for this new technology. G hopes that the current pressure from environmental groups and governments will lead to large volume sales.

Increasingly, electronic component manufacturers are under pressure to manufacture close to the locations of their customers, the automobile manufacturers.

The research and development (R&D) director has decided that there is a need to open a research facility abroad, to work in partnership with the facility in the home country and capitalise on the benefits that a foreign base could offer. If this venture were successful, G would open a manufacturing facility next to the proposed overseas R&D base.

The board of directors recognises that different countries will offer different potential advantages and disadvantages. It has been decided that the ideal characteristics and factors for the chosen country should be determined, so that potential choices can be screened effectively before a final decision is made.

Required

(a) Advise what ideal characteristics and factors should be present in the chosen country. **(15 marks)**

(b) Recommend the nature and sources of information that G should use when evaluating potential countries. **(10 marks)**

(Total = 25 marks)

Questions 5

STRATEGY DEVELOPMENT AND STRATEGIC OPTIONS

Questions 4-28 cover strategy development and strategic options, the subjects of Parts A and B of the BPP Study Text for Paper E3.

4 Digwell Explorations — 45 mins

Eastborough is a large region with a rugged, beautiful coastline where rare birds have recently settled on undisturbed cliffs. Since mining ceased 150 years ago, its main industries have been agriculture and fishing. However, today, many communities in Eastborough suffer high unemployment. Government initiatives for regeneration through tourism have met with little success as the area has poor road networks, unsightly derelict buildings and dirty beaches. *Digwell Explorations*, a listed company, has a reputation for maximizing shareholder returns and has discovered substantial tin reserves in Eastborough. With new technology, mining could be profitable, provide jobs and boost the economy. A number of interest and pressure groups have, however, been vocal in opposing the scheme.

Digwell Explorations, after much lobbying, has just received government permission to undertake mining. It could face difficulties in proceeding because of the likely activity of a group called the Eastborough Protection Alliance. This group includes wildlife protection representatives, villagers worried about the potential increase in traffic congestion and noise, environmentalists, and anti-capitalism groups.

Required

(a) Discuss the ethical issues that should have been considered by the government when granting permission for mining to go ahead. Explain the conflicts between the main stakeholder groups. **(12 marks)**

(b) By use of some (mapping) framework, analyse how the interest and power of pressure and stakeholder groups can be understood. Based on this analysis, identify how *Digwell Explorations* might respond to these groups. **(13 marks)**

(Total = 25 marks)

5 CTC – Strategic objectives (*MABS*, 11/06) — 45 mins

CTC, a telecommunications company, has recently been privatised by the government of C after legislation was passed which removed the state monopoly and opened up the communications market to competition from both national and overseas companies – a process known as deregulation.

Prior to the deregulation, CTC was the sole, protected, supplier of telecommunications and was required to provide 'the best telecommunications service the nation can afford'. At that time the government dictated the performance levels required for CTC, and the level of resources it would be able to bring to bear to meet its objectives.

The shares were floated on the C Stock Exchange with 80% being made available to the population of C and up to 20% being made available to foreign nationals. The government of C retained a 'golden share' to prevent the acquisition of CTC by any foreign company. However, the privatisation meant that many of the traditional ways in which the industry had operated would need to change under the new regulations. Apart from the money received from the flotation, the government privatised CTC in recognition of both the changing global environment for telecommunications companies, and the overseas expansion opportunities that might exist for a privatised company. The government recognises that foreign companies will enter the home market but feels that this increased competition is likely to make CTC more effective in the global market.

You have recently been appointed as the management accountant for CTC and have a background in the commercial sector. The Board of Directors is unchanged from CTC's pre-flotation days.

Required

(a) Explain to the Board of Directors why the objectives of CTC will need to change as a result of the privatisation of CTC and the deregulation of the market. **(10 marks)**

(b) Produce two examples of suitable strategic objectives for CTC, following its privatisation and the deregulation of the market, and explain why each would be an appropriate long term objective. **(4 marks)**

(c) Advise the Board of Directors on the stages of an appropriate strategic planning process for CTC in the light of the privatisation and deregulation. **(11 marks)**

(Total = 25 marks)

6 EEE – Stakeholder analysis (*MABS*, 11/06)   45 mins

EEE is an established chemical company extracting flavours and oils from plant materials and supplying them to the flavours and fragrances industries. The shareholders include institutional investors (20%), employees and pensioners of the company (20%) and the descendants of the family (30%) who founded the business approximately 100 years ago. The remainder of the shares are in public ownership. The company is reasonably successful but, recently, there has been pressure on margins and its future is not guaranteed.

The majority of the Board of Directors are members of the founding family who have always taken an active part in the management of the business.

When the company was originally started, the surrounding area was mainly used as agricultural land but, over time, a residential area has developed around the factory. Although many of the workers in the factory live locally, some of the housing is quite expensive and has attracted affluent residents from the local city.

The chemical engineers at EEE have recently developed, and patented, a new process which would allow EEE to extract onion oil and garlic oil at far better yields than those obtained by existing processes. The market for these oils is very profitable and presents a significant opportunity for EEE to gain a real competitive advantage in its industry.

Unfortunately, as with all extraction processes, there will be some leakage and, although perfectly safe and compliant with all safety legislation, the smell of the oils will offend some of the more affluent residents who have complained to local government officers.

There is very little other industry in the area and EEE is a large contributor to the local economy. One of the trade union representatives working in EEE is also an elected council member serving in the local government.

Required

As management accountant you have been asked to:

(a) Advise the Board of Directors of the advantages to EEE of conducting a stakeholder analysis in the context of the proposed investment decision. **(5 marks)**

(b) Analyse the principal stakeholders in EEE in the context of the proposed investment in the new process. **(15 marks)**

(c) Recommend an acceptable course of action to the Board of Directors in the light of the stakeholder analysis conducted in (b). **(5 marks)**

(Total = 25 marks)

7 Island stakeholders (MABS, 5/07)   45 mins

E is a developing country in a group of islands where each island is a separate country. A number of the islands formed a trade bloc five years ago and cooperate economically and in their terms of trade.

Those countries that are in the trade bloc impose no tariffs on imports and exports between member countries but impose a common rate of import duty on any goods or services brought into the group. The trade bloc jointly advertises the attractiveness of the area for inward investment, exports and tourism, and this has been reasonably successful recently. At present, each island has a different currency but full monetary union has been proposed for the future.

E does not belong to the trade bloc at this point in time and is the least developed of the islands in the group although, geographically, it is one of the largest.

There is a fairly large volume of trade between the islands and the majority of E's exports of agricultural products and light engineering products go to other countries in the group of islands. Since the other islands are more industrialised than E, they are not self-sufficient for foodstuffs.

The school system of E produces well-educated children, many of whom go to a nearby industrialised country, F, to take degrees. F is not part of the trade bloc. Only 10% of those students return to E and usually work in their parents' business or other small firms. The average age of the population of E is some ten years higher than that of the islands in the trade bloc.

Although E is an attractive location, there is a limited tourism industry in E and there is very little in the way of service industry, although the government has recently received a grant from the World Bank to improve the telecommunications infrastructure of the island.

Required

(a) Identify those internal and external stakeholders who would be interested in E's decision to join the trade bloc and discuss the nature of their interest. **(12 marks)**

(b) Discuss the advantages and disadvantages that could be experienced by the stakeholders based in E if the country were to enter the trade bloc. **(13 marks)**

(Total = 25 marks)

8 Genetically modified plants (MABS, 5/09)   45 mins

Genetically modified (GM) plants are produced by adding a gene from another species. This is so that the plants are more resistant to weed killer or pests, and are able to grow with less water or in other difficult conditions. GM crops are substantially more profitable for farmers than normal crops because they produce far larger yields per acre. GM crops are seen by many as the great hope for ending starvation around the world.

There are concerns, however, especially in Europe, about the possible long-term negative impact of genetically modifying crops. There is further opposition based on fears that conventional crops growing in fields some distance away from a GM crop can be damaged by the GM crop's DNA.

B is a privately owned biotechnology company based in Europe. B has developed a process which makes seeds pest resistant **without** genetically modifying those seeds. Up to now, the company has only operated at the laboratory scale and has no production facilities capable of producing commercial quantities of the seeds.

Due to the nature of the biotechnology industry, B has been very secretive about the research work it is conducting. However, the news of the recent invention has caused a lot of excitement in the scientific community. Within this community this non-GM technology, developed by B, is seen to have the potential to contribute significantly to both the economy and the well being of populations in poorer countries.

Recently, however, B has faced increasing protests from environmental lobby groups and elements of the local community near its laboratories. These groups want B to stop developing and testing these non-GM seeds. These stakeholder groups claim, incorrectly, that the seeds are genetically modified.

The government of the country in which B is based is currently conducting an enquiry into the safety of GM crops. The enquiry is not likely to reach a conclusion for another 18 months. The expected conclusion is a ban

on the research and development of GM crops. Some other countries have already banned research and development into GM crops, whilst other countries have approved such research.

Although B does not genetically modify seeds, the Board believes that the company will suffer from the adverse publicity that will result from a ban on research and development into GM crops.

The Board of B is considering the following options:

1   The company could work to convince the stakeholders that it is not genetically modifying seeds and that it is in the best interests of everyone that it is allowed to carry on with its research.

2   The company could move to a country where there is a more tolerant attitude to research and development in the area of biotechnology.

Required

(a) Discuss the corporate responsibility that B has towards the government, the environmental lobby groups and the local community as stakeholders. **(8 marks)**

(b) Recommend how B can improve relationships with the government, the lobby groups and the local community. **(9 marks)**

(c) Discuss the corporate social responsibility (CSR) issues relating to B's option to relocate, using the four dimensions of CSR; legal, ethical, economic and philanthropic. **(8 marks)**

(Total = 25 marks)

9 Tobacco planning (*MABS*, 11/05) — 45 mins

The MTM Group (MTM) is a major tobacco products manufacturer. As a global organisation, MTM has production facilities on every continent, and a highly sophisticated distribution network. MTM uses the 'rational planning model' to produce a strategic plan for each country in which it operates. The plan states any assumptions about the business environment in that country, then forecasts retail price levels, the market size and market share of MTM for each of the next five years. This plan is then used as a basis for next year's budget for that country. The budget is fixed at the beginning of the year, and used for control and reporting for the year.

The directors of MTM are currently formulating the organisation's strategy relating to a small Asian country (referred to as the SAC) where the government is known to be considering the introduction of a ban on all tobacco advertising. At present, the probability of such legislation has been estimated at 40%, and the marketing department has estimated that the effect of the ban would be to reduce MTM's profits in the SAC by 20%. Such a reduction would be significant enough to threaten the viability of MTM's operations in the SAC. The marketing manager has therefore suggested that the strategic plan should assume an 8% reduction in profits from the SAC (40% × 20%).

Required

(a) Discuss the limitations of the use of the expected values technique in the context of a single strategic decision such as this. **(6 marks)**

(b) Recommend how the planning processes of MTM, for the SAC, should be modified to take account of the possible new legislation. **(12 marks)**

(c) Evaluate different methods that MTM might use to influence the government of the SAC. **(7 marks)**

(Total = 25 marks)

10 Timber company (*MABS*, 11/07) — 45 mins

D is an international logging company, which cuts down timber and supplies sawmills where the timber is seasoned and then cut to appropriate sizes for use in a range of industries. D will work with any timber, ranging from softwoods used in construction or paper manufacture to exotic hardwoods used in expensive furniture. Its usual approach is to secure the rights from a landowner, or in some cases a national government, to cut timber. This can often involve the payment of large initial cash deposits to these suppliers, money which D usually

borrows. A logging team then cuts down the trees as quickly as possible and hauls the timber to a convenient river where it is floated to a sawmill. Moving on rapidly to the next site, the loggers usually leave considerable surface damage behind them.

Since an increasing proportion of the company's work has been in the tropical rainforest, it has recently come under pressure from environmental groups that have protested that it is not socially responsible to act in this way. Whilst the softwood forests can be regenerated in a couple of decades by replanting, hardwoods in tropical forests take far longer to mature.

The Chief Executive of the company has argued that he is not concerned about these protests since, as far as he is concerned, the company always acts ethically, as it has the agreement of the national government in any country in which the company operates.

A recent development in the timber industry has been the harvesting of timber from the bottom of reservoirs which have been created by flooding valleys. Although the capital equipment required for this approach is significantly more expensive than that used in conventional logging, the operating costs are lower. Waterlogged trees in reservoirs have balloons attached, are cut, float to the surface and are towed to a sawmill. The underwater process is quieter and less disruptive to wildlife and the environment.

It has been estimated that there are over half a billion trees, or 20 years' supply, submerged in reservoirs across the world, but it can take considerable research and expense to find them.

As long as the timber has remained submerged deeply enough, it is of the same quality as timber harvested from the land. There is currently only one company conducting underwater logging, although a number of other companies are also considering this development.

Some of the board of directors feel that D should pursue this underwater approach and abandon land based logging. The Chief Executive and one other director feel that the underwater approach carries too high a risk.

Required

(a) (i) Briefly explain the differences between business ethics and corporate social responsibility (CSR). **(5 marks)**

(ii) Discuss the CSR issues relating to D's business and how the company might improve its CSR position. **(8 marks)**

(b) With reference to D, evaluate the two approaches to logging and recommend which you think is more appropriate for D. **(12 marks)**

(Total = 25 marks)

11 FFF – Competitor analysis (*MABS*, 11/06, adapted) 45 mins

FFF is a manufacturer of specialist portable communications equipment, which is designed for use in hazardous and dangerous conditions. Developments of new technology in recent years, such as wireless mobile telephony, infra-red thermal imaging and global positioning has allowed FFF to create new products.

The market for such equipment has grown significantly over the past five years. The customer base includes fire services, oil and chemical companies and the government. FFF now recognises that, during this period of rapid growth, the market has attracted a number of new entrants and may even be reaching a level of overcapacity.

The directors feel that they do not know as much as they should about the existing, and new, companies in the industry. The market is now maturing and, although FFF is managing to maintain its margins and leading market share (45%), it is likely that the characteristics of the industry will change.

Required

As management accountant you are required to:

(a) Advise the board of the advantages of carrying out competitor analysis. **(10 marks)**

(b) Advise the directors of the stages in a formal competitor analysis process and identify any information that would need to be gathered at each stage for FFF. **(15 marks)**

(Total = 25 marks)

Questions

12 Water charity (*MABS*, 5/08) — 45 mins

Based in a European country, BBB is a charity which raises funds to provide portable equipment to remove the poison arsenic from drinking water in villages, in less developed countries. Run by a Board of Trustees, the organisation operates on 'laissez-faire' management principles. There are few full-time paid employees and BBB is heavily dependent upon the work of volunteers. Although these volunteers are dedicated, many have said that they do not feel the organisation knows where it is going and have said that they are not confident about the future of BBB.

Funding comes from appeals to the general population, which are made through newspaper advertisements. BBB does not use the Internet to promote or raise donations and, generally, does not use available technology to any extent in its organisation. Additionally, BBB receives corporate donations, most of which come from old school friends of the trustees. There is no government funding.

Recently BBB has had difficulty in attracting donations and is at risk of not being able to carry on its work. The charity industry has become more competitive and many other organisations within it have become more aggressive in their marketing and promotion.

None of the Board of Trustees has a commercial background. The Chairman of Trustees has recently been to a number of conferences where the value of foresight and the need to conduct a frequent and thorough 'environmental analysis' have been discussed.

The Chairman has accepted that there is a serious gap in the knowledge that the trustees have about the environment in which BBB operates. Recognising that BBB needs a more proactive approach to the environment in which it operates, your help as a management accountant has been sought.

Required

(a) Discuss how conducting a frequent and thorough environmental analysis would help the Board of Trustees of BBB. **(14 marks)**

(b) Explain the concept of foresight and two techniques for the development of foresight. **(5 marks)**

(c) Discuss the difficulties that BBB might, as an organisation, experience in developing a process of environmental analysis. **(6 marks)**

(Total = 25 marks)

13 Scenario planning (*MABS*, 5/07) — 45 mins

B is a media company, publishing lifestyle magazines for the consumer market. These lifestyle magazines contain articles and advertisements about fashion, health and beauty products, homes, furniture, and hobbies and are bought by people aspiring to a high standard of living.

Increasingly, consumers are turning to other media for the information and entertainment traditionally provided by this type of magazine.

Traditionally, 60% of B's revenue has been derived from selling advertising, the balance being provided by the cover price of each magazine. Over the last four years both the revenue and profits have declined as there has been a steady reduction in the sale of both advertising space and the number of magazines sold.

The industry is very dependent upon the level of discretionary disposable income. If this income is at a low level, fewer luxury goods are advertised. However, people still buy the magazines to read about these goods.

The company has tried to expand abroad but has failed, expensively, to achieve this. Similarly, attempts to enter other segments of the home market, particularly teenage magazines, have failed. Both of these failures have come as a surprise to the Board of Directors who thought that they understood the respective markets well enough to make the appropriate decisions.

New technology, in the form of digital media, has also affected the magazines industry. These changes have been felt in both production methods, such as broadband distribution of proof copies, and the choice of media, such as the Internet, available to consumers. To a large extent, the speed of these developments was a surprise to the directors of B.

Required

As management accountant, you have been seconded to work with the organisation's forecasting and planning function, to improve its long-range planning.

(a) Evaluate the benefits to B of implementing a process of systematic environmental analysis. **(12 marks)**

(b) Describe the essential stages that should be included in a scenario planning process that could be introduced by B. **(13 marks)**

(Total = 25 marks)

14 GC — 45 mins

GC is a conglomerate which comprises five strategic business units (SBUs), all operating as subsidiary companies. Information relating to each SBU (and the market leader or nearest competitor) is given in the following table.

	Current Market Share			Market growth expected by GC
	GC %	Market leader %	Nearest competitor %	
Building brick manufacturer (*Declining profitability*)	3	25		Small
Parcel carriage service (*Long established, faces strong competition. Turnover and profitability over last three years have been stable but are expected to decline as competition strengthens.*)	1	6		Nil
Food manufacturer producing exclusively for household consumption (*Long established with little new investment. High levels of turnover and profitability which are being sustained.*)	25		5	Slowly declining
Painting and decorating contracting company (*Established three years ago. Continuous capital injections from group over that period. Currently not making any profit.*)	0.025	0.5		Historically high but now forecast to slow down
Software development and supply company	10		8	Rapid
(*Acquired two years ago. Market share expected to increase over next two years. Sustained investment from group but profitability so far is low.*)				

Required

(a) Discuss on GC's overall competitive position by applying the Boston Consulting Group Growth/Share Matrix analysis to its portfolio of SBUs. **(10 marks)**

(b) Discuss how GC should pursue the strategic development of its SBUs in order to add value to the overall conglomerate group. **(15 marks)**

(Total = 25 marks)

15 Value activities (*MABS*, 5/06) — 45 mins

2B is a medium-sized retailer of sports equipment and leisure clothing. 2B was established in 1987, and currently operates from three retail shops in town centre locations.

The management team of 2B is very careful about how it recruits staff. In addition to the specific skills required to do the job, any applicant must also have a 'passion' for sport. This has resulted in 2B gaining a reputation for excellent customer service and enthusiastic staff. A large proportion of staff time is also devoted to training, both on the product range and customer service techniques. According to a recent survey conducted by the store managers, the customers believe that 2B employees are 'helpful and knowledgeable'. The customers also praised the 2B shops for being 'well designed' and said that it was 'very easy' to find what they were looking for.

Another feature of 2B that is appreciated by the customers is the range of goods stocked. By developing close relationships with the major manufacturers of sports goods and clothing, 2B is able to stock a far wider range of items than its rivals. Control of this stock was made easier, last year, by the development of a sophisticated computerised stock control system. Using the system, any member of staff can locate any item of stock in any of the shops or the warehouse. If the required item is not 'in stock' at 2B, it is also possible to automatically check the availability of stock with the manufacturer.

At a recent management meeting, one of the store managers suggested that 2B consider developing its very basic website into one capable of e-retailing. At present, the website only gives the location of stores and some very basic details of the range of stock carried. Although the development of the website would be expensive, the managers have decided to give the suggestion serious consideration.

Required

(a) Using the value chain model, explain those activities that add value in the 2B organisation, BEFORE the e-retail investment. **(10 marks)**

(b) Identify those activities in the value chain of 2B that may be affected by the e-retail investment, explaining whether the value added by each of them may increase or decrease as a result of the e-retail investment. **(15 marks)**

(Total = 25 marks)

16 Benchmarking in a charity (*MABS*, 5/05) — 45 mins

E5E is a charity concerned with heart disease. Its mission statement is to:

- Fund world class research into the biology and the causes of heart disease
- Develop effective treatments and improve the quality of life for patients
- Reduce the number of people suffering from heart disease
- Provide authoritative information on heart disease

E5E obtains funding from voluntary donations from both private individuals and companies, together with government grants. Much of the work it does, in all departments, could not be achieved without the large number of voluntary workers who give their time to the organisation and who make up approximately 80% of the workforce.

E5E does not employ any scientific researchers directly, but funds research by making grants to individual medical experts employed within universities and hospitals. In addition to providing policy advice to governmental departments, the charity's advisors give health educational talks to employers and other groups.

The Board recognises the need to become more professional in the management of the organisation. It feels that this can be best achieved by conducting a benchmarking exercise. However, it recognises that the introduction of this process may make some members of the organisation, particularly the volunteers, unhappy.

Required

As Financial Controller:

(a) Discuss the advantages and disadvantages of benchmarking for E5E. **(8 marks)**

(b) Advise on the stages in conducting a benchmarking exercise in the context of E5E. **(13 marks)**

(c) Advise on how those implementing the exercise should deal with the concerns of the staff, particularly the volunteers. **(4 marks)**

(Total = 25 marks)

17 Product portfolio (*MABS*, 5/06)   45 mins

3C is a medium-sized pharmaceutical company. It is based in Asia, but distributes and sells its products worldwide.

In common with other pharmaceutical companies, 3C has a large number of products in its portfolio, though most of these are still being developed. The success rate of new drugs is very low, as most fail to complete clinical trials or are believed to be uneconomic to launch. However, the rewards to be gained from a successful new drug are so great that it is only necessary to have a few successful drugs on the market to be very profitable.

At present 3C has 240 drugs at various stages of development; being tested or undergoing clinical trials prior to a decision being made whether to launch the drug. 3C has only three products that are actually 'on the market':

- Epsilon is a drug used in the treatment of heart disease. It has been available for eight months and has achieved significant success. Sales of this drug are not expected to increase from their current level.
- Alpha is a painkiller. It was launched more than ten years ago, and has become one of the leading drugs in its class. In a few months the patent on this drug will expire, and other manufacturers will be allowed to produce generic copies of it. Alpha is expected to survive a further twelve months after it loses its patent, and will then be withdrawn.
- Beta is used in the hospital treatment of serious infections. It is a very specialised drug, and cannot be obtained from a doctor or pharmacist for use outside the hospital environment. It was launched only three months ago, and has yet to generate a significant sales volume.

The directors of 3C meet every month to review the product portfolio and to discuss possible investment opportunities. At their next meeting, they are to be asked to consider three investments. Due to a limited investment budget, the three investments are mutually exclusive (that is, they will only be able to invest in ONE of the options). The options are as follows:

- The directors can invest in a new version of Alpha, Alpha2, which offers improved performance. This will allow 3C to apply for a new patent for Alpha2, and maintain the level of sales achieved by Alpha for an additional five years. Alpha2 has successfully completed all its clinical trials, and can be launched immediately.
- The directors can invest in a major marketing campaign, to promote the use of Beta to specialist hospital staff. While this investment should lead to a significant growth in the sales of Beta, 3C is aware that one of its competitors is actively promoting a rival product with similar performance to that of Beta.
- The directors can invest in the final stage of clinical trials for Gamma. This is a 'breakthrough' drug, as it has no near rivals on the market. Gamma is used in the treatment of HIV, and offers significantly better success rates than any treatment currently available. The team of 3C specialists managing the development of Gamma is confident it can successfully complete clinical trials within six months. The team also believes that Gamma should be sold at the lowest price possible, to maximise the benefits of Gamma to society. However, the marketing department of 3C believes that it would be possible to earn very large profits from Gamma, due to its success rate and breakthrough status.

Required

(a) Briefly explain how the product life cycle model can be used to analyse the current product portfolio of 3C (that is, BEFORE the planned investment). **(8 marks)**

(b) Evaluate the potential impact of each of the three investment options (Alpha2, Beta and Gamma) on the product portfolio of 3C, referring to your answer to part (a) above. **(9 marks)**

(c) Discuss the social responsibility implications of each of the three investment options, for the directors of 3C. **(8 marks)**

(Total = 25 marks)

18 Chemical manufacturer (MABS, 11/06)   45 mins

DDD is a relatively small, specialist manufacturer of chemicals that are used in the pharmaceutical industry. It does not manufacture any pharmaceutical products itself since these are made by different processes and under different conditions. DDD obtains its raw materials, which are quite simple, from large chemical companies, and modifies them by a number of patented processes before selling them on to a few pharmaceutical companies. DDD makes significantly higher margins than its suppliers, which manufacture in bulk.

Several patents are due to expire in the next three years.

The large pharmaceutical companies, which are DDD's customers, are suffering reduced profits as governments reduce the price they are prepared to pay for drugs. As a result, the pharmaceutical companies are pressuring DDD to reduce its prices.

The majority of the shares are owned by members of the family which started the business some years ago and who still take an active part both as managers of the business and as development chemists. There is a share option scheme for the employees and this is well supported.

Required

As management accountant for DDD you have been asked to:

(a) Advise the Board of Directors of the possible threats related to the patent expiries **(10 marks)**

(b) Evaluate suitable courses of action that DDD might take to maintain its profits in the face of the threats identified in (a) **(12 marks)**

(c) From your analysis recommend, with a brief justification, the most appropriate course of action for DDD **(3 marks)**

(Total = 25 marks)

19 Competitor benchmarking   45 mins

PAL is a banking group specialising in loans for home purchase. It has a network of shops, cash machines and other outlets in and around the capital city (where it has its headquarters) with all outlets within 70 miles. It monitors interest rates offered by competitors and strives to match or better the lowest rates. This strategy has been successful, but in order to compete more fully, it has introduced a range of additional customer services, including home insurance.

A dedicated unit was established to extend existing benchmarking of price to other aspects of customer requirements. Following a survey, the following factors in addition to price have emerged as being relevant to customers.

- Delivery
- Technical content of literature
- Customer service and correspondence.

Required

(a) Discuss the use of appropriate performance measures which home insurance could use as part of the proposed competitor benchmarking exercise. For each measure, advise on ways in which subjectivity might be dealt with. **(12 marks)**

(b) Analyse the strategies followed by *PAL* so far and evaluate the possible effects of actions arising from benchmarking in supporting these strategies. **(13 marks)**

(Total = 25 marks)

20 Printing company (MABS, 5/09) — 45 mins

D is a printing company that was founded by three people 20 years ago. At that time, the company used a new technology which had been developed by one of the founders. Another founder member was a finance professional. The third person is Mr Z, who has a strong, dynamic, personality. Mr Z has been the driving force behind the development and growth of the business to its present size of 350 employees. With a charismatic leadership style, Mr Z was very proud of the fact that he knew all employees by their first names and considered everyone to be part of one big team. Everyone understood exactly what the company stood for and how things should be done.

As the company has grown, Mr Z feels he is not in touch with newer members of staff and that they do not understand his, and the company's, values.

In addition, the technology used by D is no longer considered innovative and there are a number of other competitors operating in exactly the same way. D is still market leader within the industry, but only by a few percentage points. Mr Z feels that the industry has reached the maturity stage of its lifecycle.

An acquaintance of Mr Z, a management consultant, has suggested that the company should have a published mission statement and a clear set of strategic objectives.

Required

(a) Identify the characteristics of the maturity stage of the industry lifecycle. **(5 marks)**

(b) Discuss the issues that the management of D would need to consider when creating an appropriate mission statement. **(15 marks)**

(c) Discuss the characteristics of strategic objectives that would be appropriate for D at this stage of the industry lifecycle. **(5 marks)**

(Total = 25 marks)

21 Conglomerate value (MABS, 5/08) — 45 mins

CCC is an established company in public ownership comprising the following divisions; construction and building, engineering and machinery, real estate. Although the company has traded profitably, its earnings have been subject to wide variations and some of the shareholders are concerned about the Board's policy of 'conglomerate diversification'.

In the last year the company had the following earning figures:

	Earnings $m
Division	
Construction and building	50
Engineering and machinery	20
Real estate	30
Group	100

Note. It should be assumed that the above divisional earnings are stated after tax.

	Current average market sector P/E
Industry	
Construction and building	8
Engineering and machinery	13
Real estate	23

CCC is currently valued on the stock market at $1,000 million, and proposed/current dividends are approximately half analysts' expectations.

Construction and building

This activity represents the original business before CCC started to make acquisitions. The divisional management has described the business as 'mature, stable, and offering the prospect of modest but sustained growth'.

Engineering and machinery

This activity represents the first acquisitions made by CCC whereby a number of small companies were bought and consolidated into one division. The divisional management has described the business as 'mature but offering the prospect of profit growth of 10% per annum'. Additionally the division has a broad customer base servicing a number of government agencies – minimising the risk of cash flow problems.

Real estate

This division represents the most recent acquisition made by CCC and has provided profit growth of over 20% per annum in the three years since it was formed. The divisional management, which is recognised as the most dynamic management team within CCC, feels that this rate of growth can be continued or surpassed.

HQ Organisation

Each division has its own headquarters office in a different town and the group headquarters, which has the responsibility for raising capital and operating a group treasury function is also separately located. The group headquarters is located in the capital, is quite luxurious and has a staff of 50 including the main board directors. Group headquarters, and the staff, is funded by a management charge on the divisions.

Investors

An informal group of institutional shareholders, which holds approximately 20% of CCC's equity has requested a review of the Board's strategy and a rationalisation of the company's portfolio. These shareholders feel that the Board of Directors has destroyed value and that the company should take the opportunity to dispose of the real estate division, reduce costs by closing the group headquarters and relocate the board and treasury functions to one of the divisional headquarters. This, they have said, would allow the company to pay a large, one off, dividend to reward shareholders for their tolerance of poor past performance.

The Board of Directors feels that the suggestions are unreasonable and that its strategy has served the best interests of all shareholders.

Required

(a) Explain the term 'conglomerate diversification'. **(3 marks)**

(b) (i) Evaluate the comments made by the institutional investors that the Board 'has destroyed value'.
(3 marks)

(ii) Evaluate the suggestions made by the institutional investors that

' the company should take the opportunity to dispose of the real estate division, reduce costs by closing the group headquarters and relocate the board and treasury functions to one of the divisional headquarters'. **(7 marks)**

(c) Identify and evaluate alternative methods available to the Board for the disposal of the real estate division, should it decide to do so, and recommend the method of disposal most appropriate to CCC.
(12 marks)

(Total = 25 marks)

Questions | 17

22 Telecommunications joint venture (MABS, 5/09)   45 mins

The telecommunications market in C, a developing country, has recently been deregulated and opened to foreign competition. The national telecommunication company was split into four separate companies, each of which has approximately 25% of the local market. The national telecommunication company was using old equipment and was in need of considerable capital investment. Each new company is individually quoted on the local stock market and the shares are held by both institutional shareholders and members of the general public.

The government of C made the decision to open the telecommunications market up to private investment to ensure that the country benefitted from the recent improvements in communications technology. There was some strong resistance to the privatisation from other stakeholders in C and the government is under political pressure to ensure that the country benefits from any foreign involvement.

Y is a successful and well established international telecommunications company. It has grown by acquiring companies in established markets. The company wishes to expand into C and is considering how to achieve this. If successful, this will be the first time that Y has entered a market at such an early stage of market deregulation.

The managing director of Y has stated that she would prefer to acquire one of the existing companies in C because this is the approach Y has always used.

However, other members of the Board of Directors have suggested that the best way forward may be to form a joint venture with one of the existing companies in the market. If Y were to adopt this strategy, this would be the first strategic alliance into which the company had entered.

The managing director of Y is concerned about the risks involved in joint ventures and has said that she is concerned about the reported lack of success of joint ventures.

Required

(a) Explain the characteristics of a joint venture. (5 marks)

(b) Discuss the benefits to country C of a joint venture between Y and one of the telecommunication companies in C. (10 marks)

(c) Evaluate the risks that Y should consider before entering into a joint venture with one of the telecommunications companies in C. (10 marks)

(Total = 25 marks)

23 Plastics manufacturer (MABS, 11/07)   45 mins

F is a leading manufacturer of plastics. Its major products are beer crates and small containers for food sold in supermarkets. Together these two product ranges constitute 90% of F's business, the remainder coming from selling more technologically sophisticated products.

The company is faced with a number of difficulties and may have to issue a profits warning in the coming year. Although the profit levels have been uneven for the past five years, this is the first time that F will have to report significantly reduced profits.

F has been adversely affected by the aggressive marketing of foreign companies importing beer crates into the market, such that F's market share has fallen from 80% to 60% in the past three years. Consolidation in the brewery industry has meant that profit margins for crate manufacturers have been squeezed.

The company is heavily dependent upon the home market, which accounts for 75% of its total sales. Exports have been mainly of food containers for supermarkets in neighbouring countries.

F has invested heavily in research and development (R&D) and, although there is one exciting proposition in electro-plastics, most expenditure has been on projects selected by R&D managers who have little commercial awareness. There is the possibility that some new products may be developed from the electro-plastics research.

F is highly centralised, with many decisions taken by the 20 members of the board of directors. The workforce is highly unionised, with a number of different unions represented. Each factory has several negotiating committees set up to agree pay and conditions. Negotiations are often time consuming and confrontational. This has resulted in very precise job definitions, which are strictly adhered to. This has further resulted in considerable inflexibility, together with a complicated system of labour grades.

The directors have had little communication with stock market analysts and investors, who have little knowledge of the company other than what is shown in the published accounts. An informal group of institutional shareholders has asked for a strategic review and has suggested that F should withdraw from the beer crate market.

Required

(a) (i) Discuss the main difficulties faced by F. **(5 marks)**

(ii) Identify and evaluate alternative strategies that F could adopt to address its difficulties and recommend those that are most appropriate. **(12 marks)**

(b) Explain why the failure to keep the shareholders more informed is a significant weakness for F. **(8 marks)**

(Total = 25 marks)

24 Biotechnology company (*MABS*, 5/08) — 45 mins

DDD is a biotechnology company which develops drugs. It was founded seven years ago by three scientists when they left the university medical school, where they had been senior researchers. The Company employs 10 other scientists who joined from different universities. All of these employees are receiving relatively low salaries but participate in a share option scheme. This means that when DDD is successfully floated on the stock exchange they will receive shares in the company.

DDD currently has a number of new, innovative drugs in development, but the earliest any of these drugs might come to market is two years from now. It is expected that there would be one successful drug launched in most years after that for at least six years. However, successful drug launches are never guaranteed, due to the speculative nature of biotechnology and the long period of clinical trials through which any new drug must pass. DDD has to invest a significant amount of resources into the development of each potential drug, whether they are successfully launched or not. Currently, it has 12 drugs in development, a number of which may not be successfully launched. Due to the speculative nature of the industry, companies such as DDD are unable to obtain bank loans on commercial terms.

DDD is funded by an exclusive arrangement with a venture capital company. However, there is only sufficient cash in place to maintain the present level of activity for a further nine months. The venture capital company owns 15% of the equity of the company. The rest is owned by the three founders. It has always been the intention of the venture capital company and the founders that, once the company has a sufficient number of drugs in production and on the market, the company would be floated on the stock exchange. This is expected to happen in five years' time.

Recently there have been a number of approaches to DDD which might solve its cash flow problems. The three founders have identified the following options:

1   The venture capital company has suggested that it will guarantee the cash flow until the first drug is successfully launched in commercial quantities. However, it would expect its equity holding to rise to 60% once this offer is accepted.

2   A large pharmaceutical company has offered to buy DDD outright and retain the services of the three founders (in research roles) and a few of the staff.

3   Another biotechnology company has offered to enter into a merger with DDD. This company has also been established for seven years and has one drug which will be launched in six months. However, of the four other potential drugs it has in development, none are likely to be commercially viable for 5 years. This company would expect the three founders to stay with the newly merged company but feels a rationalisation of the combined staff would be needed.

As the financial advisor to the three founders you have been asked to comment on the approaches that have been made.

Required

(a) Describe the 'Suitability, Feasibility and Acceptability (SFA) framework as used for evaluating strategic options. **(6 marks)**

(b) Using the SFA framework, evaluate the strategic options identified by the founders. **(12 marks)**

(c) Identify and evaluate one other strategic option that the founders might pursue. **(5 marks)**

(d) Recommend the most appropriate strategic option based on your analysis above. **(2 marks)**

(Total = 25 marks)

25 Internet strategy (*MABS*, Pilot paper) — 45 mins

The SDW Company has been trading for one year. It provides rail travel services between three major cities in the country in which it operates.

Mr M, the majority shareholder and Managing Director, is keen to expand its operations and, in particular, to use the Internet as the major selling medium. He has discovered, for example, that doubling sales on the Internet usually results in no additional costs. However, doubling sales using a call centre normally results in a doubling of staff and an increase in costs.

All tickets are currently sold via the company's call centre. The company has an Internet site although this is used for publicity only, not for sales or marketing. Competitors currently use a mixture of selling media, although detailed information on the success of each medium is not available to the SDW Company.

Mr M has asked you, as a qualified management accountant, to assist him in upgrading the company's Internet site and, in particular, showing how this will help to reduce operating costs.

Required

(a) Advise Mr M on how to establish and implement an appropriate Internet strategy for the SDW Company. **(13 marks)**

(b) Discuss the key customer-orientated features of an Internet site, showing how these can be used to meet the objective of cost reduction required by Mr M. **(12 marks)**

(Total = 25 marks)

26 Sole supplier (*MABS*, 11/05) — 45 mins

C is a large multinational car manufacturer. It has factories in five countries and sells its products through networks of independent dealerships throughout the world. As part of its strategy of reducing unit costs and improving quality, C has entered into a number of 'sole supplier' agreements. This means that, on a worldwide basis, C buys all of its requirement for a specific material or component from a single supplier organisation. Such contracts are normally for a five year period.

S is a specialist manufacturer of safety equipment. It has recently been invited, by C, to submit a tender to supply all of the 'airbag' safety devices to be installed in C's cars. This will be the biggest order for which S has ever tendered and, if won, would require a two hundred per cent increase in production capacity (that is to three times its present scale) for S. In return for this large order, S would have to agree to deliver the required parts to each C factory twice a day. Any failure to deliver on time would lead to S being liable for the cost of lost production.

As part of the contract, C would allow S access to its extranet. This would mean that S was able to see C's forecast production schedules on a real-time basis. C maintains detailed forecasts of the number of each model of car being produced in each factory. This information is available on an hour-by-hour basis for the next month, on a day-by-day basis for the following five months, and a week-by-week basis for the subsequent 18 months. This means that S would be able to view detailed production forecasts for a two year period. The extranet also has a 'virtual trading room' where suppliers bid for new contracts. It also contains a lot of car industry information, some of which is not available to organisations that do not supply C.

Required

(a) Discuss the advantages and disadvantages, to S, of the sole supplier arrangement described. **(15 marks)**

(b) Evaluate the benefits, to S, of access to the C extranet. **(10 marks)**

(Total = 25 marks)

27 IT outsourcing (*MABS*, 5/05) — 45 mins

The insurance industry is characterised by large organisations producing, packaging and cross-selling a number of different 'products' to their client base. Typical products include life insurance, health insurance, house insurance and house contents insurance. Therefore, cost efficiency, repeat business and database manipulation are of significant importance.

BXA is a medium sized insurance company that has grown over the past fifty years by a number of relatively small mergers and acquisitions. Its business is focused on life, automobile and private property insurance. Over the last few years the insurance industry has undergone significant change with increasing consolidation and the squeezing of margins.

The Board of BXA recognises that it is quite old fashioned in its approach to business, particularly in its attitude to information technology. Much of the computing is done on personal computers, many of which are not networked, using a variety of 'user written' programs. There are a number of different computer systems in the organisation that have been inherited from the companies that have been acquired in the past. However, these computer systems have not been fully consolidated. It is recognised that this lack of compatibility is causing efficiency problems.

BXA has recently been approached by CXA, an insurance company of a similar size, with a view to a merger. Although BXA has never combined with an organisation of this size before, the Board recognises that this merger could present an opportunity to develop into a company of significant size but that this may also present further problems of system incompatibility.

BXA has decided to proceed with the merger, but the Board recognises that this might only make the situation worse with regards to information management strategy of the resulting combined company.

The Finance Director has asked you, as project accountant, to investigate the potential of outsourcing the information technology function as part of the post-merger consolidation process.

Required

(a) Discuss the advantages and disadvantages of outsourcing the IT function for the merged organisation at each of the strategic, managerial and tactical levels of the organisation. **(15 marks)**

(b) Briefly describe the characteristics of the supplier that BXA will be looking for in the selection of the contractor to take on the outsourcing. **(5 marks)**

(c) Identify the factors which should be included in the service level agreement with which the contractor will be expected to comply in achieving the levels of performance that BXA will require. **(5 marks)**

(Total = 25 marks)

28 Supplying and outsourcing (*MABS*, 5/07) — 45 mins

C is a major pharmaceutical manufacturing company producing and supplying a variety of prescription drugs in its home market. C currently uses its own fleet of vehicles to deliver to the wholesalers. There are six competitors who supply drugs which can be used to treat the same diseases as those produced by C.

Up until three years ago, the supply chain for the industry consisted of the manufacturers, and a group of ten wholesalers which covered the whole country and which supplied approximately 4,000 independent pharmacies. These independent pharmacies are all small companies which source their drugs from the wholesalers.

Traditionally, patients would see a doctor who would write a prescription for the correct dose of the required drug which the patients had to take to the pharmacy to get their supply. This was the only way they could obtain their medication. Because of a government subsidy, regardless of the medication prescribed, all prescriptions are charged at a fixed rate.

Three years ago, the legislation changed and for the first time supermarkets were allowed to employ a qualified pharmacist and to supply prescription drugs. Because of their size and buying power, the supermarkets are now refusing to deal with the wholesalers and are insisting on being supplied directly by the pharmaceutical manufacturers.

These changes have not been well received by the independent pharmacies. There has been a significant volume of comment in the press about pressure groups which see this as another encroachment by 'big business' on the small independent traders. Some government ministers have also expressed concern about the increasing market power of the supermarkets.

C is considering changing its distribution network so that it no longer supplies the wholesalers but will sell directly to all the independent pharmacies and will share the wholesalers' margin with them.

Although the transport manager has said that he believes the arrangements can be dealt with in-house, some of the Board of Directors feel that it might be better to outsource all the transport function.

The Board of Directors recognises that there would need to be significant changes in the way the company operates were either, or both, proposals to be implemented. These changes would also have a significant effect on the stakeholders of the business.

Required

(a) Discuss the advantages and disadvantages, to C, of the proposal to supply directly to the independent pharmacies. **(10 marks)**

(b) Discuss the advantages and disadvantages, to C, of the proposal to outsource the transport function should the proposal to directly supply independent pharmacies be adopted. **(8 marks)**

(c) Advise the project team how C might best communicate the decision, to directly supply independent pharmacies, to each of its principal stakeholders. **(7 marks)**

(Total = 25 marks)

CHANGE MANAGEMENT

Questions 29-34 cover change management, the subject of Part C of the BPP Study Text for Paper E3.

29 Contact Services — 45 mins

An increasing number of people in Vizland, a European country, are wearing contact lens rather than traditional spectacles (glasses).

In Vizland, customers who need contact lenses visit an optician (eye doctor) who assesses the type and strength of lens they need, and then writes a prescription to enable the customer to buy the relevant lenses.

Customers then have to take their prescriptions to a pharmacy (chemist) to get the lenses made up. This can sometimes take a long time and customers have to call back to collect the lenses a few hours later. This annoys customers who prefer a 'while-you-wait service', and so the larger pharmacies are encouraging their regular customers to order their prescriptions online so that the lenses can be prepared in advance of the customer collecting them. Recently, a number of pharmacies have also been encouraging the opticians to send the prescriptions directly to them electronically so that the lenses can be prepared in advance ready for the customer to collect.

Contact Services is a privately owned software company which has developed a specialised software package for the pharmacies to deal with the prescriptions from the opticians and from customers ordering online. Contact Services' current corporate objective is to be a 'skilled professional company providing high quality, dedicated software services to the pharmacy industry.'

In recent years, Contact Services has been reasonably successful in selling its software, and has experienced a gradual growth in turnover and operating profit. However, it is not the only company which offers software solutions for the pharmacy industry, and it currently only holds a market share of around 25%.

Contact Services has three directors, each of whom has a significant amount of shares in the business.

The chief executive is an entrepreneur whose natural tendency is to identify opportunities and take any risks necessary to exploit them. He joined Contact Services just over a year ago, and feels the time is right to expand the company to a size and profitability that makes it an attractive acquisition target, thereby providing him with an exit route to cash in some or all of his investment in Contact Services.

The sales and marketing director also feels that Contact Services needs to expand into new markets to increase its growth. However, the software development director does not share this enthusiasm for expansion.

The chief executive feels that Contact Services can grow by developing a generic software package which can be used more widely by the retail industry. He thinks that by removing the specific references to contact lenses and pharmacies, the software package could be adapted for use in other retail sectors. The existing pharmaceutical package would be retained but it would be marketed as a specialist version of the generic package.

The software development director resists this proposed change of strategy very strongly. His team of developers are already under constant pressure to meet the demands of the existing pharmacy customers. The pharmacies regularly request updates to the software to allow them to implement technical innovations that improve customer service.

The software development director would like additional resources to be devoted to developing a more standardised software package for their current customers. He is annoyed at the way Contact Services' salesmen regularly commit the company to producing customised software solutions for individual customers and promising delivery dates that the software delivery team struggle to meet.

The rush in development work is leading to users reporting an increasing number of faults in the software. As a result, Contact Services' reputation is suffering, and several large pharmacies who are key customers have recently expressed dissatisfaction with the quality of their software package.

Required

(a) Analyse the type of change the chief executive is proposing for Contact Services. **(10 marks)**

(b) Discuss the internal factors at Contact Services that may influence the success or failure of the chief executive's proposal to develop a generic software package. **(15 marks)**

(Total = 25 marks)

30 Brian Jolson — 45 mins

The residents of Newdon, the second largest city in its country, are very concerned with the level of antisocial behaviour and the number of minor crimes in their city. Although the individual crimes are relatively minor, they are making living, working, travelling and socialising in the city centre increasingly unpleasant.

There has been a significant decline in the number of tourist visitors coming to the city in recent years, and in the latest national poll, Newdon was voted as one of the five worst cities to live in. Residents are also unhappy that the police are not asking them their views and working with them to resolve these problems. There is little contact between the residents and the police.

The city is split into a number of police districts, each with its own senior officer in charge. The senior officers focus on designated Key Performance Indicators (KPIs) such as the response times to emergency calls and solving serious crimes in their districts, rather than the less urgent crimes affecting everyday living in the city.

Each police district has little sense of being part of an overall city police force, and there is little sharing of information and experience between the different districts forces.

The failure in policing antisocial behaviour in the city is blamed by the residents on the police having a shortage of resources.

Brian Jolson has recently been appointed as the overall head of the city police force, and is keen to address the residents' concerns about policing in the city.

He is also aware that there are a number of important groups who have an interest in any changes he makes, and the degree of support or resistance to the changes is likely to vary between the groups.

Key players include: police officers, the mayor of the city anxious to improve the reputation of the city, the city law courts and the city's press. The city law courts have warned Brian that bringing antisocial behaviour cases to court would significantly increase their workload and they would be reluctant to support such a move. The city's press are traditionally used to highlighting police failures, but they could play an important role in broadcasting any successes Brian's new policies might have.

Brian is aware of the complexity of the problem of trying to improve the quality of life of the city residents through the way the city is policed. However, he has an impressive track record of delivering change in his previous appointments, and is confident that he can bring about the necessary changes to do this.

Required

(a) Discuss the issues Brian should consider when changing the way the city is policed in order to improve its quality of life. **(15 marks)**

(b) Analyse the styles of managing change Brian should use to bring about the desired change. **(10 marks)**

(Total = 25 marks)

31 Heritage Trust — 45 mins

The Heritage Trust is a charity which was founded in 1830 with the aim of acquiring buildings of national interest and preserving them for the public to visit, along with the art collections and antiques within them. The Trust now owns over 200 houses nationwide, many of which also have large gardens.

Historically, about 30% of the Trust's income has come from government grants, reflecting the importance the Government attaches to preserving the nation's heritage. About 50% of the Trust's total income comes from membership fees. (Members pay an annual subscription which then allows them free entry to any of the Trust's properties.) The remaining 20% comes from a combination of admission charges (which non-members pay to visit the properties) and sales in the gift shops and restaurants which many properties have.

The income is used for the continued preservation of the properties and their art collections, as well as paying for the administrative costs of the Trust, including staff costs. Each property has a salaried manager, who lives on site, although a number of volunteers also help with the upkeep of the properties.

The Trust is governed by a Board of Trustees, who are well-known and respected figures in the field of heritage and the arts. The Trust's strategy is developed by the Director General (DG) in conjunction with the Trustees.

The Board of Trustees and the DG have always believed that there are a number of 'flagship' properties which people want to preserve and support. These properties encourage people to become members of the Trust and to renew their memberships each year, regardless of whether they actually visit the properties.

In the annual budget, a share of the central membership income is allocated to each individual property. The amount each property receives depends on whether or not it is a 'flagship' property, and how important the collections within the property are believed to be.

Being the manager of a 'flagship' property is considered an important position and enjoys many privileges, including spacious private accommodation within the property itself, and a dedicated personal assistant.

Recently, the government has announced plans to halve its grants to the Trust, meaning the Trust will have to significantly increase its income from commercial activities to make up the shortfall in funding. The DG resigned in protest at the government's actions. However, the Trustees recognised the scale of the problem facing the Trust, and appointed a new DG from the private sector to develop a new business strategy. The new DG was previously the CEO of a major retail chain.

The DG has produced a strategic planning document, which includes a number of controversial proposals:

- In future, the central budget will be allocated to properties according to visitor popularity. This is designed to stimulate properties to come up with interesting and innovative ideas to increase visitor numbers.

- Removing the property managers' personal assistants, and giving them IT training where necessary so that they can do their own administration

- Recruiting five regional business development managers to increase commercial income by selling a wider range of souvenirs from the gift shops, and hosting open air concerts and theatre productions in the grounds of the properties

- Recruit an e-commerce business manager to develop an online store

The 'flagship' property managers have reacted furiously to the DG's suggestions. The idea of linking budgets to visitor numbers has been greeted with dismay, and the DG has been accused of devaluing the historical significance of the properties in a search for popularity.

A number of these managers have written to individual members of the Board of Trustees with their concerns about the DG's proposals, while others have contacted local television companies and the local press and have given interviews which are critical of the DG's proposals.

All the managers across the Trust have also been particularly critical of the lack of consultation about the proposed changes. They argue running the Trust is very different to running a retail chain and the new DG hasn't taken time to understand the culture and values of the Trust before publishing her plans.

The new DG has been shocked at the strength of opposition to her plans and has asked you to help her deal with it.

Required

(a) Explain the role of a change agent in leading change. **(5 marks)**

(b) Discuss **five** underlying organisational cultural issues that have led to the resistance to the Director General's proposals. **(15 marks)**

(c) Recommend the steps that could be taken to overcome the resistance to the proposals. **(5 marks)**

(Total = 25 marks)

32 Goldcorn (45 mins)

Goldcorn is a multinational company that manufactures automobiles which it sells in the low- to medium-price sectors of the market. It is listed on an international stock market.

Goldcorn manufactures three different types of product: small cars, large cars, and trucks.

The company currently has four manufacturing sites: one in western Europe, one in eastern Europe, one in Asia, and one in North America. Each of the factories currently manufactures all three products and, in general, sells them in the region of the world in which that factory is located.

While sales are internationally diversified, market research has shown that different geographical regions require different designs and features. As a result, each factory has developed each of the products separately with different features and capabilities which are appropriate to the market in its own geographical region.

Each of the factories operates as a separate profit centre. However, profitability has declined in all four of the factories in recent years meaning that profitability for the company as a whole has also fallen steeply.

The central board has attempted to improve matters by reviewing costs, and applying a series of cost reduction programmes. It has also carried out some internal benchmarking exercises on costs and efficiencies.

The benchmarking exercises have shown that some of the factories can produce some vehicles at a lower cost than others, but the results are not consistent. For example, the Asian factory produces small cars more cheaply than any of the other factories, but it is the highest cost producer of large cars.

What is more, when there is a major change in exchange rates, the whole cost comparison exercise changes.

The CEO is concerned that although Goldcorn has repeatedly engaged in cost reduction programmes by selective redundancies, reducing capacity, changing reporting structures and outsourcing the production of various components, there has been no permanent cost reduction of any significance.

There has recently been an unexpected major new entrant into the industry from South East Asia, which has low costs and sells its vehicles at low prices. The CEO believes that if Goldcorn is going to be able to compete with this new entrant it will have to reduce costs much more significantly than it has been able to do in the past.

In response, the finance director has suggested that Goldcorn considers globalising production.

The key features of his proposal are that:

- Each of the three products would be made in only one basic design, and all of the world production of each product would be made at a single factory. Consequently only three factories would be needed, so one would be closed.

- Each factory would be a cost centre rather than a profit centre. Responsibility for sales and marketing would be centralised functionally worldwide.

Given the perceived significance of the threat of the new entrant, the finance director argues that these changes should be pushed through urgently, with the aim of completing the change programme within six months.

He believes that that larger scale specialist production would significantly reduce production costs. However, he has suggested that the situation should be reviewed in two years' time given the uncertainties involved in such a major change.

Required

(a) Critically analyse the type of change programme envisaged in the finance director's current proposal compared to those carried out in the previous cost reduction exercises. **(10 marks)**

(b) Discuss the reasons why Goldcorn should communicate the nature of the changes to the key stakeholders affected by the finance director's change programme. **(8 marks)**

(c) Analyse the possible barriers to change that may arise and cause resistance to the implementation of the finance director's proposal. **(7 marks)**

(Total = 25 marks)

33 ChemiCo (45 mins)

Chemico is a chemical engineering company, based in an eastern European country. It is the largest and most important employer in the region, which is a relatively poor area with only one small town in reasonable commuting distance.

Chemico's main shareholders are international financial institutions, who have also provided finances in the form of loans.

At the moment, the company is performing well. Annual sales and profits have been increasing, the share price is strong, and the company has a number of large orders on its order book. It also has a favourable reputation among customers, which include some major household names.

However, Chemico's directors realise that the company's profitability is likely to diminish in the longer term, because new engineering technologies are being developed which will reduce (although not eliminate) the demand for their products.

The directors have been considering the option to diversify by developing a new product, using the same basic engineering and chemical processes as the existing products. However, this new product can present higher risks of toxic incident, and environmental campaigners have written to the local authorities highlighting the inherent risks involved in developing the new product.

Chemico's directors are also aware that one of its competitors is also developing a similar new product. Initial scientific research has concluded that Chemico's new product is generally more effective than its rival's in the process it was designed for. However, the rival product doesn't pose any toxic risk.

Chemico's director's are currently considering the possibility of entering a strategic alliance with the competitor for the joint development of the new product.

Chemico is also considering a move into manufacturing specialist plastics. The plastics manufacturing business is one of the major users of Chemico's current products. However, Chemico would need to develop completely new manufacturing processes for it to be able to be able to make the plastics in house.

The directors feel the investment required could be justified because there is strong growth in western Europe for the plastics, and the margins earned would be much higher than on their current products. However, initial investigations have also shown that Chemico could enter the market by buying a small local plastics company from the current owner who wishes to retire.

Required

(a) Assume Chemico decides to pursue the first proposal and develop the new chemical product itself. Discuss the main stakeholders' likely reactions to that proposal, and the degree to which they are likely to resist the proposal. **(9 marks)**

(b) Evaluate the issues which Chemico's directors should consider with respect to entering a strategic alliance with the competitor for the joint development of the new product. **(7 marks)**

(c) Discuss the change implementation issues which are likely to arise if Chemico decides to acquire the plastics company. **(9 marks)**

(Total = 25 marks)

34 ProfTech (45 mins)

ProfTech is a privately-owned training college which specialises in providing courses in business subjects such as accounting, marketing and law.

It is currently the largest training college in its country, but its market position is increasingly coming under threat from Youtrain Co which has developed an electronic learning (e-learning) facility which is proving very popular with students. Students value the flexibility it gives them as to when they choose to learn.

ProfTech's directors are keen for ProfTech to develop its own e-learning product, and have approved the budget for the investment in the electronic hardware and software required to support such a product. However, the e-learning programme also requires considerable investment in tutor time to convert the existing taught materials into electronically accessible modules.

The directors have said that within two years they want all students to have the option of having either face-to-face or online tuition for every course that ProfTech offers. Some of the tutors who are in favour of e-learning have already developed their online courses, and are offering them for students, but a number of tutors have yet to do so.

The majority of ProfTech's tutors argue that the best way for students to learn is through face-to-face contact with tutors, and they remain unconvinced of the benefits of e-learning. Very few of the tutors have taken advantage of the in-house courses which have been arranged for them to show them how the e-learning software works, and how to prepare e-learning materials. Consequently, many of the tutors don't understand how the software works, yet they still automatically blame the IT department if any problems arise with the e-learning material they are preparing.

Not surprisingly, the impact of e-learning at ProfTech is very varied. Some courses make extensive use of online learning and technology, while others are still taught largely by traditional classroom methods. A number of students have commented critically on this variation.

ProfTech's directors are worried about imposing e-learning on their staff in the face of known resistance. However, they are equally concerned that the impression ProfTech is giving to current and prospective students, in an increasingly competitive and international marketplace, is far from impressive.

The current partial and unsystematic use of e-learning is becoming a significant competitive disadvantage.

Required

(a) Briefly discuss how ProfTech's directors could use force field analysis in connection with the e-learning facility. **(6 marks)**

(b) Discuss the reasons why the tutors are opposing e-learning. **(6 marks)**

(c) Advise the approaches the directors may take to ensure that the change to e-learning is successfully implemented. **(13 marks)**

(Total = 25 marks)

> **IMPLEMENTATION OF STRATEGIC PLANS**
>
> Questions 35-42 cover implementation and control, the subject of Part D of the BPP Study Text for Paper E3.

35 Operating theatre (*MABS*, 5/06) — 45 mins

4D is a large teaching hospital. While it offers a full range of hospital services to its local community, it also has a large staff of professors and lecturers who teach and train all kinds of medical student. 4D has a very good reputation for clinical excellence.

One of the areas in which 4D is very highly regarded is the training of surgeons. Three of the nine operating theatres in the hospital can be observed from a gallery, though only a limited number of students can watch any operation due to space constraints. This allows the students to watch an experienced surgeon carry out a procedure and then ask questions of their lecturer or the surgeon. Later in their training, students can use the same facilities to carry out operations while being observed by experienced staff and fellow students.

The IT department of 4D has just developed a new Information System for use in operating theatres. This system (OTIS – the Operating Theatre Information System) uses web technology to allow students anywhere in the world to videoconference with a lecturer during an operation. The students can observe the operation and the surgical team, and discuss the procedure with the surgeon and their lecturer. The system also works 'in reverse' so a surgeon at 4D can watch a student perform an operation elsewhere in the world, and provide guidance and support. The OTIS system is currently being tested, prior to introduction.

Required

(a) (i) Distinguish between Business Process Re-engineering (BPR) and Process Innovation (PI), and explain the role of information technology in each of these techniques. **(6 marks)**

 (ii) Discuss whether, in your opinion, the Operating Theatre Information System (OTIS) implementation is an example of BPR or PI. **(4 marks)**

(b) Evaluate THREE benefits to 4D and TWO benefits to society, of the Operating Theatre Information System (OTIS) **(15 marks)**

(Total = 25 marks)

36 Transfer prices — 45 mins

P plc is a multi-national conglomerate company with manufacturing divisions, trading in numerous countries across various continents. Trade takes place between a number of the divisions in different countries, with partly-completed products being transferred between them. Where a transfer takes place between divisions trading in different countries, it is the policy of the Board of P plc to determine centrally the appropriate transfer price without reference to the divisional managers concerned. The Board of P plc justifies this policy to divisional managers on the grounds that its objective is to maximise the conglomerate's post-tax profits and that the global position can be monitored effectively only from the Head Office.

Required

(a) Explain and critically appraise the possible reasoning behind P plc's policy of centrally determining transfer prices for goods traded between divisions operating in different countries. **(12 marks)**

(b) Discuss the ethical implications of P plc's policy of imposing transfer prices on its overseas divisions in order to maximise post-tax profits. **(13 marks)**

(Total = 25 marks)

37 Royal Botanical (MABS, Pilot paper) — 45 mins

The Royal Botanical Gardens has been established for more than 120 years and has the following mission statement:

'The Royal Botanical Gardens belongs to the Nation. Our mission is to increase knowledge and appreciation of plants, their importance and their conservation, by managing and displaying living and preserved collections and through botanical and horticultural research.'

Located toward the edge of the city, the Gardens are regularly visited throughout the year by many local families and are an internationally well-known tourist attraction. Despite charging admission it is one the top five visitor attractions in the country. Every year it answers many thousands of enquiries from Universities and research establishments, including pharmaceutical companies from all over the world and charges for advice and access to its collection. Enquiries can range from access to the plant collection for horticultural work, seeds for propagation or samples for chemical analysis to seek novel pharmaceutical compounds for commercial exploitation. It receives an annual grant in aid from Central Government, which is fixed once every five years. The grant in aid is due for review in three years' time.

The Finance Director has decided that, to strengthen its case when meeting the Government representatives to negotiate the grant, the Management Board should be able to present a balanced scorecard demonstrating the performance of the Gardens. He has asked you, the Senior Management Accountant, to assist him in taking this idea forward.

Many members of the board, which consists of eminent scientists, are unfamiliar with the concept of a balanced scorecard.

Required

(a) For the benefit of the Management Board, prepare a briefing on the concept of a balanced scorecard, which also analyses its usefulness for The Royal Botanical Gardens. **(10 marks)**

(b) Discuss the process you would employ to develop a suitable balanced scorecard for The Royal Botanical Gardens and give examples of measures that would be incorporated within it. **(15 marks)**

(Total = 25 marks)

38 Management styles (MABS, 11/07) — 45 mins

B is a multinational company with more than 20 divisions operating in various light engineering industries supplying automobile and aircraft manufacturing companies. Each division is managed by a chief executive officer (CEO) reporting directly to the board of directors of B.

B has recently acquired C, a smaller company with only 5 divisions which also operate in light engineering and supply similar customers to B's existing businesses. Each division is managed by a CEO reporting to the board of directors of C.

In the previous acquisitions that B has made, the acquired companies have been allowed to continue operating independently. This is despite the fact that there are overlapping or competing divisions in the combined enterprise. There is no certainty that this approach will continue.

Using Goold and Campbell's classification, B operates a system of 'strategic planning', and C operates a system of 'strategic control'.

B has announced that the board of directors of C will retire and each of the former divisions of C will report directly to the board of B.

The board of directors of B recognises that this will represent a considerable change in culture, working practices and expected behaviour for the CEOs of the divisions of C. It is concerned that there may be problems in ensuring the commitment of those CEOs to both B and its 'strategic planning' style.

As part of the acquisition team you are responsible for the transition to the new structure.

Questions

Required

(a) Discuss the differences between 'strategic planning' and 'strategic control'. **(4 marks)**

(b) Discuss the impact that the change in planning culture is likely to have on the CEOs of the former divisions of C. **(11 marks)**

(c) Explain how the changes to the reporting arrangements could be implemented to ensure the commitment of those CEOs to B. **(10 marks)**

(Total = 25 marks)

39 Performance measurement (*MABS*, 5/07) — 45 mins

D is a management consultancy partnership providing complex computer modelling services to utility companies. Three partners started the business ten years ago but rapid growth in the past four years has seen it increase to fifteen partners. Each partner has a team working exclusively for, and reporting directly to that partner. Competition between the teams is fierce and, sometimes, heated. The loyalty of each team to its respective partner is very strong.

Members of each team are rewarded with an annual team bonus based on the amount of new business they bring in each year. However, recently it has been discovered that teams have been competing with each other for the same potential new client.

Partners recruit all consultants as trainees, usually after they have obtained a doctorate in pure mathematics or economics. After a six months probationary period they are either confirmed in post or asked to leave. The rewards for those that stay are high with at least 60% of income derived from the team bonus. Typically a basic salary of $40,000 would be boosted to $100,000 if the team has worked aggressively and found new clients.

The service that the partnership provides is highly specialised and at the forefront of available technology. Each team will write computer simulations to address its clients' problems. These models are not made available outside the company and, on some occasions, have not even been shared with other teams in the consultancy.

At a recent partners' meeting, it was agreed that the inter-team rivalry was not working in the partnership's best interest, since teams were competing in such a way as to damage the firm's reputation, profitability and its prospects for growth. Recognising that the current performance measurement system encouraged this behaviour, the partners agreed that an appropriate performance measurement system should be introduced which was less one-dimensional. The partners believed this would encourage better practice in terms of knowledge sharing and a coordinated approach to their existing clients and potential clients. They have recognised that the introduction of a multi-dimensional performance measurement system will involve a significant training programme for their teams to redirect their current focus away from only finding new business.

Required

As a first stage in this process, you have been appointed as management accountant and practice manager.

(a) Advise the partners of the functions that an effective performance measurement system will perform for D.

Note. You are not required to describe, in detail, any particular system. **(10 marks)**

(b) Recommend the process that should be used in developing the performance measurement system to be used within D. **(15 marks)**

(Total = 25 marks)

40 International acquisition (*MABS*, 5/08) — 45 mins

EEE is a divisionalised company, based in F, where it is quoted on the stock exchange. EEE manufactures and sells small electrical equipment products. As a country, F is more highly developed than the neighbouring countries. EEE has enjoyed a strong home market and has exported to the neighbouring countries.

EEE has had a reputation for producing high quality products. Recently, it has come under increasing competitive pressure from new, privately held, companies based in the neighbouring countries.

It appears that competitors based in these neighbouring countries have been selling lower quality products than EEE and have been undercutting it quite significantly in terms of price. Sales in both EEE's home and export markets have been badly affected by the actions of these competitors in the neighbouring countries.

EEE has looked at a number of possible solutions to this situation and has decided to acquire a manufacturing company in one of the neighbouring countries and move all of its production there, completely closing the manufacturing division in F. This would mean that EEE would purchase one of the companies that has recently become a competitor. EEE would maintain its present divisionalised structure within its home country F and treat the acquired company as a new division.

The Board of Directors recognises the need to carefully select a suitable acquisition target company. The Board also recognises that careful consideration will need to be given to the most suitable approach to performance management once the acquisition has been made. The Board is considering an approach based on either Return On Investment (ROI) or Residual Income (RI).

Required

(a)   Advise the Board on what information would be required to assess the suitability of an acquisition target.
(15 marks)

(b)   (i)   Discuss the difficulties that EEE may experience with the performance measurement of its division, post acquisition. **(6 marks)**

    (ii)   Discuss the disadvantages that EEE may experience if it chooses to use ROI as its primary performance measure. **(4 marks)**

(Total = 25 marks)

41 Computer company (*MABS*, 11/08)   45 mins

DD is a research company operating in the computer hardware industry. It has been established for three years. The company employs 30 scientists and engineers working in three research teams. One of those teams has invented an innovative processor which is significantly faster than any processor that is currently available commercially. It is likely that the new processor will be usable in computers used for industrial and, possibly, gaming purposes. The other teams are working in similar areas, developing processors.

The company is privately funded by an entrepreneur (Mr X), who made $350 million from the sale of his previous computer business.

Although all of the researchers have done new and innovative work, which has led to a number of published academic papers, no patents have been filed since the company started. Therefore, none of DD's innovative products has ever become commercially available.

Mr X has, to date, allowed his research staff to conduct research which is focused on creativity rather than commercial viability. He does not want to lose any of the current research staff but now wants to encourage them to be more commercially aware.

Mr X has decided that the company must now capitalise upon the innovative computer processor that one of the DD teams has invented. He intends that some of the focus should shift to the development of commercially available products rather than purely research activities.

Mr X recognises that this will be a significant change in strategy and culture for the company and that the change will require significant planning and management. Mr X intends to hire marketing staff and five additional engineers to bring the processor, and any other potential products, to market as soon as possible.

Currently there is no performance measurement system in place within the company. Mr X believes that the Balanced Scorecard might be the best performance measurement system for DD.

Required

(a) Explain the components of the Balanced Scorecard model. **(4 marks)**

(b) Recommend, with reasons, two measures that DD should use in **each** of the components of the Balanced Scorecard model. **(16 marks)**

(c) Discuss how the Balanced Scorecard should be introduced and used, in order to help DD achieve the proposed change in strategy and culture. **(5 marks)**

(Total = 25 marks)

42 Global environmental charity (*MABS*, 5/09) 45 mins

E is a global environmental charity. E is internationally recognised for its work in the area of sustainable development and the protection of endangered species and habitats.

Some supporters of E have criticised the organisation for its lack of clear direction in an increasingly competitive environment. Donations to charities have been declining, year on year, for the past five years.

The structure of E is unusual in that there is an autonomous division in each country in which the charity operates. There are 45 autonomous divisions, each headed by a CEO. It is the responsibility of each divisional CEO to report to the Supervisory Board of 10 trustees, which is based in a European country. Four times a year, the 45 CEOs meet for two days to discuss performance and their plans for the future. The meetings usually finish with no clear decisions about a unified direction for the charity to take. The divisions act independently for the next three months. This has led to a number of crises, both financial and non-financial, in the past five years.

As a result, the Supervisory Board has recognised that the charity cannot continue with the existing lack of direction, control and accountability. The Supervisory Board has decided to introduce a performance measurement and control system which will help it to implement a clear strategic direction for the charity. The Supervisory Board recognises that this will be a significant change for the CEOs and managers, and the Board expects considerable resistance.

A consultant has suggested E should introduce a balanced scorecard system of performance measurement and control.

Required

(a) Discuss the advantages and disadvantages for E of introducing a balanced scorecard system of performance measurement. **(12 marks)**

(b) Discuss **four** reasons why the CEOs of E might resist the proposed changes. **(8 marks)**

(c) Recommend the steps that could be taken to overcome the resistance to change. **(5 marks)**

(Total = 25 marks)

PRACTICE SCENARIOS

Questions 43 to 51 provide some practice case study questions, taken from the old syllabus Management Accounting – Business Strategy (P6) exams.

However, please note, these case studies are not split into pre-seen and unseen material and so are included here to help you practise answering question study questions rather than trying to replicate the real E3 exam format. In your **E3 exam**, the 50 mark section A question will be based on a combination of **preseen** and **unseen** case study material.

43 Pipeco (*MABS*, 5/05) — 90 mins

Pipeco, a wholly owned subsidiary of an international company (the parent group), has for the past twenty years manufactured, by an extrusion process, large bore plastic pipe for use in water, sewage and gas plumbing systems. (Extrusion is a process whereby hot plastic is forced through a die and takes the shape of the die.) Based in Western Europe, Pipeco has been the major supplier to the infrastructure building projects in most surrounding countries. Pipeco has operated from a single site. All projects, which typically last three or four years, are won by competitive tender and Pipeco has had a success rate, for many years, of over 80% of the contracts for which it has bid. Pipeco's dominant position, in a very competitive industry, has been achieved by cost effectiveness and the high technical skill of its sales engineers.

In the last three years, revenue and profits have declined as existing building programmes have neared completion and no new projects have become available from current markets.

The directors of Pipeco feel they cannot maintain the dividend to the parent group at the present levels beyond the current year. The parent group has made available to Pipeco a budget of $2 million for investment and has suggested a hurdle rate of 10% on any project undertaken. Although the parent group takes a strategic, long term view it is currently under pressure from the shareholders to at least increase the overall profitability of the group and maintain the dividend.

The parent group is particularly concerned about profitability over the next five years because of the cost of the expansion plans in other subsidiaries.

There are a number of possibilities that Pipeco wishes to consider, including:

Option 1

Pipeco could expand geographically to countries which are beginning to improve their infrastructure. The recent expansion of the European Union is considered to be an opportunity over the coming years.

Preliminary investigations have identified two possible countries to which some of the existing extrusion plant and equipment could be relocated leaving sufficient capacity to finish existing orders.

Country A would involve an initial capital investment of $1.5 million and Country B would involve an initial capital investment of $2.0 million. Sales volumes, in tonnes *per year*, are as follows:

Years	Country A tonnes	Years	Country B tonnes
1 to 5	42,000	1 to 8	63,000
6 to 10	64,000	9 to 14	51,000
11 to 15	20,000		

Each tonne would sell for $90 and there would be variable costs of $85 per tonne.

Option 2

Pipeco could move into other areas of plastics, producing pipework and fittings for use within buildings. The manufacture of fittings would involve moulding, a very different manufacturing process. There are a number of established firms in that industry, although this is considered to be a strong growth industry within Western Europe, particularly at the prestige design end of the business where gross margins of 55% are quite common. Sales within the industry are made to retail outlets or, for larger building projects, by presentation to the architect.

Pipeco recognises that this a different business model to that currently used and the approached used by some departments, notably marketing, will need to change. Research has shown that Pipeco could enter the market by investing an initial $1,450,000 in plant and equipment followed by a further $425,000 for plant and equipment payable at the end of the first year of operation. The market entry would be achieved by buying a small, underfunded company from the owner who wishes to retire. The purchase price is included within the total of $1,875,000. This company is based in Pipeco's current home market.

Research has shown that the project would give the following projected probabilities and cash contributions from sales per year for the next ten years:

Year	$'000	$'000	$'000
1–10	300	435	265
Probability	0.5	0.3	0.2

These figures will only be achieved if the investment in plant and equipment outlined above is carried out and do not reflect the level of performance under current ownership. The directors recognise that Pipeco will need to market more proactively and have decided to consider adopting relationship marketing for this option should it be selected. Pipeco realises that the adoption of relationship marketing would represent a significant change to the way the company operates.

Summary

Whichever option is chosen, Pipeco believes that, with the exception of depreciation, which is based on gross capital expenditure, there would be no increase in fixed costs. All capital expenditure is depreciated on a straight line basis over ten years.

Pipeco has a good employment record, with low staff turnover, and would prefer to retrain and possibly relocate (depending on the option selected) staff rather than make them redundant. It believes the staff would welcome this approach.

Required

As the management accountant of Pipeco:

(a) Make reasoned recommendations on the selection of Options 1 and 2.

Note. Up to 16 marks will be awarded for calculations. **(29 marks)**

(b) Identify the additional information that would need to be gathered to compare and contrast the suitability of the two countries identified for possible relocation in Option 1. **(6 marks)**

(c) (i) Briefly describe relationship marketing and explain how the approach would benefit the company. **(6 marks)**

(ii) Advise how the changes associated with the introduction of relationship marketing and the acquisition should be implemented if Option 2 is adopted. **(9 marks)**

(Total = 50 marks)

44 Island transport (MABS, 11/05) — 90 mins

S Company provides transport by sea and air between a country's mainland and a small group of islands 30 miles off shore. The company operates two ships, which make daily return trips to the islands. One ship carries only freight and provisions while the other transports freight and passengers. The islands are a popular holiday resort.

In addition to the ships, S operates some aircraft which convey passengers to and from the islands on a daily basis. While other airlines also fly to the islands, S is the only operator of ships to the islands, though some tourists visit in their private yachts. During the winter months the ships are repaired and maintained. However, the two ships are never out of service at the same time. The only other time the ships do not sail to the islands is in extreme weather conditions when it is considered unsafe to make the voyage. Major aircraft repairs are undertaken by S itself.

The Islands

The main industries on the islands are agriculture and tourism. Due to their location, the islands enjoy a climate that enables them to successfully cultivate crops ready for market much earlier than can be achieved on the mainland. The islands have established a reputation for growing flowers and vegetables, which they supply to retailers on the mainland. Some of these flowers and vegetables are exported to other locations throughout the world. Much of the produce is transported from the islands on board the ships operated by S.

A strong tourist industry has developed on the islands, peaking during the months of July and August. Most islanders are engaged in tourism, either by providing accommodation, boat trips, catering or retailing. The tourist trade declines sharply after September of each year until the following April. During this period the islanders are mainly engaged in agriculture.

The Company

S has 750,000 ordinary shares in issue, which are owned by the directors and employees of the company.

Over the years the company has established a good reputation for reliability and safety in its passenger services. The passenger ship operated by S was launched in 1979. It can carry a capacity of 200 passengers and can accommodate some cargo. The company charges the same price of £120 per person for a return trip irrespective of whether the passenger is an islander or visitor. This charge per passenger has increased steeply in recent years and considerably reduced the difference that, at one time, existed between the fares for travel by air and sea. Similarly, the other airlines operating to and from the islands do not differentiate between visitors and islanders in their charging policies.

S has secured mooring rights at ports on the mainland and on the islands. However, these are negotiated on a periodic basis and are due for renewal in one year's time. In the last financial year, the company achieved an after tax profit of £120,000 on a turnover of £4.8 million. S has experienced a gradual reduction in profit over time, as it has not been able to cover all its continually increasing operating costs by increasing its passenger and freight charges.

S owns the two ships, which had a net book value of £1.6 million at the end of the last financial year. At the same point in time, S had in its accounts a net book value of £2.9 million for all property, plant and equipment.

Potential Development

A few years ago, a mainland holiday company (M) applied to the government of the country and islands for permission to build a holiday complex on one of the uninhabited islands. The complex was planned to accommodate a maximum capacity of 500 people constantly throughout the year, and intended to incorporate numerous entertainment facilities associated with water and beach sports. In addition, the complex was planned to have indoor swimming facilities as well as its own golf course and bars. The application was refused by the government on the basis that the development would be out of character with the local environment. This decision was well received by the local island communities.

Since the application was made, there has been residential holiday accommodation built on two of the other uninhabited islands. This has been in the form of high quality hotels and apartments. Since these developments have taken place, the government has undertaken an initiative to increase the revenue generated by tourism, and has indicated to M that it would now view its development proposals more favorably. If the development was in a similar style to the other accommodation, the government would not oppose the scheme. M has indicated to the government that it wishes to proceed with a development similar to that previously proposed (that is, for 500 guests). M is preparing to invite quotations, from S and others, for the transport of building materials from the mainland to the site and the subsequent transport of tourists once the complex is operational.

Implications for S

The directors of S are aware that M intends that its visitors would travel to the complex by both air and sea. In order to prepare for a quotation, the directors have recognised that they would need to be willing to increase their sea passenger capacity. They would need to replace their existing passenger ship if they were awarded the contract. A replacement ship with sufficient capacity would cost £7 million and would be bought in two years' time. The scrap value of the existing ship would be £250,000. The directors estimate that the cash running costs of the replacement ship would be £12 per passenger, the same as for the existing ship.

In order to moor the new ship, extensive building works would be required at the major port on the mainland. S's directors expect that this will cost approximately £1 million and will take one year to complete. These works will commence immediately upon the contract being agreed with the holiday company, which is expected to be in one year's time. There will be no increase in passenger numbers until the new ship is bought in two years' time.

If awarded to S, the contract for the transportation of passengers will be for a duration of five years. It is expected that 90% of the visitors attending the complex will go by the sea route rather than by air. On average, the visitors travelling to the holiday complex will each remain there for two weeks and, due to the extensive entertainment provision at the complex, there will be constant demand throughout the year. There is sufficient capacity available for the existing airlines servicing the islands to carry the extra passengers who wish to travel by air.

If awarded the contract for the conveyance of passengers, the directors of S expect that S will obtain an additional contribution of £2 million for transporting the materials necessary to build the holiday complex. This contribution can be assumed to arise two years from now.

The contract terms (for the conveyance of passengers only) will be that S will receive from M an equal payment each year over the life of the actual contract. Payments to the successful bidder will commence in three years' time and run for a period of five years. It may be assumed that S will also charge each passenger £120 for a return trip throughout the period of the contract.

S requires a return of 20% on this project, to reflect the degree of risk involved. The directors believe that the value of the new ship will have fallen to £4 million by the end of the contract. All cash flows can be assumed to arise at the end of the year to which they relate unless otherwise stated.

Required

(a) Explain the threats to S from changing market conditions. **(10 marks)**

(b) Identify what price per year the directors of S should quote to M for the contract to convey the additional passengers. You should use the annuity approach to determine the equivalent annual value required. **(15 marks)**

(c) Discuss what financial and non-financial control measures could be implemented by S during the bid process and the operation of the contract to convey passengers to the holiday complex. **(15 marks)**

(d) Identify how S could develop its business in the long term by extending its operations beyond the transport services it provides. **(10 marks)**

(Total = 50 marks)

45 Specialist cars (*MABS*, 5/06) — 90 mins

CCC is a specialist car manufacturer, based in Y, a country in Europe. Three ex-employees of a major car manufacturer founded CCC in 1992 as a private limited company. CCC has never required further finance to aid its expansion, and remains a private company owned by the three founders. The three, who are all engineers, decided to leave their former employer in order to establish a business producing hand-built high performance sports cars for wealthy customers. The major car manufacturers are not able to supply such vehicles, as their systems are all based on the assumption that they will produce each car model in sufficient numbers to benefit from significant economies of scale.

CCC has always been profitable, and has grown significantly in recent years. It is now the second largest specialist car manufacturer in Europe and employs 300 staff at its head office and factory near the capital city of Y.

The specialist car industry

The customers who buy specialist cars are very status-conscious, and want a car that is totally unique. They are prepared to pay a very high price for their new car, in comparison to 'top of the range' models from the major manufacturers, but require extremely high quality and service levels in return. At present there are fewer than twenty specialist car manufacturers in Europe, and only six of these (including CCC) produce sports cars. The others specialise in off-road vehicles, armour-plated cars or limousines. As the cars are produced to customer order, there has historically been little price competition between the various specialist sports car manufacturers.

CCC, in common with other specialist car manufacturers, has invested a significant sum in creating the design of its two car models. It also spends a large proportion of its annual budget on sales promotion and marketing. This includes placing expensive advertisements in upmarket car magazines, and attending many car shows and exhibitions. CCC also has a reputation for paying higher than average salaries to its senior designers and production staff. As a result, staff turnover at CCC is virtually non-existent.

Customers, who are often loyal to a particular manufacturer, can specify modifications to the basic design, such as minor changes to the body shape of the car, or major changes to the engine performance and driving characteristics of the car. The directors of CCC have always assumed that their customers are not particularly price-conscious, as they are often wealthy individuals with high disposable incomes. For these customers, the alternative to buying a car from CCC might be to purchase a yacht or go on a round-the-world cruise.

CCC manufactures most of the components of its cars in-house. The main exceptions are electrical and control equipment, wheels and tyres. The only major bought-in component is the car's engine, which CCC buys from a major car manufacturer and then sends to SSS (a subcontractor) for modification and performance upgrades. While the engine is relatively expensive, it is the work of SSS that represents the single most significant cost of producing each car. CCC has, on occasions, paid SSS the equivalent of 25% of the final sales price of a car.

The board meeting

At the most recent board meeting of CCC, the directors discussed the worsening financial position of the organisation. Having spoken to the Sales Manager they came to the conclusion that, with the economies of Y and neighbouring countries in recession, customers had recently become more aggressive in negotiating down the purchase price of their cars. This had put pressure on the profit margin of CCC for the first time in its history. The directors therefore felt it was necessary to commission an independent review of their industry.

The Finance Director provided the following summary of CCC's performance:

€million	2005	2004	2003	2002
Revenue	11.75	11.12	10.06	10.10
Pre-tax profit	0.88	1.43	1.55	2.01
Dividend paid	0.08	0.50	0.50	0.50

The directors were particularly alarmed that SSS, the engine modification sub-contractor, seemed to be making almost as much profit on one of the engines as CCC was on the whole car. The Purchasing Manager of CCC said that it was impossible to negotiate a lower price with SSS, as most of CCC's customers specified that their car must have its engine prepared by SSS. The Sales Manager agreed that one of the 'unique selling points' of CCC's cars was the work done by SSS. At present, SSS does not supply engine modification services to any of CCC's competitors, but there is no contractual obligation to prevent it from doing so. The Purchasing Manager reported that CCC has no long-term supply contract with SSS, and the owner-manager of SSS had declined the offer of such a contract, believing that to enter into such an agreement would not be in the best interests of himself and his seven staff.

SSS

The Purchasing Manager has obtained the following information relating to SSS.

Extracts from the financial statements of SSS Ltd

	2005 €000
Revenue	2,455
Cost of sales	1,398
Other costs	867
Profit before tax	190
Profit after tax	133
Dividend paid	65

	At 31 Dec 2005 €000
Non-current assets	894
Inventories	232
Receivables	146
Cash	32
Payables	244
Equity share capital	100
Retained earnings	960

Information obtained from the Motor Trade Association

Automotive component and service suppliers:
Average P/E ratio (for those suppliers with quoted share prices)	7.5
Average annual growth rate in reported post tax profits (1995-2005)	2.5
Average pre-tax profit margin	4.3%
Average pre-tax return on capital employed	11.2%

Average receivables days	65
Average payables days	28
Average revenue per employee	€128,500

Required

(a) Using Porter's 'five forces' model as a framework, evaluate the competitive environment in which CCC operates. **(15 marks)**

(b) Evaluate the financial position and performance of SSS, as at 31 December 2005.

Note. There are up to 12 marks available for calculations in this part of the question. **(25 marks)**

(c) Advise the directors of CCC how the organisation might overcome the bargaining power of SSS. **(10 marks)**

(Total = 50 marks)

46 AAA (*MABS*, 11/06) — 90 mins

Introduction

AAA is a large manufacturing company that specialises in the design and manufacture of televisions. It was formed in 1985, following the merger of two rival companies, and is now one of the three largest TV manufacturers in Asia. AAA employs over 2000 staff at its head office and four manufacturing plants, which are all in the same Asian country, Jurania. AAA is listed on the Juranian stock exchange.

The production system

TV manufacturing is a mass production industry, with high volumes of identical or similar products being made on a production line basis. The products are generally made to order for customers, who are either other electrical manufacturers (who put their name on the product and re-sell it) or large electrical retailers. The manufacture of televisions is still a relatively labour-intensive process, as many of the components need to be assembled in a precise way. Most of the electrical components used in AAA's process are bought in from suppliers, as is the TV screen and cabinet (the plastic case in which the screen and components are contained). The staff who assemble the components are mainly semi-skilled, and have been trained by AAA to perform fairly simple, repetitive operations. When completed, quality assurance staff test the TV sets, and any that are found faulty are returned to the production line to be re-worked.

Components received from suppliers are also tested by the quality assurance staff of AAA. As they do not have the time to test every component, they test a sample of components from each batch delivered. If they find more than one faulty component in every twenty tested, the whole batch is rejected and returned to the supplier.

Business Performance

The following is a summary of the performance of AAA last year. AAA reports its performance in the currency of its home country, the Juranian dollar (J$):

Last Year

Financial Performance

	Actual J$m	Budget J$m
Sales revenue	1,793	1,941
Gross (Factory) profit	1,177	1,320
Pre-tax profit	652	790
Capital employed (average)	2,835	2,550
Cash (closing)	179	485
Finished goods inventory (average)	38.2	20.0
Raw material inventory (average)	11.4	9.5
Work in process (average)	0.8	0.3

Last year

	Actual	Budget
Other performance indicators		
Share price (closing) (J$)	334.50	400.00
Earnings per share (J$)	46.00	50.00
Number of employees (average)	2,259	2,128
Sales (million units)	2.35	2.40
Number of finished units re-worked	54,000	30,000
Percentage of purchases from suppliers rejected(by value)	4.25	3.00
Average production cost of sales per unit (J$)	262	259
Average sales price per unit (J$)	763	809
New product lines developed	12	10
New product lines successfully launched	1	4
Products returned from customers as faulty (per 1,000 units sold)	28	20
Warranty claims (per 1,000 units sold)	56	30
Number of working employee-days lost to industrial disputes	2,500	3,200

The board meeting

At the most recent board meeting of AAA, the Chief Executive Officer asked for suggestions as to how the management of AAA might be improved. One of the non-executive directors suggested that the use of the balanced scorecard might assist in controlling the business, as it had in another company of which she is also a non-executive director. The marketing director mentioned that he had compiled some information about another organisation in the television manufacturing industry, BBB, and asked if that might be of use. The purchasing director mentioned that he had recently been at a conference where a speaker had suggested that the introduction of 'knowledge management' was improving the performance of many organisations. As far as the other directors present at the board meeting were aware, this was not an approach used commonly in their industry.

BBB

BBB is a major rival of AAA, and is based in a neighbouring Asian country, Mesnar. BBB is a private company, owned by a wealthy industrialist. BBB compiles its accounts in the local currency of Mesnar, the Mesnari Riyal (RM). Both the Mesnari Riyal and the Juranian Dollar are freely traded currencies, and the current spot exchange rate between the two is J$1:RM2.50. There is free and unrestricted trade between Jurania and Mesnar.

The following information has been obtained from BBB's filed accounts from last year, and from the trade association of which both AAA and BBB are members.

Last year

Sales revenue (RM million)	1,400
Total production cost of sales (RM million)	435
Profit before tax (RM million)	557
Capital employed (RM million)	1,589
Closing inventories (RM million)	17
Number of employees (closing)	740
Number of units sold	780,000
Number of warranty claims in the year	19,800

Required

(a) Prepare a balanced scorecard appraisal of the performance of AAA last year.

Note. There are up to 10 marks available for calculations in this section. You are not required to compare the performance of AAA with that of BBB in this section. **(25 marks)**

(b) As the management accountant of AAA, prepare a benchmarking report for the directors that compares the performance of AAA last year with that of BBB for the same period. You should refer to your answer to part (a) in making your comparison.

Note. There are up to 8 marks available for calculations in this section, and up to 2 marks for the use of an appropriate report format. You are not required to reproduce the calculations from your answer to part (a) in this section, but may do so if you wish. **(15 marks)**

(c) Advise the directors of AAA how the introduction of knowledge management might lead to AAA developing a sustainable competitive advantage over BBB. **(10 marks)**

(Total = 50 marks)

47 AFR (MABS, 5/07) — 90 mins

Introduction

AFR is a large retailer of furniture, based in an Asian country. It has three strategic business units (SBUs) which specialise in office, bedroom and lounge furniture. Each SBU is responsible for the design, procurement and retailing of its own range of furniture. AFR sells all its product ranges through a chain of large 'furniture superstores' throughout its own country. Each store sells all three furniture ranges.

AFR has been in existence for over twenty years, and has always been profitable. Recently, the organisation's profitability has been slightly higher than average for the furniture retail sector.

All the furniture that AFR sells is designed 'in house'. Design staff from each of the three SBUs work in a centralised research and development (R&D) department, where all designs are developed. Production of the designs is outsourced to a number of small local manufacturers. This ensures that AFR can keep close control of product features, style and quality, while negotiating down the unit cost of production.

Segmental analysis

The following figures are extracts from the report and accounts of AFR for 20X6. AFR reports its performance in the local currency, the dollar.

		$m
Sales revenue	Office furniture	4.23
	Bedroom furniture	3.20
	Lounge furniture	6.04
	TOTAL	13.47
Contribution	Office furniture	0.81
	Bedroom furniture	0.44
	Lounge furniture	0.75
	TOTAL	2.00

Market conditions

The market for office furniture is estimated to be growing at a rate of about 15% each year. The market leader is DS with a reported sales revenue from this sector of $6·35 million. DS sells a much narrower range of 'basic' office furniture than AFR, through a chain of specialised office furniture stores. Most of its products are mass produced in large factories elsewhere in Asia, and it is therefore able to sell at much lower prices than AFR.

The market for bedroom furniture is considered to be declining by about 5% each year. AFR is market leader in this segment, ahead of NKO (with sales revenue of $2·85 million) and MK ($2·14 million). AFR has a good reputation for the style and quality of its bedroom furniture, and customers report very high satisfaction levels.

The market for lounge furniture, such as sofas and easy chairs, is growing at a rate of about 2% each year. AFR is a relatively small player in this market which is dominated by MK with its sales revenue of $14·25 million. The second placed competitor is TSC ($11·96 million), closely followed by NKO ($8·94 million). Despite having tried to increase its market share in this segment, AFR has had little success. Much of AFR's lounge furniture is made to order, with customers allowed to choose from a wide range of styles and fabrics.

The following information has been provided by the Government bureau of economic statistics:

		$m
Market volumes	Office furniture	23.60
(20X6)	Bedroom furniture	12.80
	Lounge furniture	70.00

Dining furniture

The research and development (R&D) manager of AFR has noticed that the market for dining furniture, such as dining tables and formal dining chairs, is growing at a rate of about 10% a year. Furthermore, he is aware that neither DS nor MK has any dining furniture products. This market segment is served by many small retailers, each of whom sells a similar range. Most of the dining furniture currently on sale originates from a few large manufacturers.

The R&D manager has proposed to the Board of AFR that the organisation develop its first ever range of dining furniture. The R&D manager has provided the following estimates of project cost and revenue.

	$m
Depreciation (per year)	24,000
Other fixed costs (per year)	80,000
Variable cost (per unit*)	560
Average sales price (per unit*)	800

* A unit is one table and six chairs.

The R&D manager has calculated that, to breakeven, AFR must sell just over 400 units per year. He believes that such a level of sales is almost certain due to the stylish designs he has been working on.

The marketing manager is not sure. She feels that sales need to be closer to 500 units each year if AFR are to make a profit. The marketing manager also believes that demand is unlikely to exceed 500 units for such unusual designs. She is also concerned that the new dining furniture may be overpriced at $800 per unit.

The managing director asked the R&D manager how much investment in new capital equipment would be required, and the R&D manager said that the investment cost of $120,000 was already taken into account in the depreciation figure.

AFR evaluates projects over a five year period.

Required

(a) Evaluate the existing product portfolio of AFR.

Note. There are up to 7 marks available for calculations in this requirement. **(15 marks)**

(b) Recommend an appropriate strategy for each existing product range. **(9 marks)**

(c) Advise the Board whether to invest in the new range of dining furniture. You should assume a cost of capital of 10% for this project, a project life of five years and no taxation.

Note. There are 6 marks available for calculations in this requirement. **(14 marks)**

(d) Recommend appropriate control measures, assuming none are currently in place, for:

(i) the three existing product ranges **(6 marks)**

(ii) the project to develop the new range of dining furniture should it go ahead. (The project, for the purpose of this question, may be assumed to be the design of the new product range and production of prototype products only.) **(6 marks)**

(Total = 50 marks)

48 Food manufacturer (*MABS*, 11/07) — 90 mins

Introduction

AA is a large food manufacturer, making a range of basic canned and bottled foodstuffs. With a turnover of almost €500 million, AA is a major employer throughout Western Europe. While a few AA brands are recognisable market leaders, notably a range of canned fish and a 'household name' tomato ketchup, most of AA's products are in the second tier of food products. The company also produces a wide range of 'own brand' products for major supermarket chains (these are products in packaging bearing the name of the supermarket retailer, rather than the producer).

Financial performance (20X7/X8)

The following information is taken from the October 20X7 management accounts of AA. It relates to the budget and latest forecast for the full financial year ending 31 March 20X8:

Questions

	Year to date €m	Latest full year forecast €m	Full year original budget €m
Sales revenue from major supermarket chains	177.0	357.0	
Sales revenue from wholesalers	42.9	89.4	
Gross sales revenue (after returns)	219.9	446.4	495.6
Discounts given	(9.9)	(20.1)	(15.6)
Net sales revenue	210.0	426.3	480.0
Gross profit*	36.2	68.2	99.0

* The prices charged to customers are calculated to generate a gross profit margin, before any discount, of 20% (that is, 495.6 x 20% = 99).

After much discussion about the possible causes of this year's poor performance, the most recent board meeting of AA discussed possible solutions. The following initiatives were identified, which should increase forecast sales revenue in the five remaining months of the current financial year:

- The Marketing Director stated that the effects of a major advertising campaign, aimed at wholesalers, had been omitted from the most recent forecast. This would be launched shortly, and should result in an increase in sales revenue from wholesalers of 8% for the remainder of the year.

- The Business Development Director proposed that a new product line, planned for launch in 20X8/9, should be launched early. The new products are already in stock, and should generate gross sales revenue of €8.4 million by year end, without affecting the sales of other products.

- The Sales Director announced that a new wholesale customer had just been won, in an Eastern European country. This new customer should generate about €12 million of net sales revenue in the remaining five months of the year. This revenue was not included in the latest forecast, as the Sales Director had not expected to win the contract.

Customer strategy

The directors of AA are concerned about the high cost of servicing some of its major supermarket customers. During a recent brainstorming session, they identified the following possible strategies to deal with the least profitable of these customers:

1. Stop selling to them. This will mean that the customers, if they wished to sell AA products, would have to buy them through a wholesaler.

2. Persuade the customers to reduce the number of cost generating activities (as identified in the forecast data below).

3. Introduce new technologies to reduce the cost of the cost-generating activities.

The Sales Director of AA has provided the following information relating to three of AA's major supermarket customers:

Forecast for 20X7/X8

	S1	S2	S3
Sales revenue (before discounts and returns) #	58	24	108
Average discount given (%)	3	2	8
Number of sales visits made	12	15	218
Number of purchase orders processed*	59	26	760
Number of 'standard'** deliveries made	104	318	602
Number of 'rush'*** deliveries made	7	2	158
Damaged products returned (% of sales revenue)****	2.1	2.0	3.4

Notes

\# The prices charged to customers are calculated to generate a gross profit margin, before any discount, of 20%.

* Purchase orders are paper documents, specifying items and quantities required, and the expected date of delivery.

** A 'standard' delivery is one that is ordered and scheduled in the normal way, that is, at least 24 hours before the delivery is required.

*** A 'rush' delivery is one that is ordered and scheduled for delivery on the day of order. This normally happens as a result of unexpectedly high demand causing a supermarket to run out of stock, or due to a customer error in calculating order quantities.

**** Customers are given a full refund for all damaged goods. These goods cannot be re-used or re-sold.

The Operations Accountant has provided the following costing information:

	Cost €
Forecast averages for 20X7/X8	
Making a sales visit	685
Processing a purchase order	148
Making a 'standard' delivery	2,250
Making a 'rush' delivery	6,475

Required

(a) (i) Briefly explain what is meant by 'gap analysis' in the context of strategic analysis. **(4 marks)**

(ii) Briefly explain the use of the Ansoff product/market growth strategies model in strategic planning, providing examples relevant to AA to illustrate your explanation. **(6 marks)**

(b) (i) Calculate the effect of the three initiatives (identified at the board meeting) on the full year net sales revenue gap. **(4 marks)**

(ii) Categorise each of the three initiatives in terms of the Ansoff growth strategies. **(3 marks)**

(c) Calculate and analyse the forecast net customer account profitability of each of the three major supermarket customers of AA, during the 20X7/8 financial year.

Note. There are 18 marks available for calculations in this requirement. **(25 marks)**

(d) Evaluate the three alternative strategies proposed for the least profitable of AA's major supermarket customers and recommend which of these strategies you believe AA should adopt. **(8 marks)**

(Total = 50 marks)

49 Machine components (*MABS*, 5/08) 90 mins

Introduction

AAA is a small manufacturer of replacement machine components for machinery used in the mining and oil exploration industries. It is based in an African country. It was formed in 1952, as a partnership between two engineers, and incorporated in 1977. AAA now employs 120 staff, and has an annual turnover equivalent to one million US dollars. AAA is proud to offer the very highest levels of customer service. Much of the machinery used by AAA's customers is quite old and, as a result, components are no longer available from the original equipment manufacturers (OEMs), most of which are large multinational companies. AAA mostly supplies parts directly to the end-users but also receives a small but significant proportion of its business from OEMs, who then supply the components to their customers.

The current business model

AAA has always run its business in a very traditional way. The sales manager receives most orders by telephone or fax. The order specifies the OEM part number that the component is to replace. If AAA has previously supplied that component, the sales manager checks the price list and tells the customer the price. AAA holds very low levels of finished goods inventory, and then only of the most commonly ordered components.

Where AAA needs to make a component for the first time, an AAA 'estimator' (a qualified engineer, responsible for producing an estimate of the material and labour involved in manufacturing the item) obtains the original drawings of the component, either from AAA's extensive archives or from the OEM. The estimator then produces detailed engineering drawings, a list of materials and parts required, and an estimate of the labour hours likely to be used at each stage of the manufacturing process. The estimate is passed to a costing clerk in the accounts department who calculates the likely product cost (labour, materials and overheads), adds a 'mark-up' of 50%, and advises the sales manager of the price. If the customer accepts the price, an order is passed to the production department, which schedules and completes the work. If the actual cost of production is significantly different from that estimated, the price list is amended to reflect the actual manufacturing cost.

Very occasionally, a customer sends (or brings in) an old component, which cannot be traced back to an OEM. The sales manager gives the component to an estimator, who dismantles the component and produces the necessary engineering drawings and estimate. This process is called 'reverse engineering', and is common in the component manufacturing industry. Reverse engineering currently accounts for about 5% of AAA's business.

When an order is fulfilled, the component is delivered to the customer, together with an invoice. Most customers pay within 30 days, by cash or cheque. AAA does not have a problem with bad debts. An increasing proportion of AAA's business is now transacted in US dollars, as African currencies tend to be unstable.

AAA prides itself on the personal service it provides. The close contact it has with its customers means that AAA receives a significant amount of repeat business. AAA has never advertised its services, but grew significantly until 2005 as a result of 'word of mouth' recommendations by satisfied customers. AAA, however, has not experienced growth for the last two years, although turnover and profit have remained stable.

AAA uses only very basic Information Systems (IS), and reports its performance using a simple comparison between budget and actual, which is produced using a spreadsheet package. AAA's accounting system is not automated, and transactions are recorded in traditional ledgers.

Project E: Computerised accounting and e-commerce systems

The sales manager of AAA has noticed that customers are increasingly mentioning that they would like to be able to order online. He knows that there has been a significant growth in business-to-business (B2B) e-commerce in recent years. The sales manager has recognised that in order to grow and to make a move into e-commerce possible, AAA's accounting system will have to be updated to a computerised one.

Having spoken to a number of potential suppliers, the sales manager has now received a proposal from SSS, a local company, to supply tailored 'off-the-shelf' systems for both accounting and e-commerce. SSS has provided a detailed breakdown of its proposal, to be known as Project E, which is summarised below.

The sales manager believes that, following implementation of the new systems (likely to be 12 months from contract agreement) e-commerce should lead to an increase in the company's turnover of 10% in its first year of operation. Thereafter, the turnover resulting from e-commerce should grow at a rate of 10% each year for the foreseeable future.

The sales manager also thinks that any increase in indirect costs as a result of this higher volume of business will be fully offset by a reduction in administration workload as a result of the new computerised accounting system. The gross margin earned from e-commerce business can therefore be used as the effective cash inflow for evaluation purposes. The current turnover of AAA is, as stated earlier, $1 million a year. The mark-up on products sold by e-commerce will be the same as at present (that is, 50%).

However, the sales manager thinks that a cautious approach should be taken to the evaluation of the proposal, and that any benefits after 5 years from implementation should be ignored. AAA has a weighted average cost of capital (WACC) of 15%.

The following information has been provided by SSS, the preferred systems supplier:

Project E

Item	Timing	Cost (US $)
'Mage Gold' accounting package	On agreement of contract	14,000
Tailoring of the above	During the first 6 months	20,000
'Sellit Online' e-commerce package	On agreement of contract	11,000
Tailoring of the above	During the first 6 months	8,000
Populating the e-commerce database	During the first 6 months	5,000
Training	During months 7–12	10,000
Support	Split over the five years following implementation	25,000
Hardware, networking and connection	During the first 12 months	40,000
Broadband service costs	Split over the five years following implementation	20,000
Total cost		153,000

Note. You should assume that all cashflows arise at the end of the period to which they relate, for example 'Tailoring' at the end of 6 months, and 'Training' at the end of 12 months.

Required

(a) Briefly explain how e-commerce has impacted on the way business is conducted. **(5 marks)**

(b) Briefly discuss how a new Information System (IS) strategy might impact upon corporate, business and functional strategies. **(8 marks)**

(c) Prepare a financial evaluation of Project E.

Note. You should ignore the effects of inflation and taxation. **(12 marks)**

(d) Evaluate the strategic and competitive benefits to AAA of the proposed e-commerce system. **(15 marks)**

(e) Advise AAA, based on your answers to part (a) and (d) above, whether or not to invest in the proposed e-commerce and accounting project.

Note. You are not required to reproduce the detail of your arguments from earlier parts of this question. **(4 marks)**

(f) Discuss how AAA might use its e-commerce system to increase the volume of business from 'reverse engineering' projects. **(6 marks)**

(Total = 50 marks)

50 Training college (*MABS*, 11/08) — 90 mins

Introduction

AAA is a privately-owned training college, which specialises in providing courses in business subjects. AAA was founded in 1992 by its current Chief Executive, who is a qualified lawyer. AAA grew rapidly to become one of the largest and most highly regarded colleges in A, an Asian country.

The general situation in A

The last two decades have been a period of rapid social change for the residents of A. The country's economy has developed from being mainly based on subsistence agriculture (that is, agriculture carried out with the aim of feeding the farmer and his/her family), to being much more progressive in all respects. The population is now fairly well educated, with literacy levels much higher among the under-20 age group than in the older population. This is partly as a result of government policy (introduced in the 1970s) aimed at making education to age 16 available to all citizens of A. While subsistence agriculture has declined sharply, commercial agriculture still contributes about 40% of the country's Gross National Product (GNP). The fastest developing sectors are manufacturing, food production, tourism, financial services and retail.

A is now regarded as a developed Asian economy, with a well-established business and financial community. A is home to many large industrial and commercial corporations, many of which operate globally. Recently, the economy of A has been growing at a rate of about 15% each year. This is better than the growth rates in neighbouring countries. A has a stable, democratic, political system. Its government has been in power for the last six years. A general election is expected at some time in the next two years, and the government is concerned that the main opposition party may be elected. Unlike a number of other countries in the region, A has no recent history of violent unrest or terrorist activity.

The business training market in A

The business training industry is dominated by three major colleges (of which AAA is one). There are also a number of smaller colleges. The estimated market shares are shown below.

Market shares %	AAA	BBB	CCC	Smaller colleges
• Finance & Accounting (F&A) courses	40	15	30	15
• Marketing courses	15	40	15	30
• Law courses	35	30	25	10
• Human Resource Management (HRM) courses	20	25	40	15
• Other courses	–	40	20	40

AAA has grown to its current size by means of organic growth. Both BBB and CCC, on the other hand, have made several acquisitions of smaller colleges in the last five years. Indeed, there have been rumours of a possible merger between BBB and CCC, but there is no evidence to support this. BBB was founded in 1990 by a group of academics from a university. CCC was founded in 1994 by an ex-director of BBB, to specialise in Finance courses. CCC has since recruited a number of experienced tutors from elsewhere in the industry, including an ex-director of AAA.

An independent survey, reported in the press in early 2008, made the following comments about the market:

"The business training industry in A is very buoyant in most sectors. Demand for courses in Law and HRM is rising quite rapidly, while the market for Finance courses is also growing (though at a slower rate). Marketing is the only sector in decline, possibly as a result of the growth in online 'e-learning' courses provided by The Marketing Institute".

'The Marketing Institute' (mentioned in the comment) is the professional body responsible for the development of marketing professionals in A. It is not a college. Currently it is the only professional institute in A to offer its own courses, whether online or 'face-to-face'. Other institutes are known to be considering the provision of online courses. BBB is known to be developing online courses, though AAA has no plans to do so.

The structure and performance of AAA

The Board of Directors of AAA now consists of the Chief Executive and four other directors. They are all senior tutors. Each of the four directors is responsible for a 'faculty' of the college, each of which provides courses in a specialist professional area.

The courses provided by AAA range from one day 'insight' or 'update' courses, on a theoretical or practical topic, to much longer courses leading towards exams for academic and professional qualifications. Courses for diplomas, degrees and professional qualifications require students to attend the college for up to 60 days in any one year. AAA does not provide any full time courses and does not provide any student accommodation.

Almost all the students on one day courses have their courses paid for by their employers. Some students on longer courses are also funded by their employers, but approximately half pay their own tuition fees. The college does not discriminate on price between employer-funded students and those who pay their own fees on individual courses. However, some large employers receive a discount for 'bulk purchase' of places on courses. The performance of the college during its most recent financial year is summarised below.

Year Ended 30 September 2008	Actual	Budget
Sales revenue (A$ Million)		
• Finance and Accounting (F&A) faculty	4.2	4.5
• Marketing faculty	0.8	1.0
• Law faculty	4.0	4.0
• Human Resource Management (HRM) faculty	3.1	3.5
Total for AAA	12.1	13.0
Profit (before interest and tax) (A$ Million)		
• Finance and Accounting (F&A) faculty	0.6	1.0
• Marketing faculty	−0.1	0.5
• Law faculty	0.6	1.0
• Human Resource Management (HRM) faculty	0.4	1.0
• Corporate and central costs	−1.4	−1.2
Total for AAA	0.1	2.3
Estimated Market Share (% market revenues)		
• Finance and Accounting (F&A) faculty	40	
• Marketing faculty	15	Not budgeted
• Law faculty	35	
• Human Resource Management (HRM) faculty	20	

Year Ended 30 September 2008	Actual	Budget
Staff numbers (equivalent full time employees)		
• Finance and Accounting (F&A) faculty	23	
• Marketing faculty	6	
• Law faculty	26	Not budgeted
• Human Resource Management (HRM) faculty	18	
• Corporate and central staff	14	
Total for AAA	87	
Student-day numbers (a student-day is one student attending for one day)		
• Finance and Accounting (F&A) faculty	2,030	2,000
• Marketing faculty	410	450
• Law faculty	2,100	2,000
• Human Resource Management (HRM) faculty	1,150	1,500
Total for AAA	5,690	5,950

The recent Board meeting of AAA

At a recent Board meeting, the following issues were raised:

- The directors responsible for the F&A and Marketing faculties each raised concerns about a small number of large employer organisations which represent a significant proportion of their faculty's business. These organisations are starting to demand discounts in excess of 20%. This is far higher than the discounts given to other corporate customers. The director of the Law faculty said that one of the law firms she deals with often books up to half of the places on a course, but now demands a discount of 20%.

- The director responsible for the Law faculty reported that two of her tutors had recently resigned, in order to take up positions with BBB.

- The Chief Executive expressed concern at the poor financial performance of AAA, when compared to the budget for 2007-08. He asked for a volunteer to take responsibility for financial planning and control for the new financial year. The director of the F&A faculty said that he could not help, as he was too busy teaching students and dealing with clients. There was no volunteer, so the Chief Executive reluctantly agreed to continue overseeing the work of the three finance staff.

Required

(a) Using the Boston Consulting Group (BCG) matrix, evaluate the product portfolio of AAA. **(8 marks)**

Note. There are up to 2 marks available for calculations in this requirement.

(b) (i) Produce a quantitative analysis of the performance of AAA. **(14 marks)**

Note. All 14 marks are for calculations in this requirement.

(ii) Using your quantitative analysis, identify and evaluate the 'strengths' and 'weaknesses' of AAA's performance. **(12 marks)**

(c) Produce a qualitative analysis of the strategic position and performance of AAA, with each of your findings categorised as either a 'strength' or a 'weakness'. **(8 marks)**

(d) Analyse the main 'opportunities' and 'threats' to AAA in its business environment. **(8 marks)**

(Total = 50 marks)

51 European Bank (MABS, 5/09)   90 mins

Introduction

AAA is a large banking group, based in a European country. AAA is stable and financially sound. It has several hundred local branches, and has a large number of personal and business customers. A personal customer is a private individual, and a business customer is a commercial organisation (such as a sole trader, partnership, limited company or not-for-profit organisation).

The Personal Banking Division of AAA is based at Head Office, and is responsible for establishing policy and procedures for the way AAA deals with personal banking customers. In addition to normal bank accounts, the Personal Banking Division also offers customers credit cards, loans and insurance products. The Business Banking Division offers the same services to business customers. All branches of AAA deal with both personal and business customers. The branches are responsible for implementing policies set by the two divisions.

Each branch manager within AAA is responsible for the control of the costs, staff, business and premises of their branch. The branch manager must comply with the policies and procedures established by the senior managers of the two divisions. Part of the cost of each Head Office division is allocated to the branches, in line with activity levels. The branch managers participate in a bonus scheme, based on the profitability of their branch. Senior managers in each of the divisions participate in a separate bonus scheme, based on the overall profitability of the Bank.

The 'Student Account' Campaign

For the last three years, the Personal Banking Division of AAA has run a campaign to recruit university students as account holders. As an incentive, AAA offers student account-holders 'free banking' while they remain in full-time study. Typically this is for three years. At the end of the free banking period, student accounts become subject to the normal terms for personal account holders.

The student account campaign is very unpopular with branch managers, as student accounts are effectively loss-making for the period during which free banking is offered. This has an adverse impact on the profitability of the branch, and therefore on the level of performance bonus earned by the branch manager. This issue has recently become more significant to AAA, following the resignation of the manager of Branch 32.

A typical student lifecycle

A new student account customer costs €30 to recruit. This cost is an apportionment of central marketing costs, which is passed on to the branch that opens the account. An additional administration cost of €20 is incurred in the branch for opening the account. Thus, the total initial cost is €50.

The student account holders typically pay no bank charges for the first three years. After this they pay bank charges of an average of €200 each year. The cost in the branch of maintaining any account is €60 each year. In each year, the bank assumes that the probability of any customer 'defecting' (that is, closing the account and moving to a competitor) is 20%. Such defections can be assumed to happen at the beginning of each year, including the first year. AAA operates at a cost of capital of 10%.

The competitive environment

AAA is one of five major banks in the country. There are also a number of smaller banks, some of which specialise in either personal or business banking. Each bank offers a wide range of incentives to attract and keep personal customers. Personal customer defection is quite common, as they 'shop around' for the best deals. Business customers, however, tend to be loyal to the bank and branch at which they open their first account.

Banks recognise that personal customers often require a wide range of 'add on' services, such as loans, insurance and credit cards. These products can be very lucrative for the bank, so they are often marketed aggressively to personal customers.

At present, three of the other major banks offer free banking to new student customers for between one and three years. One of the smaller banks offers three years of free banking to students and, additionally, gives each new student customer vouchers worth €30 for music downloads from a major Internet-based music distributor.

Branch 32

Branch 32 of AAA is located on the edge of a small city, only one kilometre from a large university campus. From 2002 until March 2009, the manager of Branch 32, was Ms A. In each of the years 2002 to 2005, Ms A received a performance bonus equivalent to about 20% of her basic salary. In 2006, Ms A's bonus was only 8%, and in the last two years she received no bonus at all as Branch 32 did not achieve the 'base level' of profitability necessary to trigger a bonus payment.

In February 2009, Ms A attended a regional management meeting, where all the branch managers in the region met with senior managers from the two divisions to discuss the financial performance of their branches and business policy. The Marketing Manager of the Personal Banking Division explained, to the regional meeting, that the student account campaign is based on the concept of 'customer relationship marketing'.

Ms A was shocked to find that she was the only manager in the region not to receive a performance bonus. As a result, Ms A resigned from the Bank and has since joined a competitor. A replacement manager for Branch 32 is now being sought, but no applications from within AAA have been received. The deputy manager of Branch 32 has also been offered promotion to manager but has declined. He has said that he would prefer to wait for another branch management job.

The next senior management meeting of the Personal Banking Division The Marketing Manager of the Personal Banking Division has approached you, as Management Accountant of the Division, and asked you to attend the next senior management meeting of the Personal Banking Division. He wishes you to help him to explain why the student account campaign should be continued. He is keen to persuade his colleagues that, rather than abandon the campaign, other policies and procedures should be changed to ensure its success.

Required

Produce a **report** to the senior managers of the Personal Banking Division, covering the following:

(a) Explain what is meant by the term 'customer relationship marketing', and how it differs from 'transactions marketing'. **(4 marks)**

(b) Discuss the advantages and disadvantages, to AAA, of adopting a 'customer relationship marketing' approach to dealing with student account holders. **(12 marks)**

(c) Briefly explain the concept of 'customer lifecycle value' and how it might be used to justify the 'student account' campaign. **(4 marks)**

(d) Calculate and analyse the customer lifecycle value of a student account, based on the information provided, over **the first ten years** of the customer life. Assume that all cashflows, with the exception of the recruitment cost, occur at the end of the period to which they relate. **(14 marks)**

Note: There are 10 marks available for calculations in this requirement.

(e) Discuss **five** changes that might be made to the branch managers' bonus scheme, if AAA chooses to continue with its customer relationship marketing approach to student accounts. **(10 marks)**

(f) Advise the senior managers of the Personal Banking Division whether to continue with the student account campaign and, if so, which of the changes to the bonus scheme (discussed in (e) above) should be adopted. **(4 marks)**

Marks for use of an appropriate report format **(2 marks)**

(Total = 50 marks)

SECTION A CASE STUDIES

Case study questions 52 – 54 combine pre-seen and unseen material in the same way they will be combined for the E3 exam.

52 ReuseR — 90 mins

Strategic level pre-seen case material

Background

The marketplace

Recycling has two significant impacts on the global environment. First, the use of recycled materials reduces the consumption of the world's natural resources. Second, recycling waste avoids the over-use of landfill refuse sites, which in turn reduces the level of potential pollution or contamination. Additionally, manufacturing costs can be reduced, as energy savings of around 5% can be achieved when, for example, new cans are manufactured using recycled aluminium.

Glass recycling is very efficient because a glass container is 100% recyclable and can be recycled over and over again with no loss in quality or purity. Another significant area of recycling is paper. Of Western Europeans' household waste, around 40% is paper waste, and paper is currently one of the fastest growing recycled products.

More and more businesses are also seeing the sense in selling off their waste paper and many new companies are entering into, or expanding their own, recycling business. Additionally, in today's business world, a company's image is one of its most important assets. A company that has a positive environmental profile will attract quality customers, employees and suppliers. It can also command a share price premium, as corporate investors are increasingly aware of the demand for "green" investments. There is also increasing external pressure to demonstrate effective environmental practices and to recycle waste.

Over ten years ago, recycling companies were small and operated only within their home country, but with the freedom to operate across boundaries within the EU, many of the larger recycling companies have made acquisitions to strengthen their position and to expand into new markets. Additionally, many large multi-national organisations have become more aware of waste and "green" issues and have established their own recycling departments, which recycle waste materials from other parts of the company.

Most European governments have established a variety of ways in which both domestic and industrial waste can be minimised and materials recycled.

Reuse Refuse (ReuseR)

Reuse Refuse (which trades as ReuseR) is a quoted company operating in a northern European country, with subsidiary companies across Europe. The company collects waste and recycles a wide range of products, but its single largest recycled product, which is also one of its most profitable, is recycled glass. It currently supplies recycled glass to twelve customers spread over eight countries in Europe. It sources its recycled glass supplies from hundreds of sources, including its many contracts for the collection and recycling of domestic waste. ReuseR also recycles a range of other waste products, including wood, paper, metal, tyres and a number of other materials.

ReuseR has expanded its operations across Europe through the acquisition of many smaller recycling companies. Since 20X0, with the pressure on governments and the general population to recycle waste materials, it has introduced several innovative ways in which various types of waste are collected for recycling and sold to a range of manufacturing companies.

In the late 1980's the company became listed and the current directors and employees collectively own over 53% of the shares. The rest of the shares are spread over a wide range of investors with no large shareholdings.

There is a small, strong head office team and there are also finance teams in each country where ReuseR operates. In each of these countries, a separate subsidiary company manages ReuseR's operations and acts as an autonomous business unit. Communication between some of the finance teams in the subsidiaries and head office needs to be improved.

Human resources

The company has experienced problems with recruiting, and also retaining, employees, despite providing training, good rates of pay and allocation of free shares for staff after two years of employment. The company is still experiencing a high staff turnover in some countries and in certain sectors of the business. HR and operational management are looking at ways in which team building and more flexible working could improve staff retention and commitment to the company.

Cost control and international logistics in ReuseR

The ReuseR Board has asked the Financial Director to investigate why the increased volumes and increased turnover have not resulted in corresponding increases in margins. At the December 20X8 Board meeting the FD tabled an analysis of costs. This demonstrated that the current level of spend on improved IT facilities was one of the contributing causes of the lower than expected margins, together with training and recruitment costs of new staff, which, he explained, was an ongoing high cost as the company was continuing to expand.

Two of ReuseR's main costs are staff costs, in respect of the collection of waste, and secondly distribution costs associated with recycled materials. As the volume of waste collected has increased, the collection costs have reduced as a proportion of the volume of waste collected, due to economies of scale. However, ReuseR has identified that its distribution costs of recycled materials have increased significantly more than changes in volumes of materials handled would justify in recent years.

Transportation costs have also increased significantly, while waste sorting and handling costs have fallen, mainly due to the introduction of new recycling plants in some countries. The bulk of some types of recycled products, some of which have a low resale value, have contributed to the reduced margins that ReuseR has experienced in the last few years. The finance director is investigating which materials are not cost effective to transport and recycle, so that the company can take a strategic decision not to handle these products.

ReuseR shareholdings, share price and earnings per share (EPS)

At the end of November 20X8 there were 200 million authorised shares, with a nominal value of €0·20 per share, and 90 million shares were issued and fully paid up.

The share price of ReuseR has risen slowly during the last 25 years and during 20X8 ranged from €1·91 to €2·61. ReuseR has a current P/E ratio of 10. The industry average P/E ratio is 9. The company achieved EPS of €0·24 in 20X8. The company plans to increase its EPS, in accordance with its five year plan, to €0·39 per share by 20X9.

Appendix 1 shows an extract from the accounts for ReuseR.

Establishment of ReuseR's first recycling operations in the Middle East

ReuseR opened a recycling plant in October 20X8 in a country in the Middle East. The move is to a stable country in the region, which has a very high record of recycling. This country is keen to establish itself as an example of high recycling levels to the rest of the world. ReuseR had wanted to establish a base in this country before the market for waste became too competitive. This would enable ReuseR to establish its name as a leading waste recycling company.

However, it is forecast that this new plant will result in operational losses for the first two years. The company has had many meetings with the large companies operating in this country and to date has signed two contracts for the recycling of waste.

Potential acquisitions by ReuseR

ReuseR has expanded its operations in the past mainly by acquisition, both by expanding into recycling different products and also into other countries. ReuseR is planning to make a number of further acquisitions to grow the business and also to give it access to new markets in other EU countries, and elsewhere, in which the company does not currently operate.

The ReuseR Board has set the following criteria as a guideline for possible acquisitions:

- Gross margins (defined as sales less all direct costs, variable and fixed) must be similar or higher than achieved by ReuseR (ReuseR gross margin is over 50%)
- Sales revenue of between €10 – €30 million per annum

- Must be a stand alone company, rather than a recycling division of a larger company. ReuseR has historically found it quite difficult to manage the merger of operations post acquisition, when it has acquired the recycling division only of a larger company
- Must be willing to be acquired (for cash or share exchange), as ReuseR's management do not want to pursue a hostile take-over.

The business development department of ReuseR, has identified a list of thirty possible targets for acquisition, of which most are operating in EU countries. However, some potential acquisitions are operating in countries in which ReuseR does not currently operate, as well as some countries outside of Europe.

Date: The current date is 1 May 20X9.

Appendix 1

ReuseR

	As at 30 November			
	20X8		20X7	
Statement of financial position	€m	€m	€m	€m
Non-current assets (net)		131.9		123.3
Current assets				
Inventory	20.8		19.9	
Trade receivables	46.5		39.1	
Cash and short term investments	6.4		4.1	
		73.7		63.1
Total assets		205.6		186.4
EQUITY AND LIABILITIES				
Equity				
Paid in share capital	18.0		18.0	
Share premium reserve	21.6		21.6	
Profit and loss reserve	109.8		95.1	
		149.4		134.7
Non-current liabilities				
7% Loan notes (redeemable in 20Y1)		20.0		20.0
Current liabilities				
Trade payables	22.5		19.6	
Tax	6.1		5.9	
Accruals	7.6		6.2	
		36.2		31.7
Total equity and liabilities		205.6		186.4

Note. Paid in share capital represents 90 million shares at €0·20 each

Income Statement

	Year ended 30 November	
	20X8	20X7
	€m	€m
Revenue	214.2	184.0
Total operating costs	185.0	155.9
Operating profit	29.2	28.1
Finance costs	(1.4)	(1.4)
Tax expense (effective tax rate at 22% after allowances)	(6.1)	(5.9)
Profit for the period	21.7	20.8

Statement of changes in equity year ended 30 November 20X8

	Share capital €m	Share premium €m	Retained earnings €m	Total €m
Balance at 30 November 20X7	18.0	21.6	95.1	134.7
Profit for the period	–	–	21.7	21.7
Dividends paid	–	–	(7.0)	(7.0)
Balance at 30 November 20X8	18.0	21.6	109.8	149.4

[TURN OVER]

Question 52 Part 2 – ReuseR

Unseen Case Material (Exam day material for Paper E3 only)

Background

ReuseR has expanded across Europe by acquiring smaller companies, and is currently looking to grow further. However, the company has also recognised the importance of controlling costs, and the Board are taking a keen interest in the profitability of different products.

Product profitability

At a recent board meeting, the Finance Director produced a summary of the costs (including directly attributable staff costs) associated with each material for the last year (20X8). He had grouped these costs into three headings: costs of collecting materials for recycling (collection costs); the cost of sorting and recycling (recycling costs); and the costs of distributing recycled materials to customers (distribution costs)

20X8 figures (actual)

	Sales revenue $m	Collection costs $m	Recycling costs $m	Distribution costs $m
Glass	79.8	7.1	21.5	7.3
Wood	42.3	4.7	14.0	5.1
Paper	46.5	3.7	13.0	4.2
Metal	14.1	1.4	5.4	2.0
Tyres	12.4	0.9	3.5	1.2
Others	19.1	1.5	5.5	2.1
	214.2	19.3	62.9	21.9

The finance director also summarised the forecast for 20X9 and highlighted the following key points:

- Sales revenue is expected to change as follows: Glass + 3%; Wood – 2%; Paper – 5%; Metal + 13%; Tyres + 1%; Others + 4%

- The decline in paper revenues reflects a newspaper publisher setting up its own recycling plant. Wood sales have been declining for a number of years now as the market is contracting.

- Demand for recycled metal is growing rapidly in the short term due to the high prices of new metal.

- Collection costs are expected to be 2% higher than 20X8 for all products, and no additional economies of scale are expected.

- Recycling costs are expected to rise 4% for glass and metal, but remain unchanged for the other products.

- Distribution costs are forecast to be 5% higher than 20X8 for all products.

The Operations Director made the suggestion that ReUseR should focus only on its most profitable materials, and should stop recycling any materials which are not forecast to make a contribution to operating profit of greater than 45%. (ReUseR defines contribution to operating profit as sales revenue less collection costs, recycling costs and distribution costs).

Strategic Control

The Board are concerned that the autonomy currently given to each of the business units is contributing to cost inefficiency. They argue that, by negotiating local contracts with suppliers, the business units are not necessarily getting best value for money. The Board also argue that the poor communication between the subsidiaries and the head office, and the lack of timely management information being provided by the subsidiaries, makes it very hard to monitor, and therefore control, costs.

The Board are considering curtailing the business units' autonomy, and centralising a number of key functions – including marketing and procurement. In addition, they are considering conducting a benchmarking exercise to assess performance across all the business units.

However, the HR director warned any decisions about centralisation need to be considered very carefully because of the impact they could have on the morale of the local managers and their workforces. He has stressed that if the business is restructured, the business units' bonus schemes must be adjusted to reflect the changes to the aspects of business performance they can control.

Potential acquisition

The Board are keen that the list of thirty possible acquisitions be reduced to a shortlist of three potential targets. The guideline criteria have already been applied and this has reduced the list of targets from thirty to ten. ReuseR's senior managers have been asked to attend a series of strategic planning meetings in the next two months, so that a shortlist of three target companies can be presented at the Board meeting in August 20X9.

Required

(a) Discuss the further factors (ie additional to those already covered by the initial screening) that the senior managers should consider when deciding which three of the ten targets they should select for their final shortlist. **(15 marks)**

(b) Calculate the *forecast* contribution to profit for each product for 20X9, and, in the light of this, evaluate the Operations Director's proposal to discontinue any products which make a contribution to operating profit of less than 45%. **(15 marks)**

Note: There are 8 marks available for calculations in this requirement.

(c) Assuming the Board decides to curtail the business units' autonomy, explain how this change could be implemented to ensure that the business unit managers remain committed to ReuseR. **(10 marks)**

(d) Evaluate the contribution the proposed benchmarking exercise could make to ReuseR.

(10 marks)

(Total = 50 marks)

53 Domusco — 90 mins

Strategic level pre-seen case material

Background

Domusco was formed 42 years ago, and became a listed company 30 years ago, in its home country of Zee, a fictitious country in Southern Europe. Zee is not in the European Union (EU).

The Domusco group structure comprises a number of wholly-owned subsidiary companies operating in different construction business segments. The three construction business segments that Domusco has are:

- Major construction projects
- Office building construction
- House building

Domusco's major construction projects subsidiary company is structured around the type of project undertaken.

The Domusco office building subsidiary company manages all office construction work in Zee, other areas of Europe and the Middle East from its Head Office based in Zee.

Domusco's house building subsidiary company is structured differently, as it has separate subsidiary companies for geographic areas. It has house building subsidiary companies based in Zee, another European country as well the USA, to enable management to be closer to the markets in which they operate.

Domusco has established itself as a builder of high quality housing and apartments at the top and middle segment of the market. The Domusco group has been able to command premium prices, because of its good designs and quality specifications. Domusco has not been involved in any low cost or social housing projects to date.

Chief Executive of Domusco

Will Umm, the Chief Executive, has seen the company's revenue grow at over 15% per annum for most of the last ten years. He has personally been the driving force behind many of the large construction projects that Domusco has been awarded over the last few years.

Will Umm has good government connections and has always found time to deal with many personnel matters. He is considered to be fair in his business dealings and has been able to maintain Domusco's reputation as being scrupulously fair in its contract negotiations. He is very much in touch with his workforce and is well liked and respected by most of the Domusco Board as well.

It is only the Finance Director, Martyn Lite, with whom he has not established a good rapport. This is primarily because Martyn Lite often argues that what Will Umm wants to do is not in the shareholders' interests. Martyn Lite often states that a project that appears to be profitable can be too risky, or that Domusco has taken on too much construction work and has insufficient management resources. On most occasions, Will Umm has over-ruled him, and although he respects Martyn Lite, he considers him to be too conservative.

Recent developments

In each of Domusco's subsidiary companies, the staff numbers in the sales and marketing departments vary greatly. Most of the construction work undertaken by the Major Construction Projects and Office Building subsidiary companies is specifically commissioned and these Domusco group companies have only a small sales and marketing support team.

Within the last five years, Domusco has been involved in the construction of many smaller office buildings which had not been specifically designed and built for a company prior to commencement of construction, but were instead sold during the construction period. The construction of these smaller edge-of-town office buildings has increased the working capital requirements of Domusco's office building construction subsidiary, but has improved the office building construction subsidiary's sales revenue and profitability.

Each of the house building subsidiary companies requires a large sales and marketing team to secure sales and ensure that all properties are sold before completion of construction work, or shortly after all work has been completed. Domusco has seen the type of house building change in the last decade, with a higher percentage of lower priced houses and apartments being built and fewer larger houses being constructed.

House building companies also attempt to sell some of their properties "off-plan" as soon as the building plans have been approved. Off-plan purchase of houses or flats is defined as a customer committing to purchase the housing unit, and paying a deposit, prior to any construction work commencing on the housing unit. During the last decade, Domusco has seen a change in the timing of when customers purchase their houses or apartments. They are making their decisions later in the construction process and the level of off-plan sales has fallen. All of these factors have adversely affected cash flows within Domusco's house building subsidiary, although profitability has increased year-on-year within that subsidiary.

Economic growth in Zee

The country has been a democracy for over 50 years and is experiencing a period of growth in consumer spending. Annual inflation has remained at a little over 4% per year for the last few years and the GNP is forecast to grow at 4% per year over the next few years. The country is a net importer, marginally, and its principal export market is the EU. The country's currency is the Zee dollar (Z$) and the exchange rate at 30 June 20X5 is Z$3.25 to US$1 and Z$2.55 to €1.

Competitor analysis

In Domusco's home country of Zee, there are eight large construction companies, some of which only operate within Zee, whereas Domusco and three other companies are involved in construction work internationally. Domusco is one of three leading house builders in Zee, and during 20X4, Domusco completed 6,924 housing units (one unit is equal to one house or one apartment) in Zee. On the basis of completed units, it constructed a little less than 12% of all new units during 20X4 in Zee. Its operations in some European countries and in part of the USA are very small compared to other international companies, and Domusco is likely to build less than 1% of all new housing units in these countries.

Domusco's international office building work is very small compared to many other international companies. However, Domusco has a substantial market share in the office building market in its home country. However, the volume of new office construction in Zee has fallen in the last five years, although Domusco has achieved around 20% of new office buildings in Zee during the last three years.

Domusco shareholding and share prices

Domusco has 441.6 million shares of Z$0.50 each in issue and has a total of 800 million authorised shares. Its share price at 30 June 20X5 is Z$13.82, which is at an all-time high for the company, due partly to its good 20X4 results. Institutional shareholders own over 80% of its shares, with no single large shareholder. Domusco's directors, staff and the general public own the rest of Domusco's shares.

Major construction projects currently under construction

The Major Construction Projects subsidiary company within Domusco had five main contracts under construction during 20X4. These were:

- The construction of a sports stadium in the Middle East (in a country where it has undertaken many projects before), which is due for completion in February 20X7. The total profitability on this project is forecast to be Z$78 million over four years.

- The construction of motorways and bridges in the neighbouring European country of Wye.

- The construction of a motorway in a different country in the Middle East, which is due for completion in September 20X5. The overall updated forecast profitability on this project is Z$380 million over 2.4 years.

- Road and motorway construction and road improvements in Zee. The project spans two years, is due to be completed by mid-20X5 and its forecast profitability is Z$220 million.

- Construction work on a new marina in Zee. Work commenced in August 20X4 and is due for completion in November 20X5. The total project profitability is forecast to be Z$270 million.

Domusco's staffing levels and sub-contractors

Most companies operating in the construction industry use a mix of their own employees and sub-contractors. The mix varies by country and also by construction segment. In the house building segment, Domusco employs its own staff for site surveying and site management, as well as for a proportion of the house building construction work. Specialised sub-contractors undertake the rest of the house building construction work. Domusco also directly employs all of the sales and marketing teams and administrative support for Domusco's house building subsidiary companies. The majority of the sub-contractors that Domusco uses have worked closely with Domusco for several years.

In major construction projects, particularly motorway construction, specialised sub-contractors undertake the majority of the construction work. The location and the level of staffing required varies enormously with each major project and Domusco does not wish to employ large numbers of staff that may be located in the wrong area or with unsuitable skills. The use of sub-contractors gives Domusco flexibility.

Domusco's operational management has, however, experienced problems with the use of some sub-contractors. Although Domusco has repeatedly used the same sub-contracting companies as on previous occasions, the make-up of the teams used on projects that undertake the work change far too often. Despite supervision by the sub-contractors' management and subsequent inspections by Domusco's project management, there are large numbers of unskilled workers who are not capable of completing certain stages of construction to the required standard, which causes delays while the extent of the faulty work is identified and rectified. Additionally, as sub-contactors are paid a fixed fee for various stages of construction, they want to complete the job in the least possible time, so that their employees can move onto the next job. This leads to jobs being rushed and not thoroughly or professionally completed.

Domusco always uses its own staff for project management and surveys and inspections. Domusco's management are currently reviewing a report which suggests that Domusco's house building companies should increase their staffing levels, so that their dependence on sub-contractors would be reduced.

Date: The current date is 1 November 20X5.

Appendix 1

Domusco: Statement of financial position, Income Statement and Statement of changes in equity

	\multicolumn{2}{c}{As at 31 December}			
	\multicolumn{2}{c}{20X4}	\multicolumn{2}{c}{20X3}
	Z$m	Z$m	Z$m	Z$m
Domusco Statement of financial position				
Non-current assets (net)		124.8		120.3
Current assets				
Inventory (including land bank, work-in-progress and inventory of materials)	5,339.6		4,470.5	
Trade receivables	841.2		727.1	
Cash and short term investments	501.6		98.2	
		6,682.4		5,295.8
Total assets		6,807.2		5,416.1
EQUITY AND LIABILITIES				
Equity				
Paid in share capital	220.8		220.8	
Share premium reserve	327.6		327.6	
Retained earnings	2,880.8		2,469.6	
		3,429.2		3,018.0
Non-current liabilities				
9% Loan notes (redeemable in 20X7)		324.0		324.0
10% Loan notes (redeemable in 20X8)		696.0		696.0
9% Loan notes (redeemable in 20X9)		900.0		–
Current liabilities				
Trade payables	747.4		728.0	
Tax	296.6		259.8	
Accruals	414.0		390.3	
		1,458.0		1,378.1
Total equity and liabilities		6,807.2		5,416.1

Note. Paid in share capital represents 441.6 million shares of Z$0.50 each.

Income statement

	Year ended 31 December	
	20X4 Z$m	20X3 Z$m
Revenue	6,216.0	5,810.8
Total operating costs	5,104.8	4,861.5
Operating profit	1,111.2	949.3
Finance costs (net)	(128.4)	(98.1)
Tax expense	(296.6)	(259.8)
Profit for the period	686.2	591.4

Statement of changes in equity

	Share capital Z$m	Share premium Z$m	Retained earnings Z$m	Total Z$m
Balance at 31 December 20X3	220.8	327.6	2,469.6	3,018.0
Profit for the period	–	–	686.2	686.2
Dividends paid	–	–	(275.0)	(275.0)
Balance at 31 December 20X4	220.8	327.6	2,880.8	3,429.2

Appendix 2

Extract for the next 5 years from Domusco's 10 year plan

	Actual	Plan				
	20X4 Z$m	20X5 Z$m	20X6 Z$m	20X7 Z$m	20X8 Z$m	20X9 Z$m
Revenue						
Major projects	2,592.2	2,748	3,022	3,264	3,493	3,842
Office building	768.0	1,248	1,473	1,811	1,902	1,997
House building	2,855.8	3,541	3,896	4,246	4,671	5,231
Total revenue	6,216.0	7,537	8,391	9,321	10,066	11,070
Pre-tax operating profit						
Major projects	576.0	616	684	746	805	894
Office building	86.1	138	158	195	205	215
House building	449.1	561	629	691	774	883
Total pre-tax operating profit	1,111.2	1,315	1,471	1,632	1,784	1,992
Post tax profit for the period	686.2	783	876	999	1,121	1,274
Shareholder capital employed (Equity)	3,429.2	3,900	4,424	5,023	5,696	6,460
Loans (at end year)	1,920.0	2,420	2,420	2,096	1,900	1,900
Number of shares (million)	441.6	441.6	441.6	441.6	441.6	441.6
Earnings per share (EPS) Z$	1.55	1.77	1.98	2.26	2.54	2.88

Note. Plan approved by Domusco Board in November 20X4 and includes construction work for all contracts signed at that date.

[TURN OVER]

Question 53 Part 2 – Domusco

Unseen Case Material (Exam day material for Paper E3 only)

Three important issues have been raised at a recent Board meeting.

1   New development at Metsa

The Zee government has recently announced proposals for a major new development at Metsa. The Zee government is pleased with the way that Domusco is managing its existing projects in Zee, and has invited Domusco to undertake the development.

The Domusco project manager analysing the potential new government project believes that the construction costs cannot be forecast with any accuracy until detailed survey work has been undertaken. Because the terrain in the area is quite rugged, initial land preparation could be difficult and expensive.

However, the project manager has prepared two levels of cash flow depending on what problems Domusco might encounter during construction. He cannot give any indication of the chances of either scenario happening though.

Cash outflows for Metsa construction project

	20X6 Z$m	20X7 Z$m	20X8 Z$m	20X9 Z$m	Total Z$m
High cost scenario	275	350	375	350	1,350
Low cost scenario	130	160	340	380	1,010

The proposed revenues inflows, mainly from housing, but with some office buildings, are forecast as follows:

	20X6 Z$m	20X7 Z$m	20X8 Z$m	20X9 Z$m	Total Z$m
Housing	80	510	790	880	2,260
Office buildings	30	50	60	50	190
	110	560	850	930	2,450

Although the Sales & Marketing Director believes these inflow figures are reasonable, the Finance Director thinks they are too optimistic. He believes sales of new housing in Zee cannot be expected to continue at their current rate, and thinks that the figures for housing are over-stated by 10%. Consequently, he has produced alternative total revenue projections for the project as follows:

	20X6 Z$m	20X7 Z$m	20X8 Z$m	20X9 Z$m	Total Z$m
Revenue					
Houses & offices	102	509	771	842	2,224

(Note. All the cash flow figures are shown before tax, and all the cash flows are assumed to occur at the end of the year to which they relate.)

The FD believes that Domusco will need to take out an additional loan of Z$600 million to fund the project. The loan will need to be drawn down at the start of the project to fund the construction costs before any sales are made. Domusco's bank is prepared to lend them the additional amount required.

The FD has stated that an appropriate discount rate for evaluating this construction project should be 12%, to allow for the risk involved.

Domusco's public relations director is concerned about the development, however, due to concerns from environmental groups. The Metsa area is home to several rare plant species, and contains a number of sites of archaeological interest. Local opposition groups have already started campaigning against the development of the Metsa area, and the campaigns have attracted the attention of the international media.

However, the Zee government has publicly stated that the development of the Metsa area is required to help Zee sustain its economic growth.

2 Employee survey

Domusco has undertaken its fourth employee survey and the management is now considering the findings. One of the key points raised it that Domusco employees are very unhappy about the quality of the work undertaken by sub-contractors.

The employees are also aware that some sub-contractors are paid a larger daily fee than their own salaries, and feel that they are under-valued.

Domusco's employees report an increasing number of the sub-contract firms are employing workers with insufficient training or inadequate experience. Zee is experiencing a construction boom at the moment and inexperienced people are seeking work in the construction industry.

Domusco's employees are concerned that some of these inexperienced contract workers demonstrate a lack of awareness of the importance of safety. Some Domusco employees have even refused to work at one site where there have been a number of accidents caused by sub-contractors.

3 Performance measurement

Domusco has traditionally used return on capital employed (ROCE) as its main measure for assessing performance. However, the managing director (MD) of the house building subsidiary has complained this is misleading.

He claims that the ROCE in the house building companies has been depressed by the purchase of land for future developments (land bank). He also feels that ROCE focuses too much on internal, financial measures, and doesn't take account of market conditions as a whole.

There are also two other influences on the ROCE that is achieved:

- One is the size of the housing development. Generally, smaller developments achieve lower returns that a larger quantity of housing units that are constructed at the same site.

- The second is that the type of housing influences the returns achieved. Large apartment blocks generally achieve a higher ROCE than medium priced houses.

In the light of this, the MD has asked whether some new performance measures can be introduced.

Required

(a) In the light of the MD of the house building subsidiary's comments, evaluate the use of ROCE as a measure of divisional performance at Domusco, and advise the directors of alternative performance measures they could use. **(13 marks)**

(b) Analyse the forecast profitability of the potential development at Mesta for Domusco. **(15 marks)**

Note: There are 10 marks available for calculations in this requirement.

(c) (i) Briefly explain the concept of corporate social responsibility. **(4 marks)**

(ii) Discuss the potential corporate social responsibility issues which Domusco should consider when deciding whether or not to accept the Mesta contract. **(8 marks)**

(d) In the light of the recent employee survey, analyse the issues which the directors should consider when deciding whether to continue using sub-contractors or to recruit additional construction staff.
(10 marks)

(Total = 50 marks)

54 Zubinos   90 mins

Strategic level pre-seen case material

Market overview

The number of chains of coffee shops in the UK has increased rapidly in the last decade, with thousands of branded coffee shops now operating around the UK. The total turnover for all branded coffee shops in the UK exceeded £1 billion (£1 billion is equal to £1,000 million) during 20X5. Over the last few years a number of UK-based branded coffee shops have emerged to compete with the internationally recognised coffee shop brands.

The range of products offered has changed over the last few years and branded coffee shops are now meeting customer demand for a larger range of foods and better quality products by using premium ingredients. Furthermore, branded coffee shops are able to command a higher average price for their products by using quality and service as differentiators, as price appears not to be a particularly sensitive factor.

In addition to the branded coffee shops, there are a large number of non-specialist food and beverage outlets including department stores, supermarkets and bookshops, which continue to expand their own cafes. They are enjoying the success of the "coffee culture" that has been established by the branded coffee shops.

Zubinos

Luis Zubino opened the first Zubinos shop in June 20X1 in London, in rented premises. He fully understood that it was location and convenience that would be critical to the success of the coffee shop.

Most coffee shops only serve a selection of hot and cold drinks and a small range of snacks and cakes. What distinguished Zubinos from many of the other branded coffee shops back in 20X1, was that Zubinos also sold a range of freshly made sandwiches, with high quality fillings and other food items. Zubinos also sold a specialised brand of ice cream, which Luis Zubino imported from Italy, as he considered that the quality and taste were far superior to many other ice cream brands available in the UK. He was convinced that ice cream, which is a product that is kept frozen, could generate high margins, as it would have very little waste and none of the problems associated with the short shelf life of other foods.

The growth of Zubinos

Within six months, the first Zubinos shop was generating a high turnover and had established a high level of repeat business. Within two and a half years, by the end of 20X3, Luis Zubino had opened a further five coffee shops, which was twice as fast as his original business plan had envisaged. All five shops were in rented premises to reduce the initial set-up costs, but Luis Zubino did not reduce the level of expenditure on the coffee shops design and fittings. The atmosphere that the coffee shop design had created was good, and was attractive to the target market of young people. Early on, from his market research, and from personal experience in his parents' business, Luis Zubino wanted his coffee shops to appeal to the 20-to-35 year old age range. This was for several reasons:

- The target age range market segment has more time and more disposable money
- They attracted other people of similar ages into the coffee shops, as they become the place to meet up
- The target age range would be attracted to the "trendy" atmosphere that Luis Zubino has created at Zubinos

There were eighteen coffee shops in total operational by the end of 20X5. The geographical split of Zubinos coffee shops was ten in London and eight coffee shops outside of London. Zubinos has not had any problems with building up its customer base after each new shop opening in the smaller towns and cities into which it had expanded.

The Zubinos business has a high turnover. However, profitability has been lower than some of its competitors, for several reasons as follows:

- High rental costs for three of the ten London coffee shops
- High staff costs, as good customer service remains a high priority for Zubinos

- Lower than average gross margins on some products due to the higher than average procurement cost of the quality ingredients that Luis Zubino has selected
- Lower margins on coffee products as over 80% of its coffee beans are procured from suppliers who deal only with "Fair Trade" coffee producers (see below)

Fair Trade produce

Luis Zubino, having a strong social conscience, felt that the coffee beans that Zubinos coffee shops should use should be bought from suppliers of Fair Trade coffee. Additionally, from his initial research into the industry, he was convinced that Zubinos could charge a price premium for the use of Fair Trade coffee.

When the first Zubinos was opened in 20X1, Luis Zubino bought 100% of his coffee from Fair Trade suppliers. As the range of coffees expanded in Zubinos coffee shops, he found that some coffee and cocoa beans were unavailable through Fair Trade suppliers. On average, Zubinos now procures over 80% of its produce from Fair Trade suppliers. Luis Zubino would still like this to be 100%.

IT development

Zubinos' IT director commissioned an IT company in early 20X5 to completely update the Zubinos website. The total cost of this IT work was forecast to be £220,000, but the final cost was a little over £300,000 including some new hardware equipment. The new website has helped to create stronger brand awareness.

The new Zubinos website also has an on-line communications area which allows users to "chat" on line. Since November 20X4, a range of Zubinos merchandise can also be ordered on-line. This range of merchandise includes coffee machines and coffee supplies, which have been selling well, despite little direct publicity.

Introduction of a business investor

By summer 20X4, Zubinos had eight coffee shops open and had found suitable locations for two more. However, Zubinos' bankers, Kite Bank, were reluctant to increase the level of loans. At the end of June 20X4, Zubinos had three loans in place, totalling £600,000. All loans were at 12% interest per year. These were:

- An initial five-year loan for £300,000 taken out in December 20X1
- A second five-year loan for £200,000 taken out in December 20X2 to fund further expansion
- A third five-year loan taken out in April 20X4 for £100,000, to cover a shortfall in working capital due to all cash resources being used for expansion

Instead, the bank introduced Luis Zubino to the manager of the bank's private equity provider, who is Carl Martin. Carl Martin and Luis Zubino established a good working relationship early on in their business meetings and Carl Martin was impressed with the business plan and the growth of the Zubinos business in the last few years. He felt confident that if Kite Private Equity (KPE) were to invest in the Zubinos business, the additional private equity finance, together with less expensive loan finance, would allow the Zubinos business to expand far more rapidly.

After many discussions and the preparation of additional, more detailed business plans, KPE agreed to invest in the Zubinos business in January 20X5.

KPE invested £2.4 million in equity finance initially, but the agreement was to also provide loan finance when required by expansion plans. The agreed value of loan finance was up to £5.0 million over the next 4 years at an annual interest rate of 10% per annum, secured against Zubinos assets. KPE appointed Carl Martin as its representative on the Board of Zubinos.

The statement of financial position, income statement and statement of changes in equity for Zubinos for the last two financial years are shown in **Appendix 1**.

Shareholdings at December 20X5

Since the formation of Zubinos in 20X1, Luis Zubino and five other directors have purchased shares in Zubinos. They have paid between £2 and £5 per share, based on the agreed fair value at the time they acquired shares.

KPE purchased 400,000 shares at £6 each (£1 each plus a share premium, based on an agreed fair value, of £5 per share). KPE owns 40% of Zubinos' 1,000,000 shares.

The Zubinos Board comprises the six shareholders plus Carl Martin, KPE's nominated representative. Luis Zubino is Chairman of the Board in addition to his role as Managing Director.

Analysis of gross margin

The board commissioned a new IT system in October 20X5 that will capture and analyse sales and cost of sales data without all of the manual intervention and spreadsheet analysis that is currently required to produce management information. The system is due to be operational in early 20X6.

The analysis of the gross margin across the eighteen Zubinos coffee shops for the year to 31 December 20X5 is shown as follows. It should be noted that the figures below are for all eighteen Zubinos coffee shops, but eight of them were operational for only part of 20X5.

	Coffee products £'000	Other drinks £'000	Sand-wiches £'000	Ice cream £'000	Other foods £'000	Total £'000
Sales revenue	4,734	1,344	3,584	896	3,360	13,918
Cost of food and drinks	(926)	(642)	(1,260)	(182)	(1,962)	(4,972)
Gross margin	3,808	702	2,324	714	1,398	8,946
Gross margin %	80%	52%	65%	80%	42%	64%

Zubinos' expansion plans

The current five-year plan was approved by KPE, and subsequently the Zubinos Board, in December 20X5. This plan includes the expansion of Zubinos to 75 coffee shops by the end of 20Y0. An extract from this current five-year plan is shown in **Appendix 2**.

Much of the expansion planned is due to be financed by cash generated by operations, as well as additional loan finance from KPE. The amount of loan finance will be determined by whether the new openings will be in rented premises or whether the company will be required to purchase the site. Much will depend on the location selected and the alternatives available in each town or city targeted for expansion.

Proposed expansion of Zubinos overseas

Luis Zubino and his Business Development Director believe that during 20X7, when Zubinos plans to have over 25 shops open in the UK, it will be in a position where it could consider expanding overseas. Already, a number of contacts of Luis Zubino, who live in Europe, are keen to operate Zubinos coffee shops in Europe.

The current five-year plan (Appendix 2), which was approved by KPE and the Zubinos Board in December 20X5, is based on operating 50 coffee shops in the UK by 20Y0 and 25 coffee shops in Europe.

However, Luis Zubino would like to have more than 25 coffee shops operating in Europe by 20Y0. There are a number of reasons why Zubinos should consider expanding abroad and these include:

- **Saturated home market** where competition is so intense that it can no longer gain any significant market share improvement
- **Competition may be less intense** in a different market
- Comparative **advantage in product against local competition**, particularly in areas dominated by British people living and holidaying abroad, which is becoming increasingly popular in some areas of Europe, especially Spain.

Date: The current date is 1 May 20X6.

Appendix 1

Zubinos' Statement of financial position, Income Statement and Statement of changes in equity

Note. All data in this appendix is presented in international financial reporting format

Statement of financial position

	As at 31 December			
	20X5		20X4	
	£'000	£'000	£'000	£'000
Non-current assets (net)		7,025		2,958
Current assets				
Inventory	420		395	
Trade receivables and rent prepayments	209		124	
Cash and short term investments	391		85	
		1,020		604
Total assets		8,045		3,562
EQUITY AND LIABILITIES				
Equity				
Paid in share capital	1,000		600	
Share premium reserve	2,630		630	
Retained profits	1,751		854	
		5,381		2,084
Non-current liabilities				
Loans				
Bank loan at 12% (repayable in 20X6)	300		300	
Bank loan at 12% (repayable in 20X7)	200		200	
Bank loan at 12% (repayable in 20X9)	100		100	
KPE loan at 10% (repayable in 20Y0)	300		–	
		900		600
Current liabilities				
Trade payables	1,367		689	
Tax	283		160	
Accruals	114		29	
		1,764		878
Total equity and liabilities		8,045		3,562

Note. Paid in share capital represents 1 million shares of £1.00 each at 31 December 20X5

Income Statement

	Year ended 31 December	
	20X5	20X4
	£'000	£'000
Revenue	13,918	7,962
Total operating costs	12,651	7,225
Operating profit	1,267	737
Finance costs	(87)	(69)
Tax expense (effective tax rate is 30%)	(283)	(160)
Profit for the period	897	508

Statement of changes in equity

	Share capital £'000	Share premium £'000	Retained earnings £'000	Total £'000
Balance at 31 December 20X4	600	630	854	2,084
New shares issued during 20X5	400	2,000	–	2,400
Profit for the period	–	–	897	897
Dividends paid	–	–	–	–
Balance at 31 December 20X5	1,000	2,630	1,751	5,381

Appendix 2

Extracts from Zubinos 5-year plan

	Actual	Plan				
	20X5	20X6	20X7	20X8	20X9	20Y0
Number of coffee shops:						
Start of the year	10	18	26	36	48	60
New openings	8	8	10	12	12	15
End of the year	**18**	**26**	**36**	**48**	**60**	**75**
Average number of coffee shops for the year	14	22	31	42	54	68
Analysis of new shop openings:						
UK	8	8	9	5	5	5
Overseas	–	–	1	7	7	10
	£'000	£'000	£'000	£'000	£'000	£'000
Coffee shops revenue	13,498	22,176	37,072	57,378	82,553	110,751
Revenue from new product launches in each year	420	1,560	2,200	2,900	3,800	4,800
Total revenue	**13,918**	**23,736**	**39,272**	**60,278**	**86,353**	**115,551**
Pre-tax operating profit	**1,267**	**2,160**	**3,613**	**5,606**	**8,203**	**10,977**
Capital expenditure	**4,800**	**2,700**	**3,400**	**3,800**	**4,100**	**5,000**

[TURN OVER]

Question 54 Part 2 – Zubinos

Unseen Case Material (Exam day material for Paper E3 only)

Background

Luis Zubinos started his coffee shop business in London in 20X1, and he has seen the business grow rapidly since then. He is now keen to expand the business into Europe.

Franchising proposal

An international franchising company, GlobalFranch (GF) has approached Luis Zubino with a proposal to assist Zubinos to expand via franchising. Luis Zubino's initial response is favourable.

GF has stated that it has over thirty franchisees ready to open franchised outlets, and it considers that the Zubinos business could be a very successful franchised business.

GF's proposal is to franchise out the Zubinos coffee shop brand and expand both in the UK and internationally, particularly in the rapidly growing Far Eastern market. GF would like to offer its services and experience to recruit and manage franchisees, who would then operate franchised Zubinos coffee shops in the UK, Europe and the Far East.

GF insists on a minimum contract period of 5 years, with a one-year notice period.

GF has proposed that for each franchised shop, Zubinos would receive 6% of the gross sales revenue of the shop. Zubinos would also supply all of its regular coffees and own brand product lines to franchised shops at agreed prices, which would include a mark up of 5% on cost.

GF has estimated that the shops will make a gross margin of 60%. The gross margin is calculated as gross sales less the cost of food and drinks which are all supplied by Zubinos.

GF has stated that its fees for locating franchisees and managing the franchising business would be an initial fee of £25,000 for each new shop opened, plus an annual fee of 3.5% of the franchised revenue for the contract period.

GF has prepared the following forecast for the 5 years from 20X7:

Franchised shops	20X7	20X8	20X9	20Y0	20Y1
Number of shops opened	20	30	50	80	120
Cumulative franchised shops	20	50	100	180	300
Total sales revenue (£m)	10	40	90	185	315

The franchise idea was discussed at the last Board meeting, and the majority of Board members thought it looked interesting and was worth examining in more detail. However, two dismissed it as misguided, arguing that Zubinos should retain total control of its brand.

At the same meeting, these two directors also suggested that Zubinos needed to develop a mission statement to help guide its strategic planning.

Product promotion

In 20X5, Zubinos launched a new product line, selling exclusive coffee machines to customers for their homes or offices. These are sold on Zubinos' website and also in Zubinos' coffee shops. Initially they were not well-marketed, but following a promotional campaign the coffee machines have sold particularly well, and customers have repeatedly bought further coffee supplies from Zubinos.

The coffee machines have been procured from a leading coffee machine manufacturer on an exclusive contract for Zubinos. The machines use specially designed sachets of coffee that can only be bought from Zubinos coffee shops, or from the Zubinos website. The unique selling point is that customers can enjoy their favourite type of Zubinos coffee in the comfort of their own home.

Zubinos' marketing director noted the success of the promotional campaign and is keen to run further campaigns online, arguing that online advertising is a good way of reaching the 20-to-25 year old age range which is Zubino's target age range.

Required

(a) Discuss the advantages and disadvantages for Zubinos of producing a mission statement. **(8 marks)**

(b) Calculate the forecast net income to Zubinos from entering into the proposed franchise arrangement with GlobalFranch (GF)

Note: Net income is franchise income payable to Zubinos less franchise fees payable by Zubinos to GF
(8 marks)

(c) (i) Analyse the issues which Zubinos should consider before deciding whether or not to accept GF's offer.
(15 marks)

(ii) In the light of your analysis above, recommend whether or not Zubinos should accept the offer.

Note: You are not required to reproduce the detail of your arguments from earlier parts of this question in (c) (ii). **(7 marks)**

(d) Discuss how Zubino's marketing manager could use the internet as part of his marketing activities as the business expands. **(12 marks)**

(Total = 50 marks)

ANSWERS

1 Industry analysis

> **Text reference**. Environmental analysis and five forces are assumed knowledge for E3. They are summarised briefly in the 'Introductory' chapter at the start of the BPP Study Text for E3, but are covered in more detail in E2.

Part (a)

> **Top tips**. The key to answering this question successfully is understanding what the examiner means by the phrase 'industry analysis'. You might consider this to mean something like 'analysis of the industry or market in which a given company operates'. The Examiner, however, uses the phrase here to mean general environmental analysis covering both the task environment and also the wider macro environment, so this may have meant you misinterpreted the requirement.
>
> Fortunately, about three months before the exam sitting in which this question appeared, the CIMA student magazine had published an article on environmental analysis by the Examiner in which he used the phrase in this way.
>
> There is an important lesson to learn from this: always read articles in the CIMA magazines which could be relevant to your exams.
>
> **Easy marks**. Stating the components of the PEST and five forces models and what they are used for would be worth two marks.
>
> **Examiner's comments**. The Examiner criticised candidates who concentrated on explaining the nature of the models but who failed to explain why they were suitable aids to carrying out an analysis.
>
> A common error was to answer part (b) of the question in part (a); that is, to be very specific about an environmental analysis for the subject company rather than explaining the general principles involved. Although you should always apply your knowledge to the scenario when you can, part (a) of this question only asks for an explanation of the general principles. Part (b), however, needs them to be applied to the scenario.

A company carries out environmental analysis in order to be familiar with the external factors that are likely to have an influence over its activities. In the simplest terms, these factors are those that may give rise to **opportunities** or to **threats**. The magnitude and urgency of such opportunities will vary almost infinitely, so environmental scanning and analysis should be a continuing activity.

The environment may be divided into concentric layers, with the physical nature of the world forming the outermost layer, the business macro environment appearing next and the micro or task environment forming the closest layer.

The **physical environment** is often taken for granted as its influence tends to change only over the very long term. However, it cannot be ignored, since such factors as extreme weather and the supply of fossil fuels have obvious importance.

PEST analysis – The wider business environment is often analysed into elements based on the **PEST** mnemonic; that is, the political, economic, social and technological components. Other acronyms have been proposed, such as PESTEL, which emphasises the importance of environmental concerns and legal influences. When carrying out such an analysis, it is important to understand that the **environment cannot actually be split into distinct parts**: the elements are intimately entwined, influencing both businesses and each other in a complex fashion. Government policy, for example, in developed nations is deliberately structured to influence economy, society and technology, though the results are frequently other than what was intended or expected.

Porter's Five Forces – The existing and potential influences of the PEST environment merge into the more immediate forces making up the **task environment**. *Porter* analyses this layer into **five competitive forces** that between them determine an industry's potential to provide superior profitability. Each of the five forces is, in effect, an aspect of competition. Using five forces analysis can help a company to identify both threats and opportunities. They are listed below.

- The bargaining power of suppliers
- The bargaining power of customers
- The extent of competitive rivalry within the industry
- The threat of new entrants into the industry
- The threat of substitutes from outside the industry

Part (b)

> **Top tips**. Note that this question is not actually asking you for an environmental analysis for 2XA. Not only would that be a huge task (worth far more than 10 marks) but you do not have the necessary information to do so. Instead, what the Examiner appears to be looking for is a brief account (with examples relevant to the scenario) of the sort of thing that such an analysis might contain.
>
> However, the emphasis must not be on the detail of the examples and their relevance; the idea is to explain the overall nature of the various elements of the information required.
>
> The marking guide indicates that up to three marks would be available for each factor identified and explained, so four well-made points should produce a comfortable pass mark.
>
> **Examiner's comments**. See comments on (a) above about applying your knowledge to the scenario. Another common error was to use inappropriate models such as SWOT, the value chain and the BCG portfolio model.

Technology

2XA operates in the aviation and specialist car industries. Both of these industries use sophisticated **designs and materials** to achieve the high performance they require. Generally, 2XA's customers will know exactly what they want and will expect the company to be able to provide it promptly and efficiently. Technological standards and developments will therefore be of great importance to 2XA in maintaining its business. **Quality assurance** will be a vital aspect of the company's business processes and any **legal or regulatory developments affecting safety** will have an immediate impact.

Society

Production output is likely to be made to order and in small batches. It is likely to require a highly skilled workforce because of the technical sophistication outlined above. It will therefore be important for the company to take what steps it can to safeguard its access to skilled labour. To some extent, this will depend on the general standards of technical education in its home country, but a more important factor is likely to be any changes taking place in its local labour market. If the company is located in a large centre of population with a significant amount of employment in engineering, it will be easier to recruit staff than if it is located in a small, rural town.

New entrants

2XA is finding that aggressive competitors are entering its existing markets. 2XA is domiciled in a EU country and the existence of the single market in goods is becoming well-developed. There is therefore every reason for the company to proceed on the basis that this new competition will continue and probably intensify. 2XZ needs to know as much as it can about its new competitors and their products so that it can analyse the threat in detail. Detailed knowledge may also reveal opportunities, such as the possibility of specialisation in areas neglected by bigger companies. 2XA should also consider what it can do in the way of barriers to entry: these would have to be very specific, since the company is quite small and barriers based on major investment, such as a very specialised technology are likely to be beyond its means. A good example would be the exploration of the possibility of obtaining protection for intellectual property in the form of new designs.

Bargaining power of customers

The technical sophistication of the industry in which 2XA operates should make it possible for it to avoid competition on price. Its selling effort should be built around the possibility of technical partnership with customers and joint development of products to satisfy customer needs. Such a strategy would require the company to identify those customers to whom such a course of action would be attractive. It may also require an enhancement to its own design and development capability: there is an interaction with the skilled labour problem mentioned earlier.

Bargaining power of supplier groups

2XA should exploit its location within the EU by examining its upstream costs. If its marketing practices are anything to go by, the company will probably find that there is considerable potential for controlling its costs by exploring a range of new suppliers, both in its home country and in neighbouring ones. Information that would help here will be specific to the its industry, rather than the wider environment.

Part (c)

> **Top tips.** Obvious sources of information such as the press and the Internet are valid answers here, but they would only be worth half a mark each if you simply mention them. You are asked to 'advise the directors...' and 'advise' is a level 5 verb. Therefore to score well on this requirement you need not only to identify the sources of information but also to **explain** their relevance to the scenario.
>
> There is an opportunity to mention Knowledge Management systems here too.
>
> **Examiner's comments.** Simple bullet point lists of sources were a common approach and would not produce a pass mark. Internal sources of information are as valid as external ones.

National and local governments provide a great deal of information free of charge on such matters as economic and demographic trends; trade volumes and values; and current and proposed government expenditure. National governments usually have departments concerned with the promotion of exports; such departments produce regular reports on foreign industries and markets.

All industries have their specialist trade publications that provide information on new developments. **National and local newspapers** can also be sources of important news; the local press in particular can provide useful information on major competitors and customers.

Trade associations generally have technical intelligence gathering, analysis and dissemination among their functions. These services may be accessible free of charge to members or may require the payment of a subscription.

Technical regulatory bodies can have a major influence on an industry, particularly where safety is a concern: this is obviously an important consideration in both aviation and the motor industry. Generally, proposals for new regulations and requirements are exposed for consultation and it is possible to make appropriate adjustments in good time.

Industry analysts provide reports on a commercial basis. Most large financial institutions have their own analysts and there are also independent agencies that provide reports on a commercial basis. 2XA should consider subscribing to such a commercial service, but should be prepared to read the reports provided critically to ensure that they are useful.

Consultants often provide reporting services of the type mentioned above and will also produce tailored information as required by clients.

Most companies have considerable information about their markets stored within their own **record-keeping systems**, in the form of order and invoice records and, possibly, past submitted tender records.

2 Qualispecs

> **Text reference.** SWOT analysis is assumed knowledge for E3, because it is covered in the E2 syllabus.
>
> **Alternative answers.** This question is a good illustration of the fact that there is usually no single right answer for a strategic level answer. In particular, the requirement to 'Produce a corporate appraisal' provides scope for a variety of different approaches. The first answer tries to show a wide range of strengths, weaknesses, opportunities and threats for its corporate appraisal. However, we have also presented a second answer (in a text box) which shows less factors but describes each in more detail. This approach – of focusing on the key points and explaining them clearly – is a good way of scoring well under the time pressures you will face in strategic level papers.

Part (a)

> **Top tips.** To score well in this requirement you need to note that requirement involves two distinct parts, separated by the word 'and'.
>
> The first part requires you to 'produce a corporate appraisal' and the post-exam guidance makes it clear that the Examiner was expecting a SWOT analysis approach rather than one based on environmental scanning and internal appraisal. How were you to know this? Firstly, there is not really enough data available for you to be able to carry out a thorough external and internal review. Secondly, the material given is in a significantly summarised form, which is ideal for the SWOT analysis approach.
>
> The second part of the requirement asks you to 'discuss the key strategic challenges'. In effect, this means breaking down the SWOT into a small number of key risks or threats.
>
> Also, make sure you look at both parts (a) and (b) of the question before answering it so that you do not repeat yourself. It is important that you decide how the parts are different. Part (a) asks you to describe the present situation of Qualispecs. Part (b) asks you what to do to improve that situation.

Qualispecs corporate appraisal

Strengths

- New CEO with good track record in the industry, intimate knowledge of a major competitor and willingness to take vigorous steps
- Reputation for quality products helps maintain margins and goodwill
- Celebrity exposure which can help increase awareness and sales
- Strong financial position including large cash reserves permits long-term investment in strategic developments.

Weaknesses

- Failure to utilise new technology that could cut costs and improve service
- High production costs that put them at a price disadvantage
- Failure to use reward system for motivation to build customer focus
- Over-centralisation prevents local initiative

Opportunities

- Formal celebrity endorsement
- Fashion 'eye-wear', including designer frames and sunglasses could improve margins and customer retention
- Availability of new production technology to cut costs and improve service throughout
- Aging population means increased need for spectacles as sight can deteriorate with age
- Increased spending among 18-30 year old customers especially on fashion products

Threats

- Effects of economic slowdown on discretionary spending such as fashion goods
- Decline in customer loyalty/increasing competition from innovative rivals using new technology
- New technologies such as laser treatment that dispense with need for spectacles
- On-line providers able to make up and provide spectacles and contact lenses to customer prescriptions

Key strategic challenges

Qualispecs is in danger of being left behind by its competitors. The erosion of its customer base shows that it can no longer allow its product to 'speak for itself'. Unless it takes vigorous steps, its rivals will draw further ahead and its decline will accelerate.

1. **To embrace new technologies.** If Qualspecs doesn't reduce its costs and prices whilst also improving its speed of service it will become increasingly uncompetitive.

2. **To become more dynamic and customer centred.** Its unimaginative **reward policy** reduces the productivity of its staff and managers and their willingness to provide good ideas that could enhance the company's success.

3. **To reach out to new customers.** Its established reputation gives Qualispecs a reliable income. To increase this it needs to find new customers such as higher-spending younger customers.

Part (b)

> **Top tips**. This part of the question requires you to recommend specific strategies. The Examiner's suggested solution was based on converting threats to opportunities and weaknesses to strengths; matching strengths with opportunities and remedying weaknesses. It would probably also be possible to base an answer on Porter's generic strategies. The Ansoff matrix could also provide some useful ideas for new products and markets.

Qualispecs is fortunate in that its finances are sound and it has large cash reserves. It would be appropriate to use some of that financial strength to make investments that will improve the company's competitive position. *Qualispecs* should seek improvements in three main areas of its operations.

- Innovation
- Performance management
- Distribution

Innovation

Two areas are ripe for innovation: **products** and **production methods**. In both areas, *Qualispecs* has to catch up with its competitors. The economic downturn means that growth will be most easily achieved in the 18-30 year old market. Fashion-consciousness is important here, so the design and variety of prescription spectacles and sunglasses must be improved. At the same time, suitable promotion must be undertaken, perhaps making use of sports star endorsement.

Production methods must be examined for opportunities to reduce cost and improve efficiency. The one hour laboratory approach should be considered, as discussed below.

In addition to these two matters, it would be appropriate for *Qualispecs* to begin to foster a **culture of innovation**. Given its existing stagnation, there are almost certainly several other aspects of its operation that would benefit from new ideas. Such cultural change is linked to our next area of consideration.

Performance management

We mentioned performance management in our earlier discussion of key strategic challenges. The principle could also be applied in the form of **management bonuses** based on the overall performance individual shops and regions and individual pay increases and bonuses related to sales and profit performance. Such a change would require greater autonomy for managers at shop level in particular if it were to have significant effect, so there would have to be some delegation of control over such matters as working conditions, job roles and pay rates.

Distribution

Qualispecs must do something about the wide variation in its shops' performance. A careful examination of costs and revenues is needed. There is also a need to look at the shops estate from a marketing point of view. The estate may be in need of renovation or even complete redesign. The company should aim to make its shops pleasant and interesting places to visit. *Fastglass* has entered into partnership with a high-street shopping group. This may be an innovation that *Qualispecs* could imitate as part of its attention to product development. A **fashion retailer** would be a good choice of partner for a new group of in-store shops concentrating on the new designer styles, for example. A partnership approach to costs and revenues may be possible and appropriate.

Qualispecs must also examine the *Fastglass* mini-lab approach with an open mind. This method may be worth adopting, assuming the technology is not protected, but caution should be employed: a full examination of costs and market prospects should be carried out and implications fully explored.

Alternative approach to answer for Question 2: (see note above)

> ### Part (a)
>
> **Strengths – (Internal)**
>
> Reputation
>
> The company has an excellent reputation for quality products. This will enable the company to launch new products with confidence that existing customers will have faith in their products and services, thus increasing market penetration.

Financial strength

The company is on a sound financial footing, including large cash reserves. This is advantageous as it will allow Qualispecs (Q) to make investments in new technologies such as those used by Fastglass, (F) without the need to secure external finance.

Weaknesses – (Internal)

Technology

The technologies employed by Q appear dated, as the company has 'failed to utilise advances'. This has resulted in a lack of competitive edge against companies such as F resulting in lost customer loyalty as well as a higher cost base.

Poor internal control

The company produces internal information that shows variable profitability and lack of control over job roles. The failure to act upon this information means that the company has continued to trade from shops that are not very profitable and hence drag down the company's results. The lack of control over job roles may lead to confusion amongst staff creating inefficiency and lower levels of customer service.

Opportunities – (External)

New technologies

The technologies that Q has not utilised may be employed using Q's cash reserves. This will allow the company to compete more effectively against F and stem the tide of lost customer loyalty. Additionally, the new technologies should lower the currently high production costs.

Youth market

Although there is a predicted slowdown in the economy we are told customer spending will rise in the 18-30 year olds market segment. Q could target its product development and marketing approaches to this segment to gain market share in a demographic that is known to contain high spending and image conscious consumers. This could be aided by the endorsement of the popular sports star.

Threats – (External)

Competition

Q faces increased competition from companies such as F employing superior technologies. The intense competition that Q faces will cause problems such as a falling customer base, which will result in lower repeat custom and falling economies of scale. The Q brand may also suffer in comparison to successful industry rivals.

Market slowdown

The national economy is predicted to slow down which could affect Q's sales. Even though consumer spending is predicted to be strong this will primarily benefit the stronger competitors with differentiated products and services. As Q is currently uncompetitive it stands to miss out on any increase in spending whilst seeing the economy shrink as a whole.

Key strategic challenges

Uncompetitive technologies

In order to become competitive Q needs to invest in newer technologies. Its current technologies make its production methods slow and expensive.

Outdated marketing

Letting 'the product speak for itself' is an outdated marketing concept. A failure to research, understand and supply customer needs allied to promotional activities undermines Q attempts to be more competitive.

Disjointed structures

The lack of cohesion over pay and job roles is undermining Q's ability to provide a consistent service offering. Failure to do so will confuse staff which my impact upon customers and harm the brand.

Part (b)

<u>Invest in new technologies</u>

One hour technology capability will solve a number of the issues discussed above. It will enable the strengths of Q, beings it brand and cash, to be matched to the opportunity of new technologies. Additionally, the weaknesses of uncompetitive technologies resulting in slow and expensive production costs, will be reduced or eliminated. This measure will also allow Q to compete on an equal footing with F, and if it invests in even more recent innovations perhaps out-compete F in the growing youth market too.

<u>Marketing Campaign</u>

Q could attempt to arrange celebrity endorsements with sports, music or film stars in order to enhance their brand. The famous sports star endorsement appears to have been a fortunate accident, the benefits of an official endorsement could be huge in terms of brand exposure, customer loyalty and maybe premium pricing.

Particular emphasis could be placed on the growing 18-30 year olds market segment. There will be a cost in terms of payments to the celebrities and marketing campaign. Marketing, however is an area that is currently both a weakness of Q that can be eliminated and an opportunity that can be exploited.

<u>Focus on profitable locations</u>

Q appears to operate some stores that are profitable whilst others are not, which drags down overall group profitability. Q should conduct a review of each site's historic and potential future profitability and focus its resources where it is most likely to make maximise returns for shareholders.

For example those sites with very high rental should have their leases reviewed to see if they can be broken or notice served to either look for alternative premises in the town or the store closed. In this way Q will be maximising its returns in respect of a key constraint (floor space).

3 Automobile components

Text reference. Porter's 'diamond' is assumed knowledge for E3. It is summarised briefly in the 'Introductory' chapter at the start of the BPP Study Text for E3, but is covered in more detail in E2.

Marking scheme

			Marks
(a)	Each characteristic or factor identified, 1 mark each	Up to 5	
	Description of characteristic or factor identified and why it is important in the choice of location, 1 mark each	Up to 5	
	Relating characteristic or factor to the scenario material, 1 mark each	Up to 5	
		Total up to	15
(b)	Each source of relevant information identified, ½ mark each	Up to 2 ½	
	Nature of information from each source, and how it will be useful to G when evaluating potential countries	Up to 7 ½	
		Total up to	10
		Total	25

Part (a)

> **Top Tips.** The scenario should have given some ideas to use in your answer. However, more importantly, the reference to 'ideal characteristics for the chosen country' should have indicated that Porter's diamond would be a valuable theory to use here, although alternative models such as PEST could also help you to structure a good answer
>
> The reference to ideal characteristics and factors is effectively asking you to apply your knowledge of the aspects of the competitive advantage of nations (Porter's diamond) to the specific situation G is facing.
>
> However, note the question does not ask you to describe Porter's diamond, and you unlikely to get marks for doing so. Rather you should use the headings and ideas given in the diamond as a framework on which to construct your answer. And remember, you must link the characteristics and factors, specifically to the scenario: G is looking to open a research facility in the foreign country, with the possibility of opening a manufacturing facility next to it at a later date.
>
> **Easy marks.** The information provided in the scenario should have given you a good start to this question, not least because it gave you clear pointers to the relevant theory to use. If you had used this, and then thought of a wide range of issues which would be relevant to a high technology industry, you could have scored well in this question.
>
> **Examiner's comments.** Most candidates used Porter's diamond to structure their answers to (a) and demonstrated a good understanding of the model. However, some still failed to apply their answer to the scenario material sufficiently.

According to Porter's Diamond there are four types of 'characteristic and factor' which G should consider when choosing the preferred location for its overseas based: factor conditions; demand conditions; firm strategy, structure and rivalry; and related and supporting industries. These, in turn, are all supported by a fifth factor: government policy.

Factor conditions

Basic factor conditions. These include the availability of natural resources, raw materials, support staff (semiskilled and unskilled labour) and a pleasant climate and location. These basic factor conditions are inherent in a country.

If G wants to send some of its research staff to work at the overseas base, the quality of life available in the chosen country will be an important factor in choosing a location.

Advanced factor conditions. These include high speed transport linkages, highly educated personnel – including university educated research scientists – and modern digital communications and internet penetration.

The transport linkages will be particularly important if G is looking at using the base as a hub for linking to potential export markets.

Whereas the basic factor conditions are often inherent in a country, the advance factor conditions require significant, and continuing, investment from the host country to maintain them.

Demand conditions

G will not be selling director to end-user consumers, but to automobile manufacturers. Nonetheless, the demand for its parts will be determined by the **demand for environmentally friendly vehicles**. So G should be looking to locate in countries with a strong environmental lobby, advocating the use of these vehicles.

Affluence. Because the environmentally friendly vehicles are still a new development it is likely that **they will be expensive.** Therefore G should be looking to locate in a country where the population is sufficiently well-off to be able to afford the cars.

Economic growth rate. Another factor G may wish to consider is the rate of growth of the economy in the country. A fast growing market is likely to encourage early adoption of state-of-the-art technology.

Sophisticated buyers. G should be looking for a country with sophisticated and demanding buyers, who will be attracted by the prospect of owning vehicles made from the latest technology. The presence of discerning consumers will in turn **lead to continuing innovation and improvement** if they provide feedback about the cars.

Market size. The size of the potential market is also important. Although, the vehicles are still currently in a development phase, once this is complete it will be important to supply as large a market as possible because this will allow **economies of scale** to be earned. Ultimately this market could be international as well as in the host country, again reinforcing the importance of good transport linkages.

Firm strategy, structure and rivalry

Structure. National cultural factors mean that countries tend to specialise in certain industries rather than others. G should aim to move to a country which has a strong market for high technology products, in which the competition between the existing producers forces them to remain competitive.

Perhaps most importantly, it should also look to move to a country with an established automobile market, and a number of established automobile manufacturers. It is these manufacturers who are likely to be G's customers.

Strategy. Because G is dealing with a high technology, market-leading product it should look to locate in a country with an established capital market. This will mean that either it, or any automobile manufacturers it partners in the country, will have access to funding if they need them to expand.

Also, G should also try to locate in a country where the existing businesses adopt long-term planning horizons.

Related and supporting industries

G should aim to locate its R&D base close to a number of existing high technology, innovative companies. Such a concentration of high technology companies should create **external economies of scale,** because there will be a **clustering of skilled workers** in the area.

G will be more likely to succeed in its new location if it has a **supporting cluster** around it. The cluster will facilitate the transfer of knowledge, which will be critical in the development stage of the new technology.

Government

A number of the factors mentioned above will be influenced by national government. Government policy will affect **education** and the **provision of services and infrastructure**.

However, G should also look at the government policies which will directly affect its financial position – for example, **taxation, managed exchange rates, tariffs or subsidies.**

G should also consider the country's **attitude to inward investment**. Some countries encourage foreign investment through development grants, although it is unlikely that development grants will be available in areas which have already established high technology clusters.

Finally, G should look at the **political stability** of the country. If there is a danger that the current government may lose office soon, then it needs to be assured that any successor governments will still support foreign investment.

Part (b)

> **Top tips**. There is a danger that your answer to (b) will just become a list of possible information sources, but you need to make sure this doesn't happen.
>
> Simply listing information sources is not what is required, and will not score well. If you just make a list of information sources, the maximum marks you could earn for this requirement is 2 ½. The requirement actually contains two aspects: the *nature* of information G should use, and the *sources* of this information. Therefore it is important for you to recommend what sort of information G should be looking at, as well as indicating where it can find this information.
>
> A good answer will indicate why the information will be useful to G – again, making your answer directly relevant to the scenario.
>
> **Examiner's comments**. A number of candidates just discussed sources of information with no reference to what information was actually required.

G should look at a range of economic, social and legal information while evaluating potential countries.

Economic indicators. G should look at a number of basic economic indicators to assess the strength of the economy in the country. These include GDP, inflation, interest rates, exchange rates. These indices should be available from the relevant government departments in the target country, and G should expect to be able to find this information on a government website. If G cannot obtain the information directly from the government, it should be able to find it from a third party data source such as The Economist Intelligence Unit, or the OECD statistics portal.

Industry review. G should review the trade press for any reports about high technology content similar to that which it is developing, to see if there are any countries which already host similar companies.

G should also look at the annual reports or websites of any national companies based in the target countries to get an indication of the professionalism and quality of the work they are doing. This would be particularly relevant for automobile manufacturers so that G could assess the possible market for its product in the country.

Consumer market. G needs to assess whether there is an end-user market for environmentally friendly cars in the country. It may be able to find out useful information about market trends from marketing agencies in the country, or through consumer research groups such as Mintel.

Transport infrastructure. G will need information on the quality of the road network in the area, and on access to airports. It can find the physical data from an atlas, but should also look at the websites for the nearest airports to see whether they will be able to accommodate its freight needs.

Education. The quality of the higher education system as a potential source of skilled labour can be gauged by looking at the research papers which are produced by the local universities and the level of international research grants that they win each year. The scientists in G's own R&D department may also know about the quality of the universities.

Internet access and other electronic infrastructure. The quality of the information networks and internet access can be found by looking at statistics for internet and broadband penetration. There are a number of websites which show this information.

Legislation and regulation. G should be able to obtain information about legislation and trade regulations from the government of the potential host countries. G should also consult is own financial advisers about the tax regimes in the various countries, especially if its financial advisers already have offices in those countries. Similarly, G should consult its legal advisors about the legal structure in the countries.

Financial markets – G should find out about the quality of financial markets as sources of capital for investment and development through discussions with its own bank and financial advisers.

Political structure and stability. G should talk to the government in its own country to find out about the political structure and stability in the possible countries. G should also contact the department responsible for international trade in its own government to assess the target country as a destination for foreign investment and trade.

Regional economic groupings. Finally, G should consider whether the country is part of a larger free trade area or regional grouping. In time, G will be hoping that the market for the environmentally friendly cars develops and they can be exported. Therefore, it should be looking at the level of exports the country currently makes, and its trade links with other countries. This information can be obtained from the International Trade Centre of the World Trade Organisation.

4 Digwell Explorations

> **Text reference.** Social responsibility and stakeholder analysis are covered in Chapter 2 of your BPP Study Text.

Part (a)

> **Top tips.** When approaching this requirement you need to be aware that there are two parts to the question: (i) discussing the ethical issues the government needs to consider; (ii) explaining the conflicts between the main stakeholder groups.
>
> Although the ethical interests are more to do with conflicts of interest than simply notions of 'right' and 'wrong' you must make sure you don't duplicate points between the two parts of the requirement.
>
> Note also that you must examine the ethical considerations from the *government*'s perspective – not Digwell, the business concerned.

> Note that for the second part of the requirement you are required to *explain* the conflicts between the main stakeholder groups – not just identify them. To obtain a good pass mark, you would have to explore the implications of the various points of view in some detail. Make sure you give a balanced account of the interests of the various stakeholders.

Ethical issues to be considered by the government

Ethics is 'the science of morals' and is concerned with doing the morally right things. The government has a duty to exercise fairness in balancing the wishes of different stakeholders.

The government has granted permission for Digwell to undertake mining, in the context of submissions from a number of stakeholders affected by the proposal. The decision is likely to have been taken with a number of **political** considerations in mind, notably the power of the various interest and pressure groups. However, the key **ethical** issues can be summarised as follows.

(i) Ownership of national resources

One of the arguments raised by the 'anti-capitalism groups' is likely to be that corporations should not be given private ownership and exploitation rights over resources that could be regarded as under '**common ownership**', such as land and the minerals contained in it. There is, however, the contrary ethical argument of '**stewardship**': that is, that since natural resources belong to the nation, there is a duty to exploit them in the public interest, rather than 'wasting' them in their undeveloped state.

From the government's point of view, this is an on-going ideological conflict (unresolved within the British political system) but also a more focused conflict between the claims of **economic sustainability** and **environmental sustainability**.

(ii) Economic sustainability

One of government's key priorities is to secure the sustainability of economic activity and the increase of prosperity, particularly in under-developed areas. This is an 'ethical' issue in that it addresses the basic economic welfare of local citizens: should rights to work and a share of economic benefits be compromised by environmental considerations (which may not have been raised by local people)?

There is a recognised need for **economic regeneration** in the Eastborough area, but the attempt to meet it through tourism – dovetailing environmental amenity and economic activity – has found little success. The granting of mining rights could result in **jobs**, a boosted local economy – and perhaps also **corporate investment** in local infrastructure and environmental regeneration (with opportunities to revitalise the tourism initiative).

(iii) Environmental sustainability

This is the primary argument against the mining operation. It addresses a range of ethical values such as **stewardship of the environment** (the duty to preserve it for future generations), the protection of habitats and **biodiversity** (eg the danger to rare birds), community rights to '**amenity**' (preservation of living conditions and enjoyment of the environment) *and* compliance with national and international law (for example, EU regulations) and regulation on environmental protection.

The government will have its own policy guidelines in regard to environmental protection and sustainability, within which the decision to grant Digwell permission should be made.

(iv) Secondary stakeholder interests

The purpose of democratic government is to represent stakeholders in society – and the process of application for mining rights is designed to ensure that stakeholder voices are heard and taken into account. By definition, a 'stakeholder' has a *legitimate* interest in a process or outcome, but there is a particular concern that otherwise voiceless or powerless stakeholders should be fairly heard: the needs of the local villagers and the claims of the (supremely voiceless) flora and fauna.

There is also a justice or equity issue involved in the concept of '**externalities**': environmental and other impacts/costs of corporate activity need to be taken into account – if not formally accounted for within the economic model – since they are borne by secondary stakeholders who may not reap the benefits.

Conflicts between main stakeholder groups

The issues discussed above account for the main sources of conflict between the stakeholder groups.

(i) Conflict between economic interests and environmental pressure groups

This conflict is focused between Digwell and some elements of the 'Eastborough Protection Alliance': the wildlife protection representatives and environmentalists. It is a systemic conflict, arising from competing ideologies and priorities in regard to social responsibility.

Digwell's focus on **maximising shareholder returns** is legitimate within its own terms. It may also be supported (although this is not stated in the scenario) by community groups on the grounds of creating employment, and benefiting the community through taxation, investment and the 'trickle down' affect of economic activity.

Environmental pressure and interest groups, however, focus on a **different set of priorities**: the need to protect rare species from extinction, the need to preserve scenic beauty for future generations and so on. Mining is a worldwide target of such groups, because of its often traumatic impact on environments (eg through open cast mines, pollution of river systems and watersheds and so on). The pressure groups may or may not be representative of local community interests: supporting the 'bigger picture' of the environment at the expense of local economic sustainability.

(ii) Conflict between local residents and Digwell

A second conflict arises from the villagers' fear of loss of residential amenity as a result of the mining activity. This may partly be legitimately focused on the risk of **traffic congestion and noise**, but there may also be an underlying **fear of change** and cultural erosion. Economic progress and development (although desirable to some) may represent the loss of an agricultural way of life and a 'small village' culture that has endured for 150 years.

While Digwell may agree that **congestion and noise** should be minimised as part of its social responsibilities, it is clearly committed to industrial development and resource exploitation, and would presumably argue that such a position benefits not only its shareholders, but the local community as well through the creation of jobs and related investments in the local economy.

Part (b)

> **Top tips.** The obvious model to use here is *Mendelow's* matrix. This should be a simple analysis, but the Examiner remarked that students frequently either failed to relate the matrix to the scenario, or placed stakeholders in the wrong quadrant. A further common error was to fail to identify how Digwell might *respond* to the various groups, as explicitly required.
>
> Although the question does not ask you to show the matrix, it asks you to analyse the 'interest' and 'power' of the stakeholder groups. Therefore, including the matrix in your answer and the plotting the position of the stakeholders on could act as an efficient and effective way of doing this.

Mendelow's mapping framework classifies stakeholders on a matrix whose axes are power/influence and interest in the organisation's activities. These factors will help define the need for Digwell to invest in managing any given stakeholder group, and how they can best be managed. The key stakeholder and pressure groups identified in the scenario might be placed in a power/interest matrix as follows.

Level of interest

Power/influence	Low	High
Low	Quadrant A Anti-capitalist groups	Quadrant B Local residents
High	Quadrant C Digwell's shareholders & directors	Quadrant D Environmental groups? Government

(i) Anti-capitalist groups

These are likely to have **relatively low power** (with relatively low numbers and credibility in relation to more directly affected stakeholders) – and relatively low interest (given the local scale of the mining operation, compared to, say, G8 summits).

Mendelow's recommended strategy for quadrant A is to **expend minimal effort**. However, Digwell can prevent these groups graduating to quadrant C by separating the concerns of legitimate stakeholders from those of the anti-capitalists.

(ii) Local residents

Local residents have a **high legitimate interest** in Digwell's plans, both positive, in terms of employment and development, and negative, in terms of loss of amenity. They have **relatively low power**: although they have influence (as voters) on local government, their position is weakened by internal conflicts of interest and by their relatively small numbers. However, because of their high interest, there is a risk that they will co-opt more influential stakeholders (such as the media and interest/pressure groups).

Mendelow's recommended strategy for this quadrant is **consultation and information**: Digwell should show its willingness to **take local residents' concerns into account by open consultation with them**, and promote the economic and social benefits of the project – co-opting this group as supporters rather than resisters.

(iii) Environmental groups

The various groups (considered together for the purposes of the analysis) have a **high interest** in the project, as it concerns the area of their specific remit and concern, and may even be seen as a 'test case' for other mining protests. Some individual groups may fall into the low-power category, but others may have considerable public credibility, media influence and lobbying power: grouped together, they may exert pressure for government to impose restrictions, or for public protest to disrupt Digwell's activities and ability to secure local labour and services.

Therefore, taken together, environmental groups should be considered as having relatively **high power**.

Mendelow's recommended strategy for quadrant D 'key players' is to ensure that strategies are acceptable to them. Digwell should prepare an **environmental audit and impact statements,** and make plans to protect rare species, regenerate land, minimise pollution and so on.

(iv) Government

Government has a **high official interest**, as the approver of mining grants: it also has an interest as **beneficiary** in the economic/social benefits to the area – and in the concerns of voters which pose a political risk. It has **high power** to revoke permissions and to monitor and enforce environmental and local government regulations.

As a key player, government should be the target of **ongoing stakeholder management**, through proactive issues and crisis management and promotion of benefits (perhaps reinforced by extra community investment and political support).

(v) Digwell shareholders and directors

These groups have a **high degree of power** over Digwell's **strategy**, as the strategic decision makers – and those to whom they are accountable. However, they may have relatively **low interest** in the **specifics** of the project: their interests are more generally in the performance of the company.

Mendelow's recommended strategy for Quadrant C is 'keep satisfied'. As long as Digwell **upholds its reputation for maximising shareholder returns**, is able to **demonstrate compliance** (and consideration for any CSR values its shareholders particularly care about), it should be able to avoid arousing more specific interest in opposition to its plans.

5 CTC – Strategic objectives

> **Text reference.** Strategic objectives, which are relevant to parts (a) and (b), are dealt with in Chapter 2 of your BPP Study Text. Stakeholders are also discussed in Chapter 2.
>
> **Top tips.** Neither the scenario nor any of the requirements make use of the word 'stakeholder', but it should spring to your mind as soon as you begin thinking about this question. CTC has some very important new stakeholder groups to consider and their interests will be the main formative influence on what the company sets out to do. Stakeholders will be a major consideration for both part (a) and part (b).

Part (a)

> **Top tips.** When answering this question you need to think of the contrasting aims and objectives of private sector organisations with those in the public sector. Simply saying what the new objectives should be will not be enough to pass this question. Instead you need to think in terms of **change,** and consider what the company's objectives were before privatisation, and how these will change after the company is privatised.
>
> Don't overlook the demands of corporate governance; this is about both what is to be done and also how it should be done.
>
> The solution below adopts a stakeholder approach. An alternative approach would be to make a series of points related to the primacy of profit in a commercial firm compared to a state monopoly, the need to hold market share at home, the need to gain sales revenues by expanding product range and providing services abroad and the need to protect its share price by good corporate governance and adequate communication with investors.
>
> **Examiner's comments.** Most candidates mentioned the pre-privatisation objectives of economy, efficiency and effectiveness and identified the new role of shareholders and their importance in setting objectives. However, many candidates failed to recognise the importance of overseas expansion as an objective.

As a state monopoly, CTC's role was expressed in terms of its **service to the nation as a whole**. Its focus was on the public sector aspirations off **efficiency, effectiveness and economy**, but it was **not subject to market discipline** and its finances were controlled by government. The lack of market input and the highly technical nature of its operations make it likely that its main operational concern was **engineering competence**, rather than customer interests. However, the government, as principal stakeholder, imposed requirements around performance and service levels to be achieved.

Shareholders as new stakeholders

CTC now has a new and important class of **stakeholder** in the form of its **shareholders**. They will have firm ideas about their requirements in the form of growth, earnings and dividends.

Importance of customers

The company faces a de-regulated market where competition will intensify. It will need to pay great attention to the views and needs of its **customers**; they are a stakeholder group that is likely to wield far more influence than previously, since they will be able to choose new suppliers when new providers of telecommunications services enter the market following its deregulation.

Impact on objectives

These influences will affect objectives at all levels in the organisation and will require a significant realignment of attitudes. In particular, there will be **pressure to reduce costs; to develop new and attractive products**; and to **improve customer service**, particularly in the matter of installing new equipment and dealing with faults.

The **respective requirements of shareholders and customers** also highlight a potential conflict which will need to be addressed by the directors when setting the company's objectives.

Shareholders will want to **maximise profitability** which may be achieved by raising prices. But customers will seek the lowest price they can get.

Although the **government** is no longer the main external stakeholder, it will still be interested in CTC's performance. The company will continue to make a large contribution to the economy of C as a major employer and taxpayer; it also has the potential to develop as a major centre of technological excellence.

While government will step back from direct involvement in the running of CTC, it is likely that it will retain an interest in its overall success, and possibly a closer involvement in such matters as the promotion of technological development and overseas expansion, which if successful could increase CTC's **tax liability** to the government.

Corporate governance

A final influence on the strategic objectives of the privatised company will arise in the field of **corporate governance**. As a quoted company, CTC will be subject to the normal regulations and codes of practice laid down by its quoting stock exchange. It may also be subject to special **government regulation** designed to prevent it from using its size and current dominant position to discourage competitors. These influences are also likely to have a marked effect on the directors attitudes and practices.

Overall, the objectives of CTC will need to change to **focus on profitability and shareholder reward**, as well as customer satisfaction which becomes increasingly important in a deregulated market. Alongside this, the directors will need to ensure the business' controls and governance are adequate to comply with its new regulatory requirements.

Part (b)

> **Top tips**. You must think carefully here. First, note that you are being asked for objectives *not* a mission statement: the objectives you select must be strategic (long term, not short term), but they can be very specifically aimed at particular aspects of strategy. Approaching the problem from the stakeholder angle would be a good way to proceed here, but make sure you explain *why* the objective is appropriate to CTC.
>
> The second important point is that the objectives you provide must be SMART.
>
> However, note (b) is only worth four marks so do not spend too long on this requirement.

Objective 1

To achieve an average of 5% annual growth in share valuation for the next five years or until competitors achieve a total of 25% market share.

This objective is relevant to the concerns of shareholders. It is specific, measurable and time-bounded. It is also realistic, in that it acknowledges that the company's existing privileged position is likely to be damaged by the entry of competitors into its markets.

Objective 2

To create, within twelve months, an affordable and humane restructuring plan that will reduce staff costs by 20% and to implement the plan over the following three years without provoking a major labour dispute.

This objective addresses the continuing strategic need for cost efficiency to allow CTC to compete effectively in a deregulated market. It recognises the need to balance that need against the interests of the existing employees and the practical difficulties of implementing a headcount reduction.

Part (c)

> **Text reference**. An overview of strategic planning models is given in Chapter 1 of your BPP Study Text.
>
> **Top tips**. As you will be aware, there is a range of views about how strategy is and should be made. You will not have time to consider them in detail here!
>
> There are 11 marks available for this requirement, which is too few for a wide discussion and too many for a simple answer based on one of the partial theories such as incrementalism or emergence.
>
> The key to resolving this dilemma is to use the **rational model** to **guide your answer**, with passing reference to the other approaches as you go. The Examiner gives you a clue that the rational model is relevant by referring to the 'strategic planning **process**' (BPP emphasis).
>
> However, by asking you to '*advise*' the Board, the Examiner is asking that your answer be appropriate for CTC, so you must apply your knowledge to the scenario rather than simply recounting the rational model.
>
> **Easy marks**. The rational model is fairly all-embracing, but even if you cannot remember all of the detail and terminology, you ought to be able to get some of it down on paper, and then apply it to CTC.

> **Examiner's comments.** In general, this question was well answered. However, some candidates still attempted to describe the text book stages of the rational model, without applying them to CTC in the light of the privatisation.

As a very large, newly privatised company, CTC needs to use a cautious and thorough approach to developing its strategy; if it does not, it runs a severe risk of being taken by surprise by the new and rapidly developing conditions under which it will have to operate. The classic **rational planning model** should therefore form the basis of its strategic processes.

This model will guide it through a series of logical stages. However, it is important to understand that although the rational model is linear in appearance, it is most effectively used if **feedback** between the various stages is created. Many of the processes involved can be run simultaneously, or even in reverse order if it becomes appropriate to reconsider earlier conclusions and decisions.

Company mission

CTC should give careful attention to what it is trying to achieve as a company. It should attempt to define its overall mission, and the strategic objectives that support that mission. Stakeholder interest and influence should be considered as part of this process, and any potential conflicts should be identified and resolved.

Environmental analysis

The company must ensure that it understands the ways in which it is affected by, and affects, the **environment in which it operates**. This will be a major task, since its comfortable state monopoly position has been disrupted; new competitors are very likely to enter its markets and, as a result, its customers are likely to discover that they have acquired significant bargaining power. CTC should analyse its wider environment using a 'PEST' analysis, and should consider the immediate industrial or task environment using Porter's Five Forces model as a guide. Environmental analysis is one of the stages of the rational model that is never complete; the company should undertake a policy of **continuing environmental scanning** for threats and opportunities.

Position audit

At the same time as it is seeking to understand its environment, CTC also needs to appraise its own internal **strengths** and **weaknesses**, and to understand its **core competencies** and **competitive position**. Its competitive advantage depends primarily on the possession of assets or competences that competitors cannot easily obtain or imitate; for instance, its network of telephone lines; intellectual property in the form of patents and proprietary designs; and the experience and knowledge of its staff.

The company should include in this phase an analysis of just how it creates value, using the **value chain** model.

Corporate appraisal

Environmental scanning and position audit permit the preparation of a SWOT analysis summarising the most important strengths, weaknesses, opportunities and threats pertaining to the company. This should then help CTC identify its strategic options.

Strategic options

CTC should consider its options in the context of *Porter's* analysis of generic strategies: **cost leadership** and **differentiation**. (The narrow **focus** strategy is inappropriate to such a large business).

Advantages also accrue to a company that achieves **lock-in**; this is the condition of owning the industry standard as proprietary technology. This is likely to be very relevant to CTC with its recent monopoly and large installed technology base.

Given the opportunities for growth in the global telecommunications industry, which lay behind the government decision to privatise CTC, CTC may also consider its strategies for **product** and **market development** as described in the Ansoff matrix.

Evaluation of strategic options

Having generated a range of possible strategies, CTC should assess them for **suitability**, in terms of its overall strategic mission and posture; **acceptability** to stakeholders; and **feasibility** in terms of the resources required. The selected strategy should also be **sustainable** in the longer term, and contribute to the company's longer term competitive advantage.

Strategy selection

It will also be necessary to consider CTC's **structure and means of growth**. CTC might choose to expand **organically** or by **takeover**. The latter option might be a sensible way to expand internationally, for example. Other options include **alliances** and **joint ventures**. There may also be subsidiary part of the current organisation that are actually distractions and could usefully be divested.

Strategy implementation

Once a strategy has been selected, it must be implemented, and the implementation must be controlled. **Implementation** will require the development of functional and departmental strategies and plans. CTC's development from its current status as a recently privatised monopoly is likely to create significant complexity in its human resources management function, for example. Control will require the identification of **critical success factors** and the design of suitable strategic **performance measures** linked to them.

Review and revision

As noted earlier, strategy development is not a linear process and it does end with strategic control. A very important role for feedback lies in the potential stimulation of reconsideration of the earlier stages of the model as outlined above, particularly as the reality of the market begins to be felt.

Also CTC should be aware that strategy may not actually develop in the ordered, linear way the rational model suggests. By contrast, CTC is more likely to experience an **emergent** process, with modifications being made to its strategy development in response to changing environmental factors or other constraints.

6 EEE – Stakeholder analysis

Text reference. Stakeholder analysis is covered in Chapter 2 of your BPP Study Manual.

Top tips. This question is obviously built around Mendelow's work, but you need to be clear in your mind exactly what it is asking for. There is no part of any of the requirements that asks you to explain in detail what stakeholder analysis is, or what Mendelow's matrix is. This question requires the **application** of knowledge to the scenario described, though see our top tip to Part (a) below.

Part (a)

Top tips. Although the answer to this question does not require a definition of 'stakeholder analysis' writing one on your plan would have helped you focus your mind on what is relevant and what is not.

Note you were not required to identify or discuss any individual stakeholders in the part of the question. That was the requirement for (b), and should have been kept separate from this part of the question.

Easy marks. While there will be no marks for explaining Mendelow's analysis, knowledge of its form will provide you with two important ideas about stakeholders that you need to bring out in your answer: the extent of their power and the level of their interest.

EEE's Stakeholders are persons or groups with an interest in what EEE does.

Stakeholder analysis establishes who the organisation's stakeholders are and the various discrete categories into which they fall; the nature of their 'stake', or interest, in the organisation, and therefore their probable objectives; and the extent of their power to influence the organisation's behaviour.

Advantages

(a) **Identify potential backers** of the proposal to develop the new extraction process. This will help the Board to approach them and gain their support.

(b) **Identify potential blockers** of the proposal. The Board can take action to reduce the resistance of blockers or, if too powerful, to modify or abandon the proposal before money is wasted on it.

(c) **Demonstrate good corporate governance.** Management is increasingly being asked to consider the interests of stakeholders beyond shareholders as part of firms' commitments to corporate social responsibility (CSR).

If EEE does decide to proceed, it will then also have to **manage the reactions** of the various groups given that some will support the project while others will oppose it.

Part (b)

> **Top tips.** To answer (b) well you have to apply your knowledge of stakeholder mapping to the specific context of the **organisational decision**. Note that you are not simply asked to analyse the principal stakeholders of EEE as an organisation, but specifically in relation to the proposed investment in the new process.
>
> The information provided in the scenario should have pointed you towards the principal stakeholders, and you should then have analysed them using the concepts of 'power' and 'interest' (from Mendelow's matrix).
>
> Note also the examiner's comment below about potential overlaps between groups. This again illustrates the importance about **thinking about the practical context** of the scenario.
>
> **Easy Marks.** If you knew the form of Mendelow's matrix, and related the stakeholders identified in the scenario to it, you should have been able to make a number of relevant points. Several of the stakeholder groups should have been both easy to identify from the scenario and easy to allocate to the matrix – for example, employees, and local government.
>
> **Examiner's Comments.** The examiner noted that many candidates focused too much on the stakeholders' influence on EEE as an organisation rather than on the decision itself. The examiner also noted that in a situation like this it is important to recognise the complexity of stakeholder analysis and the potential overlaps between different groups; for example a number of employees are also likely to be local residents.

An analysis of EEE's stakeholder groups using *Mendelow's* criteria of power and influence is shown below.

Key players (high degree of both interest and influence)

(a) The **founding family** forms a majority of the board and holds 30% of the share capital; it therefore, collectively controls the company. Its members are likely to give strong support to adoption the new process since it will confer a definite competitive advantage.

(b) If **local government** operates as in the UK, it will have extensive power to regulate industrial processes and developments. It will be very interested in EEE because it is a major element in the local economy and in the new process because of the complaints of the local residents. The council will therefore have mixed feelings about the new process.

(c) EEE's **employees** depend on the company for their livelihood and make a major contribution to its success. They also control or influence 20% of the shares in the company. Their interest lies in the successful introduction of the new process, since the competitive advantage its gives should also be to their benefit in terms of job security and, possibly, pay.

Note. The **trade union representative** who is also a local councillor falls into two of these categories: like the council itself, he may have mixed motivations, to the extent that he suffers from a **conflict of interest** that he should formally declare to his fellow councillors.

Keep satisfied (low degree of interest, high degree of power)

The **institutional shareholders** control 20% of the share capital; the extent of their activity in relation to the running of the company is unknown, but is likely to be minor. They will probably be content if EEE continues to operate reasonably successfully. However, they have the capacity to become interested if a major and costly problem arises.

Keep informed (high degree of interest, low degree of power)

Local residents fall into two sub-categories. Both will be directly interested in the new process, but any influence they can bring to bear on the company will be mediated through intermediaries.

(a) The **affluent residents** that have complained can only have significant effect through the local council and, possibly, by a media campaign. The effectiveness of either route will depend on how well EEE manages its press and public relations. In addition, the ambivalence of the council already commented on will limit this group's power. However, this group could seek to cause problems for EEE in the future if they are antagonised and so EEE should treat them with respect.

(b) **Other local residents** may also be concerned about unpleasant odours, but many of them are likely to be connected to the company through the employment of a family member; this group is more likely to be sympathetic to the new process.

Minimal effort (low degree of interest and influence)

The remaining **shareholders** own 30% of the shares but are unlikely to be particularly interested in the new process or to act as a group.

Part (c)

> **Top tips.** You should not have simply repeated suggestions made in (b) in this part of the question. Instead you should have used your analysis from (a) and (b) to **recommend** how EEE should proceed. As ever, your recommendations should be practical rather than theoretical: to go ahead with the decision or not; and how to manage with the public relations message arising from the decision.

The **economic advantages** of the new process are such that all of the key players are likely to agree that it is very desirable for EEE to adopt it on a large scale. However, the company cannot afford to ignore the feelings of those local residents that object on grounds of amenity. People can be very stubborn and **a campaign against the company** could, eventually, be very damaging.

The company should therefore adopt the process but should also take two important steps to safeguard its position.

First, it should be prepared to make a reasonable investment in developing the technology in a way that will **minimise the objectionable odours**. This might involve further chemical processing or filtering or merely something as simple as only using the process on days when the wind is in an appropriate direction. This will both reduce the potential for actual dispute and provide a basis for the second step, which is **careful PR management**.

EEE should ensure that its operations are presented in the best possible light, stressing the **economic benefits** to the area and the company's efforts to be a good neighbour. This will assist the local council to take a positive view of the company and will discourage the formation of a **single-issue pressure group** by the objecting affluent residents.

EEE could also consider some more pro-active PR events such as sponsoring local events or facilities, to build up its image as a good neighbour.

7 Island stakeholders

> **Text reference.** Chapter 2 of the BPP Study Text covers stakeholders which this question is all about.

Marking scheme

			Marks
(a)	Each stakeholder identified (provided the stakeholder is directly related to the case material)	1	
	Discussion of why each stakeholder would be interested in the decision	Up to 2	
		Total up to	12
(b)	Each advantage or disadvantage discussed	1	
	Illustration of each advantage or disadvantage with reference to specific internal stakeholders	1	
		Total up to	13
		Total	25

Part (a)

> **Top Tips.** The scenario should have given you a lot of ideas to use in your answer. However, it was important to read the requirements carefully before you started so that you didn't duplicate material between (a) and (b).
>
> This first part of the question asks you to identify the stakeholders who would be interested in E's decision and to identify what their interests might be. It does not ask you to discuss the likely impact on their interests of joining the trade bloc.
>
> The way the question is worded could help you with the structure of your answer: identify internal stakeholders who would be interested and discuss the nature of their interest, then identify external stakeholders and discuss the nature of their interested.
>
> This question certainly does not require you to discuss stakeholders in terms of their position in Mendelow's matrix, and you should not have wasted time doing so.
>
> The solution below is structured under the headings of the various stakeholders. In some cases the interests of a given stakeholder may be affected in several ways.
>
> **Easy marks.** The amount of information provided in the scenario should have given you a good start to this question, because it gave you clear pointers to a number of stakeholders you could identify. If you had used this and then thought of a good range of issues affecting from them, you could have scored well in this question.
>
> **Examiner's comments.** Most candidates identified a wide range of relevant stakeholders in (a), but some wasted time analysing each stakeholder using Mendelow's matrix.

(a) Internal stakeholder groupings

These are individuals and institutions resident in country E.

1 Businesses in E

These will be concerned at the impact of membership on competition and profits. They will see the abandonment of tariffs as opening up the markets within the bloc.

They will also be interested in the impacts of changes in regulations from removal of tariffs and other protectionist measures but also from the potential increased economic integration promised in the next step.

Businesses trading outside the bloc will be concerned at the **responses of external countries** to the bloc, such as protectionism. They will also be concerned at the **impact on the costs of imports**.

2 The tourism industry in E.

E currently only has a limited tourism industry. It will be interested in potential **increased numbers of visitors.** These will provide additional employment and increased earnings for the tourism sector.

3 Residents

E's population will be interested in the impact on **economic growth,** the availability of **jobs** and the possibility that more of the nation's educated young will choose to return to E after qualifying.

They will also be concerned at the **impact on their way of life** of increased tourist numbers and possibly also the **environment** of the island.

4 Government of E

The government will be interested in the impact of membership on the **political and economic development** of E. They will also be interested in the **public response** to the membership and ensuing impact on quality of life.

Ministers, other politicians, and senior civil servants will be personally interested in the impacts of closer integration with other countries on their **influence and their careers**. Will they lose power, or perhaps will they gain senior posts in an enlarged economic and political union?

External stakeholder groupings

These are individuals and organisations resident outside E.

1   Businesses outside the trade bloc

These will be concerned on the **impacts on their profits** of the adoption by E of the common external tariff. If this tariff is higher than E presently charges this will make it **harder to sell in E**.

They may also be interested in whether they should **establish production facilities in E** to get inside the bloc and gain advantage. Businesses who import from E will not longer have to pay import duty on their imports. This will increase their profits.

2   Businesses from other islands in the bloc

They will recognise that open markets will affect the competitive balance in the islands. They will be interested in the **markets that will be opened up** to them in E but also in the **new competition coming from firms in E**.

They will also be interested in whether this will hasten the progress to economic and political union and the effects this will have on regulation, growth and currency stability.

3   Residents on other islands in the bloc

Residents will hope to benefit from **reduced retail prices** for goods.

They may be concerned at the implications of more open markets, and the progress towards economic union, on the prospects for jobs and industries moving to different islands.

4   Potential investors

Because the trade bloc will promote E as a destination for inward investment, investors from inside and outside the bloc will look for **opportunities to invest** there.

Part (b)

Top tips. Your answer to (b) must not simply repeat points from (a).

(b) requires you to discuss the advantages and disadvantages to internal stakeholders as a whole, whereas (a) required you to look at the interests of individual stakeholders.

It is important that you recognise the distinction between the two parts, because this will affect the way you structure your answers. Your headings in this part should be advantages and disadvantages, whereas the headings in part (a) should have been the stakeholders who would be interested in E's decision to join.

Note that you are asked for both advantages and disadvantages so you should try to present an balanced account of both sides, rather than focusing too heavily on one or the other.

The points in text boxes at the end of the 'advantages' and 'disadvantages' are relevant points which would have earned you marks if you included them, but you could have still passed the question without including them.

Examiner's comments. Weaker answers merely repeated points in (b) that had already been made in (a) – and didn't score any marks in (b) for points which were repeated in this way.

If E decides to join the trade bloc, this decision will have both advantages and disadvantages for the stakeholders based in E which we have identified in part (a) (i) above.

Advantages

- Businesses who export to countries in the trade bloc should see an **increase in the volume of their exports**, because their goods will become cheaper in their destination markets following the removal of the import tariff.
- E currently only has a limited tourism industry despite being an attractive location, and the trade bloc's promotion of E as a **tourist destination** should help the growth of this industry.
- **Other local businesses may also benefit** as a consequence of the income and jobs generated through an increased tourism industry stimulating demand for their goods and services.
- **Inward investment in the economy**, allied to a well-educated population, should generate economic development on the island. Because the population is well-educated, the inward investment on E should

provide higher value jobs than investment which goes to undeveloped countries to take advantage of cheap labour rates.

- The investments in E should also generate additional **growth in support industries** associated with them, and the increase in the number of jobs should stimulate economic growth overall through the **multiplier effect**. Coupled with increased tourist revenues, this should allow the residents to benefit from increased standards of living.

- The improved employment opportunities resulting from new investments may **reduce the brain drain** which is currently experienced when well-educated children remain overseas to work once they have completed their degrees.

- The growth in exports, tourism and new businesses should **increase the tax revenues** available to the government. This will provide the government with additional funds to improve the infrastructure and hence become even more attractive to foreign investors.

- The government could also use some of the additional tax revenues to establish higher education facilities, thereby reducing the need for well-educated young people to look overseas for their degrees. This should help to reduce the brain drain even further.

- If we take all these advantages together, we can see that there is a further advantage the government. It will be in charge of a successful, growing economy which will make it popular with the electorate at home and will increase its status on the broader international political spectrum.

Disadvantages

- Businesses who export to countries outside the trade bloc are likely to see a decrease in demand for these exports because of the imposition of the tariff, or else they will have to reduce their selling price to keep the import price constant after the tariff has been applied. Either way, the tariff is likely to **reduce the profit earned from exports outside the bloc**. However, because the majority of E's exports are within the group, the advantages to export business from joining the trade bloc are likely to outweigh the disadvantages.

- Also, businesses who import from countries outside the trade bloc will have to pay **import duties** on these imports as a result of the common external tariff. This will either reduce their profit margins if they choose to absorb the additional cost, or it will lead to **higher prices for the consumers**. Depending on the level of imports affect, and their elasticity of demand, this could lead to an increase in **inflation levels** on the island.

- The rapid levels of growth on the island could also create **inflationary pressure**, especially if demand for key resources – in particular labour – exceeds supply.

- Although inward investment is potentially advantageous through creating jobs and economic growth, **foreign investment may not actually deliver the benefits E is hoping it will**. The foreign investors may simply want to move to E to take advantage of relatively cheap, well-educated labour, rather than creating the linkages with local suppliers which are needed to maximise the benefits to the local economy.

- Similarly, it is possible that inward investment may also have a detrimental impact on local businesses if multinational corporations move to E and **crowd out the existing local businesses**.

- For some of the local residents, increased numbers of tourists may be an undesirable intrusion onto their island and their way of life, particularly if they are accompanied by **increased levels of noise and pollution**. The same is also true of the inward investment by foreign companies.

- While joining the trade bloc could confer increased prestige on the government in the short term, there could be longer-term disadvantages of joining, especially if the trade bloc develops into a full economic union. This would significantly **reduce the government's control over E's economy**.

- The government should also be aware that if the inward investment doesn't create the beneficial multipliers it had hoped, tourists damage the residents' quality of life, and inflation levels rise significantly after joining the trade bloc, their political popularity could fall very quickly.

8 Genetically modified plants

Text reference. Corporate social responsibility and stakeholders are discussed in Chapter 2 of your BPP Study Text.

Top tips. In parts (a) and (b), three key stakeholder groups are identified in the question requirements: the government, environmental lobby groups, and the local community.

In both parts of the question, a sensible approach would be to look at each of the separate groups in turn. So, for part (a) you should have looked at B's corporate responsibility towards: (i) the government, (ii) the environmental lobby groups, and (iii) the local community.

Similarly, for part (b) you should have divided your answer into three parts and looked at how B could improve relationships with: (i) the government, (ii) the lobby groups, and (iii) the local community.

One of the key issues here seems to be communication. Although B's work does not involve the genetic modification of the seeds the lobby groups and the local community, incorrectly, believe they do. If B can make the groups understand what it does more accurately, that could well improve relationships with the groups.

Note, however, that you were not required to undertake a detailed stakeholder analysis, and so you should not have wasted time doing so.

Part (a)

Responsibility to the government

Legal obligations – B has a duty to comply with all the legislation which is currently in force in its country. This will include employment laws and health and safety laws, for example governing the working conditions in which B's staff work.

However, B does not have any direct responsibility to the government in respect of the seeds it produces. Not only are B's seeds not genetically modified (GM), but also the national government has not actually passed any legislation banning the research and development of GM crops.

Financial obligations – B has a responsibility to pay corporate taxes on its profits and account for the relevant payroll taxes on its staff.

Innovation and leadership – Although the primary responsibility in developing the non-GM technology is to the international community and to poorer farmers as a whole, rather than the government, B might be seen to have a secondary responsibility to the government as an industry leader. If B can develop the new technology and develop it so that the seeds can be produced on a commercial scale, this could be a source of new jobs and additional revenue for the government. Moreover, it will establish B's country as the leader in this field, generating prestige and a favourable international reputation.

Responsibility to environmental lobby groups

Explain seeds are not genetically modified – The lobby groups' opposition to B's work comes from the fact that they believe B's seeds are genetically modified. However, as this is incorrect, B should explain to the lobby groups that it is not genetically modifying the seeds.

Although B does not have to explain any details of its work which could be commercially sensitive, it should nevertheless explain the nature of its work sufficiently to illustrate that it is not genetically modifying the seeds in the way the lobby groups believe. Although B cannot stop the lobbyists opposing its work, it does have a responsibility to ensure that the lobbyists are aware that it is not actually genetically modifying seeds.

Highlight the potential benefits of its work – There is a danger that by trying to stop B developing the seeds, the lobby groups will be preventing the development of a product which could be beneficial to society as a whole.

To this end, B should highlight the potential benefits of its seeds, and, in particular, how they could be a major benefit to populations in the developing countries of the world.

Responsibility to the local community

Explain the nature of its work – In the same way that B needs to explain to the lobby groups that it is not genetically modifying seeds, so it also needs to explain this to the local community to try to reduce their opposition to its work. Again, B needs to explain that opposing its work could prevent B from developing a product which could be very beneficial to society as a whole.

Responsibility as an employer – B is also likely to have a responsibility to the local community as an employer of local people. As an employer, B contributes jobs and income to the local community, and it should consider the potential impact on the local community if its moves to a new country.

Good corporate citizen – More generally, B has a responsibility to the local community to be a good corporate citizen. For example, as a research and development company with highly skilled staff, B could support some educational initiatives in local schools and colleges.

Part (b)

One of the main problems B seems to be facing is that key stakeholder groups do not really understand the nature of its work. Therefore, **educating them** about its processes will be crucial for B to improve relationships with them.

The government

Explain benefits – B should explain to the relevant government minister the potential benefits that the research could bring to the country. It is vital that B explains that its process does not involve genetic modification, and therefore offers a possible **commercial alternative to GM crops**.

If B carries on with its research, and subsequently produces its seeds in commercial quantities, this could have significant economic benefits for the country. B could generate significant **export earnings**, and as production grows, the local economy would also benefit through the **creation of jobs and supporting services.**

Explain the science – The government is likely to employ scientists of its own, particularly as it is currently conducting an enquiry into the safety of GM crops. B's scientists should try to develop good relationships with the government scientists to explain that B's technology is safe, and that its processes do not involve genetically modifying the seeds.

Co-operate with government enquiry – It is also important that B is seen to be co-operating with the current government enquiry into GM crops. This might make the government and other key stakeholders view B more favourably, and it will give B the opportunity to show its processes do not involve genetic modification of crop seeds.

Nonetheless, B should not disclose information which is commercially sensitive, because this could allow competitors to obtain details of its work, and develop similar processes of their own.

Environmental lobby groups

Explain processes do not involve genetic modification – The lobby groups remain convinced that B's work <u>does</u> involve genetically modifying crops, and B has to persuade them this is not the case. It is likely that the lobby groups, like the government, have scientists working for them, so B could look to **explain the principles of their work to the scientists** to get them to appreciate that B's processes do not involve genetic modification.

Explain wider benefits – As well as explaining its processes, B should be looking to explain the wider benefits of its work. If it can develop pest-resistant seeds, this will allow farmers (particularly in developing countries) to grow better crops and hopefully also improve their standard of living. This could also bring wider environmental benefits: if the farmers can improve the yield of their current land, this might reduce deforestation rates and erosion, because there will be less pressure to bring extra land under cultivation.

The local community

Press and media stories – Many people in the local community will not understand the detail of what B does, but will only be aware of B's work through the stories reported in the press and the media. It is therefore important that B increases its communications with the media, so that they can present B's side of the story as well as is opponents' views. To this end, B could hold regular press releases, and possibly could even invite some journalists to see some of its processes, to highlight that they do not involve genetically modifying any crops. Again though, B has to strike a balance between giving people more information and preserving commercial sensitive details.

Local government – The local government could be another important stakeholder in the local community, so B should also look to improve communications with it. If the local government (and in particular any local government scientists) accept that B's work is safe and doesn't involve any genetic modification, then the local community may also be more likely to accept it.

Support community projects – B might also be able to improve its relationship with the local community by getting more involved with local people. For example, it could sponsor some local events, or provide some financial support to community projects.

Part (c)

> The question for part (c) also gives you a clue about how to structure your answer, by listing the four dimensions of CSR. A sensible approach would have been to look at each of these four dimensions in turn. There are 8 marks available, and 4 dimensions, so you should look to score 2 marks for each aspect.
>
> However, your answer should have related the four CSR aspects specifically to B's decision to re-locate. General discussions about aspects of CSR would not have scored well.

Legal

B has no legal obligation to be based in one country as opposed to another. Therefore, if it chooses to move to another country it is free to do so.

Clearly, B will still need to comply with the laws and regulations of the country it moves to, but it is unlikely these will be more rigorous than those it currently has to follow.

One issue which B will need to be aware of, however, is that if there are any **international standards** governing genetic engineering processes and practices, then it will need to ensure it complies with these whichever country it is based in.

Ethical

The main ethical issue in this scenario appears to be that the lobby groups feel that B's work is unethical because it allegedly involves the **genetic modification** of seeds. B's own directors know that their work does not involve genetic modification, and so the ethical objections are not justified on scientific grounds. However, it is likely that the lobby groups will continue to object to B's work, wherever it is located.

B's motive for moving to a new country is that it the new country is more supportive of biotechnology research and development. So there may be a perception in this country that the **greater good** of being able to produce seeds which help to feed people better outweighs the concerns that some groups have about genetic modification. In which case, if relocating helps B develop the product and then produce it commercially, the move should be supported.

Economic

Demand for genetically modified food is growing worldwide, and this looks to provide B with good opportunities for economic growth. B has an economic objective to **generate a profit for its owners** and so if moving to a new country helps it to **grow and achieve more profit**, then that is a valid reason for moving.

Moreover, if B grows and becomes a successful business, its success will also benefit its new host country. The government will benefit from **tax revenues**, and the local economy could benefit through B's **investment** in it, and through the demand for supporting goods and services.

Ultimately, if B becomes very successful, it could prompt other similar companies to move to the country, and could lead to the development of a biotechnology cluster there. This again would be economically beneficial to B's new host country.

Philanthropic

Although the new country has a more tolerant attitude to research and development than B's current country, some locals may still be unhappy about the potential impact of a new business on their amenities and their way of life. However, B should be keen to work with the local community so that the community supports it rather than resents it.

One of the ways B can gain the local community's support is by improving people's quality of life, and **giving something back to society**. For example, B could support some local education projects: either by helping to fund new schools or colleges, or by running some education programmes for local farmers.

9 Tobacco planning

Text reference. Strategic planning processes are discussed in Chapter 1 of BPP's E3 Study Text. Corporate Social Responsibility (CSR) is discussed in Chapter 2.

Marking scheme

			Marks
(a)	Each relevant limitation discussed, up to 2 marks each	Up to 6	6
(b)	Analysis of the problem (risks from new legislation) Up to three modifications, worth up to two marks each Two relevant recommendation, worth up to two marks each	Up to 2 Up to 6 Up to 4 Total up to	12
(c)	Identify the importance of the ethical dimension of the discussions Up to 2 marks for each method of influencing the government Conclusion (and recommendation), if given	Up to 2 Up to 6 1 Total up to	7
		Total	25

Part (a)

Easy marks. This short first part is entirely dependent on theoretical knowledge: it is an easy question if you are familiar with the theory and effectively impossible to answer if you are not.

Limitations of expected value techniques for a single strategic decision

1   Use of average values

    An expected value is an average value – and averages are only useful as a means of considering a range of values as a whole. The use of an expected value to assess a project is only valid if the project is one of a number of similar projects (or, as in this case, a number of similar government decisions). The legislation will either come into force or it won't. Therefore profits will fall by 20% or they will stay unchanged. There is no in-between position of an 8% reduction.

2   Attempted quantification of unquantifiable factors

    The assignment of probability to political decisions is **highly subjective**. Even if there were a series of historical and regional precedents to draw on, the conditions in the SAC, the internal and external pressures on the government and so on are likely to be both highly complex and highly volatile. MTM's strategic planning approach appears to gather systematic environmental data for five-year plans. Factors may have intervened since the last environmental scan that would render the critical values inaccurate.

3   Limited approach to strategy evaluation

    The risk of an individual strategy should also be considered in the context of the overall portfolio of investment strategies adopted by MTM. A single strategic decision should not be considered on its own as a stand-alone decision.

Part (b)

> **Top tips.** The way to approach this question is to break the requirement down into two parts:
>
> - How should MTM's planning processes be modified in general?
> - How should it plan for a possible ban on tobacco advertising (the new legislation)?
>
> The fact that there are 12 marks available for this question should have alerted you to the fact that you needed to do more than simply recommend that two alternative plans are prepared.
>
> However, note that the question requires you to recommend improvements that are specifically applicable to MTM's planning processes: the question is not an invitation to discuss possible improvements to the rational model in general.
>
> Also, note that if you are asked for improvements to an existing situation, it is a good idea to give a brief summary of what is wrong before making recommendations.
>
> **Easy marks.** The obvious requirement is for MTM to build a great deal more flexibility into its planning and it could do that in a variety of ways; you ought to be able to think of and explain at least one.
>
> **Examiner's comments.** This question was answered poorly. Many candidates recommended modifications to MTM's plans, rather than its planning *process* which is what the question required.

Need increased flexibility

MTM's existing method of strategic planning produces plans that do not have sufficient **flexibility** to deal with the changes inherent in its environment. As each year progresses, the dynamism and uncertainty present in the environment will make the current plan less and less relevant and control reports based on it will deteriorate in their usefulness.

There are several approaches that MTM could adopt to deal with this problem. They would all require a behavioural shift on the part of **senior management**, away from the spurious security of a detailed, fixed plan towards embracing more **emergent** strategies to deal with the opportunities presented by the changing environment.

Flexible budgeting

A simple change would be to use a system of flexible budgeting, adjusting the plan as required from time to time to reflect new circumstances. This would improve the relevance of performance reports and make the plan more usable as an aid to decision-making.

Rolling budgets

MTM already has a system of **outline planning** for the five-year time horizon, which forms the basis for more detailed annual plans. Further responsiveness could be incorporated by a system of **rolling budgets** with revisions to both longer- and shorter-term plans at intervals of three or six months. Strategic planning could thus be carried out continuously but only in as much detail as was necessary to support decision-making. Major investments, for example, would need outline plans that looked several years into the future, while decisions about sales targets and semi-skilled labour might only require seasonal plans. Shorter-term plans would be based on and would support the longer-term plans already in place, except to the extent that those longer-term plans needed revision.

Scenario planning

Scenario planning might be useful for a global company such as MTM, which faced with significant environmental change in the political and social environments. The proposed tobacco advertising ban in SAC is only one example of the modern movement to restrict smoking. MTM could prepare a **range of scenarios to reflect possible futures**, each based on different assumptions about what the future holds for all aspects of the business and its environment.

A **scenario approach** would be a useful way to approach the current problem of planning for the SAC market. Two outline plans could be prepared, one incorporating the effects of the possible legislation and one without. The 'no legislation' case could be used to develop a full budget for current operations, with work continuing on the other plan so that it would be ready for use if the ban were to be introduced. **Contingency planning** could be adopted. This means that management will have a response ready for each future scenario. For example if the legislation is passed in SAC they should have an alternative promotional strategy ready and, perhaps, be ready to shift unsold production to other markets.

Part (c)

> **Top tips.** Although this question tests your ability to suggest proactive ways a business can deal with the government, it also introduces important social responsibility issues.
>
> First, when talking about influencing government (or anyone else) your recommendations must conform with CIMA's ethical guidelines (so, for example, bribery is not an option). Second, the medical evidence against smoking is very strong and should not be ignored by MTM.
>
> Also note the verb used is 'evaluate' – so you need to look at how likely the different methods are to succeed, and what their possible limitations might be.

As a global company, MTM must ensure that its attempts to influence government are both **legal** and **ethical**: corrupt practices are not only wrong in principle, they are also hostages to fortune and may rebound in the form of large-scale and extremely bad publicity.

However, MTM does have a number of options it should consider.

1   **Direct lobbying** of politicians and influencers can be undertaken discreetly and effectively by professional lobbyists. The chances of influencing currently undecided legislators will depend to some extent on the reasonableness of the stance taken by the company on matters discussed below

2   **Influence public opinion** towards opposition to the ban. They could emphasise the impact on jobs, or taxation earnings. Influence could be sought through such means as press briefings emphasising the libertarian arguments, direct press advertising, sponsorship and celebrity endorsement.

    The usefulness of this approach will depend on the current political situation in SAC, but, in general, politicians in democracies are wary of annoying voters.

3   **Establish or support libertarian and smoker's action groups** or establishing and funding some if none already exist. The value of such groups would depend on **public perceptions of their independence**, so this tactic would have to be used with care.

4   **Offer a voluntary code of practice on promotion.** MTM could offer to avoid advertising when children could be influenced, and to avoid associating smoking with health and success. They could agree to carrying health warnings on promotion and packaging.

5   **Offer to sponsor social schemes**. MTM could agree to donate part of its profits to improving education and health facilities in SAC to offset some of the social harm done by smoking. This might well be an attractive option for the government, because it provides some benefits to society as a whole.

Any of these approaches could, of course, be undertaken **jointly with other tobacco manufacturers** and distributors.

10 Timber company

> **Text reference.** Chapter 2 discusses corporate social responsibility, and also summarises the differences between business ethics and corporate social responsibility.

Marking scheme

				Marks
(a)	(i)	Explanation of business ethics (BE)	2	
		Explanation of Corporate Social Responsibility (CSR)	2	
		Explanation of the difference between BE and CSR (CSR is a much broader concept that BE)	1	
			Total up to	5
	(ii)	For each valid issue discussed regarding D's CSR position	1 mark each	
		For each valid suggestion about how D could improve its CSR position	2 marks each	
			Total up to	8

(b)	For each relevant point relating to the new approach, well evaluated	2 marks each
	For each relevant point relating to the current approach, well evaluated	2 marks each
	Clear recommendation on which option should be taken, justified by evaluation of the two approaches	Up to 2
	Total up to	12
	Total	25

Part (a)

> **Top tips.** Whilst, in general, strategic level question requires you to use the information provided in the scenario to inform your answer, (a) (i) is knowledge-based requirement. The key to doing well here is to present a clear definition of, first, business ethics and then corporate social responsibility, before highlighting the differences between two.
>
> However, the way to approach (a) (ii) is to draw information from the scenario to shape your answer. You should have related the corporate social responsibility (CSR) issues specifically to the scenario given. A general discussion of how companies can deal with CSR would not have scored well.
>
> **Easy marks.** The scenario should generate a number of issues for you to talk about; and for the majority of the question, the examiner wanted you to relate your answers specifically to the scenario. However, if you knew the subject material well, (a) (i) would have offered 5 easy marks.
>
> **Examiner's comments.** This question was reasonably well answered, and candidates demonstrated a sound understanding of CSR.

(i) Business ethics and corporate social responsibility

The notion of corporate social responsibility (CSR) has become used interchangeably with the term ethics.

However, the two are not the same.

Business ethics can be defined as behaviour which supports justice, integrity, honesty and goodness, and is guided by ethical theory.

Corporate social responsibility (CSR) is a broader concept. It includes a commitment for businesses to act ethically, but also to act in a way what provides benefits to society. This benefit to society can be related partly to economic development, but CSR also extends to look at the ways companies deliver environment improvements, community projects, or any other measures to improve quality of life.

In this context, we can see that business ethics only forms one part of corporate social responsibility. A company also has **economic** and **legal duties**, in addition to its **ethical duties**. However, the major value of corporate social responsibility is that it encourages companies to take account of **social costs and benefits** when they are fulfilling their economic duties.

(ii) CSR issues facing D's business

Environmental damage. The loggers usually leave considerable surface damage behind them once they have finished felling the trees. Because they are working as quickly as they can to move onto the next money-making job, they are relegating environmental concerns below purely financial ones.

Sustainability of forests. One of the major issues surrounding D's business is the sustainability of the timber it is harvesting – particularly the hardwood timbers. Again, the logging process is concerned more with obtaining timber to sell rather than considering the longer term environmental impact of the actions.

Acting in the best interests of society. Although D claims it always acts ethically because it has the agreement of the national government in any country in which it operates, this assumes that the government and D are the only two stakeholders with an interest in the projects. Moreover D's claim assumes that national governments always act in the best interests of society.

However, in practice, neither of these cases are always true. Also the methods used by D to get the government's agreement to logging should be appropriate. If D offered inappropriate inducements to government ministers in a country then it will have acted unethically by corrupting ministers.

Ways to improve CSR position

When considering these issues D should remember that it is a commercial organisation, and it has a **responsibility to its owners** (shareholders) as well as the environmental stakeholders. So, D's management needs to balance the aims of continuing profitability with those of environmental sustainability.

Review logging practices. At the operational level, D should review the ways the trees are felled to ensure that **ecological damage is minimized**.

Restore habitat. As far as possible, once the lumberjacks have finished logging, D should aim to restore a habitat to the condition it was in before logging started.

This should include **replanting areas** which have been deforested with appropriate trees to improve the sustainability of the forest.

D should also seek to minimise any impact its work has on **indigenous populations** living in areas where it works. If villages have to be relocated as a result of the logging works, D should support those whose livelihoods have been destroyed.

Work with environmental groups. At a more strategic level, D should work with the environmental groups that have criticised them, and consult with them about ways in which it can **reduce its negative environmental impact**.

One of the ways it may be able to do this is to **restrict its logging to sustainable forests only**.

Ensure safety and working conditions of employees. Logging is a dangerous industry to work in. D should ensure safe working practices, even if these are beyond the minimum legal standards in each country. It may be possible for D to exploit workers in some countries by giving low pay and inadequate facilities. D may fulfil its CSR obligations better by improving standards for its workers.

Giving something back. Simply taking the natural resources of a country may not be a good example of CSR. D could consider building schools to provide education to the children of lumberjacks in an effort to assist development of the country. Medical care may also be valuable.

Part (b)

> **Top tip.** This question again requires you to relate your answer specifically to the question, and the issues facing D. You were asked to *evaluate* the two approaches to logging, and so your answer should include a balanced argument 'for' and 'against' each approach. However, remember that this is a *business strategy* paper, so your answer should include business issues as well as environmental ones.
>
> Note you were also asked to *recommend* which strategy you think is more appropriate to D so you must present a conclusion based on the relative merits of the approaches evaluated to get full marks.
>
> The Examiner commented that the main weakness in student answers was the failure to make a recommendation about which of the two approaches is most appropriate for D.

Logging on dry land

Continuity of working practices. One of the advantages of continuing to work on dry land is that it means D will not have to change any of its working practices, and will not have to retrain any of its staff.

D's current working practices appear profitable, and it has no problems obtaining finance from the bank, therefore if it continues with its existing practices it should be able to continue generating profits for its owners.

However, in order to continue with its existing practices, D needs a continuing source of trees to fell.

Diminishing timber resources. Perhaps the most critical problem it will face in the medium to long term will be a reduction in the supply of trees to fell. This will be particularly true for hardwood resources. Hardwood trees take a long time to grow, and so even if they are replanted now the forests will take decades to regenerate.

Price increases. As a consequence of this shortage of supply, D may find the price it has to pay landowners or national governments for the rights to cut timber will increase. While D may pass on some of these higher costs to consumers, it is likely that a shortage in timber supplies will adversely affect D's profitability.

Current logging practices – with timber being logged faster than trees are replanted, and with little concern being given to environmental impact – are increasingly unsustainable. If D were to adopt this approach, it would face

increasing pressure from environmental groups to adopt a more socially responsible approach to logging. And this social responsibility needs to take account of the rights of local populations as well as the timber resources.

Moreover, **other corporate stakeholders** – such as banks – are now taking corporate social responsibility increasingly seriously. Therefore if D is not seen to be acting in a socially responsible manner it may find it harder to raise loans.

Underwater business

Less environmental damage. One of the main overall benefits of the underwater business is that it has less negative environmental impact than logging on dry ground.

Also, estimates suggest that there is a **plentiful supply of timber** (20 years' supply) submerged in reservoirs.

As land based timber resources become scarcer, the underwater business will become increasingly attractive. If D moves into this area now and becomes an expert underwater harvester it may be able to develop a **competitive advantage** as the market leader.

Favourable CSR reputation. D will also get a good reputation if it follows this more socially responsible approach. There may also be **financial benefits** if end-users switch to using timber from the reservoirs because it is an environmentally friendly resource. In addition, D may be able to secure cheaper funding from its banks as a socially responsible company.

Serving environmentally conscious consumers. As the recycled paper and other industries demonstrate, many consumers are prepared to seek out and pay a premium price for products which have not caused environmental damage during their production. Providing timber harvested underwater to manufacturers and merchants will enable a premium price to be charged and a competitive advantage gained.

D is also likely to get some (international) **public relations exposure** from taking this new approach to socially responsible timber harvesting.

However, there are some significant issues to consider with the underwater business.

Initial costs. The new venture will require significant initial capital investment to acquire the equipment needed to harvest the timber underwater. This equipment is significantly more expensive than the equipment needed for logging on dry land.

The underwater business will also **need staff with different skills**. D will either need to retrain its existing staff, or possibly hire new staff (making its existing staff redundant if its discontinues its existing business on dry land).

Risk. There may be **operational difficulties with actually finding the timber**. Although estimates suggest that, globally, there are over half a billion submerged trees, D will need to locate them precisely in order to be able to harvest them efficiently. It may be able to do this with remote sensing equipment, but again, it is unlikely to have these skills or expertise currently, and these skills will take time to acquire.

Recommendation

Although there will be practical issues involved in changing the business' approach, the underwater business provides an attractive alternative to D's current land based operations. It will provide D will a source of sustainable supplies, and will allow it to demonstrate its corporate social responsibility.

11 FFF – Competitor analysis

Text reference. Competitor analysis is covered briefly in the 'Introductory' chapter of the BPP E3 Study Text because it is covered in detail in E2. However, competitor analysis is an important part of strategy development, which is why this question has been included in the E3 Kit.

Marking scheme

			Marks
(a)	For each of advantage of competitor analysis identified and discussed	Up to 2	
		Total up to	10
(b)	Identification of each stage of in the process of competitor analysis ½ mark for each stage identified	Up to 5	
	Description of each stage, and identification of information required ½ mark for each stage	Up to 5	
	Justification of why each stage would be necessary; ½ mark per stage	Up to 5	
	To score the full marks available, clear references must be made to FFF		
		Total up to	15
		Total	25

Part (a)

Top tips. The scenario for this question is quite brief, so there is not a great deal of detail for you to use in your answer. However, competitor analysis is a key syllabus area so you should have been able to make some sensible suggestions as to why FFF should undertake it given the industry characteristics identified in the scenario.

To score well you should have considered how FFF could **use** the information it finds out about competitors to shape its **own** strategies.

In effect, this question is about the importance of FFF's management knowing about the position of its competitors and their strategies. What are the benefits to FFF of knowing about its competitors when planning its own strategy?

Even if you are not very familiar with the detail of competitor analysis, you ought to be able to say that competitors are a very important feature of FFF's competitive environment – a passing reference to the force of competitive rivalry (from Porter's five forces) could also be useful here.

Better answers would explain how competitive rivalry can harm a firm's prospects, for example because they rob FFF of sales and profits; because they frustrate its product launches; because competitors' innovations make FFF's products prematurely obsolete; and because sometimes competitors might even try to acquire FFF.

Examiner's comment. Many candidates failed to recognise the importance of competitor analysis on FFF's own strategies. Candidates focused on finding out information about competitors, without recognising how this information could help FFF formulate its own strategies.

Competitors are one of the main elements in a company's immediate **task environment** and it is essential that FFF should acquire as much information as possible about them, especially as the market is now maturing.

If FFF introduces a formal process of competitor analysis it would have the following **features**:

1 Designated staff with responsibility for collecting and monitoring data
2 Defined objectives for monitoring, ie. which competitors will be monitored
3 Defined methods for storing and disseminating competitor information

The benefits of undertaking competitor analysis, monitoring and analysing information about competitors are as follows:

Understand the basis of competitive advantage

If FFF analyses its value chain compared to its competitors' it can assess the ways in which each firm adds value for its customers. Given that the market is becoming increasingly competitive, such analysis will be useful for FFF in determining whether its current competitive strategy is sustainable, and which of its processes will need improving to enhance competitiveness.

Understand competitors' strategies

If FFF analyses its competitors' current strategies and how they have developed over time this may give it some insight into its competitors' future strategies. This could help FFF plan how to compete and preserve its market position, rather than simply having to react to its competitors' actions.

Identify risk of new entrants

As well as using it to analyse current competitors, FFF can also use competitor analysis to identify possible new entrants into the specialist communications equipment market. Given that the market is reaching a level of overcapacity this could be useful to FFF to assess how barriers to entry could be strengthened to deter the potential new entrants from joining the industry.

Develop future strategies

FFF can use the information it finds out about its competitors to help determine its own strategy. FFF is currently the market leader and so it needs to develop strategies to maintain its market share in a changing and increasingly competitive industry. For example, could FFF afford to reduce prices in order to increase market share, or are competitors likely to respond in kind, meaning FFF doesn't increase market share, but instead both FFF and its rivals are left with lower margins? Are there certain competitors who are likely to be more aggressive than others, in which case should FFF target growth in specific sectors of the market to avoid those competitors? Competitor analysis could help answer these questions and thereby help FFF determine its business strategy.

Improve forecasting

By improving FFF's understanding of its competitors' behaviour and how it will affect FFF's sales, competitor analysis will also enable FFF to improve its forecasts and business plans.

Part (b)

> **Top Tips**. A large part of (b) was grounded in theory, so if you knew the stages of the competitor analysis process you could have scored well. However, you should still have applied to it FFF wherever possible.
>
> Also, note that there were two parts to the requirement: (i) to advise the directors of the stages; (ii) identify the information that would need to be gathered at each stage.
>
> The examiner noted that 'most candidates' failed to address this second requirement. This is not only careless but also proves, yet again, that failing to read the question properly costs marks.

Appoint staff responsible for the process of gathering data on competitors

Although competitor analysis can benefit from tacit knowledge from many sources in the organisation it is important that a person or department be appointed to co-ordinate this data. They will set up process for gathering, verifying, and disseminating the intelligence received.

Identify competitors

Before FFF can begin its detailed analysis it needs to identify who the competitors are. This might be quite difficult in such a rapidly developing and diverse industry. In particular, it seems unlikely that there will be many suppliers that offer an exactly equivalent range of products or serve exactly the same market segments.

Identify competitors' current strategy

Having established the companies that are to be investigated, the next stage will be to **assess their current strategies** by observing their activities in the market. It may be fruitful to use such models as *Porter's* generic strategies and *Ansoff's* product-market analysis to assess what kind of strategy the competition are using – for example, cost leadership or product differentiation.

Identify competitors' objectives

A more difficult task, but a worthwhile one will be to attempt to establish the competitors' **aims or objectives** in relation to the industry. This is where a careful assessment of the extent to which they compete head-on will be useful, since a company that sees the segment of FFF's market it competes in as a sideline is unlikely to constitute a major threat, for example, while a company that aims for rapid growth in several of FFF's market segments will be worth much closer attention.

Establish competitors' assumptions about the industry

It will be important to **establish competitors' assumptions** about the markets they operate in, since these will play a large part in determining their future activity. For example, a competitor that agreed strongly with the view that there was overcapacity in the market might contemplate exit. These assumptions exist largely in the heads of senior managers and knowledge of their personal business histories and preferences will be desirable.

Identify competitors' unique competences and assets

Competitive advantage depends in large part on the possession of **unique competences and assets**. Establishing the extent to which competitors have these will be the next stage of the investigation. In FFF's industry, ability to exploit a range of technologies in order to develop and bring new products to market will be particularly important. However, this stage of the competitor analysis process is absolutely critical. FFF needs to understand as much as possible about its competitors' capabilities so that it can gauge the level of threat which it poses. Continuing the previous example, competitors who are good at innovating and developing new products are likely to be a serious threat to FFF over time.

Predicting competitors' behaviour

Having gathered the information outlined above, it should be possible to begin the process of **predicting how competitors might behave** in a range of possible future circumstances, including changes in the market brought about by FFF's own potential future strategies. Such predictions should then be presented to FFF's senior managers in a suitable format.

Competitor analysis is not a once and for all process: monitoring of behaviour and activity should continue and steps taken to identify new or potential entrants or any new product developments from competitors.

12 Water charity

Study Reference. Environmental analysis (PEST analysis) and Porter's 'Five forces' model are assumed knowledge for E3 because they are covered in the E2 syllabus.

Foresight is covered in Chapter 3 of the BPP Study Text for E3.

Marking scheme

		Marks
(a)	Identification of benefits of environmental analysis to BBB, up to 2 marks each	Up to 4
	Each valid example of how knowledge of the 'Five forces' will help BBB, clearly related to BBB, up to 2 marks each	Up to 8
	Each valid example of how knowledge of PEST factors will help BBB, clearly related to BBB, up to 2 marks each	Up to 8
	Total up to	14

(b)	Definition of foresight		1	
	For each well explained foresight technique (up to maximum of two techniques), up to 3 marks each		Up to 4	
			Total up to	5
(c)	Each difficulty well discussed and relevant to BBB, up to 2 marks each		Up to 6	
				6
			Total	25

Part (a)

> **Top tips**. The question requirement doesn't specify which models to refer to in conjunction with environmental analysis, but the examiner's own answer uses Porter's Five forces and PEST analysis.
>
> The question does not ask you to discuss environmental analysis itself, or PEST or Five forces as models. Instead it asks you to discuss how environmental analysis would help the Trustees. So the way to approach this question is to use the models to generate ideas, but then apply those ideas specifically to BBB's circumstances. It is the application which will earn you the marks in this question.
>
> PEST is the most obvious model to use when considering environmental analysis. However, the scenario doesn't provide a great deal of information about the general environmental, so you should have realised that there wasn't sufficient scope to score 14 marks on PEST analysis alone.
>
> Moreover, the reference in the scenario to the increasing competitiveness of the industry should have alerted you that Porter's Five forces model is also relevant here. One of the key issues the charity is facing is how to attract donations in an increasingly competitive industry. How could the ideas behind the Five forces model be useful to the Trustees here?
>
> **Easy marks**. PEST and Five forces analysis are both core models so you should be able to use them in conjunction with the information from the scenario to identify some benefits to BBB from conducting environmental analysis.
>
> **Examiner's comments.** There are still some candidates who fail to apply their knowledge as required in the question. This question did not require candidates to write all they know about PEST or the five forces. Instead they should have identified the benefits of environmental analysis to BBB – but many candidates failed to do this.
>
> A common error students made was to prepare a PEST or Five Forces analysis without considering how they could help BBB address its opportunities or threats.

If the trustees of BBB conducted a thorough environmental analysis, this would allow them a better understanding of the **environmental factors** (political/legal, economic, social/cultural, technological) and **competitive forces** affecting their organisation. Understanding these factors and forces would help BBB shape its own strategy to help it survive and develop, not least by improving the information it has available to assist it in its decision-making.

Environmental factors

Political factors – BBB receives **no government funding**. This may be because it has not applied for any funding, or because government policy is not to make grants to charities. By reviewing government policy – either at national or EU level – BBB make be able to identify opportunities which will allow it to qualify for government funding. BBB should also review policies and legislation to see if there are any **tax breaks** available to it which it is not yet taking advantage of.

Economic factors – Because BBB relies entirely on voluntary donations (either from individuals or corporations), consumer confidence and economic growth are likely to affect the level of donations it receives. In an economic downturn, people and corporations are likely to look at ways of reducing their **discretionary spending**, and reducing charitable donations may be one way of achieving this. Therefore, BBB may be able to improve the accuracy of its **revenue forecasting** by taking account of general economic trends.

Also, by looking at economic trends and industry sectors' financial performance more closely, BBB may be able to target its appeals for donations more effectively. For example, if some **industry sectors are performing well**, then BBB would be better advised to approach companies in that for donations rather than companies in sectors which are performing poorly.

Social/cultural factors – It is likely that different social groups will have different **attitudes towards charitable donations,** and in particular to charitable donations towards overseas causes. If BBB was able to identify which groups in society give most generously, it may then be able to target its advertising campaigns more effectively. For example, particular towns and cities may have large ethnic populations with **family ties to the areas which BBB is seeking to help**; in which case, placing advertisements in the local press in those towns may be an effective way of increasing donations.

Technological factors – At the moment, BBB does not use the internet at all in its advertising campaigns. However, **online advertising** could be a cost-effective way of reaching potential donors, not least because online advertising has a **global reach** which BBB's current newspaper advertising is unlikely to have.

BBB could also investigate whether it could get some banner adverts or click-throughs on the websites of some of its existing corporate donors, linking in to the way the companies fulfil their corporate social responsibilities.

It is also important for BBB to be aware of any **technological advances** which could **improve the equipment** they provide to decontaminate the water, or which could provide **alternative ways of removing the arsenic** from the water.

Competitive forces

Although Porter's five forces model is usually applied by commercial organisations, it is still relevant to BBB especially since the charity industry is becoming increasingly competitive. By considering it, the trustees would be aware of the following factors which could impact their charity:

Competitive rivalry – BBB should consider what other charities are providing similar water aid to less developed countries. In particular, it should look at the **ways they are raising funds**, given the difficulty BBB has had in attracting donations. Part of the reason for this could be that people are **giving to other charities instead of BBB**, responding to the **advertising campaigns** of those other charities in preference to BBB's. BBB may be able to get some insights from competitors' campaigns to make its own adverts more effective.

New entrants – The increase in competition may reflect the **emergence of new charities**, and BBB needs to be aware of new charities with similar aims and goals to it starting up. If BBB knows about any new charities starting up it can **time some of its campaigns and promotions to coincide with the launch** of the new charity – thereby retaining its own donors rather than seeing them give money to the new charity instead.

Donors – Donors are the equivalent of buyers in Porter's model, because they are the people who provide BBB's revenue. Because **donations are discretionary**, the buyers have quite a **significant influence over BBB's performance**: if they choose to reduce their donations, BBB is relatively powerless to stop them doing so.

Substitutes – In theory, any **alternative ways which donors may choose to spend their money** could be seen as substitute products and services to BBB. This means that the threat of substitute products and services affecting BBB's revenue is quite significant.

One significant threat to BBB is that donors will switch to make donations to other charities or good causes; for example, a donor may invest in medical research rather than supporting BBB.

It will be particularly important to BBB that it retains its large corporate donors, and recognising the threat of substitutes should alert BBB to the importance of making sure these donors keep giving to it rather than other good causes. As part of this, BBB could consider producing a periodic report for its donors which shows how their money is helping the villages, thereby illustrating the value and importance of its work.

Part (b)

> **Top tips.** The Examiner wrote an article on foresight and foresight techniques in *'Financial Management'* magazine the month before the exam in which this question was set. This serves as an important reminder that you should read any articles in CIMA magazines which are relevant to E3 as part of your preparation for the exam.
>
> The question itself is a test of knowledge and does not need to be related to BBB. If you had read the Examiner's article, it should have offered you some easy marks.

Foresight can be described as the art and science of **anticipating the future,** by looking at how present actions could shape the future. Unlike forecasting, foresight does not attempt to predict the future, but rather to **identify a range of possible outcomes based on an understanding and analysis of current trends**. This could allow organizations to be better prepared for the future because they have anticipated possible changes which could affect them.

An organisation can use a number of techniques to improve its foresight. These include:

> **Tutorial note.** Note the question only asks for two techniques which could be used to develop foresight. Therefore you should only have included **two** in your answer. However, we have included a wider range of techniques in the text box below for learning purposes. Any two of these would have earned you the marks available here.

Scenario planning – In scenario planning, organisations look at the factors, trends and uncertainties that could shape their industry, and then develop a range of plausible scenarios based on the key areas of uncertainty. These scenarios illustrate a range of possible futures for the organisation, so that it can consider the implications of those futures on its business, and can develop possible strategies to deal with the uncertainties it may face.

Delphi technique – A number of experts are asked to independently and anonymously give their opinions and insights on a particular trend and how it may develop. These initial results are summarised and the summary is returned to the experts. They are then asked to reconsider their original answers and respond again in the light of the responses from the group. This process is repeated until a consensus is reached.

Morphological analysis – The attributes of a product or strategy are listed as column headings in a table, and then as many variations of each attribute as possible are list in each column. In effect, a matrix of components is created. One entry from each column is then chosen to create a new mixture of components. This new mixture could represent a new product or strategy. The range of possible new mixtures illustrates the range of possible new products or strategies.

Visioning – An organisation's management develop an image of a possible or desirable future state. This image may initially be quite vague, but it is then developed into a more definite goal, accompanied by a strategic plan for how to achieve that goal. For visioning to be useful for an organisation, the image or goal articulated has to be a realistic and achievable alternative to the current state, and one which is preferable to the current state.

Opportunity mapping – An opportunity map is a qualitative and experience-based analysis aimed at identifying gaps in the current user experience of an organisation's product portfolio. By comparing the desired qualities of a product or strategy against the current qualities, an organisation may be prompted to change its priorities and strategies in order to deliver those desired qualities.

Trend extrapolation – This is a projection technique based on the assumption that certain social, economic or technological trends or patterns identified in the past will manifest themselves again in the future. The logic is that it is possible to forecast future trends by observing how certain patterns have changed in the past and projecting or extrapolating those changes into the future. The impact of those changes on the organisation should be considered, along with possible ways the organisation can respond to them.

Part (c)

> **Top tips.** One of the keys to answering this question is to note that none of BBB's Trustees have a commercial background and so they are unlikely to have any experience of developing a process of environmental analysis. This lack of experience is likely to cause them problems as they try to carry out an environmental analysis for the first time.
>
> The organisation's culture and structure are also important: for example, how will the laissez-faire management style or the fact that BBB is primarily staffed by volunteers affect the introduction of an environmental analysis process?
>
> As always, make sure your answer draws directly on the material in the scenario. This question isn't about the problems of carrying out environmental analysis in general, but is about the specific difficulties BBB will face in doing so.

BBB currently operates on laissez-faire management principles and there is no focus on where the organisation is going. In order to implement a process of environmental analysis, BBB may have to make changes in a number of aspects.

Data management and technology. Environmental analysis often involves gathering and analysing significant amounts of information. BBB does not currently make use of available technology to any extent in its organisation. The apparent aversion to technology could inhibit BBB's attempts to develop an environmental analysis process.

Staff resources. BBB is staffed primarily by **volunteers**, and has very few full-time paid employees. Moreover, it is likely that the volunteers are **field-based**, concentrating on either raising funds for BBB's working or managing aid projects. However, environmental analysis will best be carried out **by office-based analysts** with access to the IT resources required for data analysis. It is debatable whether BBB currently has anyone suitable for this work.

Leadership and management. For the benefits of environmental analysis to be maximised, there will need to be a clear focus and direction to the analysis; for example, the key environmental factors to focus on will need to be defined. However, the current management approach appears to be one which does not give clear **focus or direction**. Therefore, developing a process of environmental analysis may require a change in the **organisational culture** (at least, among the senior management), and the introduction of more formal **structures and processes**.

However, it is debatable whether the current senior managers have the necessary **management skills** to implement such a significant **change management** programme.

Lack of experience. Because none of the Trustees has a commercial background it is unlikely that any of them has any experience of developing a process of environmental analysis. This, again, could lead to problems in defining both the aims and goals of the process, and also the practicalities of how it is introduced.

13 Scenario planning

> **Text reference.** Environmental analysis, including PEST analysis, is assumed knowledge from E2. Scenario planning is discussed in chapter 3 of the BPP Study Text for E3.

Marking scheme

		Marks
(a)	For each benefit of implementing a process of environmental analysis	1
	For applying the benefit to the case material	1
	For evaluating each benefit given	1
	Note: Students can only be awarded a maximum of 5 marks if no *evaluation* of benefits is provided	
	Total up to	12

Answers 109

(b) For each stage described, up to 1 mark each but limited to ½ mark
each if only presented as a bullet point   1

An additional 1 mark for each stage if it is clearly linked to the question
scenario   1

                                                        Total up to   13

                                                        Total   25

Part (a)

> **Top tips.** It is important to distinguish what the two parts of this question are examining. (a) is a general assessment of the benefits of environmental analysis; (b) is much more narrowly defined and relates to a specific management tool – scenario planning process.
>
> The key to doing well in (a) is to stick to what the question asks. It asks for an *evaluation* of the benefits of a system of environmental analysis. It does not ask for an explanation of what it is, and so it does not require you to carry out a PEST analysis. However, an evaluation should include discuss the limitations of the benefits as well their positive sides.
>
> When this exam was sat, some students interpreted (a) to mean evaluate the benefits to B of implementing a process of systematic environmental analysis of the publishing industry as a whole. Others interpreted the question as asking for an evaluation of the benefits of implementing a process of systematic, rather than ad hoc, environmental analysis. Although these were both minority interpretations, the Examiner accepted them as valid.
>
> However, the model answer below is based on the majority interpretation of the question – with the systematic environmental analysis relating to B itself, and the comparison being between implementing the systematic environmental analysis and not having any environmental analysis at all.
>
> **Examiner's comments.** In (a), many candidates chose to provide a detailed 'PEST' or 'Five forces' analysis rather than answering the question set; such an approach earned very few marks, because it was largely irrelevant.

Understanding the company's strategic environment

B has recently tried to diversify into new market segments and to expand its business overseas, but both of these ventures have failed despite the Board thinking they understood their target markets well.

This suggests that the Board's awareness of the environment in which the business is operating is not as good as it thought it was. Moreover, it suggests that the business failures could have been avoided with a better understanding of the business environment.

Similarly, the directors have been surprised by the speed with which new technology has been adopted by the magazine industry. This again suggests that the Board's awareness of the external technological environment is not as good as it needs to be for B to compete successfully in the industry. For example they could be overtaken in the advertising market by media owners able to offer a combined print and internet advertising capability.

Internal versus external focus

The fact that the technological changes in the industry have come as a surprise to the directors indicates that they have been focusing too narrowly on their own business rather than also being aware of their strategic environment. Business strategy is concerned with maintaining and improving the fit of the organisation with its environment. Lacking knowledge of its environment means that B's management are in no situation to develop successful strategies.

Therefore B would benefit from gathering information on the general environment in which it is operating to help redress the balance between the internal and external focus of the business.

Benefits from systematic environmental analysis

Identifying Opportunities – B would be aware of new opportunities so that it could capitalise on them rather than seeing their competitors take advantage of them. This is crucial to the long-term success of the business, because if B does not successfully identify new opportunities its business will not be able to grow.

The converse is also true. If B does not undertake environmental analysis, there will be a threat that its publications or their formats will become obsolete and ultimately that it will go out of business.

Understanding the market – B's recent attempts to expand overseas and to diversify into new domestic markets (teenage magazines) have both failed, at significant cost to the business. If the company had had a better understanding of these markets it may not have chosen to try to enter them. Similarly, if it had a better understanding of the range of potential new markets it may have chosen alternative segments to target.

Understanding the customers – We have seen that consumers are increasingly turning to new media away from traditional publishing media. If B was aware of its customers changing needs it could respond to them, and thereby hope to reverse the decline its sales and profitability.

Similarly, if there were particular niches in the market where there was unsatisfied demand, B may be able to move to fill them.

Market analysis – By looking at the market as a whole, B would be able to analyse trends in the industry and benchmark its performance against its competitors.

Technological advances – B needs to be aware of the technological developments in its industry so that it can adapt to them. This will allow it to take advantage of new production possibilities, and will also mean that the directors are not surprised by the speed of developments in the industry.

Strategic Intelligence

When they are all taken together, these benefits will provide B with a level of strategic intelligence to inform strategic decisions which it currently does not have. On the one hand, strategic intelligence will give the directors greater knowledge about B's business environment and enable them to anticipate change, which in turn will hopefully allow it to reverse the trend of declining sales and revenues which it has suffered over the last four years.

On the other hand, and equally importantly, once it has improved strategic information B will hopefully be able to avoid the costly failures it has suffered due to failed expansions into new markets.

Limitations of systematic environmental analysis

Although environmental analysis will allow B the possibility of improved strategic information, the company should also beware some of the problems attached to it.

The speed of technological change, particularly in digital media, means that there is a danger B's analysis will quickly become out of date. Consequently there is a risk that business decisions could be made based on invalid assumptions. Therefore rather than introducing a formal process of environmental analysis, B may be better served by a more informal process of information gathering about its competitors' activities and its markets.

A more informal process will also be cheaper to implement, particularly if B was thinking about using external consultants to prepare the formal analysis for them.

Part (b)

> **Top tip**. A number of different methods have been proposed for how to produce scenario plans so there is no single 'right' answer. The solution shown here uses a 10 point plan (after Schoemaker) and this is the method discussed in the BPP Study Test.
>
> However, provided you have described the stages of any similar plans (for example, Mercer), following a logical structure, you would get credit for this. You could also have considered contingency planning scenarios as well as scenarios about long-term futures insofar as they follow the same approach. However, if you merely presented the process headings without *describing* them you would not score enough marks to pass this requirement.
>
> Again, the verb is very important – you are asked to describe the stages, not simply to list them.
>
> Note also that the question only asks for the stages of a process that 'could be introduced by B' it does not ask for any specific references to B's industry. Although we have used references to B to help illustrate the stages we have described in our answer, the marking grid for this question did not allow any marks for specific references to the industry. You should not have spent time trying to think of specific references where you were not required to do so by the question.

Answers   111

Scenario planning process

Scenario planning does not try to predict the future. Rather it attempts to describe a range of plausible scenarios, and the action plans required if they do occur.

B's management should create a team to develop the scenarios, including a range of staff from across the company.

There are a number of methods of producing scenario plans (for example those proposed by Mercer, or Shoemaker) but the following are the key stages B should consider in building scenarios.

1   **Define the scope of the scenario**. This will include an assessment of the time frame involved, and the range of products and/or markets it wants to include in the scenario. Scenario planning could be used for a specific product, or extended to look at magazine publishing as a whole, so it will be very important to define the scope of the scenarios which the company wishes to look at. However, the key issue is to decide what insights are likely to be the most valuable to the company, and to set the scope so that it focuses attention in those areas.

2   **Identify the major stakeholders** that drive change or affect the industry (within the scope of the scenario identified in stage 1). Stakeholders should be both internal and external, including B's competitors.

3   **Identify the basic trends** affecting the industry and the business environment. For B, one of the key trends to consider will be technological change and the impact electronic media and the internet are having on magazine publishing. Again though, the trends should be relevant to the scope identified in stage 1.

4   **Identify the key areas of uncertainty** and their drivers. Uncertainties in scenario planning should be viewed as future possibilities, and should be based upon the political/legal, economic, social/cultural and technological (PEST) factors identified in the environmental analysis which B has been advised to undertake. In addition, the uncertainties should also consider B's own organisational competencies and capabilities.

5   **Construct initial scenarios** based on the key areas of uncertainty. The scenarios should be created by shaping the key uncertainties into coherent themes. For example, for B one scenario might be that a slowdown in economic growth reduces the uptake of digital media distribution channels due to companies rationing capital investment. An equally valid scenario might be the reverse, with continued economic prosperity fuelling an increasing propensity for lifestyle features to be distributed through digital media including interactive television.

    Each scenario will have different implications for B, and this is a critical aspect of scenario planning – the outcomes of the scenarios can then be used to assist business planning and forecasting.

6   **Check for consistency and plausibility**. For the scenario planning process to be useful, the scenarios presented must be able to happen, in the timescale identified in the scope of the scenario.

7   **Develop learning scenarios**. At this stage, the initial frameworks identified in stage 5 should be expanded into full descriptions of the scenario as if it were actually occurring.

    B's senior management should become involved in the process at this stage, and should start considering the implications of each scenario in terms of the potential impacts they could have on their business.

8   **Identify research needs**. As a result of the work done in stage 7, B should be able to see which aspects of potential scenarios present risks and threats to its business. However, in order for it to be able to assess whether the risks are materialising, it must have some key indicators by which to measure them. For example, monitoring the percentage of households which have internet connectivity would give B an indicator of the extent to which paper-based publishing can be superseded by digital media.

9   **Develop quantitative models**. This stage builds on stage 7, to put together business models to forecast the effects of different scenarios on B's activities and future profitability/cash flow.

10 **Use scenarios to formulate competitive strategy**. The value of the strategic planning process is that it assists a company's decision-making in times of uncertainty. The process should have exposed the key areas of uncertainty which B faces, and in this final stage of the process management should develop strategic courses of action which they can apply to each of the scenarios.

14 GC

> **Text reference.** The BCG matrix is covered in Chapter 4 of your BPP Study Text.
>
> **Top tips.** Practical application of the BCG matrix is the theme with this interesting question, rather than simple description or discussion of its features. Indeed, the way the question is presented forces you to apply the matrix – having to slot the different SBUs into the familiar categories, and then go on to discuss overall competitive position.
>
> We have used a diagram to present our analysis of the SBUs in a concise format, with expanded commentary below. The diagram summarises the basis of the answer and collects the easy marks.

Part (a)

Applying the BCG Growth/Share Matrix to GC's portfolio of SBUs reveals the following position.

Relative Market share

	High	Low
High Market growth	**Stars** Software company	**Question marks** Painting/decorating
Low	**Cash cows** Food manufacturer	**Dogs** Building bricks Parcel carriage

First impressions: problems

As can be seen from the matrix, the overall competitive position of GC is not strong. Only one business unit operates in a sector where strong market growth is expected. Three out of the five SBUs operate in sectors where market growth will be low, and two of these are categorised as **dogs** which are using up cash resources that would be better utilised in areas of the business which have greater potential. The painting and decorating business can be regarded as a **question mark**, historically absorbing cash in the hope of turning it into a high market share star, but the slow down in market growth may have defeated those ambitions.

Parcel carriage has become a **dog** with the expected decline in turnover and profitability as competition intensifies. The **cash cow**, food manufacture, may become the only SBU capable of delivering the cash required to finance future **stars**. Its market growth, however, is slowly declining and could eventually be nil.

The future

Currently, only the software development and supply company can be categorised as a star. While capital expenditure in this SBU has been high, its share of a growing market is expected to increase, along with its cash generation potential.

The future prosperity of the conglomerate is possibly dependent on two out of five business units, the cash from one supporting the development of the other. If cash from the food manufacturing business becomes inadequate to finance the software company as its market slows down, the position will be even more unstable.

Part (b)

> **Top tips.** The way to approach this requirement is to identify that certain strategic options are recommended for each quadrant of the BCG matrix. For example, companies are recommended to 'build' stars, and 'hold' or 'harvest' cash cows.
>
> However, while that is the basic theory behind this question, you should not simply describe the strategies recommended in the model. Instead, you need to apply these general ideas and use general commercial awareness to suggest specific strategies which are suitable for each of GC's SBUs.
>
> Make sure you consider a strategy for each of GC's SBUs in turn.

Strategic development

GC's **strategic development** of its SBUs will have to address the points noted above. The group is widely **diversified** across very different industry sectors, and the conglomerate itself is now a less usual form of business than it was, for example, in the 1980s, when companies such as Hanson had widely differing business interests. It may be possible to find **synergies** between the businesses and their **value chains** to enable further development.

GC may have to consider **divestment** of poorer performing businesses in order to concentrate resources on those areas of the business where potential for adding value is greatest. This may include further **acquisitions** in carefully chosen ventures in the future, but the immediate priority must be to address the existing SBUs.

Building bricks division

The building brick manufacturer is facing declining profitability, and expected small growth in a market where GC's share is low. If such expectations are borne out then this division will become a drain on resources, although recent reports in the British press about the South East needing over one million new houses over the next few years will give a boost to the construction industry, and demand for building bricks will obviously increase.

Unless GC can reasonably expect to be involved in such developments as new housebuilding activity, it should consider **disposing of the building bricks division**. The current market leader, with a 25% share, may be interested in acquiring its small rival.

Painting and decorating

The painting and decorating contracting company has not been part of the group for long and has received continuous cash injections. Even if it was profitable in the past (this is not known), it is currently not making any profit and market growth is forecast to slow down, which may make it difficult to gain a large enough share to ensure **sustained profitability** in the future.

The present situation in painting and decorating mirrors that of the building brick manufacturer, and the fortunes of the two are tied together on expectations of a housing boom. It may be more difficult to sell this business as the market is characterised by numerous companies with no dominant player, so GC will have to decide whether to hold on to this business and try to restore it to profitability. It may consider investing in a different area of the market (for example, branching into commercial contracts if it has previously concentrated on residential) to try and expand its market share and **differentiate** itself from competitors.

Parcel carriage

The parcel carriage service faces strong competition and GC could consider ways of facing that competition before turnover and profitability decline, possibly through **improved services** or offering different ones. Although market growth is expected to be nil, the business has been long established in the market and should be able to use this **reputation** to develop other services. This could include use of the **Internet** to take customer orders and monitor delivery schedules. Services and resources for this may be developed by the software development and supply company, so GC already has the expertise that competitors may lack. Alternatively, the decision may be taken that this SBU does not warrant additional investment.

Food manufacture

The food manufacturer is facing a slowly declining market, but GC is by far the dominant business in the market and enjoys high levels of **turnover and profitability**. To ensure that this continues in the future and that **cash flows** are maintained, GC should consider producing for larger scale catering concerns (restaurants, hotels, schools and hospitals, for example) to reduce its dependence on the declining household market. Its reputation and dominance should mean that it has the resources to make this expansion successful.

Software development and supply

The development of food manufacture is very important for GC as it is the most viable source of the steady cash flows needed to finance its one 'star', the software development and supply company. This sector is highly volatile due to the speed of technological innovation, and GC needs stable resources to be able to invest in research and development and staff with the necessary expertise. This is the only way to make sure that market share grows and that it offers **innovative** products to an increasingly computer literate public. It has a close competitor (8% of market share compared with GC's 10%) and GC may be in a position in a few years' time to acquire this competitor and reinforce its position.

114 Answers

15 Value activities

Text reference. The value chain is dealt with in Chapter 4 of your BPP Study Text.

Marking scheme

			Marks
(a)	List of value chain activities OR diagram of the value chain	1 2	
	(Note: No extra marks are available if a list if provided in addition to the diagram. Total marks available for this aspect of the requirement are capped at 2.)		
	Identifying each activity that adds value in the 2B organisation, and classifying it in the value chain; for each activity	1	
	Explaining the classification of each activity	1	
	Total up to		10
(b)	For each activity: Identify the activity affected by the e-retail investment Classify it in the value chain Explain whether value is increased or decreased	1 1 1	
	Total up to		15
	Total		25

Part (a)

Top tips. The general principle in this exam is that there are few if any marks for **displays of pure knowledge**. However, in this question you will get marks for pure knowledge is and the marking guide offers either one mark for a list of value chain activities or two marks for a value chain diagram.

The Examiners have designed the scenario so that it gives plenty of examples of the way that 2B adds value. The way to approach this question is to analyse these examples in terms of the value chain model. As you know, this is most applicable to manufacturing businesses and it is only with difficulty that it can be applied to a service business such as a retailer. The Examiners admit, in a note to their suggested solution, that 2B's value activities could be classified in more than one way, 'according to interpretation'. The message here, therefore, is this: be bold in your analysis and do not worry too much about the subtleties.

You must avoid obvious error, such as calling an HRM activity a logistic one, for example, but if you can establish a link of some kind between an activity and an aspect of the value chain, you can base your analysis on it, even if another interpretation is possible (eg the allocation of recruitment both to HRM and to procurement).

Easy marks. The marks available for display of basic knowledge are mentioned above. In addition, the staff in 2B's shops are clearly a major asset, so HRM must be considered an important value activity.

Examiners' comment. A common error was failure to understand the nature of supporting activities: as their name indicates, they link to the primary activities by giving support to them.

Value chain activities

Value chain activities, using Porter's model, can be depicted as follows.

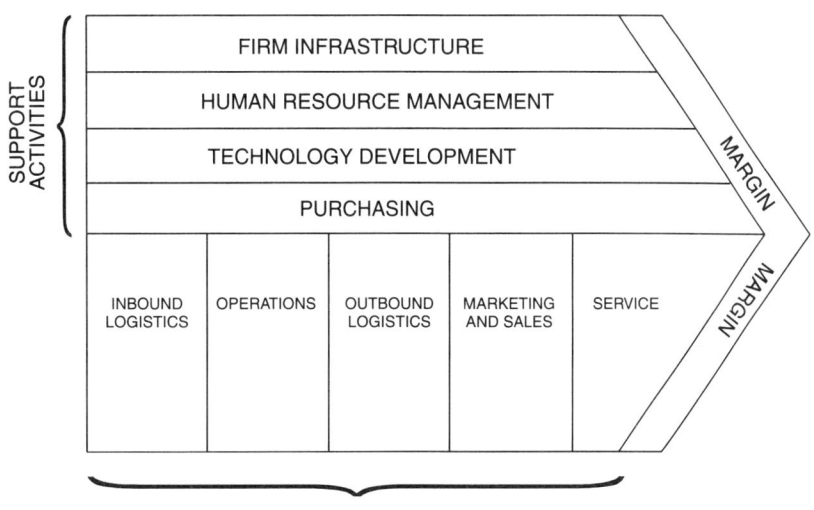

```
                    ┌─────────────────────────────────────────────┐
                    │         FIRM INFRASTRUCTURE                  \
       SUPPORT      │         HUMAN RESOURCE MANAGEMENT             \
      ACTIVITIES    │         TECHNOLOGY DEVELOPMENT                 >  MARGIN
                    │         PURCHASING                            /
                    ├──────┬──────┬──────┬──────┬──────────────────┤
                    │INBOUND│OPER- │OUT-  │MARKET│ SERVICE         /
                    │LOGIS- │ATIONS│BOUND │-ING  │                / MARGIN
                    │TICS   │      │LOGIS-│AND   │               /
                    │       │      │TICS  │SALES │              /
                    └──────┴──────┴──────┴──────┴─────────────┘
                              PRIMARY ACTIVITIES
```

(i) Firm infrastructure

The location, design and layout of 2B's shops enhance customer convenience and satisfaction and are therefore important sources of value. Firm infrastructure, as described by Porter, includes such continuing administrative activities as planning and accounting, while buildings and furnishings are assets rather than activities. However, the decision-making processes that resulted in the current benefit derived by 2B from its fixed assets certainly qualify as important value activities.

(ii) Human resource management

2B's staff are enthusiastic and knowledgeable; they are helpful and provide excellent customer service. As is heavily emphasised by the extended marketing mix, the degree of success achieved by a service business such as 2B is heavily dependent on the people it employs. 2B has both recruited and trained its employees with great care and the company's shops are now staffed by people who make a major contribution to the value it creates through the way that they do their work.

(iii) Procurement

2B's range of goods in stock is far wider than those of its competitors, which provides its customers with a greater degree of choice and an improved likelihood that they will be able to purchase items suited to their needs and wants. These factors are likely to have a positive effect on both footfall (the rate at which potential customers visit the premises) and on actual sales. 2B is in this happy position as a result of its having developed close relationships with major manufacturers, which is an important procurement activity.

The potential downside to this is that 2B's stock holding costs are likely to be higher than those of its rivals.

(iv) Technology development and inbound logistics

The company has developed a sophisticated stock control system that can be used to locate any desired item that is in stock in 2B's shops and warehouse; it can also be used to check the availability of stock with the manufacturer. This system is likely to provide significant enhancement to customer satisfaction and thus to sales.

The potential downside to this advantage is the cost of developing the system.

(v) Marketing

The managers of 2B's shops have recently carried out a customer survey. This is an important aspect of customer communications and a proper customer focus: it is important to know what customers think of the company's market offering.

Part (b)

> **Top tips.** You should not normally expect to see two parts of the same question cover much of the same ground in a strategic level paper. Therefore the apparent overlap between part (a) and part (b) should have focused your attention on what the examiner was getting at. In part (b) you need to **identify,** from the activities discussed in part (a), those which **'may be affected by the e-retail investment'**, and once you have selected them, you need to **'explain'** the effects of the e-retail investment in terms of whether the value added would increase or decrease.
>
> It is obvious that any e-commerce operation dealing with physical goods needs an appropriate system to deliver the items ordered online. This is known as fulfilment, and would be analysed in value chain terms as outbound logistics, an activity that does not exist in 2B as described in the narrative. We consider that such a comment would be entirely appropriate as part of an answer to this requirement.
>
> **Easy marks.** The Marking Guide suggests that you would earn 1 mark each for identifying affected activities *plus* another mark each for classifying them within the value chain model. In which case, it takes some of the pressure off the explanation of increase/decrease in added value.

The following, of the value added activities identified in part (a) above, are likely to be affected by the e-retail investment.

(i) Firm infrastructure

The location, design and layout of 2B's shops will remain an important source of value, although this may be reduced as **physical stores give way to 'virtual' on-line displays and sales**. In essence, 2B would move from having a purely physical infrastructure to having a mixed physical and on-line infrastructure. Sales revenue through the stores will decrease as some existing customers choose top shop on-line, but the associated costs of operating the stores will substantially remain. However, it is likely that 2B's overall turnover will increase as a result of starting its on-line store. Although there will be some cannibalisation of the existing shop sales, it should expect the on-line store to also generate some new, incremental business.

The e-retail avenue may increase the added value of **point-of-sale infrastructure**, by enhancing the perceived offering to customers (in terms of convenience, empowerment and potentially an entertaining on-line experience), generating additional sales revenue at lower administrative cost.

(ii) Human resource management

Given that customers continuing to use the retail stores will be doing so primarily because of the human service element, the capacity of 2B's staff to add value within the off-line retail segment should be increased.

This will, however, be diluted in overall terms by the shift in sales to e-retail, where customer value is not significantly added by human intervention. The focus of HR added value may shift to skills in the design and implementation of the e-retail system: the ability of IT staff to deliver a quality service at lower administrative/maintenance cost to the firm.

(iii) Procurement

The e-retail system should increase the added value of 2B's **supply strategies and inventory control systems**. It will enable the full range of goods stocked to be visible to all customers, regardless of location, maximising the value of an attribute highly valued by customers.

The e-retail system should also support better-quality information-sharing with suppliers, enabling better demand forecasting and delivery performance throughout the supply chain. This may enable 2B to add further value through **just-in-time supply strategies**, thereby reducing the amount of working capital tied up in inventories.

Meanwhile, procurement has potential to add new value through the procurement of IT infrastructure, equipment and services – perhaps through managing an outsourced IT support. There may be a further role in managing outsourced fulfilment activities: many e-retail organisations **outsource their warehousing and distribution systems** to specialists who can cope with the greater-volume of small transactions.

(iv) Technology development and inbound logistics

Integration of the e-retail system with the existing stock control system should increase its potential to add value. It will empower customers to access stock availability information, generate orders and track orders at lower cost than via sales staff intervention. The system should also allow real-time updating of stock figures – and triggering of stock replenishment – in response to on-line purchases: this increases the potential for reduced costs through fully automated and integrated e-procurement.

(v) Marketing

The addition of an e-retailing capacity has the potential to **add considerable value to the firm's marketing activities**. It presents highly flexible, controllable and cost-efficient opportunities for information, advertising, purchase incentives (eg on-line loyalty schemes and sales promotions), public relations (eg posted media releases), relationship marketing (eg gathering customer data, encouraging registration, site personalisation, e-mail permission marketing) and so on. It particularly **enhances market/customer research**, by replacing customer survey data with data about actual customer browsing and purchase patterns and preferences.

(vi) Additional value-adding activities

It should also be noted that e-retail will create potential for **new value-adding activity in the area of outbound logistics**, which currently operates within the internal supply chain only, (warehouse-to-outlets) and represents cost without generating revenue. This is a 'waste' activity, which can be reduced by supplying direct from the warehouse to the customer. Prompt, reliable and trackable delivery is a major contributor to customer satisfaction, so outbound logistics has the potential to create significant value – although the greater frequency and smaller value of deliveries will also create new costs.

In value chain terms, **service** means after sales service. No doubt this is minimal at the moment and consists largely of dealing with returned faulty goods. With e-retailing, it will be necessary to offer a more comprehensive reverse-logistics service – which again both adds value and incurs cost.

16 Benchmarking in a charity

Text reference. Benchmarking is dealt with in Chapter 4 of your BPP Study Text.

Marking scheme

			Marks
(a)	Up to 1 mark for each advantage of benchmarking discussed	Up to 4	
	Up to 1 mark for each disadvantage of benchmarking discussed	Up to 4	
	Total		8
(b)	– Senior management commitment	1	
	– Decide and understand process; develop appropriate measures	Up to 2	
	– Monitor process measurement system	Up to 2	
	– Identify appropriate organisations to benchmark against	Up to 2	
	– Analyse data; discuss results with management and staff	Up to 2	
	– Implement improvement programmes	Up to 2	
	– Monitor and control; strive for continuous improvement	Up to 2	
	Where up to 2 marks are available for each point, 1 mark is to be given for mentioning the point, the second mark is for adding detail around it and embedding it in the case.		
	Total		13
(c)	1 mark for each valid point made		
	(These may include: obvious commitment from senior management; clear explanation of purpose of exercise; focus on process not individuals; involvement of staff in mapping process, or involvement in development of KPIs; making use of staff's knowledge and expertise)	Up to 4	4
	Total		25

Part (a)

> **Top tips**. The key to answering this question well is to appreciate that while it is asking about the advantages and disadvantages of benchmarking, it is doing so in the specific context of E5E. Therefore you mustn't just write about the advantages and disadvantages of benchmarking in general, but you must apply these to the specific context of the charity.
>
> Remember also you are asked to discuss them , so you need to consider the advantages and disadvantages in some detail, not simply list them.
>
> **Easy marks**. There are very few really easy marks here. If you knew very little about benchmarking, you might be tempted to waffle on about variants of the general theme of improved efficiency (our first point below). This would not get you many marks at all, unfortunately. On the other hand, if you are familiar with the appropriate section of your BPP Study Text, a pass mark should be quite easily attainable.
>
> **Examiner's comments**. The usual frustrations: lack of application of theory to the scenario and a lack of depth – basic lists, with little explanation, do not constitute a 'discussion'.

Advantages of benchmarking

Benchmarking allows an organisation to learn from best practice; this may be found in other, similar, organisations, in very different organisations that have some point of similarity, or within the organisation itself.

One category of benefits will revolve around **improvements in economy, efficiency and effectiveness** and for a charity such as D4D will typically include some of those listed below.

- **Reduced costs** of operation,
- **Improved service** levels for all groups of stakeholders
- **Simplification of processes**
- **Improved quality**

There are further benefits.

Both full time staff and volunteers may have their **assumptions challenged**. This may be disturbing, especially in the charity sector, but can reinvigorate operations by removing complacence and improving understanding of what is worthwhile and what is not.

Charities compete with one another for funds; benchmarking allows **effective monitoring of fund raising (and spending) strategies**.

Connected with the two effects mentioned above, is the provision of **evidence to stakeholders** that the charity is fulfilling its purpose efficiently.

Disadvantages of benchmarking

There is an **increased flow of information** that must be monitored, summarised and assessed. These processes are not cost-free and they can lead to management overload. In a charity, the work involved in benchmarking can be discouraging for volunteer staff.

Overload can also occur when a successful benchmarking exercise produces a large volume of requests to participate from organisations that have themselves little to offer in potential improvements.

Benchmarking usually involves the exchange of information with other organisations. There is a threat to **confidentiality**, both commercial and personal.

Poor results from a benchmarking exercise can be disproportionately **discouraging and demotivating**, particularly to managers.

The benchmarking process itself can **distract managers' attention** from their primary responsibilities. Even when this does not happen, managers may put too much emphasis on improving the efficiency with which they do the things they have always done and fail to ask if new ways of doing things would be better overall.

Part (b)

> **Top tips**. Although the question asks you to 'advise on the stages...', the key to this question is identifying the stages of which are involved in a benchmarking exercise. However, do not simply list the stages of a benchmarking exercise: the question requirement makes it very clear you have to relate them to the specific context of E5E.
>
> **Easy marks**. Some things are obvious: partner organisations must be found; appropriate measurements must be taken and compared; improvements must be made if available. You could almost score a pass mark by discussing such ideas and relating them to the scenario.

Stage 1 – Obtain management support

The first stage is to **ensure senior management commitment** to the benchmarking process. This will only be genuinely available when the senior managers have a full appreciation of what is involved: senior people are quite capable of changing their minds when it becomes apparent that they did not anticipate the actual levels of cost or inconvenience, for example. The Board of E5E has actually proposed that a benchmarking exercise take place, but they will be as likely as any other senior management team to change their minds.

Stage 2 – Set objectives

The areas to be benchmarked should be determined and objectives should be set. Note that here, the objectives will not be in the form of aspirations for improvement to specific processes and practices, but more in the nature of stating the extent and depth of the enquiry. In E5E, for example, under fundraising, it might be decided to look carefully specifically at the security of cash collections.

Stage 3 – Identify key performance measures

Key performance measures must be established. This will require an understanding of the systems involved, which, in turn, will require discussion with key stakeholders and observation of the way work is carried out. A simple example of how this stage would be carried out within E5E might be to examine the processes for assessing applications for research grants.

Stage 4 – Choose organisations to benchmark against

Internal benchmarking may be possible where, for example, there are local fund-raising branches or shops. Where internal departments have little in common, comparisons must be made against equivalent parts of other organisations. The aim will be to find an organisation that does similar things but which is not in competition with E5E. For example, another charity that undertakes educational work, but is not involved in medical research would provide a suitable benchmark for E5E's educational work. This is a kind of **functional benchmarking**.

Stage 5 – Measure performance

Measure own and others' performance. Negotiation should take place to establish just who does the measurement: ideally, a joint team should do it, but there may be issues of **confidentiality** or **convenience** that mean each organisation does its own measuring.

Stage 6 – Compare performance

Raw data must be carefully analysed if appropriate conclusions are to be drawn. It will be appropriate to discuss initial findings with the **stakeholders** concerned: they are likely both to have useful comment to offer and to be anxious about the possibility of adverse reflection upon them. This may be particularly applicable to the volunteer staff within E5E, who may be sensitive about their amateur status.
From the performance measures identified, E5E's management should identify where improvements are needed.

Stage 7 – Improvement programmes

Design and implement improvement programmes. It may be possible to import complete systems; alternatively, it may be appropriate to move towards a synthesis that combines various elements of best practice. Sometimes, improvements require extensive **reorganisation** and **restructuring**. In any event, there is likely to be a requirement for **training**. Improvements in administrative systems often call for investment in new equipment, particularly in IT systems.

Stage 8 – Monitor improvements

The continuing effectiveness of improvements must be monitored. At the same time, it must be understood that **improvements are not once and for all** and that further adjustments may be beneficial.

Part (c)

> **Top tips.** The wording of the question gives you the clue that you need to be sympathetic to the concerns of the staff in your answer to this question. An autocratic approach clearly would not score many marks: instead you need to take a concerned, humane stance and think about the setting. Application to the scenario is vital here, because the concerns will be specific to the volunteer status of many of the workforce and to the nature of a benchmarking process.
>
> Also, think about the change management issues involved here. If you remember nothing else about change management, you should be aware of the need to tell people what is going on: rumour and speculation will become a serious problem if there is a deficit of communication.

Communication with staff and volunteers

Any type of investigation with an eye to change will cause apprehension and possibly alarm. People like to feel comfortable; they are comfortable with what they know and uncomfortable with the prospect of unspecified change. The first priority, therefore, must be to give the **fullest possible information about the purpose and nature of the benchmarking programme**. This is best done face to face by senior managers in a series of small meetings, but where this is impractical, as may be the case with volunteers running branches and shops, the information should be disseminated down the usual communication channels of the hierarchy.

Part of the message should be that **senior managers support the programme** and that they see it as important.

The communication effort should continue throughout the life of the programme, reporting on progress and improvements made.

Encouraging staff involvement

The second main route to dealing with the concerns of staff lies in the way the programme is carried out. It must be emphasised that there is no element of personal assessment: procedures and methods are being examined, not individual performance. The staff should be encouraged to contribute as much as they can to the benchmarking process. They will be able to give important information on how systems *actually* work, to help in the development of key performance measures and to assist with the evaluation of proposed new methods. Many volunteers will have **wide experience of management** and **methods in other organisations** and, as a consequence, will have much to contribute.

17 Product portfolio

> **Text reference.** The product life cycle is dealt with in chapter 4 of your BPP Study Text. Social responsibility is discussed in Chapter 2.

Marking scheme

			Marks
(a)	Diagram of product life cycle, if given	1	
	Explanation of how the product life cycle model can be used to analyse a product portfolio	Up to 4	
	Classification of 3 C's current products in the portfolio, with explanation for classification, up to 1 mark each	Up to 3	
		Total up to	8
(b)	Evaluation of each option on the product portfolio, up to 3 marks for each option	Up to 9	9
(c)	Up to four social responsibility issues and implications discussed, each worth up to 2 marks	Up to 8	8
		Total	25

Part (a)

> **Top tips.** Although the question specifies the model you are expected to refer to, you must remember that there are very few marks available for simply explaining the model.
>
> However, in this case drawing the diagram for the product life cycle would be a good place to start. If you show the positions of 3C's products on a sketch of the standard life cycle curve, you can then think what those positions tell you about 3C's portfolio.
>
> Note that this question was about the product life cycle, not the BCG matrix (see the Examiner's comment below).
>
> **Easy marks.** The life cycle model is simple and if you can get the names of the phases roughly right you should collect some easy marks. A good diagram will show both sales and profit.
>
> **Examiner's comment.** The words 'product portfolio' do not always imply that the BCG matrix should be used primarily for consideration of the *balance* of the portfolio. In the case of the life cycle model, balance means that the portfolio shows a succession of products at different stages in their individual life cycles.

The product life cycle (plc) is a simple model of the way that the sales of a product and the profits earned by it vary from its launch to its exit from the market. The model is crude in that a product's progress through the phases can be heavily influenced by marketing activity and, in any case, many products do not follow the standard pattern. Nevertheless, the concept is a useful tool for basic **portfolio analysis**.

The PLC for 3C's current product portfolio can be depicted as follows.

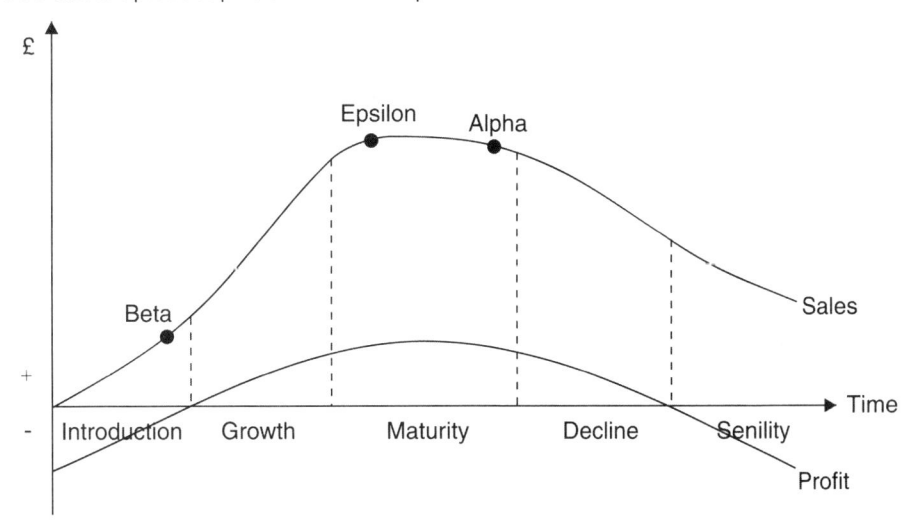

[Diagram: Product life cycle curve showing Sales and Profit curves across phases Introduction, Growth, Maturity, Decline, Senility. Beta positioned in Introduction, Epsilon at peak (Maturity), Alpha just past peak entering Decline.]

(i) **Beta** has been positioned in the introduction phase, because it has been only recently launched, and has not yet generated significant sales volume. However, Beta is likely to have a fairly accelerated Introduction stage, as it is a specialised product, for which there is already demand within the hospital market.

(ii) **Epsilon** has been positioned at the peak of the cycle. Although it has not been available for long, it has already 'achieved significant success' (and its introduction/growth curve may therefore have been steeper than shown in our 'standard curve' model). Sales are not expected to increase (hence its position at the peak).

(iii) **Alpha** has been positioned just at the point of decline. It has been available much longer than the other products, so its maturity stage may have been longer than our 'standard curve' model suggests. Decline will soon follow, because of the expiry of the patent and the entry of low-cost generic competitors: the decline/senility stage will last 12 months.

It would be usual with any portfolio analysis technique to look for **balance**: in plc terms this means that the portfolio should include products at several stages in their life cycles, so that as one declines, another is emerging to take its place.

3C's current portfolio seems adequate in this respect, in that while Alpha is expected to enter a rapid decline phase, Epsilon is generating high sales in its maturity phase as an acceptable 'cash cow', and Beta has been launched and has potential for growth.

However, the fact that Beta is unlikely to generate sales volume to replace Alpha (because it targets a specialist market niche) is likely to be of concern: hence the need to secure succession by launching Alpha2. There are also 240 drugs at various stages of development, so it should be possible to continue the succession into the future.

Part (b)

> **Top tips**. In this part of your answer you have to look into the future and consider the probable effect of each option on 3C's portfolio as a whole. It is not enough say what will happen in plc terms to the three drugs concerned. You must also say what effect each option is likely to have on the future *balance* of the portfolio. **Risk** will be an important factor to consider.

3C has three investment options. Each must be considered in terms of the risks and benefits it offers, both in itself and within the context of the product portfolio. It is also important to consider the implications of *not* choosing each option.

Alpha2

Investment in Alpha2 may be seen as extending the maturity phase of Alpha by five years – or as introducing a new product (with accelerated introduction and growth due to existing brand loyalty), giving 3C two well-performing products in that category rather than just one. The overall effect on the portfolio will be to **ensure product succession** and produce moderate improvements in both sales and profitability.

This is a **low risk strategy** since clinical trials of Alpha2 are complete and the drug could go straight into production. Moreover, Alpha2 will be able to **build on existing brand loyalty** and **present barriers to entry** to the generic competitors to Alpha (who will be a step behind again). The disadvantage of this option is that the launch of generic copies could limit Alpha2's sales and profitability, unless the improved performance of Alpha can be successfully marketed.

If Alpha2 is not chosen, 3C will rely on Epsilon for most of its sales and profits in the near to mid term.

Beta

Beta is clearly felt to have good potential for growth, being in the early stage of its life, but it is unlikely to replace Alpha in the product portfolio as the latter declines, as it is a much more **specialised niche product**. Even if the rival product is as successful as Beta, it will not be of a generic type; prices and profitability should remain high, though total sales of Beta will be hit by competition from the rival.

The current investment option is based on direct marketing/promotional competition: with 'active promotion' by the rival, there is no guarantee of added market share – but there should be significant growth in sales in the short term.

Gamma

Seen in isolation, Gamma is the **high risk, high reward option**. It has yet to complete its clinical trials and there is no guarantee that these will be successful. On the other hand, a breakthrough treatment for HIV could be confidently expected to generate an extremely large volume of sales and high profit (with no near rivals on the market). Even if the low profit, high social benefit route is chosen, the rewards could be high.

Seen from the portfolio management point of view, Gamma would be a good succession option compared with Beta: it is likely to have an accelerated introduction and growth stage (due to existing market demand and no competition), and is ultimately likely to have a higher revenue peak at maturity.

There is some logic, therefore, in suggesting that either Alpha2 or Gamma should be the chosen option, with choice largely depending on 3C's appetite for risk.

Part (c)

> **Top tips**. Although it is possible to discuss social responsibility issues in a lot of detail, it is unlikely you will have the time to do so in your exam. In the same way, the questions are unlikely to be on particularly complex areas of CSR or ethics.
>
> That is certainly the case with this question, which is about a very basic topic: for whose benefit do business organisations exist?

> You are not expected to produce a definitive answer to this question: the requirement uses the verb 'discuss', which is quite unusual. Although in some questions, you are expected to make a reasoned recommendation, that is not the case here. Here all you need to do is consider the various relevant points.
>
> Remember that you have to consider all *three* investment options though: do not concentrate solely on the dramatic potential of Gamma.

General social responsibility (CSR) implications

3C is required to operate within the confines of the **laws** of the countries in which it does business and, as an innovative pharmaceutical company, it is subject to extensive **regulation and ethical scrutiny** relating to its drug development and manufacturing activities.

There are certain key **stakeholders** in pharmaceutical development, including those who need/use the drugs. There is a general ethical obligation to alleviate suffering where possible, and uphold the public interest. However, as a commercial organisation, 3C exists primarily to make profit for its owners.

CSR implications of Alpha2

The implications of Alpha2 fundamentally rest on the issue of **fair competition** and **offering consumers value for money** for an essential product. Generic copies of drugs are often equally effective and able to be provided at lower cost (particularly in developing countries for whom the cost of importing patent brands is prohibitive): it is socially responsible to encourage basic pain-killers to be widely available. The case for Alpha2 rests on whether it bears out the claims of improved performance (which will be made by 3C's marketers) in such a way as to justify consumers paying a higher price.

CSR implications of Beta

The key implication of investment in a marketing campaign for Beta is likely to be the ethics of that campaign in its approach to medical practitioners and hospital buyers, in this specialist market (generally based on personal selling). Medical practitioners and procurement professionals have their own codes of ethics which prohibit them from altering their decisions or recommendations as a result of inducements (corporate hospitality, gifts and so on) – but this may be the 'temptation' for 3C in aggressive competition with its rival.

CSR implications of Gamma

There is already an ethics-related conflict between the aims of the development specialists (to offer a life-saving drug at the lowest possible price, to maximise the benefit to society) and those of the marketing department (to maximise profits by charging a high price for a monopoly product).

The worldwide HIV/AIDS epidemic has attracted enormous public interest both in support of individual sufferers (creating pressure to alleviate suffering where possible) and as a social justice issue (since the poorest countries are the worst affected). Many interest and pressure groups are lobbying for drugs to be made available (or patents shared) on a preferential or non-commercial basis.

3C has **responsibilities to its owners to reap optimal profits** from the drug's strong competitive advantage, in what is a high-risk, high-cost industry. However, it also has an **ethical responsibility** to make the drug as widely available as possible. Nor is this only a pricing issue: arguably, 3C would be socially responsible to invest in manufacturing Gamma – and irresponsible *not* to invest in its development, given that the drug has the potential to be successful.

There is no easy solution to the profitability dilemma, but it may be possible to compromise via differential pricing: eg making the drug available on favourable terms to medical charities in poorer countries. The problem here would be that such a dual pricing policy would inevitably attract both complaint from individuals who had to pay the full price, and arbitrage, with the attendant risk that profits would be undermined.

There is also a secondary social responsibility issue of raising the market's hopes of the new treatment *before* clinical trials have confirmed its success and safety, and rendered it legally and commercially viable.

124   Answers

18 Chemical manufacturer

Text reference. The 'five forces' model is assumed knowledge in E3, brought forward from E2.

Strategic options and the Ansoff Matrix are discussed in Chapter 5 of your BPP Study Text.

The evaluation of strategic options is dealt with in Chapter 6.

Marking scheme

			Marks
(a)	Currently, supplier and customer power are both low, and the patent acts as a barrier to entry. This could all change when patent expires	3	
	Lack of differentiation for DDD	1	
	Pressure on margins from customers and suppliers	2	
	Supplier actions	2	
	Threat of new entrants	1	
	Pharmaceuticals unlikely to backward integration	1	
	Total		10
(b)	Each relevant option identified (up to six or seven courses of action)	1	
	Each option evaluated, up to 2 marks each	2	
	Total		12
(c)	Clear recommendation, based on, and consistent with, answer to part (b)	3	3
	Total		25

Part (a)

Top tips. You need to think about this requirement carefully before you start to answer it. It may be tempting just to pick out the threats mentioned in the scenario and write them down. But a Strategic Level paper will require more than that. Look for a framework to help you make sense of the situation. The word 'threats' should make you think of the environment and from there you may decide that the five forces will provide a good framework for an answer; even though not all five of the forces are represented in the scenario. However, they will not provide an exhaustive answer. You should also read the scenario setting carefully in order to identify other possibilities that might be threatening.

Easy marks. The obvious result to expect from the patent expires is increased competition, since the patent documents themselves put the technologies involved into the public domain and there will be nothing to prevent other companies from setting up plant to imitate DDD's processes.

Examiner's comments. A number of candidates misunderstood the nature of patents, and referred to DDD overcoming the problem by renewing the patents in some way.

Potential entrants

DDD's current patent protection confers an **effective monopoly** on the exploitation of the industrial technologies concerned. This means that DDD can make monopoly levels of profit from them by charging relatively high prices.

The immediate effect of the loss of this protection is that DDD may suddenly be faced with competition from other companies manufacturing identical products made with the same processes, thus turning them into commodities.

Globalisation means that some of these entrants may have much lower cost structures and so will drive prices down to gain sales.

Bargaining power of buyers

The arrival of potential entrants will increase the bargaining power of DDD's customers by allowing them the option of using alternative suppliers to provide the chemicals they need. It is therefore highly likely that DDD's revenues will fall significantly, as the pharmaceutical companies exert pressure on it to reduce prices (and therefore margins).

Bargaining power of suppliers

A further problem for DDD is that the most likely new entrants are the large chemical companies from which it currently buys its supplies. They may well decide on a strategy of **forward integration** to manufacture the same products as DDD in order to capture more of the value created in the overall **value system**.

These companies are larger than DDD and may be expected to enjoy significant **economies of scale** in several areas of their operations. In which case, they may be able to force the price of the products down to a level that DDD cannot sustain.

Threat from substitutes

It appears that DDD has patented the processes it uses rather than the chemical products themselves. It is entirely possible that their customers may either be developing different methods of manufacture or else substitute products in order to avoid paying DDD's patent-based price premium.

If these new substitute products are launched then DDD's **market share** is likely to be significantly reduced.

Part (b)

> **Top tips**. The requirement should have indicated that the possible courses of action you consider need to relate back to the threats you have identified in (a).
>
> A sensible approach would have been to identify courses of action which could reduce the threats, and then consider whether they are **suitable, feasible** and **acceptable**. Although the question mentioned 'suitable courses of action' you should not have limited your answer look at suitability; this would not have given you enough scope to score 12 marks.
>
> Note that the question required you to evaluate the possible courses of action. This again should have prompted you to consider suitability, feasibility and acceptability. If you simply listed possible courses of action, you would have scored poorly.
>
> **Easy marks**. A consideration of the Ansoff matrix and the various basic organisational routes to growth should have provided you with some ideas for possible courses of action.
>
> **Examiner's comments.** This question was not well answered. Many answers had little structure, and failed to link back to the threats identified in (a). In addition, candidates failed to 'Evaluate' the strategies suggested, although the question clearly asks for an 'Evaluation'.

An evaluation of the strategic options available to DDD to respond to the threats it is facing should be based on the standard criteria of **suitability** in terms of the overall strategic posture; **acceptability** to stakeholders; and **feasibility** in terms of the resources required. Attention should also be paid to the need for any strategy to be based on a **sustainable competitive advantage**.

Do nothing

To do nothing is always a strategic possibility, but it seems inappropriate here. DDD's competitive advantage and its success are built on its patents which are about to disappear. To do nothing would not prevent the **decline of the company** and would rely on the threats identified in (a) not materialising. This is quite feasible, but it is unsustainable and would be unacceptable to the owners and work force.

New patented products and processes

DDD could attempt to continue its existing patent-based advantage by the development of a stream of new processes and products that would be patentable in their turn. This would be eminently suitable and a source of sustainable competitive advantage. However, feasibility looks more problematic: the developers of the original patents are still working in the company, so the technical skills required are probably available, but funding the necessary research and development might be difficult.

Answers

Market development

DDD could seek new markets for its existing products and thereby generate new revenues. In the short term this would be suitable and acceptable because it will reduce the buyer power of the existing customers, and might well be feasible. However, its potential for **longer-term sustainability would be limited**, in that the emerging competitors would be likely to follow DDD into any new market it developed unless DDD were able to find a niche market to move into. This option would still not prevent suppliers squeezing margins though, and so may not be suitable or acceptable either.

Strategic alliance

DDD might attempt to limit the potential for damaging competition by forming a strategic alliance with one of its larger suppliers. It would provide technical and commercial **knowledge** and the partner would provide an element of protection from other potential competitors by the deployment of its own scale economies. This is probably feasible, but goes a long way towards destroying the strategic rationale of the business. It is difficult to believe that either DDD's owners or the company's employees would approve of this course of action, since it would almost inevitably lead to the **absorption of DDD by its larger partner**. Consequently this option is neither acceptable nor sustainable.

Exit

If the owners of DDD feel that they have no real chance of preserving their company, they may opt for immediate exit by means of a sale of the business as a going concern, probably to one of the existing suppliers. The sale price is likely to be higher while the patent is still in place than once it has expired, so if the family did choose to sell an early sale would be advantageous in this respect. However, while a sale is feasible, it is not suitable for the company as a stand-alone entity and certainly does not count as a sustainable strategy.

Part (c)

> **Top tips**. Do not be tempted to skip over this requirement just because it is only worth three marks. Also, note how we suggest a combination of two of the discrete options discussed above. You do not have to limit yourself to a single choice from among them, but your recommendation must follow logically from your evaluation in (b).
>
> Another approach to justification of a strategy is describe how it measures-up to the evaluation criteria of **suitability, acceptability** and **feasibility.**

The single most promising choice for continuing DDD's business would seem to be the development of **new products and processes**, assuming the necessary finance can be found. This would allow the company to continue to create high levels of value and retain its independence, with consequent longer-term benefits for both owners and staff.

It might be possible to combine this with an element of **market development** to increase its customer base, thereby both increasing revenue and reducing the buyer power of its existing customers. This could be done both on the concept of niche markets for existing products and the further exploitation of new ones as they emerge. However, this would require caution as it would involve more risk and uncertainty if the new markets were in overseas countries which DDD has no experience of dealing with.

19 Competitor benchmarking

Part (a)

> **Text references**. Benchmarking is covered in Chapter 4 of your BPP Study Text for E3.
>
> **Top tips**. PAL is a service business. This makes it difficult to understand what the Examiner means by *delivery*. Clearly, it cannot mean what it would mean if there were material goods involved. So we are left with a conundrum: how does 'delivery' of a service differ from 'customer service'?
>
> We think we can resolve this problem like this: **customer service** is about dealing with enquiries and processing sales up to the point at which an insurance policy is in force; while **delivery** is about providing the practical benefits of insurance: which is to say, paying out when a valid claim is made.
>
> You may have a different idea. This is fine, so long as you make your assumption clear in your answer, as we do in ours.

CIMA's *Official Terminology* defines **benchmarking** as 'the establishment, through data gathering, of targets and comparators, through whose use relative levels of performance (and particularly areas of underperformance) can be identified. By the adoption of identified best practices it is hoped that performance will improve.' The entry goes on to define several distinct types of benchmarking, including **competitive benchmarking**: 'information is gathered about direct competitors, through techniques such as reverse engineering'. *PAL* is already carrying out this type of benchmarking in its home loans business by its monitoring of competing lenders' interest rates.

Benchmarking PAL's home insurance operation

We will look at *PAL's* activities in a logical sequence.

Technical literature

Viewing technical literature is likely to be one of the first experiences the prospective customer has of *PAL's* home insurance business. Obtaining examples of competitors' literature should be easy, as much is likely to be freely available from their premises. Material issued in correspondence later in the selling process could be obtained by *PAL* employees' pursuing specific enquiries.

It would be a mistake to divorce technical content from presentation in the benchmarking process. While technical content may be regarded as particularly important, its excellence should not be pursued at the cost of clear and attractive design. PAL's literature might be assessed against criteria such as those below.

- **Appearance and design**: attractiveness and clarity
- **Information content**: not too much, not too little
- **Accuracy**: technically and grammatically correct
- **Coverage**: no major gaps in the range

Some of these criteria are matters of judgement; avoidance of subjectivity would depend on mustering the views of a panel. This might be an outsourced service, but it would be important that the panel members were competent to judge technical content as well as presentation.

Customer service and correspondence

Customer service is a complex concept. We know good service when we see it but find it hard to define. There is a danger when assessing service of being **too specific** with performance measures. Highly specific measures, such as how long a phone rings before it is answered, are easy to use and equally easy for workpeople to target, possibly at the expense of actual service quality. It does not matter how fast a phone is answered if the query is dealt with in a slow, rude or incompetent manner.

For this reason, **benchmarking service levels is extremely difficult** and might be best undertaken with a series of in-depth **interviews** by a market research agency. This would also deal with the problem of subjectivity. Such a project could be supplemented with **mystery shopper** activity. This requires people to play the role of real customers and record the details of their service encounters. This could also be undertaken by an agency.

Areas such as those below might be investigated.

(a) **Telephone activity**. Call-waiting times, call lengths and number of calls handled would be basic data. Quality of responses, friendliness and ability to deal with unusual questions without long periods on hold and extensive transfers would be more subjective measures.

(b) **Correspondence**. Speed of response, use of simple, clear language and completeness of exchanges could be objectively measured from samples of correspondence.

(c) **Policy documentation**. Policy documentation has to fulfil both legal and marketing functions. It must state clearly the terms of the contract of insurance while, at the same time, constituting the 'physical evidence' component of the extended service marketing mix. It is thus similar to the technical literature discussed above and could be benchmarked in the same way.

Part (b)

Text reference. Both Porter's generic strategies and the Ansoff matrix are dealt with in Chapter 5 of your BPP Study Text.

Easy marks. The Examiner anticipated that candidates might make use of Porter's generic strategies and the Ansoff product/market matrix in answering this question. However, the marks available would be awarded only if the discussion clearly linked the banks' strategy with the use of benchmarking.

> It is actually quite difficult to do this, so we follow the example of the Examiner's own suggested solution and provide a general discussion of benchmarking to round off our answer. Do not be afraid to do this if you feel you have points to make but cannot quite see how to work them in to your main argument.

PAL's strategy may be analysed by reference to *Porter's* **generic strategies** and *Ansoff's* **product-market matrix**.

Generic strategy

Porter suggested that firms have two choices when seeking competitive advantage. The first is between cost leadership and differentiation.

Cost leadership enables competition on the basis of price. It requires market leading efficiency and the achievement of great scale economies. By definition, there can only be one cost leader in a market and, because of the need for scale economies, this will normally be the company with the highest turnover.

Differentiation allows the firm to overcome the disadvantage of higher costs by charging higher prices; customers believe they are receiving greater value than is available from the cost leader and are therefore willing to pay more. This belief need not be supported by objective analysis.

The second choice lies in the scope and scale of operations: a firm may choose to avoid competing in the widest marketplace by concentrating on a particular niche, defined, perhaps, by customer type, product characteristics or geography. Such a choice leads to a **focus** strategy.

PAL is a **focus player** in its restricted region and is clearly following a strategy of **cost leadership** within its home loans business – it cannot offer the best prices without achieving the lowest costs. Competitor benchmarking is crucial to this strategy, since *PAL* must have detailed knowledge of its competitors' prices if it is to equal or better them.

While it is possible for independent SBUs within a divisionalised company to pursue different generic strategies, it might be confusing for a single firm to attempt to do so. *PAL* thus runs a risk in adding new competitive ideas to its basic strategy of low price. Provision of high standards in such areas as customer service must inevitably drive up costs, thus compromising the company's cost leadership approach. On the other hand, concentrating on low costs must compromise the ability to give high levels of service. Benchmarking service quality is a symptom of this potential confusion.

Product-market vector

Ansoff analyses strategies for growth along two axes: products and markets, as illustrated below.

	Product Existing	**Product** New
Market Existing	Market penetration	Product development
Market New	Market development	Diversification

On this matrix, *PAL's* strategy would probably constitute product development, since it is reasonable to assume that the bank will target its existing customers, at least initially. Since it is also reasonable to assume that its existing market is rather cost-conscious, the possible contradiction between low cost and high service is again apparent. However, if *PAL* were to seek to **develop its markets** and sell to higher margin customers, this would not be so important and the benchmarking effort would be more appropriate.

Benchmarking generally

Benchmarking is a useful tool for an organisation that wants to become better at what it does. It can reveal the aspects of a business that are in need of improvement and to what degree they are below standard. This helps in setting priorities for managerial attention. It can be used to assist a change process and can indicate if a company is being left behind by its **competitors**.

On the other hand, benchmarking schemes impose significant costs in terms of managerial time and effort involved both in collecting the necessary data and in analysing the results. Similarly, the setting up and maintenance of the benchmarking system itself is a drain on resources.

The **aspects of performance** that are to be benchmarked must be chosen with care. If this is not done, management attention may be diverted away from the really important aspects of operations; just as is the case with purely internal performance indicators.

Much, if not all, benchmarking data is extremely **commercially sensitive**. It can indicate weaknesses that competitors might exploit, even to the extent of launching a takeover. Companies are therefore likely to safeguard such information, thus making the task of the benchmarker more difficult. One solution to this problem is the formation of a separate industry benchmarking association to collate information and distribute it under terms of anonymity.

20 Printing company

> **Text reference**. Industry lifecycles are discussed in Chapter 4 of your BPP Study Text. Mission statements are discussed in Chapter 1.
>
> **Top tips**. The verb for **Part (a)** is to 'Identify' the characteristics. 'Identify' is only a level 2 verb, so you do not need to give a detailed discussion or evaluation of the characteristics.
>
> Also, the question requirement does not ask you to link your answer to the scenario, so you do not have to do so. And remember, there are only 5 marks available for part (a), so don't spend too long on it even if you think it is the easiest part of the question! For example, you shouldn't have wasted time drawing a detailed diagram of the whole industry lifecycle.
>
> Unlike Part (a), your answer for **Part (b)** does have to relate directly to the scenario and company D. So don't just discuss mission statements in general terms, but discuss specifically what issues D would face in trying to create one.
>
> A useful way of generating possible ideas for your answer might be to think of the advantages and disadvantages of mission statements. But remember, the question isn't asking for advantages and disadvantages as such. So you must present your answer as the issues D's management needs to consider, rather than as a series of advantages or disadvantages. For example, one of the perceived problems with mission statements is that they can be too general to have any real impact on employee's behaviour. So, the relevant issues which D's management needs to consider is how to make the mission statement specific enough and relevant enough to day-to-day activities to influence employee's behaviour.
>
> **Part (c)** also requires you to apply your knowledge to the scenario. However, you could have used the idea of 'SMART' objectives as a useful framework for discussing the relevant characteristics. SMART identifies five characteristics and there are five marks available, so a brief discussion of each – in the context of D – should haveallowed you to score well on this part of the question.

Part (a)

Products – In the mature phase of the industry lifecycle, there will be a high degree of **standardisation** among the products offered by different competitors. Product quality will also be high, as producers look to offer **superior quality** products to their rivals.

Competitors – There will be strong competition in the industry, but the fierceness of the competition may force some of the weaker players to leave the industry.

Buyers – There will be a mass market, so buyers will be widespread. Brand switching will be common: because the product is standardised, buyers will only incur relatively low switching costs in switching brands.

Profits – Profits will be eroding under the pressure of competition in the industry, and due to consumers' bargaining power. Margins will also be reduced by increased advertising and marketing costs.

Strategy – The competitive pressures in the industry will lead to firms seeking ways to reduce costs to try to preserve their margins.

Part (b)

Impact on employees' behaviour – One of the main reasons for D to have a mission statement is to make its employees aware of its organisational culture. So the mission statement will need to illustrate D's basic values and beliefs, to let the employees recognise the behaviours which are expected of them.

D's culture and values are currently strongly **shaped by Mr Z's behaviour and ideas**. For example, the desire to know everyone's first names suggests an open culture and a friendly environment. But D will need to ensure the values it encourages are **appropriate to the competitive environment**.

Impact of industry lifecycle – As the printing industry enters the mature stage of its lifecycle, D may be find itself facing increasing competitive pressure and the need to reduce costs. The mission statement will need to ensure that it promotes behaviour which is consistent with this. It may be that D's management feel that maintaining the friendly working environment will help maintain staff motivation and therefore may help keep costs low.

However, the mission statement will need to make staff appreciate the need to **work efficiently in a competitive environment**, rather than simply being friendly with one another.

Practical and realistic aims – D needs to ensure that its mission statement sets realistic and attainable aims, but also that it can actually deliver practical benefits. As the industry moves into its mature phase, D will need to work harder to retain its customers. So the mission statement should also try to identify how D will give value to its customers.

To do so in a meaningful way, it needs to identify aims which staff will be able to apply, otherwise they will simply ignore the mission statement as a management gimmick.

No experience of mission statements – D, and its staff, have never had a mission statement before. Creating one for the first time could be an issue in itself, for both management and staff. It will take time and effort for management to develop the statement, so they need to feel the organisation will benefit from having it.

Equally, the staff will need to accept it and feel it is relevant to them. If they basically ignore it, its value will be significantly reduced.

Specific aims – If the staff can't relate the statement to the work they do, it will not have any effect. So the statement needs to be **specific** enough that staff can see how it applies to their everyday work. For example it should indicate how staff should treat each other, and how staff should treat customers, suppliers and other external stakeholders. One of the main criticism of mission statements is that they can be too general to have any impact what people do, so D needs to avoid this problem.

Deliver competitive advantage – One of the key elements of a mission statement is a summary of a company's distinctive capabilities and competences.

Although D has historically grown by exploiting the technology one of its founders developed, that technology is no longer new or unique. Because the industry lifecycle is in its mature stage, it is likely that many of D's competitors have now all developed similar technology to it.

Therefore, the mission statement shouldn't emphasise the current technology too much, and it could be more useful to highlight that **finding new technologies** and **developing new innovations** will be the source of new growth in the future.

Flexible to changing environment – If D does look to introduce new ideas, then the mission statement needs to be flexible enough to accommodate them. If the mission statement essentially forces D to replicate what it is currently doing, rather than to look forward and develop, then it could be counter-productive in the long run.

Appropriate to competitive strategy – D has used the new technology its founders developed to establish itself as the market leader. As such, D may initially have been pursuing a differentiation strategy. However, as the industry enters the mature stage of its life cycle, it may be more important to highlight the **cost effectiveness** of D's printing solutions, rather than their **distinctive** product features.

In this case, D's mission statement will need to make clear this change of emphasis.

Market position – D is still marginally the market leader in the industry, and so the mission statement might include a statement that it intends to maintain that market leading position. That might be a bold statement to include, however, given that its technology is no longer innovative and so its competitors can look to capture market share.

Nonetheless, the mission statement should still include an indication for D's customers and other external stakeholders of where it sees its position in the industry in the longer term.

Part (c)

D's objectives need to reflect the fact that the industry is moving into the mature stage of its lifecycle.

Specific objectives – D's objectives need to be specific so that management clearly know the key issues for them to focus on. For example, given the strong competition and declining margins in a mature market, D could set objectives about the market share and level of profitability it wants to achieve.

Measurable – D's objectives need to be measurable so that the management can measure the company's actual performance indicators and see how well they compare to the objectives. For example, D could quantity the percentage market share it wants to achieve.

Achievable – There is no point setting objectives which are not achievable, because they will be ignored. For example, in a mature market it would unrealistic for D to set a target of growing sales by 10% per year.

Relevant – Objectives need to be relevant to a company's mission. In this context, the relevance of D's objectives will depend on the mission statement it writes. For example, if the mission emphasises the continued importance of innovation for D, an objective which looks to reduce research and development expenditure would not be appropriate.

Time-related – Objectives need to have clear timetables for achieving the measures specified, so wherever possible D should prescribe completion dates for the objectives it sets.

21 Conglomerate value

Text Reference. Conglomerate (unrelated) diversification, and methods of disposal and divestment are both covered as strategic options in chapter 5 of the Study Text.

Marking scheme

				Marks
(a)		Clear definition of conglomerate diversification	1	
		Additional marks for clarifying what the definition means	2	
				3
(b)	(i)	Calculation of market capitalisation for each division	1 ½	
		Numerical demonstration that group does not add value	1	
		Interpretation of figures from institutional shareholders' perspective	1	
		Concluding remark about adding/destroying value	1	
			Total up to	3
	(ii)	Evaluation of suggestion to dispose of real estate division	Up to 4	
		Evaluation of suggestion to reduce costs	Up to 3	
			Total up to	7
(c)		Each disposal method accurately described and related to the scenario, up to 3 marks for each method, of which 1 for identification, and 2 for evaluation	Up to 10	
		Clear recommendation, justified according to evaluation	2	
			Total up to	12
			Total	25

Part (a)

Top tips. Requirement (a) is a pure test of knowledge. However, it is only worth 3 marks, so you should write a brief explanation and then move on to parts (b) and (c).

Part (a)

Conglomerate – or unrelated – diversification is a strategy in which a **business moves beyond its present industry** into products or markets which are unrelated to its present industry.

The resulting conglomerate is a collection of businesses which **do not have any real operational relationships** to each other, and do not a common identity through being part of the same group. The only connection between them is a common parent.

Because the businesses are in different industries, conglomerate diversification does not generate any operating synergies from combining the different businesses. However, the parent can **spread its risk,** or change the balance of its **product portfolio** by entering new markets or new products.

Equally, the parent may use conglomerate diversification as means of **exploiting under-utilised resources** – for example, it may buy an underperforming business, and then turn it around by introducing better management.

Part (b)

> **Top tips.** You need to recognise that both parts of requirement (b) ask you to 'evaluate' assertions made by the institutional investors. Your evaluations should identify the aspects of the assertions which you think are valid and also those which you think are not valid. A simple market capitalisation calculation would identify that the Group's valuation is significantly less than it should be.
>
> Also, note that in (b) (ii) there are two different suggestions to consider: (i) a sale of one of the divisions; and (ii) a rationalisation of the head office functions / facilities. A sensible approach would be to evaluate the two suggestions separately because there are very different issues at stake in each of them. Closing the Group headquarters is essentially a cost rationalisation exercise, but closing a division will affect revenue generation. With respect to the proposed sale of the real estate division: what will be the effect on the Group's profitability and its growth prospects? Would one of the other divisions be a better candidate for disposal?
>
> **Examiner's comments.** This question was reasonably well answered, but many candidates did not properly evaluate the institutional investors' comments by discussing whether they were valid or correct.
>
> Many candidates simply undertook the market capitalisation calculation without then discussing what it means.

(i) The institutional investors claim that the Board 'has destroyed value' implies that CCC group's overall valuation of $1,000 million is less than it should be given the potential value of each of the divisions.

	Earnings $m	Market sector average P/E	Market capitalisation $m
Construction and building	50	8	400
Engineering and machinery	20	13	260
Real estate	30	23	690
Total	100		1,350
Group valuation			1,000

The calculations suggest that if the divisions were operating separately, and were quoted separately on the stock market, their **market capitalisation would be $1,350 million**. Therefore, at face value, it seems that the Group has 'destroyed' $350 million of value.

However, because it is based on the sector average P/E ratios, this calculation assumes that the performance of **each of the divisions is in line with their sector average**. It is possible that some of the divisions are themselves under-performing, which may explain some of the shortfall.

Nonetheless the scale of the shortfall does suggest that the Board is destroying value, and so the institutional investors call for strategic review is justified.

(ii) While a review of the Group's strategy is necessary, such a review should consider all of the operating divisions as well as the Group and head office functions, rather than being limited in scope to the areas the institutional investors suggest.

Disposal of real estate division

The real estate division currently contributes 30% of the Group's earnings, and is the **fastest growing** of the divisions (over 20% per year in the last three years). The divisional management team expects this rate of growth to be sustained.

The real estate market sector also has the **highest P/E ratio**, suggesting the sector affords good growth prospects, and supporting the divisional management team's optimistic forecasts.

In terms of CCC's overall portfolio, the real estate division appears to offer **better growth prospects** than either the construction or engineering divisions, although the engineering division is likely to have relatively secure earnings by virtue of its contracts with government departments. Nonetheless, disposing of the Real Estate department does not appear to be a good strategic move.

The **Engineering and machinery division** looks a more suitable candidate for disposal, despite its government contracts. It makes the **lowest contribution to group earnings**, and has a lower growth rate than the Real estate division.

Although the **Construction and building division** has the lowest growth rate, it **generates 50% of the Group's earnings** and CCC would be unlikely to want to dispose of a division which contributes such a large proportion of earnings.

Moreover, we should also consider the **institutional investor's potential motives** in recommending the sale of the Real Estate division. They are looking for a **large one-off dividend**, which suggests a short term strategy. In this respect, it is likely that CCC could sell the Real Estate division for a much **higher price** than the Engineering division, thereby generating more cash to pay a dividend. However, that is unlikely to be in the Group's longer term strategic interests.

Relocating Group headquarters

The Group headquarters are 'quite luxurious' and located in the capital which suggests that they are quite expensive. Therefore it is likely that **cost savings** could be made, by relocating to one of the divisional headquarters. There may be reasons why the offices need to be located in the capital (for example, being close to the stock market) in which case the Board need to explain this to the investors.

Equally, there may not be space in any of the divisional headquarters to relocate all the Group staff (50) there; in which case, the Group could still look at finding **new offices where overhead costs will be lower**. This could also be a good opportunity to review whether the Group really needs 50 staff or whether the team can be streamlined.

In the context of the suggestions that the Group is 'destroying value' it should be looking to **demonstrate value for money in its spending**. Controlling costs and making cost savings will be one way of doing this. Moreover, by reducing Group costs, the management charges levied on the divisions could also be reduced.

Part (c)

> **Top tips.** Requirement (c) like (b) (ii) is also, in effect, a multi-part requirement: you need to identify alternative methods; evaluate them; and then finally recommending the most appropriate one.
>
> The approach we have used in the answer below is to look at each alternative method in turn, before making a recommendation in the light of our comments on each method. As in part (b), because the action verb asks you to 'evaluate' you need to assess both the advantages and the limitations of each potential method the Board could use for the disposal.
>
> For parts (b) and (c) you may find it useful to consider whether the 'institutional investors' (who only hold 20% of the equity) are representative of all the shareholders. Do the institutional investors' wishes for a large one-off dividend represent the interests of the other 80% of shareholders? For example, might some of the other investors prefer longer-term growth over a short-term dividend?
>
> **Marks available.** The marking guide for this question allows up to 3 marks for each disposal method accurately described and related to the scenario, up to a total of 10 marks, suggesting you are expected to suggest 3 or 4 different methods. A further 2 marks are available for recommending the most appropriate method.

> The answer below includes five alternative methods which the Board could consider. Given the mark allocation, you would not have needed all five to pass this question, but all five are valid options, and so are included for tutorial purposes.
>
> Nonetheless, whichever methods you do include, it is important that you make a recommendation as to which is the most appropriate to CCC.
>
> **Easy marks.** You should be able to identify a range of possible disposal methods. By then assessing how well they address the issues arising from the shareholders comments in the scenario, you should be able to how appropriate the possible methods are in this context.

If the Board does decide to sell the real estate division there are a range of alternative methods it could use for the disposal:

Sale as a going concern to another business

This would represent, in effect, the reverse of the transaction by which CCC acquired the real estate division. The division would be **sold to another company**, in exchange for either **cash or shares** in the acquiring company. All the responsibilities and costs of running the division would pass to the acquiring company, as would all future profits.

If the sale were made for cash, it could provide CCC with an **inflow of cash** to meet the shareholders demands for a large, **one-off dividend payment**.

However, it would mean that **CCC loses 30 percent of its earnings**, and any future earnings growth which the real estate division would have generated. This could mean that the Group's subsequent **ability to pay dividends in future years is reduced**. Moreover, stripping out the division with the highest P/E ration would cause CCC's share price to fall; in turn reducing the value of the remaining Group, and possibly again laying the Board open to a charge of 'destroying value.'

Finally, the sale of a division would mean that the Group **overhead costs** have to be apportioned over only two divisions rather than three, again reducing the Group profitability unless significant overhead savings were made.

Demerger

A demerger would mean that instead of simply being a division of CCC Group, the real estate operation becomes a **separate company in its own right**. The existing shareholders of CCC Group are likely to **receive shares in the new company** in proportion to their existing holding in CCC.

The logic behind a demerger is usually that the existing formation is creating **negative synergies**, and therefore the new company will generate greater earnings operating independently rather than being part of the Group. Given the suggestion that CCC is currently 'destroying value' this could well be the case.

However, from CCC's perspective a demerger is less attractive. As with a cash sale, CCC Group would lose 30 per cent of its earnings. But unlike the cash sale, the **demerger would not generate a cash inflow** into the business.

Therefore this option **would not provide for a one-off dividend to the shareholders**, because it is a non-cash option. If shareholders want a one-off cash boost they will have to generate it themselves by selling their shares in the newly demerged company.

However, one advantage of this approach from the shareholders perspective is that they have **shares in both companies**. If they remain dissatisfied with the performance of CCC Group, they could elect to sell their shares in it, and just retain their shares in the new real estate company.

Liquidation of assets

The real estate **division could be closed**, its staff made redundant (or redeployed elsewhere in the Group) and its **assets sold off** at market price.

However, given that the real estate is a profitable and growing business this is unlikely to be a desirable option; not least because a sale of assets is **likely to command lower prices than the sale of the business as a going concern**.

A liquidation of assets would be a cash sale, and so would provide a cash inflow to underwrite a one-off dividend payment. However, given that both options would lead to CCC losing 30 per cent of its group earnings, it is likely that it would **prefer the option which generates more cash** in return.

Moreover, there is a likely to be **negative publicity** surrounding the closure of the division, and any associated redundancies, which may have a further negative impact on the Group's performance.

Management buy-out

In a management buy-out, the **management of the real estate division would buy the division** from CCC, with the intention of driving forward its growth and increasing its profitability.

However, an important issue here is the **price which the managers would agree to pay** for the division. On the one hand, it is likely they will have to obtain **funding from venture capitalists** to support their own capital in the purchase, so they will want to keep the purchase price as low as possible to minimize their debt and future interest charges.

On the other hand, the divisional **managers are likely to know more about the business** and its prospects than the Group managers, and also any external purchasers.

These two factors together are likely to mean that the price a management buy-out team offer for the sale is **likely to be lower than the price which could be earned from an open market sale** of the business as a going concern.

Again, the Group needs to remember that after the buy-out the real estate will be a separate entity so Group **earnings will be reduced by 30 per cent**. Therefore it should not accept a sale price which is too low, particularly if it intends to make a one-off dividend payment to the institutional investors.

However, a management buy-out may be considered the most attractive option from a **public relations perspective**. The Group could present the sale of a successful division to its management positively – emphasising the way they are being given the opportunity to control the division's strategy and its future.

Management buy-in

This approach, in effect, combines aspects of a management buy-out and a sale of the business as a going concern. Like a management buy-out, a **group of people collectively buy the division**. However, unlike a management buy-out, the **purchasers come from outside the company**. So after a management buy-in the real estate division would become a privately owned real estate company.

From CCC's perspective, the management buy-in is another option which could **generate a cash inflow**, and so would provide the funds to satisfy the investors demands for a one-off dividend. Depending on the extent of the purchasers' knowledge of the business, CCC may be able to earn a higher selling price from a management buy in than from a management buy-out.

However, a management buy-in does not afford the same positive aspects in terms of public relations.

Recommendation

CCC could either look at the disposal as a means of **maximising value** from the Group, or **raising cash** to pay a one-off dividend. A de-merger is probably the option which would maximise value, but it will not generate cash. However, a management buy-out will generate cash proceeds, and, by allowing the divisional management full control of the real estate division should allow its capabilities to be exploited fully. Although the new entity will be outside the group, the public relations aspect of a sale to management will be more positive than an open market sale.

Therefore, CCC would be advised to sell the real estate division through a management buy-out.

22 Telecommunications joint venture

Text reference. Joint ventures are discussed in Chapter 5 of your BPP Study Text.

Top tips. In **Part (a)**, you are only asked to 'explain the characteristics of a joint venture.' You are not asked to relate them specifically to the scenario.

In our answer we have made some passing references to the case study, as a couple of the points provide a useful link forward to parts (b) and (c). However, you do not need to do this. Also, remember that part (a) is only worth 5 marks, so don't go into detail on points which are more relevant to the later parts of the question.

> For **Part (b)**, note you are asked to discuss the benefits to country C, not to either Y or one of the companies in C. Although a lot of the benefits of the joint venture might accrue initially to the venture partner in C, you need to think more widely about how they could then also benefit the country in general. For example, could new skills and new technology be transferred not only to the individual company, but also to other companies in C?
>
> The political context of the scenario could also help you generate some ideas. Politically, a joint venture looks more acceptable than an acquisition by a foreign company, because more of the economic benefits (and the tax revenues) are likely to remain in C.
>
> **Part (c)**. Although there is only a single requirement – to evaluate the risks that Y should consider – there are still effectively two different sources of risk for you to consider here. On the one hand there are risks associated with the Y's potential partner: for example, will it have the necessary skills to be a valuable partner?
>
> On the other hand, there are risks associated with Y itself. Y has previously always expanded via acquisitions, so what are the different issues it will face in a joint venture arrangement rather than controlling a fully owned subsidiary?
>
> Note also, that part (c) asks you to evaluate the risks of entering a joint venture, rather than entering Country C. So, for example, discussions about political or economic risks in C were largely irrelevant, because they would have applied equally if Y had acquired a company there as opposed to entering into a joint venture.

Part (a)

Characteristics of a joint venture

Joint control – A joint venture is a contractual arrangement in which two or more companies undertake an economic activity which is subject to joint control.

New company – Joint ventures often result in the venture partners setting up a separate, new organisation in which they each hold an equity stake. In a number of joint ventures, the partners have equal stakes in the new company, but this is not necessarily the case. For example, if one partner provides the majority of capital for a venture, it is likely they will also control the majority share of the venture.

Exploit opportunities – Joint ventures are often used to enable the companies to exploit an opportunity which it would be difficult for any one of them to take advantage of individually.

Joint ventures are often used as a means of entering markets which are either closed to foreign companies or difficult for them to enter. Therefore Y might see a joint venture as a good way of entering C, given that the government there is under political pressure to ensure that the country benefits from any foreign investment.

Pooling skills and competencies – A joint venture can allow the partners to bring together different skills and competencies. For example, one partner might have extensive technical expertise, while another may have local market knowledge. This could well be the case with Y and a local partner in C.

Risks and rewards – Because the joint venture involves two or more partners, the risks and rewards involved are shared between the various partners. Joint ventures allow risks and capital commitment to be shared between the venture partners, so they can be a very useful way of undertaking expensive technology projects.

Part (b)

Benefits to Country C of the joint venture

Transfer of skills – As Y is a successful international company, its staff, and particularly its managers, are likely to have more commercial skills and experience than the staff at the company in C, a developing country. The joint venture would allow staff in C to work in conjunction with Y's staff to gain knowledge and skills. This would benefit C by increasing the skills in its labour market.

Technology transfer – It is also likely that Y will be using more modern technologies than the company in C. So again, the joint venture arrangement will allow the company to become familiar with new technologies, which it could then use in other aspects of its business in C, thereby potentially improving technology in C as a whole.

Investment – The national telecommunication company in C was using old equipment and needed considerable capital investment. The joint venture arrangement with Y will mean that the cost of this investment will be shared with Y, which may accelerate the investment programme.

Also, Y might be encouraged to make more investment through the joint venture than it would otherwise do if it simply acquired the company as a wholly owned subsidiary.

This investment in the telecommunications equipment should hopefully improve the quality of service that the customers in C get.

Competitive rivalry – If the joint venture company makes a major investment with one of the four local telecommunications companies, the other three might feel compelled to match this investment so that they do not lose market share. This investment should lead to benefits for all customers in C through improved telecommunications.

Benefits of improved telecommunications – If the telecommunications infrastructure in C is improved overall this may make C a more attractive location for foreign investment by companies in other industries.

Clustering – The joint venture company might be more likely to use local suppliers and components than would be the case if Y simply acquired the existing company as a subsidiary. The joint venture arrangement could benefit the supporting industries in C, and could bring new jobs to the local economy.

Future growth – If the joint venture model proves successful, then other international telecommunications companies, or other foreign companies, may be attracted to invest in C using a similar joint venture model. Any such additional investment will provide a further boost to C's economic development.

Tax revenues – C is likely to receive a greater proportion of tax revenue from the joint venture company than it would from a subsidiary of an international corporation. For example, if Y owned the company in full, it could use transfer pricing to reduce the level of taxable profits in C, and therefore the tax revenues which would accrue to C. Such a transfer pricing arrangement is less likely in a joint venture because it is a stand-alone legal entity.

Part (c)

Potential risks from potential partner

Skills of partner – The success of the joint venture will be strongly affected by how well the partner's skills support and complement Y's. Y is **entering the market at an early stage after deregulation**, and will rely on its partner's market knowledge and marketing skills to take advantage of opportunities in the market. If the partner doesn't deliver these skills, and Y has to do the majority of the marketing itself, in a market it doesn't really know, it will take longer for the joint venture to become established in C. Consequently its potential profits are likely to will be reduced.

Y also needs to be satisfied that its partner is going to contribute actively to the venture, rather than just using it as an opportunity to benefit from a skills and technology transfer from Y.

Partner's stability – Y should consider the financial stability of its partner, and the security of its customer base. Although the four companies in C each have approximately 25% of the local market at the moment, if there is a danger that large numbers of customers may leave a supplier soon then this may make an investment with that supplier worthwhile.

Reputation of venture partner – There is a risk to Y that its own reputation could be damaged by the actions of its partner if its partner acts unethically or illegally. Y's own professional judgment and integrity might be questioned if its partner is discredited.

Objectives from venture – The joint venture partner may have different objectives from Y. For example, they may have different opinions on the level of market growth they expect, and what this will mean for the joint venture's growth prospects. Equally, there may be differences of opinion as to how profits should be used. Should they be distributed to the shareholders, or should they be re-invested in the venture's growth?

If the two partners have different objectives, this is likely to lead to conflict, which could damage the performance of the venture.

Risks surrounding Y itself

No experience of joint ventures – Y has previously always expanded by acquiring subsidiaries, and so has no experience of joint venture arrangements. The skills required to manage the joint venture will be very different to managing a takeover. In particular, Y cannot impose its culture and working practices on the new operation, it will need to be sensitive to the local staff in C. If the integration of the two cultures is not managed properly, this will lead to conflict between the two partners.

Roles and responsibilities – Y and its partner will need to define clearly who is responsible for doing what; for example, Y might be responsible for IT and technology, and the local partner for marketing. These responsibilities need to be clearly defined at the outside to remove the chance for any disagreements and conflict. Equally, the way the joint venture is going to be managed, and who will hold the management roles, need to be clearly defined to prevent any conflicts.

Financial splits – Y and its partner will need to agree how the **costs of any investments are split**, and equally how the **profits are shared**. If Y is going to contribute the majority share of the capital investments, it could look to secure more than 50% share of the profit from the venture. Any such distribution of profits needs to be clarified with the venture partner at the outset – both to avoid conflicts later on, but also to avoid the risk of Y not getting the returns it believes it is due.

Lack of clear strategy – Y needs to have a clear idea of what it wants to achieve from the joint venture. One of the key issues it needs to consider is whether it views the joint venture as a permanent arrangement, or as a stepping stone to acquiring the local partner at a later date.

These longer term strategic plans might affect Y's objectives for growth and capturing an increasing share of the market. However, if Y does not have any strategic plans, there is a danger the venture could drift, and therefore it will not generate the returns Y might have expected.

Transfer of confidential information – One of the dangers of joint ventures is that partners can gain confidential information about each other which could be subsequently used competitively by one partner against the other. One of the main potential benefits of the venture to the partner in C is the transfer of technology and skills from Y. However, there is a risk that if the local company gains too much information then it might seek to leave the venture and compete directly with Y.

Political risk in C and security of assets – The government in C faced strong resistance to its privatisation plans. Therefore there is a risk that a future government might look to reverse the privatisation, and reduce foreign involvement in business in C. If this happens, Y's position in the joint venture might be under threat, and it might be difficult for Y to recover its assets and investment.

23 Plastics manufacturer

Text reference. Chapter 5 deals with Strategic options. Chapter 2 covers stakeholder management.

Marking scheme

				Marks
(a)	(i)	Each difficulty identified from scenario information and discussed to explain *why* it is a difficulty (not just repeated from the scenario)	1	
			Total up to	5
	(ii)	Strategies to deal with:		
		Price competition (price wars)	Up to 2	
		Problems in the home market	Up to 2	
		The need for overseas expansion	Up to 2	
		Problems with the labour force	Up to 2	
		Problems in the R&D department	Up to 2	
		Clear recommendations, based on evaluation of strategies	Up to 2	
			Total up to	12
(b)		Each point linked directly to the scenario material, and well discussed	Up to 2	
			Total up to	8
			Total	25

Answers

Part (a)

> **Top Tips.** This question again requires you draw upon information presented in the scenario to inform your answer.
>
> Requirement (a) (i) clearly directs you to the scenario – you should identify the difficulties facing F, and then discuss them. It is not sufficient to simply list the difficulties you read about in the scenario; a good answer should discuss the implications of them for F.
>
> Likewise, (a) (ii) requires you to draw information from the scenario to shape your answer. Your need to identify a range of strategies that will help F specifically address the difficulties you have discussed in (a). Merely presenting a generic list of strategic options will not score well.
>
> Notice also that (a) (ii) requires you to *evaluate* alternative strategies, so your answer should include a balanced appraisal of the suitability of the strategies you suggest; before *recommending* those that are most appropriate. Again, your are required to reach a conclusion based on your evaluation.
>
> **Easy marks.** The scenario should generate a number of issues for you to talk about; and the examiner wanted you to relate your answers specifically to the scenario. If you did this (a) (i) should have offered some very easy marks, and should in turn have prompted you to identify relevant strategies for (a) (ii).
>
> **Examiner's comments.** Part (a)(i) was poorly answered because candidates 'identified' difficulties rather than 'discussing' them. Part (a)(ii) was answered better, but while candidates identified a wide range of strategies they still failed to evaluate their appropriateness or make any final recommendations.

(i) The main difficulties facing F are:

- **Loss of market share.** F is suffering a reduction of turnover and profits as a result of foreign companies aggressively increasing their share of the beer crate market. If F does not react to this, it will find that the foreign companies overtake its market share leading F to lose further profits.

- **Reduced margins in beer crate market.** Because F is heavily dependent on two major products, it is vulnerable to any reduced margins earned on those products. One of those products is beer crates, and the recent consolidation in the brewing industry, coupled with increased availability of imported crates, has meant that consumers have an increased bargaining power to key the price of beer crates low. This has affected both turnover and margins.

- **Inflexible labour force.** The workforce appears very inflexible, and this inflexibility is leading to inefficiency in the production process and probably resistance to innovation. In turn, this inefficiency is also impacting on profitability, and may ultimately prevent F from reacting effectively to the increased competition form foreign competitors.

- **R&D department is not delivering commercial success.** The lack of commercial awareness within the R&D department means that F is not developing any new products which are commercially successful. This means that it is incurring significant overhead costs (on the R&D department) without realising any benefits to turnover and margins.

- **Poor communications with institutional shareholders.** F has failed to communicate its performance properly to its shareholders. Consequently there is a risk that they will not support future plans for the business, or provide additional capital if it is required to fund future initiatives.

> **Top Tips.** Your answer to this question should include strategies to address both the external market difficulties and the internal operational difficulties F is facing. The key difficulties the examiner highlights in his past exam review are: (i) problems of price wars; (ii) problems in the home market; (iii) the need to expand, possibly overseas; (iv) labour problems; and (v) research and development.
>
> Up to 2 marks are available for each of these areas, with a further 2 for a clear recommendation as to which key strategies F should follow.
>
> The answer below covers all these areas, but we have also included some supplementary points in text boxes. Although the points in the text boxes are relevant, you could still score well in this question without including them.

(ii) Loss of market share and reduced margins in beer crate market

F's most important priority must be to reverse the decline in the profitability of its beer crate business, caused by the loss of market share and reduction in profit margins.

There is unlikely to be any significant product differentiation for beer crates, and therefore price will play the key role in the product's success.

Pricing strategy

Competitive prices. In order to retain market share, F should aim to keep its price competitive against the foreign imports as their current aggressive growth strategy continues.

Reduce costs. Alongside this competitive pricing strategy, F needs to reduce costs wherever possible to restore profitability. Unfortunately, the inflexible and unionized working practices among F's workforce are likely to make it hard to reduce labour costs.

Although the institutional shareholders have suggested that F should **withdraw** from the beer crate market, this **is not a viable strategy**. F is still the dominant manufacturer in the home market, and if it withdrew from the market it would severely reduce its total sales. This would leave it carrying excessive fixed costs and so be faced with the costs of dismissing staff and closing capacity. Moreover, such a strategy is likely to be seen as a sign of weakness, and would merely encourage other competitors to target its remaining markets.

Market expansion

Market development. By contrast, if the longer term prospects for the home crate market do not look good, then F should look to supply to other overseas markets. In this way, they could increase production volumes and benefit from **economies of scale in production**. The market for beer crates is likely to be equally competitive overseas and so F should consider exporting other containers.

As a further benefit, once F has achieved cost reductions from economies of scale it would be able to compete more aggressively on price in the home market.

Overseas expansion

Foreign manufacturing plants. The fact that foreign competitors have been able to gain market share by competing aggressively on price, suggests that they have a lower cost base than F. F may be able to counteract this by setting up an overseas manufacturing plant of its own, to take advantage of lower operating costs and overheads.

Overseas acquisition. F may be able to combine the objectives of overseas market development and lower production costs by acquiring an existing overseas plastics manufacturer. However, F is likely **to need the support of its shareholders for this strategy**. Consequently, F's management will have to convince the shareholders of the benefits of this strategy, because the shareholders have proposed a withdrawal from the beer crate market.

Problems with the labour force and inflexible working practices

Inflexible working practices. If F is going to compete successfully with its foreign competitors, it will need to **streamline the working practices** within the company and make them more **flexible**.

Reduce bureaucracy. There is currently too much bureaucracy – with negotiating committees, precise job definitions and a complicated system of labour grades.

This bureaucracy is likely to mean that F has a **higher cost base** than leaner, more flexible competitors, and is therefore likely to be contributing to F's declining performance.

F needs to make its working practices more flexible, and simplify the employment structure. However, because the workforce is unionised, F will have to **negotiate with the unions** to get them to support any changes.

Staffing levels. One of the key issues to address will be whether F has more staff than it needs. It may be able to reduce operating costs by **making some staff redundant**. However, such a decision will have to be negotiated very carefully with the staff and the unions in order that it does not provoke strike action or other unrest.

> If some staff are made redundant, F will incur a one-off charge for their redundancy payments, but in the longer term operating costs should be reduced. And if having a smaller, more efficient workforce means that F can compete more effectively in the longer term, then this one off cost is worth incurring – especially as the worst-case alternative may be that the company collapses.

Uncommercial R&D department

F is seeing its margins and market share in its core market (beer crates) come under increasing threat and so innovation and new product development could be critical in finding alternative areas for growth.

One such area could be electro-plastics, which is a much newer sector, and one in which F could potentially establish a competitive advantage if it is the first company to develop a successful product.

However, for F's new products to be a commercial success they have to **meet a market need**.

Marketing and market research. In order to identify which new products could be commercially successful, F needs to understand what sort of products it customers want.

The R&D department should then focus its time and resources on projects which are selected by the operational and marketing departments in the light of this market research information.

> **Links between R&D and marketing.** The marketing department has an important role in indicating which products the R&D department should focus on, according to customer needs. But equally, once the R&D department has developed a new product, they need to work with the marketing department to generate consumer interest in the new product.
>
> Given the current organisation structure, it is likely that there is not much communication between departments, so creating these links between departments will require a **change in the organisation's culture**.

Recommended strategies

F should focus on three key strategies to address the difficulties it is currently facing.

1 **Improve competitiveness to protect existing markets and market shares**. It should look to do this by reducing costs, in particular by reorganising current working practices.
2 **Look to develop new markets overseas** to reduce dependence on the home market.
3 **Look to develop new products**. It should do this by combining the new technological developments which the R&D department are working on, with an understanding of market needs provided by the marketing department.

Part (b)

> **Top tips.** Although this part of the question is about stakeholder (shareholder) management rather than strategic options, you should still relate your answer directly to the scenario. The reasons why F needs the shareholder support stem from the difficulties and strategies which form the basis of (a).
>
> A general answer about the importance of communicating with shareholders would have earned few marks here.

Depressed share price and unrest due to lack of information. Share prices are in part determined by expectations of future earnings. Because F has not kept its shareholders informed, they have very little knowledge about the company, its performance and its future plans. They do not know about the potentially exciting developments in electro-plastics for example. The only information they see is past performance, published in F's annual report and accounts.

As a result of this lack of knowledge, a group of institution shareholders has requested a strategic review and suggested that F should withdraw from its core market (beer crates). This is a potentially very damaging strategy, but it is one which may never have been suggested if the shareholders have been kept better informed.

Vulnerable to take-over bids. Perhaps most importantly of all, the poor results and reduced value of the company may make it vulnerable to a hostile take-over bid. If such a bid were received – even if it were under-valued – the shareholders may be tempted to accept it, because they have no information from the directors explaining why they shouldn't sell, and/or how business will improve in the future.

Alternatively, even if they were considering a sale, the directors should have been communicating any developments and issues with the shareholders so that they have an indication of what a fair value for the company would be based on the current projections.

Need for shareholder support. The Directors of F are potentially going to be faced with some major strategic decisions in the near future – foreign expansion, foreign acquisition, and workforce restructuring (which may lead to industrial unrest). The Directors will need the support of the shareholders to deliver these strategies, for example to provide additional finance in a rights issue, but if the shareholders feel alienated because of the lack of communication, they are unlikely to give their support.

No surprises. The company has reported uneven profits for the past five year, and this year it will have to report significantly reduce profits. If shareholders and financial analysts have not been informed of the reasons for this, and what F is doing to improve performance, the results are going to come as a nasty surprise. Investors and analysts do not like surprises, so the results are likely to lead to a fall in the company's value (share price).

24 Biotechnology company

Study Reference. Evaluating strategic choices (suitability, acceptability, feasibility) is covered in Chapter 6 of the Study Text.

Alternative answer. This question provides a good illustration of the fact that there may often be more valid points that you could make in answer to an E3 question than you will have time for in the exam.

In particular, there are a large number of points you could make in relation to part (b).

The first answer below tries to show a wide range of these points for tutorial purposes. However, by doing so, the answer becomes quite long. Moreover, you would not need to make all the points we do to score a good pass to this question.

To illustrate this we have also presented a second answer (in a text box after the first answer) which would have scored a good mark for this question, and was written under strictly timed conditions.

This question illustrates that there is often no single right answer to business strategy questions. If you are asked to recommend an option (as in (d)) provided your recommendation is consistent with your previous answers and is sensible you will score marks for it. The two answers we have presented make different recommendations in part (d) but both are equally valid and would have both scored the marks available.

Marking scheme

			Marks
(a)	For a full description of suitability	Up to 2	
	For a full description of feasibility	Up to 2	
	For a full description of acceptability	Up to 2	
		Total up to	6
(b)	For evaluation of the cash flow guarantee from the venture capitalist	Up to 5	
	For evaluation of the purchase by the pharmaceutical company	Up to 5	
	For evaluation of the merger with another biotechnology company	Up to 5	
		Total up to	12
(a)	Identification of any reasonable alternative option	1	
	Evaluation of the alternative option	Up to 4	
		Total up to	5
(b)	Clear recommendation based on the evaluation	2	2
		Total	25

Part (a)

Top tips. A sensible way to approach requirement (a) would be to take each aspect of the SFA framework – suitability, feasibility, acceptability – in turn, and discuss how that aspect can be used to evaluate strategic options. Note your answer to (a) does not need to be specifically related to the options facing DDD.

Strategic choices are evaluated according to their **suitability** to the organisation and its current strategic logic; to how **feasible** it will be to implement them given the organisation's resources; and how **acceptable** they will be to the organisation's various stakeholders.

Suitability – A strategy must fit with an organisation's current operational circumstances and its strategic goals. In this context an organisation should consider the choices in relation to a corporate appraisal:

- How well does it exploit the organisation's **strengths** and distinctive **competences**?
- How well does it address any **weaknesses**?
- Does it help the organisation take advantages of **opportunities** available to it?
- Does it allow the organisation deal with **threats** facing it?

Alongside these questions, an organisation should also consider whether a strategy will help it generate or maintain **competitive advantage** over its competitors.

The most suitable strategy for an organisation will be the one which allows it to do this most effectively.

Feasibility – For a strategy to be feasible, an organisation must have **sufficient resources** to carry it out successfully. In this context, resources include **money**, **technology**, **materials**, **staff** and **time**. If a strategy cannot be implemented using an organisation's existing competences, and therefore demands new competences to be acquired, it may not be feasible.

Acceptability – This aspect of the framework looks at the acceptability of a potential strategy to an organisation's various **stakeholder groups** – for example, customers, management, staff, shareholders and bankers. To assess a strategy's acceptability, an organisation should consider the values and interests of key stakeholders and then assess how well these fit with the strategy. Two key considerations when considering a strategy's acceptability will be the **financial return** it is expected to deliver, and the **level of risk** involved in adopting it.

Part (b)

Top tips. Unlike for part (a), for requirement (b) you do need to apply the SFA framework specifically to the three options identified by the founders. Therefore a sensible approach here would be to apply the SFA framework to each option in turn; ie suitability of option 1, feasibility of option 1, acceptability of option 1, suitability of option 2 etc. It is also important to identify the different stakeholders involved here: the founders, the venture capitalists and the employees. What will the potential impact of the different options be for each of them?

Note, however, that you are not asked to comment on the overall appropriateness of the options at this stage – that comes later in (d).

Easy marks. If you approach (b) in a methodical way – working through the suitability, feasibility and acceptability of each option in turn – you should be able to score a good number of marks here.

1   Cash flow guarantee from venture capital company

       Suitability

       DDD's main weakness is a shortage of cash, and the guarantee from the venture capitalists will ensure there are sufficient funds to allow DDD to continue until the first drug is successfully launched in commercial quantities.

       The injection of cash will not, in itself, add to DDD's strengths, but assuming the new drug proves commercially successful the funding could allow DDD a competitive advantage which it would have otherwise been denied.

       The venture capitalists have only agreed to guarantee DDD's funding until the first drug is successfully launched, and so there may still be question marks about the **longer term funding requirements** between that launch and DDD's flotation, unless cash inflows from the launch of that drug are sufficient to support the business' cash needs.

However, to the extent that the venture capitalist **funding will meet cash needs** in the short to medium term and bring at least one new drug to market this option is suitable.

Acceptability

Venture capitalists – This plan will see a significant rise in the venture capitalist's shareholder in the company – from 15% to 60%. As the venture capitalists have proposed the plan, we can assume it is acceptable to them.

Founders – However, the increase in the venture capitalist's shareholding will mean that the **founders' stakes in the company are significantly reduced**. This may not be acceptable to the founders, particularly in the context of the profits they might make when the company is floated in five years time.

Employees – Similarly, the plan will not be acceptable to the employees because it will reduce the numbers of shares available to them through their share option scheme. Currently, the employees are prepared to accept relatively low salaries because they will receive shares in the company when it floats. However, if this option is removed they are likely to either **want higher salaries**, or will **leave the company** altogether. If too many employees leave, DDD's ability to develop its new drug may be jeopardized.

Feasibility

This option does not, in itself, affect the internal resources of the company so there are no problems about its feasibility.

2   Purchase by pharmaceutical company

Suitability

This option will allow at least some of the drugs which DDD is working on to be brought to market, but not by DDD as a company in its own right.

Given the foundations intention to float the company on the stock exchange, it seems likely that one of the strategic goals was to **run DDD as an independent company**. From that perspective, the outright purchase by another company is not a suitable option.

Acceptability

Venture capitalists

This option is **unlikely to be acceptable to the venture capitalists**, not least because they have proposed an alternative option. However, possibly more importantly, they are unlikely to be happy that whereas they invested in DDD expecting to see significant returns when it successfully launches its first new drug, they will no longer get the benefit of these returns. We do not know the terms of the deal under which the pharmaceutical company has offered to buy DDD (for cash, or for shares) but either way it is unlikely that the venture capitalists will receive the same returns as they would if DDD have successfully launched the new drug as an independent company.

Founders

This option **may not be acceptable to the founders** either, because while they currently have the independence and status of being their own bosses, under the new structure they will simply be employees (researchers) in a much larger company. If the large company offers the founders a favourable price to acquire DDD now, (rather than them having to wait 5 years to benefit from the flotation) the relative acceptability of this option may be increased. However, this will probably be unlikely – especially if the larger company is aware of DDD cash flow problems.

Employees

The employees will be concerned about the acquisition because the larger pharmaceutical company **only intends to retain 'a few of the staff'**. Therefore there is a risk that some of the current employees will be made redundant, which will not make this an acceptable option for them.

The other issue for all the employees to consider is that they will lose the potential benefits accruing from DDD's share option scheme in the event of it floating. However, if the larger company offered them higher base salaries than DDD did, they may be prepared to accept the security of a higher salary instead of the potential benefits of the share option scheme.

Feasibility

There are no problems with the feasibility of this option.

3   Merger with another biotechnology company

Suitability

Because the other biotechnology company's new drug will be launched in six months time this will provide **a short term cash injection** to support DDD until its first new drug is launched.

However, whereas DDD is then expecting to launch one new drug in most subsequent years, the other company is not expecting to have any other new drugs commercially available for another 5 years. Therefore, it is **debatable whether the other company has the same strength in developing new drugs** as DDD. If the merger effectively means that the other company provides a short-term cash injection in return for piggy-backing on DDD's competences in the longer term, then that is unlikely to be a suitable option for DDD.

Acceptability

Venture capitalists

Again, this option is **unlikely to be acceptable** to the venture capitalists, because it would mean DDD rejects the option they have proposed. Also the merger would **dilute the venture capitalist's share** in the new company which is unlikely to be acceptable.

Founders

As with the acquisition by a larger company, the merger would **reduce the founder's independence and autonomy**, because the directors of the other company would now be jointly responsible for business decisions and strategy. This change may not be acceptable to DDD's founders. Moreover, there is no indication of how long the founders would be expected to stay with the newly merged company. If they are expected to remain for a long time, they may find this restrictive.

Also, there is no indication whether the newly merger company would still **look to float in 5 years time**. If it would not, this again may be undesirable for DDD's founders.

Employees

The merger is very unlikely to be acceptable to the employees, because the rationalization of the workforce will mean that some **employees are made redundant**.

Also, if the newly merger company does not intend to float the employees who remain will **lose the potential benefits from the share option scheme**. It is possible, that they may be offered higher base salaries to compensate for this, but this appears unlikely since the other company has fewer new drugs in the pipeline that DDD and so **on-going cash flow could still be a problem** for the business.

Feasibility

The feasibility of this option will depend on how similar the research and development practices of the two companies are. The merger is the only option which will involve the integration **of the systems from two different companies**. This could mean that there are some significant changes to DDD's operating systems, and the **time taken** to complete the merger could also be an issue.

In addition, DDD's founders have **no experience of managing a merger** process which could increase the risk of the merger being unsuccessful.

Part (c)

> **Top tips**. Requirement (c) asks you to evaluate one other option the founders might pursue. We have taken the view that DDD currently is spreading its resources too thinly over a large number of developments and so could rationalise the number of drugs in development. However, if you suggested a different alternative and evaluated its suitability, acceptability, and feasibility you would have got credit for this. For example, given the founders background as senior researchers in a university medical school might they consider whether there are any research grants which DDD could apply for to supplement its cash flow?

> **Examiner's comments.** Parts (a) and (b) were generally well answered by most candidates. However (c) was generally not well answered. Very few candidates recognised the most obvious option to improve available cash flows by reducing the number of products in development from 12 to a more cost effective level.

At the moment, DDD has 12 drugs in development, a number of which may not be successfully launched. One option which DDD could pursue is to **reduce the number of drugs in development** and concentrate funds on those drugs which can be brought to market soonest.

Suitability

This option will not in itself generate an additional cash inflow for the business. It will only be suitable if by concentrating resources on a small number of drugs they can be **brought to market quickly enough** to cover the cash short-fall in nine months time.

There may also be issues around **which drugs to stop developing**. Those which can be developed most quickly may not be the ones which will be most commercially successful in the longer term.

Moreover, as with any development, there is no guarantee that the drugs which DDD chooses to continue with will be commercially successful.

Acceptability

Venture capitalists – This option may be acceptable to the venture capital company in that it doesn't involve any dilution of their share in the company. However, if reducing the number of drugs in development reduces DDD's future earnings this may be less acceptable to the venture capitalists. DDD's perceived earnings potential will affect its value when it floats on the stock exchange.

Founders – This option will be acceptable to the founders because it **maintains their independence and does not dilute their shareholding in the company**. As with the venture capitalists, however, the founders have a vested interest in not restricting DDD's future earnings too much however, because they will be the principal beneficiaries of a successful flotation. Because this option will reduce the number of new drugs DDD is working on at any time, it may decide to delay the flotation to allow the number of drugs launched to be increased before it floats.

Employees – This option is unlikely to be attractive to the researchers working on the drugs whose development is discontinued.

From the perspective that this option will not change the company structure or the employees' share options, it may be relatively more attractive, although not if the flotation is significantly delayed.

Feasibility

There should be no problems with the feasibility of this option.

Part (d)

> **Top tips.** Requirement (d) is only worth two marks, so you should not spend too long on it. Do not repeat your answers from (b) or (c); but rather use them to reach a conclusion. You are asked to recommend one option only, so make sure you do just that!

DDD should select its preferred option by considering its impact on the three main stakeholder groups (venture capitalists, founders, employees).

Option 1 (Additional funding from venture capitalists) – This is relatively unattractive to the founders and the staff due to the reduction in shares available

Option 2 (Acquisition by large company) – This will not be acceptable to any of the stakeholder groups

Option 3 (Merger) – This is also unlikely to be acceptable to any of the stakeholder groups

Option 4 (Reduction in development portfolio) – This will be the most attractive for the founders and the staff, and should be acceptable to the venture capitalists.

Therefore, DDD should **reduce the number of drugs in development**.

Alternative answer to Question 24 (Biotechnology Company): see note above

Part (a)

Suitability

This means whether or not the proposed option makes strategic sense i.e. is it a logical fit with the company's activities. An example of this is an option that builds upon a critical success factor in which the company is proficient, or an environmental opportunity that the company is well placed to exploit.

Feasibility

Put simply, this is whether or not the company can successfully pursue the proposed option through to completion. Factors to be considered include, for example in DDD's case, regulatory approval or completion of successful clinical trials. Of more immediate concern to DDD is whether or not they have sufficient funds to bring their drugs to market.

Acceptability

This relates to whether or not the strategic option will be acceptable to the company's stakeholders. For example, in DDD the three options for funding must be assessed in the light of whether they provide an acceptable level of financial return and business control to the founder members, the 10 staff they employ and the venture capitalists.

Part (b)

Each option will be assessed using Johnson, Scholes and Whittington's framework: suitable, feasible, acceptable.

Option 1

Suitable

This option appears suitable. It would allow the company to pursue its mission to develop drugs for commercial use. Once this happens the stock market listing is much more likely to be obtained. The lack of cash is a major weakness for DDD and this option resolves this issue.

Acceptable

The founders will have mixed feelings with regards to this option. Although it appears to guarantee the immediate future of DDD, releasing some of their equity via a subsequent floatation, the amount of equity they are having to trade appears very high.

The other employees will also have mixed feelings because although it may guarantee they get the opportunity to realise their share options they may also suffer a dilution of their value.

The venture capital firm will see this as a good deal. In exchange to underwriting DDD until it becomes commercially successful they get a massive increase in their financial returns. As an organisation that thrives on high risk and high reward investments this represents an excellent opportunity.

Feasible

This option appears feasible. There is no indication that the venture capitalists do not have the funds necessary to support the company until the first drug is successfully launched.

Option 2

Suitability

This option also appears suitable for bring the drugs to market. It would provide DDD with the resource required to see its drugs through to market, and a lack of resources is its key weakness at the moment.

However, it will mean that DDD no longer operates as an independent company, and so the founders may not think this is a suitable option if one of DDD's strategic goals is to operate as an independent company.

Acceptable

Acceptability will vary according to the parties. The venture capitalists will only view this as acceptable if it represents a better financial return based upon risk when compared to options 1 and 3.

The founders may prefer to retain a degree of independence and show some concern for the welfare of the other staff due to lose their jobs. This may depend upon the terms of the buy-out.

The other staff will be concerned as this option offers limited job security and they will be concerned as to the impact upon their share options.

Feasible

There should not be any problems with the feasibility of this option, although ultimately the success of this strategy may be subject to the takeover getting regulatory approval of the takeover and the ability of the two parties to agree to the sale, and to upon price and related conditions of the sale.

Option 3

Suitable

This option appears unsuitable. The combined entity would still be suffering a shortage of cash and there is no guarantee that enough funds would be available to see the first drug to market in 6 months. Equally important is that there is no assurance as to the commercial viability of the first drug the merger partner has developed.

Acceptable

This option does not seem acceptable to any of DDD's key stakeholders.

Other staff will fear for both their jobs and share options given the cash flow issues that are unresolved and the mention of staff rationalisation.

The founders may feel that they are tying themselves to a company with more problems than their own, given the 5 year wait to maturity of the merger partner's other drugs.

The venture capitalists may view this as a less attractive company than DDD. They are being asked to take on board a company that may extend the period of time in which a successful floatation may occur. This is unlikely to appeal to them as they are potentially able to realise their current investment in DDD within two years.

Feasible

This option appears to be unfeasible. Once again, regulatory approval would be required, which may delay the merger beyond the crucial 6 month deadline. Given the uncertainty over cash flow it is also highly unlikely that the key financial stakeholders such as DDD's venture capital partners and founders would agree to such a move, unless they were offered a significantly increased holding in the combined entity.

Part (c)

Alternative strategic option

It would seem that the biggest problem facing DDD is a gap between cash resources and investment strategy. The simplest way to solve this would be to focus on fewer drugs until such time that DDD starts to generate revenues.

In order to implement this strategy DDD should undertake an immediate review of its drugs portfolio and identify those drugs most likely to be commercially successful within the shortest time frames. Any drugs that fall outside of these parameters should be either mothballed, or alternatively sold to other biotechnology firms with an interest in purchasing them, which may even boost cash reserves. With the same number of staff focusing on fewer drugs the development cycle may be shortened.

This strategy would be suitable as it allows DDD to pursue its aim of developing drugs to bring to market. The feasibility appears high as it will allow the company to continue to trade whilst preserving its limited cash reserves. The founders, staff and venture capitalists should find this acceptable as it increases the likelihood of the company surviving to the point where it becomes an attractive floatation proposition thereby allowing them to realise their investments.

The main drawback of this strategy, however, is that it increases risk by focusing the company's resource on fewer drugs. Should the assessment of these drugs turn out to be wrong then DDD has a chance of pursuing unsuccessful drugs whilst spurning potentially lucrative ones.

Answers 149

Part (d)

It is recommended that Option 1 is pursued. This option is the only one that offers some sort of guarantee that the company will be financially supported until it can start to generate its own revenues.

Although this will lead to a significant dilution of the founders' investment, a successful floatation may well make them extremely wealthy anyway. By choosing the option that maintains the operational status quo there will be little or no disruption to the company giving it the stability to focus on developing drugs.

25 Internet strategy

Text reference. Business strategy and strategic planning is covered in Chapter 1 of the E3 Study Text. E-commerce is dealt with in Chapter 7.

Part (a)

Top tips. The way to approach this question is to recognise that while its context is the impact of e-commerce on business, the question itself deals with strategic management.

You are not asked about what an appropriate Internet strategy might be for the SDW, but how Mr M might establish and implement it.

Note also that you are required to give Mr M two distinct pieces of advice: how to *establish* an appropriate internet strategy; and then how to *implement* it. You should have considered these two aspects separately in your answer.

For the first part you could adopt the headings of the rational model to organise your recommendations. In the second you may like to use some of the headings from project management covered elsewhere in your studies.

Easy marks. There are some obvious points to make in part (a), concerning the existing website, the need for strategic integration and the need for security. Generally, such points will earn a mark for a basic mention and up to perhaps two or three further marks for discussion, depending on their complexity.

Establishment methodology and issues

(i) Establish the desired outcomes

Mr M will need to start by **setting the objectives** for his Internet (and wider IS) strategy, and these objectives must be **SMART** (specific, measurable, achievable, results-focused, time-related). The strategy must support the company's wider business strategy, so it is important for Mr M to review his overall strategic position first. In particular, he should consider the **scale and scope of his operations**: if he has any plans for expanding his operations, he must ensure that his systems will be capable of handling the increased business (for example, an increase in the number of bookings made; increase in the complexity of offered itineraries; or perhaps an expansion into another market, such as entertainment bookings, that could exploit the same technology).

One important factor will be the timeframe for this implementation.

Clear strategic objectives will help Mr M to avoid piecemeal design and acquisition of his IS, which might have a dis-integrating effect on other business systems.

(ii) Position audit

The next step is to determine SDW's **current strengths and weaknesses** in terms of IT, IS and IM. The company already has a website: Mr M must decide whether he wishes to expand his existing website or start a new one from scratch, and whether this is possible. The capability, compatibility and integration of existing systems should be reviewed, alongside their potential/flexibility for further development. The availability of in-house expertise in web design and management should also be considered, alongside the costs of **developing or buying-in** such expertise.

(iii) Environmental analysis

This should embrace **market research of customer needs** and information gathering/e-commerce preferences, plus **monitoring and analysing competitor and other industry e-commerce sites**. Once this information has been gathered, SDW's system can be benchmarked against its competitors. E-commerce is well-established in the travel industry and continues to develop at a rapid pace: Mr M would be well advised to institute a **continuing review** of benchmark websites so as to avoid being left behind.

(iv) SWOT analysis

Mr M needs to **identify the gap** between the capability of his current systems and the desired future state. At this stage, a number of issues may emerge. E-commerce offers a significant opportunity to reduce administration costs, improve customer service, gather meaningful customer data and so on. However, there are also potential threats. E-commerce causes wide-spread business changes: reducing the percentage of business gained by other means, creating pressures on fulfilment, perhaps changing the pricing structure (eg through on-line booking discounts for customers), and raising issues of data and transaction security.

(v) Generate, evaluate and select options

Mr M and his technical advisers should be able to generate a range of options (for example, by using a 'TOWS' matrix) to build on strengths or minimise the effect of weaknesses, in order to capitalise on opportunities and counter threats. Each option can be screened for **Suitability** (will it achieve its stated objectives?), **Feasibility** (is it achievable given the budget, timescale, expertise and technology currently available?) and **Acceptability** (will it secure the broad support of key stakeholders including Mr M, internal users and customer users? Will it be opposed by other units such as the call centre, who may lose staff?)

At the end of this screening process, Mr M should then choose his preferred strategy.

Implementation methodology and issues

The methodology for implementing the strategy will need to:

(i) **Appoint a project manager**. This role will be responsible for taking the implementation forward.
(ii) **Determine a timescale and delegate tasks,** using internal staff, with or without external consultants, or outsourcing the project to specialists.
(iii) **Design and test control measures,** such as load testing
(iv) **Roll out the new system.** The roll out should be done in phases or else a pilot scheme should be introduced first in order to reduce the risk/impact of teething troubles. It is likely that there will be parallel running of the web based and call centre systems to help customers adapt. Later a strategy can be developed to migrate customers to the new system such as discounts or extended waits for service by the call centre.

A number of key issues will need to be addressed.

Change management – The introduction of e-commerce represents a significant (potentially transformative) **change to business processes**. This may be experienced as traumatic by internal staff affected by the change. **Call centre staff**, in particular, are likely to be apprehensive about its effect on jobs. Proper consideration must be given to an effective **human resources management** response to this concern, as well as to the manner of implementing any changes that may actually occur.

Customer communication – Similarly, **customers** will need to be carefully informed and supported through the change, while **staff** required to operate and support the new system (eg by answering customer voice queries) will have to be briefed and trained.

Customers will have to be encouraged to trial the Internet booking option. This will require extensive **publicity and promotion** prior to the launch. Existing customers could be direct mailed with information. Once customers have made an on-line booking, they must be encouraged to do it again. This will require reminder advertising, possibly by e-mail. It will also require that the booking experience is satisfying to a wide range of users. A website that is difficult or frustrating to use will drive customers away.

Internet security – The introduction of e-commerce will also have important implications for **security**, since monetary transactions will be entered into. Customers' credit card details must be safeguarded and proper attention must be paid to the security of assets: tickets must not be available without payment confirmation.

Part (b)

> **Top tips**. Note that the requirements ask you not only to discus the customer-oriented features of an internet site, but also how they can be used to reduce business costs. It is crucial that your answer addresses both parts of this requirement. You should draw on your own experience of using websites to think about how they are tailored to customer needs (customer-oriented features).
>
> This question demands both an appreciation of the ways in which business costs arise and a familiarity with the way that websites work. It is therefore a good example of the importance of drawing together your theoretical studies, your management accounting experience and your awareness of real world business methods. It is quite easy to answer if you can do that, but if any your knowledge of any of those three areas is inadequate, you will find it more difficult.
>
> **Easy marks**. You could gain easy marks by considering your own experience of using websites and thinking about their good and bad features, even if you had never studied IT strategy.

Customer-oriented features of a web site and their impact on cost saving

A key issue for the viability of SDW's e-commerce plans is whether the Internet site can be made customer-friendly (attracting on-line bookings) while at the same time fulfilling its aim of reducing operating costs. The following features of a web site may be considered key to customer/user satisfaction.

(i) Ease of use and navigation

The site must be easy to use and must have a logical structure and internal links, to avoid user frustration. If the site is easy to use it can contribute to cost reduction because customers will use it as an alternative to the call centre (with its heavier labour, overhead and operating costs).

'Ease of use' would also suggest a simple, 'uncluttered' site design, which might limit design, programming, maintenance and upload costs.

(ii) Low access speed requirements

The site should load quickly even when accessed using a dial-up connection: it cannot yet be assumed that customers will be using broad-band. It should therefore be free of complex graphics, which will keep design and programming costs down.

(iii) Financial incentives to book on-line

Travel customers have come to expect discounts for Internet bookings, recognising that the supplier incurs lower selling and administration costs. Additional loyalty incentives (eg 'train miles' accumulated with repeat purchasers) may also be possible using on-line user registration tools. While these discounts represent an opportunity cost to SDW, they may contribute to overall cost savings by diverting customers to on-line sales, further decreasing reliance on the call-centre, and allowing progressive staff, space and equipment savings.

(iv) Empowerment of customers for self-service

E-commerce is designed to empower customers to become the 'fourth leaf' of the flexible 'Shamrock'-type organisation, allowing cost savings on the provision of service via human contact, and also generating savings on the printing costs of tickets and vouchers (which can now be downloaded by customers). Information and support can be substantially offered without human intervention, in the form of FAQs, clearly signposted booking processes and on-line help messages, for example.

(v) Added-value information and services

In order to attract customers to the site and to keep their attention longer (and over repeat visits), the web site needs to be 'sticky': that is, it needs to be interesting and motivating. SDW can achieve this by a number of innovative and interactive features: 'virtual' tours of trains and destinations, flexible itinerary planning (eg by desired destination, or available budget), seasonal 'specials', and links to the sites of related attractions, accommodation and so on. Again, while incurring initial set-up costs, this should help to attract repeat and extra e-customers, reducing overall selling costs.

SDW may also be able to negotiate some **affiliate deals** with related attractions so that SDW will receive a commission for any customers who click onto a related site via its link. The income from any such affiliate deals can be used to counter-balance the cost of running the site.

152 Answers

(vi) Opportunity to give feedback

Customers often welcome the opportunity to be heard, in the form of feedback and suggestions. This information is easy to gather using on-line forms, and can contribute to cost savings by providing a cheaper alternative to telephone/mail surveys – and by providing information for service improvement, prioritisation and so on.

Also, if customers feel valued and have the opportunity to give feedback they may be more likely to become repeat users of the site. If SDW can improve **customer retention** then it may be able to make savings on the amount marketing expenditure needed to attract new customers.

26 Sole supplier

Text reference. Information systems are dealt with in Chapter 7 of your BPP Study Text.

Marking scheme

			Marks
(a)	Up to 2 marks for each advantage of the sole supplier arrangement, (up to 4 advantages)	Up to 8	
	Up to 2 marks for each disadvantage of the sole supplier arrangement, (up to 4 disadvantages)	Up to 8	
		Total up to	15
(b)	Up to 2 marks for each benefit of access to the internet, up to 6 benefits identified	Up to 10	10
		Total	25

Part (a)

> **Top tips.** You need to think carefully about both parts of this question before you start to answer part (a). If you do not do this, you run the risk of confusing the two. The essence of the difference between the two is that access to the extranet is just one advantage to S from accepting the contract. There are others. Be careful not to describe the benefits of the extranet link twice over.
>
> In part (a) you need to discuss the advantages and disadvantages of the sole supplier arrangement in general.
>
> **Easy marks.** You should be able to spot the risks inherent in massive expansion, a single, dominant customer, penalty clauses and international operations without too much difficulty.

Advantages to S of the proposed sole supplier agreement

(i) Growth

The contract holds out the prospect of **rapid growth** on a major scale. Depending on the term of the contract, increased turnover should produce increases in **profit**. In addition, growth impresses **capital markets** (which will only be relevant if S is a quoted company) and should lead to the creation of **scale economies**, with a further favourable effect on profitability.

(ii) Reputation

The contract with C would be confirmation of S's status as a sound and reliable supplier: S would then find it **easier to win further business** with other manufacturers.

(iii) Planning

The proposed contract will run for five years. All other things being equal, this should reduce the general level of business risk S suffers, thus, possibly reducing its cost of capital. It should also enhance the company's ability to plan its operations in detail and, if funds are available, to concentrate its marketing resources on further routes to expansion.

(iv) Human Resources Management

The extra certainty in S's business situation might produce desirable effects upon its staff. The company will be able to recruit, select, train and develop its staff in a coherent manner, which may produce a beneficial effect on **motivation** and thence on **productivity**.

Disadvantages of the proposed agreement

(i) Dominant customer

There is an enormous disparity in size between S and C: the contract will be vital to S's survival, but merely a convenience to C. C would be by far the more **powerful party to the contract**. This could lead to irresistible pressure on S to conform to C's wishes in a range of matters, not excluding renegotiation of the contract's terms on price and settlement. Indeed, C could simply ignore contract's stipulations from time to time with impunity.

(ii) Credit risk

Few motor manufacturers are financially healthy. While C may be too large to be allowed by its domestic government to fail, it may at some point **seek protection from its creditors**, including S. This could have a catastrophic effect on S's cash flow.

(iii) Financial risk

S will be committed to enormous expansion with a consequent enormous increase in its **requirement for capital**. We are not told anything about S Company's legal status, but, it seems unlikely that the current owners would be able to raise the necessary capital from their own resources or from a sale of equity to the public. The needed capital is likely to be met by borrowing, with a much increased level of **gearing** as a result.

This represents a major risk for the owners of S, since the **interest payments will be fixed**, but income from the contract will vary with C's fortunes in the global car market. A further risk is that **the contract may not be renewed** at the end of its five year term, in which case, S would probably be quite unable to service its debt and may be forced into insolvency.

(iv) Delivery failures

The contract requires S to compensate C for production lost if deliveries are late. The sums involved here may be very large indeed, and far greater than the revenue from the airbags supplied late. This is another aspect of the unequal effects of the contract.

(iv) Currency risk

C produces cars in five countries. Depending on the terms of the contract, S may suffer significant exchange losses if required to invoice in foreign currency.

Part (b)

Top tips. In order to answer this question well, you need to appreciate the verb requirement: evaluate. You are asked to *evaluate* the benefits to S of access to the C extranet, and so to score well your answer needs not only to explain the benefits, but also to discuss any limitations to them.

Examiner's comments. Few candidates actually evaluated the benefits of the extranet. To evaluate a benefit, it is necessary to discuss the extent to which it applies to a situation, or the likely extent of the benefit.

Benefits to the supplier of access to C's extranet

(i) Access to C's forecast production schedules

Access to the extranet will provide S with a great deal of very valuable planning information.

- **The two year forecast will permit S to plan its production requirements** and its implications for staffing and plant for that period. Where production is planned to reduce seasonally or on change of model, S will be able to plan to seek compensating business elsewhere, perhaps using its scale economies to compete on price.

- Meanwhile, the real-time information will permit detailed adjustments to production rates and the **planning of daily deliveries** to meet the terms of its contract – particularly valuable, given C's just-in-time supply requirements and S's liability for the cost of lost production through delivery delay.

The extent to which these benefits apply, and their value to S, will depend on **how far into the future C fixes its plans, and how often and how radically those plans are subject to change**. It also depends on how flexible S and its logistics providers are able to be about adjusting its own plans in response to fluctuating demand, given that it is already having to increase its production capacity radically in order to fulfil the contract.

(ii) Access to industry information

Access to information through the virtual trading room should enhance S's ability to compete for sales to other customers. This information may include details of: technological improvements; competitor and customer prospects and intentions; and industry scenario developments.

Again, however, the benefits of this access are somewhat reduced in value because: a number of network partners all have access to the same information, reducing its potential to give S genuine competitive edge; and participants are unlikely to expose information of genuine competitive importance in such a relatively open forum.

(iii) Development of network relationships

Information sharing and systems integration are part of the development of **mutual trust and collaboration** between supply chain partners. Access to the extranet should enable S to cement and deepen its relationship with S, and perhaps – through co-ordinating mechanisms – with other suppliers in C's network: this could lead to **knowledge-sharing**, value-adding service improvements, **collaboration on new product development** and other long term benefits.

The value of this benefit may be limited by S's current pre-occupation with simply matching the required order volume for its immediate contract with C, and by the long-term structural power-imbalance in the relationship between C and S: information-sharing, investment in improvement and gain-sharing may be one-way.

(iv) Access to new contracts

Through the virtual trading room, S will join the ranks of suppliers who can bid for new contracts, enhancing its opportunities to secure further business for airbags and its other safety products.

Again, however, the value of this is undercut by the emphasis on competitive bidding, which is likely to focus on price competition, rather than quality of service and buyer-supplier loyalty.

Answers | 155

27 IT outsourcing

Text reference. Outsourcing in the context of IT is dealt with in Chapter 7 of your BPP Study Text.

Marking scheme

		Marks
(a)	**Strategic level**	
	General identification of strategic level issues in relation to IT	1
	Advantages related to the IT function of the merged organisation	Up to 2
	Disadvantages related the IT function of the merged organisation	Up to 2
	Managerial level	
	General identification of managerial level issues in relation to IT	1
	Advantages related to the IT function of the merged organisation	Up to 2
	Disadvantages related the IT function of the merged organisation	Up to 2
	Tactical level	
	General identification of tactical level issues in relation to IT	1
	Advantages related to the IT function of the merged organisation	Up to 2
	Disadvantages related the IT function of the merged organisation	Up to 2
	Total up to	15
(b)	1 mark for each relevant characteristic described and applied to BXA	1
	(Relevant characteristics include: experience of similar work, capacity to do work, financial stability, cultural compatibility and fit with BXA's staff, track record of retaining transferred staff, openness during due diligence)	
	A maximum of 2 marks will be awarded for a generic list which is not applied specifically to BXA	
	Total up to	5
(c)	1 mark for each relevant factor to be included in the service level agreement	1
	(Relevant factors may include: definition of the service and required performance, charges and procedures for charging, management information to be provided, right to audit figures, compliance with key obligations, benchmarking process to be used, termination arrangements)	
	Total up to	5
	Total	25

Part (a)

Top tips. The way to approach this question is to break down the requirement into its various parts. You are asked to discuss advantages and disadvantages, and you are asked to discuss them for each of three levels of the organisation.

However, note the requirement is to look at the advantages and disadvantages of outsourcing the IT function for the *merged organisation*.

Although the terminology of strategic, managerial and tactical levels (rather than strategic, tactical and operational) is unusual, the requirement to consider three levels of management should have given you a reasonable idea of how three levels should be differentiated.

It should also be reasonably clear that the marks available for this part of the question are easily divisible by three, emphasising the nature of the answer required: 5 marks for advantages and disadvantages at each level.

> Notice how we have structured our answer: rather than working straight up or down the hierarchy, we have left the middle layer until last, since we think it is less clearly defined than the strategic and junior levels.
>
> **Easy marks**. Some of the various advantages and disadvantages should be fairly easy to identify from your knowledge: such ideas as economies of scale, specialist skills, loss of control and improved cost forecasts are basic to any discussion of outsourcing. However, to maximise the credit you get for them make sure you apply them to the scenario.
>
> **Examiner's comments**. The Examiner felt that answers to this question were generally poor: there was the usual problem of lack of application to the scenario and very few candidates were able to distinguish between the three levels of management.

The **strategic level of management** is concerned with decisions that set the overall, long-term direction the organisation is to take.

Potential advantages at this level include the following.

The supplier ought to be able to deploy **IT competences, skills and techniques of a higher order** than BXA can provide internally, thus equipping the company to handle the much greater complexity inherent in doubling in size by merger with CXA. This should also make future acquisitions easier to absorb.

Outsourcing ought to bring cost benefits through the **exploitation of the supplier's economies of scale**, though actually achieving these benefits would depend on satisfactory contract negotiations.

The merged company will have to do something about its IT strategy. Outsourcing should **reduce the risks involved** in what will be a major project.

Access to state of the art IT systems may spur a **complete strategic reappraisal** of internal methods and procedures, producing **transformational** rather than **incremental** improvement in the way the company does things. One obvious example of such change is **delayering and empowerment**. An insurance business runs on assessment of risk: much of the process can now be automated. Also, the role of middle managers as filters and processors of routine information can now be largely eliminated by the use of modern IT systems. Much flatter and more effective structures can result.

Potential disadvantages at the strategic level

There are two important strategic dangers involved in outsourcing such an important function. First, there is the **risk of losing internal IT capability**: this could stunt future developments.

Alongside this, and linked to it, is the **risk of losing control of the IT function** and the services it provides. This is a very serious problem, since IT may represent a **core competence** for a large insurance company: the growth of direct, telephone-based insurance services is a good example. A more immediate danger is, perhaps, the possibility that the chosen contractor will **exploit its position by raising charges unreasonably** at some future time.

The every day, **routine (tactical) level of management** will also be affected by outsourcing.

Potential advantages at the tactical level

Advantages should include the provision of **more capable, reliable and faster systems**, which should enhance customer service; better and faster response to operational IT problems; and a reduction in the training effort currently needed to keep the existing legacy systems in operation. Junior managers should find they have more time for non-IT related aspects of their jobs and will have more flexibility in the management of their staff, since work will be simplified and more standardised.

Potential disadvantages at the tactical level

Disadvantages will revolve around the **reliability and efficiency of the contractors and their staff**. It is at this level that there must be the greatest integration of work; contractor staff will be expected to understand and support operational rather than technical IT priorities.

The **intermediate level of management** between the strategic and the routine (the marginal level) will be affected by the levels both above and below it, since it will be responsible for implementing strategic decisions and for providing the first response to the operational problems that junior managers cannot solve.

Potential advantages at the managerial level

These will include improved **reliability and continuity** of systems, with a reduced risk of significant failure.

Access to **IT staff of a high quality for advice and assistance**: it may be possible to recruit some contractor staff for any remaining internal IT activities. **IT training resources** should also be improved.

Potential disadvantages at the managerial level

However, there will be the possibility of disadvantages too. These will be similar to those experienced by junior managers, though of greater significance.

Outsourcing would constitute a **significant change**, as would the merger with CX. The management of these changes and the stress associated with it would fall to this level of management. Staff would be unsettled and would require a clear lead. Also, staff at all levels must keep their eyes on the ball and not allow the changes taking place to distract them from their primary responsibilities to their customers. Middle managers such as department heads must make sure that this happens.

There is also a potential problem in the degree of retraining these managers would themselves require. They will tend to be older and **possibly less able to adjust** to the new methods and practices.

Part (b)

> **Top tips.** You need to take note that there are only 5 marks available for here, and you should have scaled your answer accordingly.
>
> The Examiner was quite mean with the marks for this requirement, a well-made point applied to the scenario being worth only one mark. However, this is possibly because there a quite a number of qualities that would be relevant and there are only five marks to play with.
>
> **Easy marks.** There are no complexities here: you should be able to think of lots of qualities that would be desirable in any partner organisation... but make sure they are relevant to the scenario (see the examiner's comments below).
>
> **Examiner's comments.** A comprehensive list without application to the scenario would not produce a pass mark.

Suppliers should be assessed for **general commercial suitability.** Factors to check would include creditworthiness, financial stability, length of service of key staff and cultural compatibility with BXA and CXA.

Technical characteristics should match the client's particular circumstances.

Perhaps the most important point is **track record** in similar circumstances. Suitable suppliers will have worked with other **financial services companies** and will understand the pressures and problems likely to arise during the proposed merger. As already mentioned, BXA has an opportunity to transform the way it works and the scale of its operations. Its chosen partner must have a record of **satisfactorily implemented innovation** if the company is to achieve the potential benefits of these changes.

It is likely that at least **some existing BXA IT staff will have their employment transferred** to the new contractor because of their experience and familiarity with the way the company does things. As a good employer, BXA should ensure that such staff are not disadvantaged by the move and should seek assurances from the contractor to that effect. Transferred staff should enjoy equivalent or better pay, conditions and training and career progression opportunities as they do at present.

BXA will wish to treat the contractor as a partner, since its efforts are likely to be so strategically important. The chosen contractor must therefore display **integrity, openness and commitment to BXA's plans and aspirations**. There must be no reason to doubt that a long-term relationship will be mutually advantageous.

Part (c)

> **Top tips.** 'Identify' is a low-level instruction, corresponding to comprehension. A list of simply explained points such as ours provides an adequate answer. Again, there are only five marks available here.
>
> **Easy marks.** As with the previous part of this question, there are some fairly obvious points to make, such as defining the service to be provided, reaction to faults and computation of charges.

Definition of strategic and operational roles to be discharged: this will include the call for innovation in the development of new systems.

Definition of standards of routine operational service, such as system uptime, installation of upgrades and operation of a help desk

Specification of the **basis of charging**, with a requirement that it should be transparent and subject to audit

Provision for arbitration or other alternative dispute resolution in the event of a dispute

Contract period and provision for early termination

Terms on which BXA staff are transferred

Method of **quality assurance** to be used, possibly including benchmarking and external audit

Ownership of any new **software** developed as a result of the changes planned for the organisation.

28 Supplying and outsourcing

Text reference. Chapter 4 deals with suppliers and the supply chain. Chapter 5 also contains material on outsourcing.

Marking scheme

			Marks
(a)	Each relevant advantage, related to C, and discussed (not simply stated)	Up to 2	
	Each relevant disadvantage, related to C, and discussed (not simply stated)	Up to 2	
		Total up to	10
(b)	Each relevant advantage, related to C, and discussed (not simply stated)	Up to 2	
	Each relevant advantage, related to C, and discussed (not simply stated)	Up to 2	
		Total up to	8
(c)	For each relevant stakeholder group identified	1	
	For each specific communication method relevant to the stakeholder identified	1	
		Total up to	7
		Total	25

Part (a)

Top tips. The way to approach this question is to use the information presented in the scenario to inform your answer. The key to doing well is to try to get as many ideas from the scenario as possible, and then *discuss* them. It is not sufficient to simply provide a list of advantages and disadvantages. A good answer should also present a balanced array of advantages and disadvantages.

Note, however, that the independent pharmacies are not the supermarkets, nor is there any suggestion in the scenario that the proposal to supply directly to the independent pharmacies means that C is not going to supply the supermarkets.

Answers   159

> When this exam was sat, a number of students assumed one or other of these to be the case, and consequently answered a different question to the one the examiner intended. The question is actually asking what the advantages and disadvantages are of supplying directly to the independent pharmacies rather than supplying the pharmacies via the wholesalers.
>
> There is an important message here: make sure you read the scenario carefully, and base your answer on the information given in the scenario.
>
> **Easy marks.** The scenario should generate a number of issues for you to talk about; and the examiner wanted you to relate your answers specifically to the scenario.
>
> **Examiner's comments.** Parts (a) and (b) were reasonably well answered. However, note that if the question asks for a 'discussion', a basic statement with no clarification is not sufficient to pass.

There are a number of advantages to C's proposal to supply directly to the pharmacies.

Advantages to C of supplying directly to the pharmacies

(i)   **Increased profits** – Because the wholesalers are no longer taking part of the margin, C should earn increased profits from the new arrangement.

(ii) **Customer loyalty** – By offering a share of the increased margin to the pharmacies, C should be able to build a loyal customer base, and may be able to increase sales by capturing business which previously went to its competitors in the market.

(iii) **Customer relationships** – The removal of the wholesalers will **shorten the supply chain**, and will allow C to build closer relationships with the pharmacies. This could allow them to gain a better understanding of the market.

(iv) **Good public relations** – There may also be some public relations benefits to C from the new arrangement. If they are seen to be championing the cause of the small pharmacies, this would be a positive message to sell to the pharmaceutical industry.

In addition, there may be some **political capital** to be gained from the proposal, since government ministers have expressed concern about the power of the supermarkets.

However, there are also a number of disadvantages to the proposal.

Disadvantages to C of supplying directly to the pharmacies

Supplying directly to 4,000 independent pharmacies will require very different **logistical arrangements** to supplying to 10 wholesalers.

(i)   **Higher inventory costs** – Under the new arrangements, C will have much higher inventory costs than it currently incurs, because it will have to hold all the inventories itself rather than having them held at wholesalers' premises.

(ii) **Increased distribution costs** – Equally, the new arrangements will increase C's distribution costs, as a result of servicing 4,000 destinations rather than 10. C may even have to increase their transport fleet to cope with the increased demand.

(iii) **Uncertainty of order levels** – It is also likely that the independent pharmacies ordering systems will not be as sophisticated as the wholesalers, which could make it harder for C to plan their deliveries and inventory levels in advance.

(iv) **Increased sales and marketing costs** – The new arrangements may also increase C's sales and marketing costs, because instead of dealing with 10 wholesalers it will now need to with 4,000 independent customers. It may need to take on additional sales staff to deal with this increased burden.

(v)   **Threats to market share** – C could also **lose access to the main part of the market**. Supermarkets are taking a large share of the business and by refusing to supply them C will leave the market open to rivals to take increasing market share. This will particularly important if the independent pharmacy sector declines with the growth of supermarket pharmacies.

(vi) **Bad debt risks** – C's exposure to bad debt risks will increase. C will need to assess and monitor the credit worthiness of 4,000 clients rather than 10. This will be expensive and, it is assumed, some of the 4,000 may still end up as bad debts.

The additional costs arising from (i) – (vi) are likely to significantly reduce the benefits gained from not having to pay the wholesalers a share of the margin.

C may feel the increased number of customers is not desirable from a **supply chain management** perspective, and so it may decide not to supply all of the independent customers. Instead it may choose to concentrate resources on the pharmacists which buy relatively more drugs. However, restricting the market in this way will reduce sales below the level they would be if C continued to supply all the pharmacies.

It is also possible that the independent pharmacies may prefer dealing with a wholesaler rather than the manufacturing. Therefore, if C changes its practice some of the pharmacies may stop buying from it and choose to buy their drugs from one of C's six competitors who still use the wholesaler.

At a broader level, the **competition from the supermarkets** represents a potential threat to the long-term viability of the independent pharmacies. If the supermarkets can capture market share from the independents, possibly even forcing some of them out of business, then C's sales will decline unless it also moves to supply the supermarkets.

It is possible that the supermarkets may also use their buying power to depress the cost of the drugs supplied by the pharmaceutical companies. This again will present a threat to C's future income streams.

Part (b)

> **Top tips.** Again, this requirement requires you to draw information from the scenario to shape your answer. This should have allowed you to relate the issues surrounding outsourcing specifically to the question, and this is what was required here. A general discussion of the advantages and disadvantages of outsourcing would not have scored well.
>
> We have included a number of advantages and disadvantages all of which are relevant to the decision to outsource the transport function. However, this question is only worth 8 marks, and so you would not need to cover all these points to score well. The points in text boxes at the end of the 'advantages' and 'disadvantages' are relevant points which would have earned you marks if you included them, but you could have still passed the question without including them. Nonetheless, you would need a balance of advantages and disadvantages to pass the question, because the marks available were split between them.

There are a number of advantages to C's proposal to outsource the transport function if it decides to supply the independent pharmacies directly.

Advantages to C of outsourcing the transport function

(i) **Removes uncertainty over costs** – If C decides to supply the independent pharmacies directly, then its transport costs will increase significantly. However, by outsourcing the transport costs – and agreeing a contract for a fixed price with the transport company – then any uncertainty about the level of future costs is removed.

(ii) **Avoids capital expenditure** – The decision to outsource will mean that C does not have to increase the size of its transport fleet to cope with the extra number of deliveries required to service 4,000 independent pharmacies. This could result in a **considerable saving in capital expenditure** if C has a policy of buying assets rather than leasing them.

(iii) **Focus on core competences** – C will be **concentrating on its core business** of pharmaceutical manufacturing rather than diversifying into transport and distribution which it has less experience in.

(iv) **Benefit from economies of scale** – The transport company should benefit from economies of scale in transport and distribution costs which C cannot match. Therefore outsourcing should lead to cost savings at a cost per unit basis (although not all of these will be passed on to C because the transport company will look to make a profit on its operations).

(v) **Scalability of resources** – Outsourcing will allow **flexibility in transport services** which C could not provide in its own right. The transport company will be able to scale up or scale down resources depending on demand whereas C could not do this in its own right.

(vi) **Transfer of risk**. Providing the service agreement has penalty clauses built in, C can receive financial compensation for breakdowns in logistics which, if it operated its own logistics, it would not.

However, there are also a number of disadvantages to the proposal.

Disadvantages to C of outsourcing the transport function

(i) **Transport and distribution are crucial to the success of C's business model** – Although transport is not part of C's core business, under the new proposals the success of the transport and distribution network will be crucial to the relationship between C and the pharmacies. By outsourcing the transport function,

C's control over the service delivery to its customers may be reduced, and if service levels slip then C's reputation with its customers will be affected. Management may decide that transport is too important a part of the business model to be outsourced.

(ii) **Loss of control** – The potential loss of control over the transport function is indicative of a general issue with outsourcing which C's management will need to be aware of. Outsourcing leads to a loss of managerial control, because it is more difficult to manage outside service providers than managing one's own employees.

(iii) **Redundancies and negative PR** – Because C already has a transport function, then the employees currently working in this area will be made redundant when it is outsourced, unless their contracts can be transferred to the external company. Such redeployment seems very unlikely though. The redundancies may generate negative publicity, which will reduce the PR benefits which we noted C could gain through being seen as a champion of the independent pharmacies.

(iv) **Tied in to contract** – If C signs a long-term deal with the transport company, it may find itself locked into an unsatisfactory contract, especially if it has no previous experience of arranging similar contracts.

(v) **Hidden costs** – There may also be hidden costs associated with the outsourcing contract. These could include the legal costs related to drawing up the contract for services between C and the transport company, and the time spent co-ordinating the contract.

Part (c)

> **Top tips.** Although (c) was the shortest part of this question and there are only seven marks available, there are still essentially two stages to answering this question (identify the principal stakeholders; then recommend the most appropriate form of communication). You should have remembered the mnemonic 'ICE' to help identify types of shareholders: internal, connected, external.
>
> However, because of the limited number of marks available you should have confined your answer to principal stakeholders only. Again, your answer must relate to the scenario. Any general discussions about types of stakeholders (or discussions about stakeholder mapping and Mendelow's matrix) would have earned no marks.
>
> Remember that the main focus of the question is how C might best communicate the decision to the stakeholders.
>
> **Examiner's comments.** Part (c) was poorly answered. Too many students gave a general discussion of Mendelow's matrix. This is not what the question asked for, and so any such answers earned no marks.

We recommend that the following stakeholders should be informed in the ways outlined below:

Internal stakeholders

Transport department staff – This group of stakeholders needs to be handled sensitively because this department is the one likely to be most affected by the changes. The message should be communicated by a member of the management team, accompanied by an HR representative, in a **face to face meeting** with the department.

Although we do not know whether the transport function is going to be outsourced, the staff are still likely to be concerned about the changes which the new proposals will have on their work. So the meeting should try to allay these concerns as far as possible, and show C to be a reasonable and considerate employer.

Connected stakeholders

Independent pharmacies – Initially, C should send a **letter to all the pharmacies** explaining the changes, with the letter including the date the changes will come into effect and the practical implications of them for the pharmacies' regular drugs orders. C should also consider setting up a **web-site** with some 'Frequently Asked Questions' which the pharmacies can consult to see how the changes will affect them.

Following the initial mail-out, should arrange some **area meetings**, in which the sales representative for an area invites the pharmacies in that area to come and discuss any issues with him or her. This face-to-face contact should help reinforce the relationship between C and the pharmacies.

C should also consider placing a general **announcement in the trade press** summarising the changes.

Wholesalers – The decision to stop using wholesalers should be communicated to each wholesaler individually in a meeting between a member of C's **management team** and a member of the wholesaler's management team.

C should explain the reasons behind the decision, and also agree a timetable for implementing the new arrangements.

External shareholders

Doctors' surgeries – C should **write to all the doctors' surgeries** explaining why they are changing their distribution networks, and emphasising the benefits for the local pharmacies and the local communities.

Local communities – C should consider publicity in **local newspapers** to promote their public relations message that they are protecting the local community and the local traders against the encroachment of the supermarkets.

Both of these communications to external shareholders should be designed to encourage people to use the local pharmacies, because this will in turn support C's sales.

29 Contact Services

Text reference. Types of strategic change are discussed in chapter 10 of the Study Text. Culture and the internal context of change are also discussed in Chapter 10.

Part (a)

Top tips. Part (a) asked you to analyse the type of change which the proposed strategy at Contact Services. Although you were not required to use any models in your answer, Balogun & Hope Hailey's matrix dealing with the nature and scope of change could have been a useful framework for your answer.

However, to score well you shouldn't spend a long time simply describing a theoretical model of change, but rather you should demonstrate your understanding of the model by applying it to analyse the specific type of change Contact Services is facing.

The answer below takes each of the four quadrants of the Balogun & Hope Hailey's matrix and then assesses the situation at Contact Services to see which quadrant it fits best. As with many E3 questions, there isn't a definitive right answer – is the change best viewed as adaptation or is it evolution? – but provided your argument is sensible, and you support it with evidence from the scenario, you will score marks.

Contact Services currently sells to a specialist **niche market** – the retail pharmacy market. Therefore the proposed strategic change – to sell to the **general retail market** – represents a **significant change to Contact Services' product and its market**. In this respect, it represents a **diversification strategy**.

We can analyse the type of change by applying Balogun & Hope Hailey's change matrix and looking at the nature and scope of the change.

Nature of change

The nature of a change looks at whether it is incremental or a one-off, 'Big Bang' change.

Incremental change builds on existing methods and approaches rather than challenging them. However, a **'Big Bang' change** involves a major change to existing methods, processes and cultures. Such an approach is usually required in times of crisis when rapid responses are required.

Scope of change

The scope of a change describes the extent of a change; the degree to which an organisation's business activities or its business model need changing. In this respect, a change can either be a **realignment** of a firm's existing strategy, or it can be a **transformational change** in which radical changes are made to the existing business model.

Types of change

Balogun & Hope Hailey's change matrix allows four different types of change to be identified: adaptation, reconstruction, evolution, revolution.

Adaptation is a change where the **existing business model is retained**, and the change only occurs incrementally. Because the proposed change at Contact Services represents a diversification of strategy, it is debatable whether the existing business model will remain valid.

The chief executive and the sales and marketing director may see the move to selling to the general retail industry as an adaptation of the existing model, but the reasons behind the software director's resistance to the change suggest that the change will involve a more significant transformation.

Reconstruction requires a significant, and rapid, change in the operations and process of an organisation often in **response to crisis** such as a long-term decline in performance. However, it does not involve any major change to the business model.

The proposed changes at Contact Services are borne out of a desire for growth, rather than being a rapid response to any critical problems facing the company. Therefore, they do not represent a reconstruction.

Revolution is rapid and wide ranging response to extreme pressures for change. It is likely to require a fundamental shift in the business model, and in the way a company operates. Although the proposed changes at Contact Services represent a diversification, the pace of change is unlikely to be rapid enough to represent a revolution.

Evolution is an incremental process that leads to a new business model. Evolutionary change often arises as a result of business analysis, leading to a **planned change**.

Evolution best describes the changes at Contact Services. The move into the generic retail market represents a **fundamental change in strategic direction** and it is likely that the company's processes and structure will have to change significantly to develop and sell the new packages successfully.

The change has come about due the chief executive's **desire to grow the business rather than in response to external financial pressures**. Therefore the changes are likely to be relatively incremental rather than requiring a sudden reconstruction of the business. In this respect, the proposed change at Contact Services may best be described as incremental.

Part (b)

> **Top tips.** As with part (a), part (b) did not require you to use any specific models, however the reference to 'internal factors' should have alerted you that the Balogun & Hope Hailey's eight contextual features (the change kaleidoscope) might be a use framework here. The model identifies time, scope, preservation, diversity, capability, capacity, readiness and power as features which can affect the success of a change programme.
>
> We have used this contextual features model in the answer below, but equally you could have used the Cultural web or the McKinsey 7S framework to help generate ideas instead.
>
> The key point though is that you need to discuss enough different factors to earn a good proportion of the 15 marks available here. If you work on the basis of a maximum of 3 marks for each factor you discuss, you should be looking to identify 4 or 5 different factors here, and then apply them to the specific change scenario at Contact Services to score well.
>
> **Easy marks.** If you were familiar with the contextual features model, you should have scored well in part (b) because the scenario gave plenty of clues about things that could affect the success of the proposed change: for example, the company wants to move to a bigger marketplace even though they are struggling to meet the demand from their existing marketplace; software is key to the project, but the software director is unenthusiastic about it, and appears to be alienated from his fellow directors etc.
>
> **Tutorial note.** For tutorial purposes, the answer below includes all the headings from the contextual features model because all of them are relevant here. However, on the assumption that up to 3 marks would be available for each feature, you would not need to include all 8 features to pass this question.

The context of change

The context of change is provided by the organisational setting. It has many aspects and can therefore be very complex. However, we can organise the internal contextual features of change into eight main categories, to look at the way they could influence the success or failure of the chief executive's proposed change at Contact Services.

Time

No need to rush – Many companies are forced into changes in response to difficulties they are facing in their business. However, Contact Services does not appear to be facing any financial problems are so time is not pressing in that respect. This should allow them time to plan the changes carefully before implementing them.

Development time – Given that the software development team already appears to be under pressure to deliver and upgrade the current package, it also seems unlikely that they will be able to develop the software package for the general market quickly. Therefore a longer time scale may be more realistic anyway.

Chief executive's expectations – However, the chief executive wants to introduce the changes quickly to accelerate the growth of the company and make it an attractive acquisition target. So the timetable for change could become a **source of conflict** between the chief executive and the software director and his staff.

Scope of change

Evolution or adaptation – We have already suggested in part (a) that the proposed changes represent an evolutionary change, because the change from serving a niche market to serving a general retail market represents a substantial change of focus. This suggests the proposal might be more risky than if it were for an adaptive change only.

Changes to marketing mix – Moreover, Contact Services will need to develop new marketing skills for selling to a general market rather than to a specific niche market.

One possible threat to the success of the change is if the chief executive and the sales and marketing director underestimate the scope of the change.

Preservation

Software developers – The software development team are critical to the success of the proposed changes, and Contact Services' business more generally. Therefore it is vital that Contact Services **retains as many of its key software staff as possible**.

However, the software developers are already under constant pressure to meet the demands of existing customers, and so if their workload is increased still further a number may decide to leave.

If too many of the software developers leave Contact Services, the whole change project could be jeopardised.

Software development director – Persuading the software development director to support the changes will also be crucial to their success. Not only is a supportive director more likely to lead to support from the software developers themselves (and to stop them leaving), but the director will also need to play a key role in the design of the new product.

Diversity

Diversity of experience – Making changes is likely to be relatively easier in companies which have experience of different ways of doing things. However, it appears that Contact Services has very little diversity of experience and has been following a single, specialist, strategy for many years.

Therefore, it appears that the business' current experience does not support the chief executive's ambitious plans for expansion. It has never been a large business, nor has it had external investors.

Diversity of expectations – The goals of the sales team and those of the software developers seem to conflict. The sales team is making promises to customers that the developers are struggling to meet. As a result, quality standards are falling leading to customer dissatisfaction.

As the business expands, this scope for differences and conflict between the sales team and the developers will increase. If these differences adversely Contact Services' product they could hamper its efforts to enter the new markets successfully. The diversity of expectations between the Chief Executive and the software development director has already been highlighted.

Capability

Capability to manage change – Although the chief executive and the sales and marketing director are both keen on the proposed changes, the software development director and his team are far less so.

The chief executive will need to **convince the software team of the merits of the proposals** so that they support the changes. If the software team remain unconvinced and unenthusiastic, the changes are unlikely to be successful, because the developer's input is crucial to the project.

Past experience – We do not now anything about the **directors' past experiences of managing change**. We know that the chief executive is an entrepreneur and risk taker so it is possible he has led some change projects in previous roles. However, if he or the other two directors do not have any previous experience of leading change programmes this could hinder the proposals.

Equally, we do not know if any of the software team has experienced change processes before, such that their experience could be used to increase the changes of success here.

Capacity

People – The software development director already wants to acquire further resources to support the existing product, because he feels Contact Services software team is already working to capacity. Therefore, it is likely that Contact Services will need to **recruit a significant number of suitably skilled new developers** to support the planned expansion. This will not only increase costs, it will also take **time** – to recruit new staff, and to allow them to become familiar with the existing software.

This timetable may again be problematic for the chief executive if he wants to progress quickly, and the quality of Contact Services' packages could suffer still further if developers have to start work on a product before they fully understand it.

Funding – We do not have any details about Contact Services' financial position, but it seems likely that it will have to increase its borrowings to fund the expansion. Contact Services is a private company, and so cannot raise capital through an issue of shares on the stock market. It could look to the current shareholders for additional funding, but that means essentially looking to the directors.

The software development director is unlikely to fund changes he does not support, and the chief executive seems keener on getting money out of the company by selling it rather than investing in it further. Consequently, Contact Services' plans could be constrained by the amount of additional loan funding they can raise from their banks.

Readiness for change

The software developers would prefer to improve the existing software package they offer customers rather than moving to this new generic package. Therefore it is likely that they will **resist the chief executives proposed changes rather than supporting them**.

Moreover, since Contact Services has been **growing gradually** over the last three years, there is little no evidence to suggest it is ready for the significant changes proposed.

Power

The **chief executive appears to be the dominant power** at Contact Services, supported by the sales and marketing director. However, in practical terms, the success of the changes depends on the software team and the software development director.

The software development director appears justified in being cautious about the changes. However, there is a risk that the other directors will **force through the changes**, possibly even by buying out the software director's shares and replacing him with a new director. Such an aggressive strategy is unlikely to be successful, however, and could lead to Contact Services' revenues falling rather than the business growing if the reputation of its product falls further.

30 Brian Jolson

> **Text reference**. Models of change and force field analysis are discussed in Chapter 9; styles of managing change are discussed in Chapter 10.

Part (a)

> **Top tips**. A useful way to approach part (a) is to identify the main types of issue Brian needs to consider. There are two main issues:
>
> - Identifying the context of change and key stakeholders affected by it
> - The forces driving change, and those resisting change

> Looking at these issues in turn provides a useful framework for approaching the requirement, and this is the structure we have adopted in the answer below.
>
> However, remember that while models such as force field analysis could be useful in helping to generate ideas, you should not spend time simply describing models. Instead you need to relate your ideas specifically to the scenario to score well in this question.

There are two main aspects which Brian should look at when considering how to change the way the city is policed:

(i) The context of the change
(ii) Forces facilitating and blocking the change

The context of change

The context of the change needs to be considered by looking at the **stakeholders** who will be affected by it. Their **readiness** to change or their **resistance** to it will have a significant impact on Brian's **ability to implement any changes**.

The **key players** for any project are those who have both a **high level of power** and also a **high level of interest** in the project. For any changes to be successfully implemented, they must be **acceptable to the key players**. Therefore, it is important to understand the perspectives of these groups while preparing for change.

The two most important stakeholder groups in this respect are the senior police officers; and the city's courts.

Senior police officers in charge of the city's districts will be directly responsible to implementing any changes. They will need to be convinced of the **need for change** otherwise they will not support the change and accordingly the staff who work for them are unlikely to support it either. The need for change could be demonstrated by arranging for the senior police officers to meet some of the residents who feel they have no contact with the police, and feel that the city is currently a very unpleasant place to live and work.

The **City's courts** also need to be persuaded to support the new antisocial behaviour measures. For the measures to be successful, the courts need to deal with the cases brought before them, despite this creating extra work for them. It may be possible to use the influence of the mayor and the media here to help make the courts more responsive to the ideas of change.

Although the **press** could affect how the public perceive the changes, they will not actually be involved in delivering the changes. Similarly, although the **mayor** is keen to improve the image of the city, he won't be involved in implementing the changes either.

Alongside this stakeholder analysis, Brian should also consider the **capacity** to undertake change – with particular reference to any **cost** and **time constraints** which could prohibit changes. For example, there is already a perceived shortage of police resources in the city. Will Brian be able to obtain the budget funding necessary to recruit any additional police officers required for the new proposals?

Forces facilitating and blocking change

City courts – The reference to the courts as a key stakeholder has already identified that there could be resistance to the change. A very important aspect of successfully implementing the changes required will be reducing the factors that could hinder change.

At the same time, it is important to identify those **factors that will promote change and strengthening them**.

Brian should considering analysing the various driving forces supporting change and those resisting it by means of a **force field analysis.** This will allow him identify some effective ways of introducing the changes, and to identify some possible ways of weakening the forces which are resisting change.

In conjunction with the force field analysis, Brian should also consider how he is actually going to implement the changes. In this respect, he could look at the change process as having three stages: unfreeze, change, and refreeze.

Unfreeze

This stage will involve getting the various stakeholders to **recognise and accept the need to change**. We have already identified that the crucial issues here are persuading the senior officers and the courts that the current policing policy is not serving the residents of the city well and so needs changing.

Change

Once the need to change has been recognised, Brian will need to communicate the detail of the changes to his officers, and offer support and training to them as necessary. These changes will affect the way **police resources are deployed**, and the way **crime statistics are measured** and publicised.

The new strategy will represent **a major change for policing** in the city, because it will affect most aspects of what the police force does, and how it does them. This will also include **changing the culture** of the police forces – encouraging them to work together to share information, as opposed to their current practices of working in isolation from one another.

It is likely that Brian will need to demonstrate some 'quick wins' showing the positive results which can be achieved through the new strategy to reinforce stakeholder support for it.

Refreeze

Once the new strategy has been introduced, measures will need to be put in place to **ensure that it remains in place**, and that behaviours do not slip back to the way they were before the change. This may involve introducing both rewards and sanctions to ensure that the officers and the courts continue to support the new strategy.

However, the most likely way of ensuring a **long-term commitment to the change** will be through showing how the new strategy is benefiting the city and its residents. The press could play an important part in communicating this message.

Part (b)

> **Top tips.** As with part (a), although there is a theoretical framework which you can use to help you with your answer to (b), your answer must still relate back to scenario. However, applying *Johnson, Scholes and Whittington's* five styles of change management – education and communication; collaboration / participation; intervention; direction; coercion/edict – should provide a good framework for answering this requirement.
>
> Note that the question asks you to *analyse* the styles rather than recommend a preferred style, so you do not have to suggest any single style which Brian should adopt. In fact, the key point here is to note that there *are* a variety of styles available to him, and different styles are appropriate in different circumstances.
>
> **Easy marks**. If you know the styles of change management as listed above, then requirement (b) should offer a number of easy marks because it only requires a relatively simple application of this knowledge.

The changes Brian is proposing are likely to have a significant impact on people's circumstances, and the manner in which the changes are introduced will be very important in them being implemented successfully.

There are five styles of change management which Brian should consider.

Education and communication

The reasons for the changes and the means by which they will be achieved should be explained in detail to those affected by them. This will be crucial in **getting the police officers to support the need for change**. Change will only be possible if the police officers alter their perception of the nature and size of the city centre problem.

Communication will also be important in keeping other stakeholders informed about the need for change. In this scenario, the mayor should be kept informed of the need for change, while Brian should also communicate regularly with the press, because they play a key role in determining how the changes are presented to the residents of the city.

Collaboration and participation

The people affected by strategic change should be included in the change management process.

Once Brian has convinced the senior police offers of the need for change, he then has to **motivate them to become involved in creating the new strategy**. Their involvement will bring experience and knowledge to the project and so should improve the chance of getting the best solution to the problem.

Moreover, by involving the officers in the decision-making process, they are more likely to have a **sense of ownership of the project**. Again, this will improve the chances of it being successful.

However, both education and communication, and collaboration and participation can be **time-consuming processes** so Brian will need to make sure that he does not allow them to slow the overall change management process down.

Intervention

At some points in the change process, Brian may need to **delegate certain aspects of the change process to others**, possibly some of the senior officers who have been involved in the decision-making. This should increase their commitment to the project and their sense of ownership of it.

However, Brian should continue to provide guidance to his delegates, and **retain the overall control and responsibility** for managing the change process.

Direction

At other points in the change process, it may be necessary for Brian to **take direct control** to provide **speed and clarity to the change management programme**.

Whereas the first three change management styles we have recommended are based on involving others in the process, **direction is a top-down style,** which is suitable for transformational rather than incremental change. However, while it has the advantage of speeding-up the process, it may also **lead to resistance** and **could lead to a poorly conceived strategy** if Brian implements changes without consulting enough stakeholders.

Coercion/edict

Coercion is an extreme form of direction which Brian may have to **use in times of crisis to impose change**.

Coercion is **likely to provoke opposition**, and so is likely to be the least successful means of managing change. Therefore it should only be **used in exceptional circumstances**.

It is likely that Brian will need to use a combination of all of these styles in the change management programme, taking different approaches with different stakeholders and at different times of the process. His experience from previous change management appointments should help him select the most appropriate style for each situation.

31 Heritage Trust

Study Reference. The role of change agents is discussed in chapter 10 of the study text. Culture and change (including the ideas of the cultural web) are also discussed in Chapter 10.

Part (a)

Top tips. Part (a) is a purely knowledge based requirement. You are not asked to apply your knowledge to the scenario. However, note the requirement is only worth 5 marks, so you are not required to give an in-depth analysis of the role of a change agent in leading change. Note also that the verb is 'explain' which is only level 2 in the CIMA list of verbs, unlike 'discuss' (part b) which is a level 4 verb.

Easy marks. If you knew this subject area well, Part (a) should have offered some easy marks because it did not require any application. But there are only 5 marks available here.

A **change agent** is an individual or group that helps to bring about strategic change in an organisation. The agent has to manipulate and **exploit triggers for change** so that the drive for change gains momentum in an organisation.

The precise role of the change agent varies depending on the brief they have been given, but it is likely to include:

- Defining the change problem being faced
- Suggesting possible solutions to that problem
- Selecting and implementing a solution
- Gaining support from all involved

The change agent must possess the skills to **manage the transition process**, but must also have the determination to see the change through.

The change agent needs to **encourage** those who are going to be affected by change to participate and get involved in the management of the change. This helps stimulate interest and commitment to the change, and should help minimise fears and opposition to the change.

The change agent needs to **communicate** across a range of business units and functions, and across a network of different stakeholders, so that they all work together to enable the change to be implemented.

Part (b)

Top Tip. Unlike part (a), part (b) does require you to apply your knowledge specifically to the context and the scenario. Although you are not required to use any specific models, the reference to 'underlying organisational cultural issues' should have been a clue that the cultural web could be useful to you here.

A sensible approach would be to use the cultural web as a framework for your answer, and select five aspects of the web from which to identify the relevant cultural issues and explain their impact on the strategy. Note the question specifically requires you to select **five** underlying issues, so make sure you do: no more, no less!

The scenario gives a clear picture of a number of aspects of the Trust's existing culture, and suggests that the new Director General's strategy has been opposed because it challenges these.

The model answer below uses the cultural web as its framework, but if you explored the cultural perspectives using a different framework you would still score marks – provided you link the cultural issues directly to the resistance to the Director General's strategy.

To score well in this requirement you need to identify the relevant cultural issues at the Trust, and then explain why they have led to the Director General's strategy being resisted.

Easy marks. Part (b) requires detailed application to the scenario, but if you worked methodically through the scenario you should have been able to identify a number of issues which would have caused resistance to the Director General's plans.

Tutorial note: The answer below looks at all the aspects of the cultural web to illustrate the range of valid points you could have made here. However, we have shown the sixth aspect we cover ('stories') in a text box to reflect the fact that the question only asked for five. You would have scored marks for any five relevant issues, but for five only.

One of the main reasons why the Director General's strategy has been resisted by the Trust's managers is that she **failed to understand its culture** and therefore the way its staff behaved. The Trust's culture can be assessed by looking at its **cultural web**, and from this we can identify five underlying issues which have caused the Director General's plans to be resisted.

Symbols

Symbols are the **representations of an organisation's culture** – they can be visual (for example, large offices for managers) or verbal (for example, titles given to staff).

At the Trust, symbols such as the **accommodation** and **personal assistants** for the managers at the flagship properties indicate that these people are considered very important. Moreover, these symbols clearly demonstrate that importance to other people in the Trust.

Threats to status – The proposal to **remove the managers' personal assistants** would have involved removing a key status symbol, and would therefore have been very unpopular with the flagship managers. Furthermore, by making such a suggestion and challenging their status, the Director General would have immediately **made these managers hostile** to any other suggestions she might have had.

Power Structures

The power structures of an organisation reflect who has the real power in an organisation, and who has the greatest influence on decisions and the strategic direction of that organisation.

The **Trustees** are all well-known and respected figures in heritage and the arts and so this has promoted a culture in which **aesthetic importance** is valued above popularity with visitors.

The managers of the flagship properties have done little to challenge this, so we might suggest that they also have implicitly been preserving their own power.

Threat to power structures – However, the appointment of a Director General with a background in commerce rather than heritage and the arts, threatens to **challenging the whole purpose of the organisation**. Does it exist purely for heritage and artistic purposes or does it also seek to generate as much revenue as it can?

The Trustees appear to realise the need for change, but the flagship managers are likely to be more hostile, recognising that the need for a more commercial focus could jeopardise the privileges they earn, without seemingly having to do very much to justify them.

Organisational structures

The scenario does not tell us about the current organisational structure of the Trust, but it is likely that the organisational structure is likely to reflect the power structure.

However, the DG's proposals to recruit new business development managers illustrate that **commercial activities will no longer be secondary considerations** for the Trust.

The idea of introducing **commercially focused managers** represents a significant change in the Trust's priorities, but this again is likely to be unpopular with the existing property managers, particularly the flagship managers.

Control Systems

The control systems of an organisation concern the way it is controlled. They include financial systems, quality systems and rewards. Looking at the areas which are controlled most closely can indicate what is seen as most important to an organisation.

Allocation of budgets – The budgets at the Trust again reflect the **dominance and importance given to the flagship properties**, and art or antique collections of historical merit.

However, these controls suggest a **fairly inflexible environment**. The budget seems to be allocated according to a formula rather than to reflect the needs of the individual properties. For example, there does not seem to be any scope for the less high profile properties to get extra funding even if, for example, they need it for major repair works. In effect, the system seems designed to **reinforce the importance and prestige of the flagship properties**.

Inward-looking focus – The Trust's controls indicate an inward-looking focus (budgets to maintain the collections), rather than a focus on any external indicators, such as visitor numbers. This may indicate that the Trust is not used to having to measure performance, and, perhaps more importantly, it does not use performance as a means of allocating rewards.

Change of approach – In the context of control systems, the DG's proposal is likely to be unpopular for two different:

(i) it is using an **external measure** (visitor numbers) to allocate budgets, and it allocates the budget on **actual performance** rather than status
(ii) it could be seen to be **challenging the superiority and status of the 'flagship' properties**, by offering smaller properties the chance to increase their budgets if they can increase visitor numbers.

Rituals and Routines

The behaviour and actions of people in an organisation signal what is considered acceptable behaviour in that organisation.

The property managers seem to think it is acceptable to **lobby individual Trustees** to express their concerns with the DG's proposals.

Perhaps more importantly, the Directors seem to think it is **acceptable for them to write letters to the press and appear on television** to promote their views and gather support in opposition to the DG's plans.

Lobbying to resist changes – The DG was recruited by the Trustees specifically to help the Trust adjust to its new funding position, but the managers now seem to be trying to undermine her plans.

Ultimately, this is a short-sighted position, because if the Trust does not increase its funding, it will have a 15% reduction in income compared to its current position, suggesting that it will not be financially sustainable. However, this may **reflects the power structure** in the Trust, where financial and commercial interests are seen as less important than preserving the status of the flagship properties.

Stories

Stories are used by members of the organisation to illustrate the sorts of things it values.

In the Trust, the **stories reinforce the impression given by its power structures.** We have already seen that the power structures are directed towards heritage rather than promoting the popularity of the properties with the general public.

For example, by dismissing the **idea of linking budgets to visitor numbers** and accusing the DG of 'devaluing the historical significance of the properties in a search for popularity' the flagship property managers are suggesting that the **public are undiscerning**, and therefore cannot really be expected to appreciate the value of the properties they visit.

Self-interest vs. commercial management – Overall, the stories reinforce the idea that the managers **do not really value management and commerce**. The inference that the new DG cannot understand how the Trust operates because she has only run shops before can be seen as an attempt to denigrate her commercial background.

However, the reality behind the stories is probably that the managers feel threatened by someone actually reviewing whether they deserve their positions and privileges, but they are using their stories to try and disguise this concern.

Part (c)

Top tips. The scenario highlights that managers across the Trust have been particularly critical about the lack of consultation about the proposed changes. Resistance to change is often caused when the triggers for the change have not been communicated effectively.

Therefore, communication and consultation with the managers could be vital in overcoming resistance to the plans.

This is the approach we have taken in our answer below.

However, you could also have looked at this question in terms of a force field analysis, and looked at the issues which needed to be addressed to unfreeze the existing structure in order to facilitate change.

Note, however, that the question asks you to 'recommend the steps that could be taken' so you must make sure that your answer focuses on the possible steps to overcome the resistance rather than simply analysing the causes of the resistance itself.

Communication plays a vital role in the change management process, and the fact that the Trust's management have been very critical of the lack of consultation throughout the process suggests that the way the DG has communicated the changes and the need for change has not been very effective.

The manager's resistance could be overcome by a clear communication process, which should include the following steps.

Communication. As soon as possible, the DG should explain the need for the changes to the managers, in particular that the reduction in government grants means that the Trust needs to increase the income it generates from its own commercial activities.

One of the managers' concerns appears to be that they are concerned the DG is devaluing the history and culture of the Trust. However, by explaining the context of the changes, the DG might be able to reassure the managers that the changes are not designed to undermine their status within the organisation, but are driven by the economic pressures which the organisation will face going forward.

Education. In the communication process, the DG should also explain the aims of her strategy, and how it will address the issues caused by the reduction in government grants. She should also explain how she proposes to implement it.

Consultation. However, it is important that the managers are not simply told what the strategy is and how it will be implemented, but that they are consulted about it. Not only may the managers have valuable experience or suggestions which could help improve aspects of the strategy itself, but they are also more likely to support the strategy if they feel they have been involved in developing it.

Negotiation. Despite the communication and consultation process, there will inevitably still be some managers who still feel aggrieved by the changes, and by their loss of status. The will need to be a process of negotiation with these managers, and the Trust may need to make some concessions to encourage them to accept the changes.

Manipulation. The Trust may also need to manipulate some managers by appealing to their better nature and asking them to set aside their personal ambition for the good of the Trust as a whole.

32 Goldcorn

Text Reference. Types of change are discussed in chapter 10 of the BPP study text. Resistance to change is discussed in chapter 9; change and communication are discussed in chapter 10.

Part (a)

Top tips. Note that part (a) does not only require you analyse the current change programme, but also to compare it with the previous cost reduction efforts. In what way are the changes similar and in what ways are they different?

A good way to approach this question is to consider the characteristics of the two change programmes in turn, and highlight the differences between them. The scenario gives you a number of clues about the characteristics of the changes and you should use these as a framework around which to build your answer.

For example, you could consider: the level of change (strategic vs operational); the nature and scope of change (transformational vs adaptive; on-going vs one-off); whether the change is planned or forced; and whether the triggers for change are internal or external.

The finance director's proposal is much more extensive than previous change programmes, and in large part this reflects the changing environment in which Goldcorn is operating. We can highlight how the current programmes differs from the previous ones by looking at a number of key aspects of change.

Level of change

Change can take place at different levels within an organisation: from strategic changes which affect the whole outlook of the organisation, to process changes which affect individual business processes.

Current proposal – The current proposal for the **change to global production** is a **strategic change**. This is a change that affects the long-term direction of the entire organisation both in terms of its production capability and in terms of its market competitiveness.

Previous changes – Previous cost reduction exercises appear to have been at a lower level in the company, being restricted to individual factories. They have included changes at the **structural level**, for example with changes in the reporting structures.

However, the main focus of the previous changes seem to have been at a **process level**. For example, certain processes have been **outsourced** to try to improve efficiency, and similarly there have been selective redundancies.

These previous changes have been necessary to deliver the existing business strategy more efficiently and effectively. However, they have not tried to change the Goldcorn's overall strategy, whereas the FD's current proposal does.

Nonetheless, while the new proposal is primarily at the strategic level, implementing the changes will still include changes at the structural and process levels.

Nature and scope of change

The FD's proposal also differs from the previous cost reduction exercises in terms of the nature and scope of the change required.

Adaptive changes – The previous changes are have not tried to change the overall strategy or working practices. We could argue that outsourcing constitutes a **reconstruction** rather than simply an adaptation, but the nonetheless the changes have not fundamentally changed Goldcorn's existing structure.

Continuous change – Moreover, the previous cost reduction programmes seem to be an **on-going process** of trying to make Goldcorn most cost efficient. By contrast, the FD's globalisation proposal seems to be a **one-off change**.

Transformative changes – The FD's proposal will completely change Goldcorn's current structure and working practices. It could also require a major change in culture, as the manufacturing sites move from producing a range of products to mass-producing a single design.

The threat of the new entrant means that Goldcorn needs to take rapid and drastic action, with the FD recommending that his change programme be completed within six months. This wide-ranging and fast-paced change could be seen as a **revolution**.

Triggers for change

The trigger for the FD's proposal is **external**. The threat of the new external competitor has forced Goldcorn into making changes. Although it is now making plans for how to deal with the threat (so the change is planned to an extent) Goldcorn has essentially been **forced** to act by the external threat.

However, the triggers for the previous, smaller-scale changes have been **internal**. Goldcorn has **planned** the cost reduction programmes itself to improve its efficiency.

Predictability of outcome

The scale of the FD's proposals also means that it is much harder to predict their impact on Goldcorn compared to the smaller-scale changes. For example, these proposals will disrupt all the company's supply chains, both upstream and downstream, and they will fundamentally change the organisational structure – changing the manufacturing sites from profit centres to cost centres.

The FD has recognised the **extent of the uncertainty involved**, which is why he has suggested that the situation should be reviewed in two years time.

By contrast, the previous cost reduction exercises were much more small-scale and so their outcomes were more predictable.

Part (b)

> **Top tips.** Make sure you read the question requirement very carefully before answering it. Before you can answer the requirement you need to identify who the key stakeholders are, and how the changes will affect them.
>
> However, the requirement is not primarily about identifying the stakeholders, so you should not have spent time simply explaining why certain stakeholders are key. Instead you need to identify how the changes will affect these key stakeholders, and therefore what their concerns about the changes will be. Goldcorn's communications with the stakeholders will need to reassure them about their concerns. This is one of the main reasons why Goldcorn needs to communicate with its key stakeholders.

Shareholders

Shareholders will be concerned about the triggers which has prompted the FD's programme, in particular the apparent threat to Goldcorn's market share and profitability. They will want reassurance that the new strategy can be implemented successfully and the changes will enable Goldcorn to compete and add value despite the new competition.

It will be important for Goldcorn to communicate regularly with the shareholders to explain the nature and impact of the changes. However, because Goldcorn is listed on an international stock market it also needs to ensure it complies with the regulations about insider trading. Therefore it will be important to communicate information openly and equally.

Employees

The production employees in one factory are going to be made redundant – unless they are relocated internationally which seems very unlikely. The production employees at the other three factories will also be facing significant changes, due to the way production is being reorganised.

The extent of these changes are likely to be a major concern to the workers, and are likely to hit morale among the workforce. It will be very important for Goldcorn's management to communicate effectively with its workers to minimise any negative impact from the changes. To this extent, it will be important to communicate the reasons for the changes, and also to explain how the changes are going to be implemented and how they will affect the workers.

Local management

Local management may also be made redundant in the factory which closes but may be more likely to be relocated than production staff. Other management will need to work under a new cost centre structure with less autonomy than they previously had.

However, the local managers will also be key figures in implementing change and acting as change agents. Therefore their support will be vital for the successful implementation of the change programme.

Therefore they should not only be informed of the changes, but also consulted about the best ways of actually implementing them.

Customers

Customers will need to be reassured that they will still be able to get their Goldcorn vehicles, despite the changes in production structure.

Goldcorn should run an advertising campaign in both the general press and the trade press to explain the changes, and also to highlight the benefits for the customer – for example, cheaper prices.

However, for this advertising message to be credible, Goldcorn needs to ensure that it can continue to supply all its customers during the change period. If dealers are unable to get the vehicles they want, this will render any advertising messages worthless. For this reason it may be necessary to stockpile some vehicles prior to the change.

Suppliers

Given the geographical shift in production there may need to be some changes in suppliers. These changes could be favourable to some suppliers where new production is located to their local factory, but for other suppliers the change may result in the termination of the relationship with Goldcorn.

It will be particularly important for Goldcorn to explain how the changes will affect the suppliers it continues to use, in order that those suppliers are able to guarantee the supply that Goldcorn needs from them.

Part (c)

> **Top tips.** You may be tempted to think that the answer to this question lies in the reaction the workers who stand to lose their jobs will have to the changes.
>
> However, while that is part of the answer, you shouldn't think only about individual people resisting change: aspects of the culture and structure of an organisation overall can also mean that the organisation tries to preserve its current ways of doing things rather than changing them.

Organisational culture and cultural barriers

The FD's proposal suggests fundamental changes that will affect the culture at Goldcorn. The new proposals will require the old culture based around **profit centres** and **geographical responsibility** will need to be unfrozen, and reset into a new global organisation.

However, the systems and procedures which Goldcorn has installed in the factories over the years to ensure they perform as well as they can may act as barriers to this change.

Power structures may be threatened by the redistribution of decision-making authority or resources, or the changing of lines of communication. For example, changing the factories from profit centres to cost centres indicates a reduction of decision-making authority in each factory.

This will affect the local managers in particular, and therefore they may be reluctant to implement changes which will be against their own interests.

Groups

Group inertia may block change where the changes are inconsistent with the preferred behaviour of teams and departments, or where they threaten their interests. The employees at the factory earmarked for closure are most likely to form a group to try to prevent the closure.

The marketing employees at all four factories may also form a group to resist change knowing that their jobs are most at risk from the centralisation of the marketing function.

If one or both of these groups are represented by a union they may also ask their union to support their cause as well.

However, their resistance may ultimately be futile, unless they can persuade Goldcorn that there is an alternative course of action it can follow and still fend off the threat of the new competitor.

Individual workers

Individual workers may also see the change as a threat. This may affect not only be workers in the factory that is destined to be closed, but also the employees in the other factories where there are likely to be substantial changes in work practices.

Workers will have got into **habits and routine** that they feel comfortable with, and the threat of having do things differently could make them feel uncomfortable.

For example, the globalisation and standardisation of production may mean they have to learn how to operate different machines on the production line.

Security. The workers are likely to see the change as threatening their security. For the site threatened with closure this will a loss of job security. But for workers at the other factories, the change will also lead to a loss of the security of familiarity.

The fear of the unknown could reduce worker's willingness and interest in **learning new skills**, not least because they may lack the confidence to take on a new challenge when their work practices change.

33 Chemico

Study Reference. Stakeholder analysis & CSR are discussed in Chapter 2 of the BPP Study Text; strategic alliances are discussed in Chapter 5, and change implementation is discussed in Chapter 10.

Part (a)

Top tips. The way to approach this question is to identify who the major stakeholders are, and then decide whether they will support or resist the proposal.

Note that there are effectively two aspects to the requirement:

- Identify the stakeholders' likely reactions to the proposal
- Consider the degree to which they will resist the proposal

If some stakeholder groups are likely to support the proposal rather than to resist it, you should say so.

Shareholders

Profitability – The shareholders will be keen that the **profitability** of the company is maintained because this will affect the return on their investments. Consequently, if developing the new product helps sustain profits they would be expected to support the proposal rather than resist it.

We do not know whether the shareholders are aware of the **alternative proposals** ChemiCo's directors have been considering (the alliance or the acquisition). If they are, and they think one of them would serve ChemiCo better commercially, then they may resist this first proposal in favour of one of these alternatives.

Risk of environmental pollution – As well as short term profitability, the shareholders are also likely to consider the longer term growth of their shares. In this respect, they may feel that the opportunities for enhancing the overall value of their investments would be jeopardised by the risk of toxic accidents.

Moreover, some of the larger institutional investors may decide they do not want to be associated with ChemiCo if its **corporate social responsibility** (CSR) policies are called into question.

The wider issue here is that ChemiCo must not been seen to **sacrificing safety in search for profits**.

Employees

Saving jobs – Given the lack of alternative employment opportunities in the region, keeping their jobs at the factory is crucial for the workers. So, from this perspective, the employees will support a change which seeks to preserve their jobs.

Health risks – However, avoiding health risks is also important to the workers. So the increased risk of toxic incidents attached to the new product will be a concern to them.

There is also a secondary issue here. We have assumed that the workers know about the health risks attached to the new product (because they have been highlighted by environmental campaigners). However, the directors may have convinced the workers that the risks are low, so that there are even less likely to resist the proposal.

Either way, the economic need to preserve their jobs is likely to mean that the workers are unlikely to resist the proposals.

Local residents

Conflicting interests – The local residents are likely to have the same dual interests as the staff. On the one hand, the community benefits from the **presence of a large employer** in the region (for example, people have more money to spend at local stores). If the proposal doesn't go ahead redundancies are likely, and this could have a knock-on effect throughout the rest of the regional economy (via the multiplier effect).

However, as with the employees the local residents will not welcome the introduction of a process which could potentially spill out **toxic waste**.

The residents are probably more likely to resist the proposal more than the workers, but it is debatable how much power residents alone could have to stop development.

Environmental campaigners

Environmental issues – The environmental campaigners will strongly oppose the proposals, because of the potential risk of toxic incident they present. The campaigners will be more concerned with the environmental costs of the proposal rather than the economic arguments for it.

Moreover, the campaigners have shown themselves to be **active in resisting the proposal**, and have already written to the local authorities. In terms of a force field analysis, the campaigners are likely to be the strongest resisting force acting against the proposal.

Regional government

Divided interests – Like the residents, the local authorities may also have split interests about the proposal.

On the one hand, they will want to **support ChemiCo as the largest employer** in the region, and they will want to keep income and jobs in the region. In this context, if they resist the proposal this could also discourage other potential investors who might have been looking to invest in the area.

However, on the other hand, the authorities will be aware of the **potential environmental risks** of the proposal, and will be concerned about any health risks the chemical processes might present.

Ultimately, the strength of their resistance is likely to depend on the level of toxic risk they think the new product presents.

Part (b)

> **Top tips.** A good way to approach this question is to think what ChemiCo could gain from entering a strategic alliance, but also what the logistical issues and business risks might be from doing so.
>
> The question asks you to 'evaluate the issues', so therefore you should present a balanced argument: you should look first at the potential advantages of the alliance, and then move on to look at its drawbacks. However, you must not just evaluate the advantages and disadvantages of strategic alliances in general – you must embed them in the context of the scenario and make them specifically relevant to ChemiCo.
>
> Note: you are not asked conclude whether or not ChemiCo should enter the alliance, and so you should not do so.

Sharing competences – Alliances can be a valuable learning exercise for each partner. Entering into an alliance would allow ChemiCo and its partner to exploit complementary competences for their mutual advantage. Therefore before agreeing to form the alliance ChemiCo should consider what distinctive competences both it and the potential partner are bringing to the venture. Can they be used for mutual advantage?

Risk sharing – New product development presents many uncertainties as well as opportunities. So sharing the funding of expensive research via an alliance can spread the risk. However, it also means that future profits will have to be shared.

Goal congruence – One of the most important things for ChemiCo to do before entering an alliance will be to work out where there might be potential conflicts of interest between the two companies.

Disagreements many arise of profit shares, resources invested, management issues (including project management), overall control of the specification of the product to be developed, and marketing strategy.

These issues must be resolved in advance, and agreed on a contractual basis, so that each party is clear about its rights and responsibilities.

People and culture – The directors should also consider staff and cultural issues, and whether the companies can work together. For example, it may take a while for staff from both companies to trust each other, and to share ideas with each other. If the two companies cannot develop this trust between themselves, then the alliance is unlikely to be successful.

Partnership costs – The alliance will involve sharing tangible expenses such as capital contribution, but also sharing intangibles such as expertise. Having **joint ownership of patents for products** that are developed by an alliance could lead to disputes about a fair share of future returns from them, unless the agreement is carefully and thoroughly worded. There could also be similar issues surrounding the **ownership** and **use of any intellectual property** generated by the alliance. The alliance may therefore include significant legal costs to deal with any such issues.

Business risk – ChemiCo is a big company, and so is likely to be the larger partner in the alliance. There is a risk therefore that the alliance partner might use the alliance as a means of finding out about its ChemiCo's technology.

Alternatively, ChemiCo might decide is wants to use the alliance as a stepping stone to a future takeover of the smaller company.

Part (c)

> **Top tips.** A sensible way to approach this question is to think about it in practical terms, rather than looking for theories and frameworks to base answer on.
>
> For example, effective leadership and management will be required to bring the two companies together; good communication will be important so that staff in both companies know what is happening and how it will affect them.
>
> Also, make sure you think about the specific context of the potential acquisition: a small, owner-managed business will be taken over by a much larger business. What will the implications of this be? (particularly in the smaller business).

Acquiring the plastics company would represent a **major organisational change** for ChemiCo. It will be necessary to integrate the target company's operations, techniques and people into the expanded company, while continuing to run the existing ChemiCo business.

Cultural issues – Mergers and acquisitions often fail to produce the expected benefits due to cultural incompatibilities between the two companies combining.

In this case, a small owner-managed business is being incorporated into a much bigger business. The policies and procedures which the staff from the small company are used to are likely to be very different to those in ChemiCo. If the acquisition is to be successful, the new staff will need to adapt to working within ChemiCo's structures. However, ChemiCo's management and staff can assist this process by making the new staff feel welcome into the business, and explaining how things are done.

Leadership – The success of the takeover will depend on effective leadership from ChemiCo's management.

The takeover is a **planned change**, and so the change process must be driven by the senior management. To be successful, the management must have a **clear vision** of their strategy for the merged business is going, and how to achieve it.

In turn this vision must be used to establish goals, and performance indicators, so that **performance across the whole business can be measured** against them.

Communication – Effective communication will be essential for both existing ChemiCo staff and staff from the newly acquired company to appreciate the reasons behind the deal, but perhaps more importantly to understand their roles and responsibilities in the new organisation going forward.

If staff from the local plastics company will be expected to use ChemiCo's policies and procedures then they will **need to be trained** so that they know what to do.

External communication – ChemiCo will need to decide how far the plastics business is rebranded (for example, will it be renamed ChemiCo Plastics?) and how the change of ownership is communicated to customers. It may be that the most practical solution is to allow the business to retain its current trading name, and reassure customers that business will continue as usual.

Management skills – The owner of the plastics business plans to retire, so ensuring a succession plan for running the plastics business will be essential. There may already be some managers in the business who can do this under this and effectively run it as an autonomous business unit within the ChemiCo 'group'.

It will be very important to establish what skills the staff within the business do have, because it is unlikely that ChemiCo's management know much about plastics manufacturing. Depending on the skills and commitment of the existing staff, it may be that ChemiCo have to recruit externally, to find a manager to run the new plastics division.

Redundancies – There are likely to be some redundancies after the acquisition, for example in the marketing and administration functions of the company being acquired. However, there may also be some redundancies in ChemiCo's production departments, because there is no guarantee the acquisition will completely reverse the decline in demand for ChemiCo's products.

The staff in both organisations will inevitably be apprehensive about the possibility of job losses. The best way to deal with such fears is to act as quickly as possible and determine whether any cuts are necessary. If they are, the cuts must be implemented fairly – for example, on basis of skills required going forward.

Given the lack of alternative employment opportunities in the region, losing their job will be a major problem for individual staff members. There is a chance that losing some of their colleagues will affect the morale of the staff who remain with the company.

To this end, ChemiCo could consider offering training and outplacement support to the staff being made redundant to help them try to find new jobs.

34 ProfTech

Text reference. Force field analysis and resistance to change are covered in Chapter 9 of the BPP Study Text. Styles of change management are discussed in Chapter 10.

Part (a)

Top tips. You should recognise that the scenario illustrates the forces driving change (competitive marketplace; student requirements; technology) and those resisting change (tutors).

Force field analysis will allow ProfTech's management to summarise these forces, but possibly more importantly it can provide a clear visual demonstration of the need to strengthen the driving forces and weaken the resisting forces.

Make sure you apply the force field model directly to the scenario: do not simply describe what force field analysis is. Remember, the question asks how the directors could *use* force field analysis. In this context, you should also consider whether there are any limitations on force field analysis' usefulness.

Remember though, there are only 6 marks available here and you are only asked for a brief discussion. So do not spend too long on any single aspect of the 'forces' identified in the force field analysis.

Lewin introduced the idea of force field analysis as a means of examining and evaluating the driving forces promoting change and the resisting forces acting against it.

If the e-learning facility is to be successfully introduced at ProfTech, then the **forces promoting** the change (particularly student feedback and the threat from competitors' products) need to be exploited and the **forces hindering** it (particularly staff resistance) need to be reduced.

Producing a force field analysis will require ProfTech's directors to **identify the various factors** that are promoting and hindering change.

Highlight key stakeholders

By listing the forces supporting and opposing the change, and identifying the relative strength and importance of each, forcefield analysis will identify the key stakeholders who will be affected by the change. This will include lecturers, students, students' employers, and internal functions at ProfTech such as the IT department and course material development teams.

This should prompt the directors to decide how to strengthen or weaken the more important forces as necessary.

However, although forcefield analysis can give these insights into how to manage change, it does not in itself explain how to overcome the resistance demonstrated by particular forces. So whilst the analysis will identify the tutors' attitudes as a major problem to ProfTech's e-learning facility, it will not actually show ProfTech how to deal with this resistance.

Appreciate different motives

Although forcefield diagrams show 'driving' and 'resisting' forces, they also highlight that people may resist change for different reasons. For example, some of ProfTech's tutors may resist the change because they fear it will reduce the amount of face-to-face contact they will have with their students, but others might resist it because they are afraid it will highlight their lack of IT skills.

By highlighting these different reasons, forcefield analysis will encourage the directors to realise that different solutions will be needed to manage the resistance to change.

Identify future state

The layout of a forcefield analysis diagram shows a current state and a desire future state. Having to think about the desired future state will prompt ProfTech's directors to establish more clearly the role they want e-learning to play in the future, and how the business' strategy will reflect this.

Again, though, forcefield analysis does not give a clear account of the resources needed to deliver this strategy, or a timetable for delivering it.

Part (b)

> **Top tips.** As with part (a), the scenario provides some useful clues: the tutors would rather keep the method they are familiar with and like, rather than having to learn new skills. However, alongside this fear of uncertainty, do not forget there may also be issues of power and security. Might the online materials reduce the need for classroom teachers?
>
> Also, to what extent is the resistance due to poor management and communication from ProfTech's management rather than being entirely due to the tutors? (Note this idea could also provide a link to part (c) of this question.)

The move to e-learning marks a major change in the way tutors deliver their material to students, and the potential size of the change may have prompted the tutors to resist it.

Fear of the unknown

Fear of the unknown is one of the main reasons people resist change, and it is likely to be a major reason behind the tutors resistance to the e-learning scheme. For example, if they are no longer going to be delivering lectures to students, what will they be required to do instead? Will they still have a job?

Dislike uncertainty

It appears that the e-learning project is not very clearly structured. Some tutors have introduced e-learning while others haven't. Consequently, there is likely to be a sense of uncertainty about how extensive the e-learning facility will be: for example, will e-learning modules be required for every subject area? Will students use e-learning modules alongside taught courses or will it replace them?

Any such uncertainty is likely to cause anxiety and resistance.

Potential loss of power

Some tutors may feel that the current situation of gives them a position of power and authority when teaching their students, so they may feel the change is a threat to this authority.

Potential reduction in quality

While some tutors might resist the change because of the impact they think it might have on them, others might resist it because of the impact they think it might have on the students. A number of ProfTech's tutors remain unconvinced about the benefits of e-learning and think that the best way for students to learn is through face-to-face tuition.

Cannot see the need for change

If the tutors believe that face-to-face learning is a better way for students to learn than e-learning then they will not see the need to change the current, face-to-face teaching style. For the change to be successful, ProfTech's directors will need to demonstrate the benefits of the new approach to the tutors.

In this respect, it may be that the tutors are interested purely in the quality of their teaching but have not considered the wider commercial issues at ProfTech. Students value the flexibility which e-learning offers, and Youtrain's e-learning facility is proving very popular. Whatever reservations the tutors may have about them, offering courses in a way which is convenient and popular with students will be crucial for ProfTech's success. The directors need to emphasise this point, but it would appear they have not yet done so.

Potential lack of skills

There is a wide range of attitudes among the tutors: some support the e-learning facility while others are resisting it. These differences in attitude may reflect differences in how happy the tutors are using technology. Some might be worried that the e-learning will expose that they are not very proficient with technology, and they will not be able to deliver their materials in the new format.

The tutors are used to delivering their materials face-to-face, and the new approach will present different challenges which they may be unprepared for, and so which they may not be able to carry out effectively.

Part (c)

> **Top tips.** The scenario highlights that there is a lack of clarity and focus about the project: some tutors are developing e-learning materials, but others aren't. This lack of clarity suggests not only that the vision for change hasn't been communicated to all the tutors, but also that there is a lack of urgency in introducing the changes.
>
> Establishing a sense of urgency, and communicating the vision for change are two of the eight steps in Kotter's eight set model for managing change.
>
> So, although you are not required to use this model here, it could be a useful framework for answering this requirement. We have used it as a framework for our answer below.
>
> (You might also wish to consider Kotter & Schlesinger's ideas about the different ways of dealing with change and managing resistance to change).
>
> However, if you use either of these models, do not spend time explaining the models. Simply use them as a framework which you can then apply to help answer the question which has actually been set: advising ProfTech's directors of the approaches they may take to ensure ProfTech successfully implements its e-learning programme.

Develop a sense of urgency

ProfTech is currently the largest training college in its country but its market position is being threatened by Youtrain Co. Youtrain has introduced an e-learning system of its own, and there is a danger that if ProfTech does not respond then Youtrain will continue to erode its market share.

ProfTech's directors need to ensure that the tutors appreciate this commercial aspect, and recognise the threats to the business if they do not adopt e-learning.

Ensure key groups work together

ProfTech's tutors and IT department are both key stakeholders in delivering the project successfully. However, the relationship between the tutors and the IT department does not appear to be very supportive, with the tutors seeking to blame the IT department for anything which goes wrong.

For the e-learning facility to be success, ProfTech's directors need to ensure that the two groups of people work together rather than antagonising each other.

Develop vision for change

Although the directors are keen to have an e-learning product and want ProfTech's students to be able to take e-learning courses within two years, they do not appear to have identified a vision of how the change will be introduced.

To this end, the directors need to establish a project team to manage the implementation, and also to agree a detailed project plan – including a timetable for implementing the facility.

Leadership and top level support

The introduction of e-learning represents a significant change in ProfTech's business model. Therefore it is important that the directors demonstrate to the business that they support it, and will champion its introduction.

The Board clearly support the project – the directors have approved a budget for the e-learning product, and want all students to have the option of having online tuition within 2 years. However, it is important that this support is communicated to the business.

Communicate the vision

At the moment, a number of the tutors are not committed to the direction of the change, but in large part this might be because they do not know how the changes will affect them.

Accordingly, the directors need to communicate the reasons for the new strategy to the tutors, and need to make sure the directors understand what is involved in the change.

Tackle obstacles to change

At the moment, ProfTech's directors are worried about forcing staff to adopt e-learning where they know a number of them are resisting the change.

However, in order to implement the change successfully, ProfTech's senior management will have to tackle the obstacles to change. To this end, they will have to get the tutors to support the programme.

There are a number of ways in which the managers can try to overcome the resistance to change, for example:

- **Communicating the need for change**, and explaining to the tutors how it will affect them
- Providing them with any **support** they will need to develop the new material, and encouraging the tutors who support e-learning to demonstrate to their colleagues how it can be used
- Looking at a **bonus scheme**, whereby the tutors are rewarded for adopting the new programme

New staff

It is possible that, however much support they are offered, some staff will still resist the changes and so will leave ProfTech. When recruiting new tutors, ProfTech needs to hire people who are not only good tutors but also support the e-learning project, and so will help implement the new material.

Highlighting positive feedback

Being able to demonstrate successes early in the implementation will maintain the momentum required to introduce the e-learning facility as a whole. At the moment, ProfTech's students have commented critically about the variation in the quality of the materials. However, ProfTech should highlight any positive student feedback about the e-learning material to remind the tutors why the scheme is worth pursuing.

Consolidate improvements

Where e-learning will be an increasingly important revenue stream, ProfTech should measure the amount of online business it generates as a KPI. This will sustain the focus on driving online business, and will highlight the fact that developing ProfTech's e-learning capabilities is an on-going project. ProfTech will need to upgrade and improve its e-learning material regularly to ensure it retains its market leading position.

35 Operating theatre

Text reference. Both BPR and PI are dealt with in Chapter 11 of the BPP Study Text for E3.

Marking scheme

			Marks	
(a)	(i)	Explanation of each technique (BPR and PI), highlighting differences between them	Up to 4	
		Role of IT in each technique	Up to 2	
			Total up to	6
	(ii)	Argument for and against OTIS being either BPR or PI	Up to 4	
			Total up to	4
(b)		For evaluation of three benefits to 4D, at up to 3 marks each	Up to 9	
		For evaluation of two benefits to society, at up to 3 marks each	Up to 6	
			Total up to	15
			Total	25

Part (a) (i)

Top tips. This is a tricky question, because it not only requires you to know about BPR and PI but also to be able to distinguish between them.

BPR is a fairly well-known idea and many candidates would have been able to give a reasonable account of its nature. However, the key to this question is identifying how PI is different from BPR. PI uses IT to streamline an existing process, whereas BPR seeks to achieve an enhanced outcome through a fundamental rethinking of the processes used to deliver that outcome.

Notice also the emphasis on IT in the requirement. IT is likely to play a significant role in BPR in a contemporary business, and you must not overlook the IS / IT elements of your syllabus.

Examiner's comments. Some candidates failed to mention the role of IT in the techniques. Most candidates could provide a definition of BPR, but fewer appeared to understand PI.

BPR may be seen as a late twentieth century aspect of **Scientific Management.** *Hammer and Champy* say that it is about 'fundamental rethinking and radical redesign of processes to achieve dramatic improvements in areas such as cost, quality and speed'.

The aim of BPR is **improvement** in the way things are done. It has its own philosophy, based on such ideas as focussing on **desired outcomes** rather than **existing tasks** and extending the **autonomy** of the people who perform the re-engineered tasks, and is most effective when there is a culture of **continuous improvement**.

By contrast, **PI** is not so much about the improvement of existing processes as the **development of completely new ones**. It is a more radical approach and less pervasive in that it tends to focus on a few key areas of the organisation.

Role of IT

In the BPR approach, IT is an **enabler**. Simple automation of processes is not BPR; the aim should be to **exploit the potential of IT** to enable the organisation to achieve its desired outcomes in ways that were previously impossible.

In **PI**, however, IT is often the **trigger for change**. Typically, its contribution will not be new ways of doing things so much as processes that achieve completely **new outcomes**.

A good example of the difference would be making airline reservations. Email would be an improvement to the basic technology of writing to a travel agent with details of the journeys required: it would enable faster communication. On-line booking would produce a completely new outcome in that the booking could be made, confirmed and paid for through direct access to the carrier's booking system.

Part (a) (ii)

Top tips. Since the question asks for your opinion, the important thing to achieve here is an informed and sensible line of reasoning that reaches a conclusion. It does not really matter whether you think OTIS is BPR or PI, so long as you apply the differences of principle that distinguish these two ideas and relate them back to 4D's new technology. In fact, the nature of OTIS is such that it could be argued that it qualifies under either heading.

The effect of OTIS is one of **scale** only. It does not achieve any new **outcomes**, so it is arguably not PI.

The existing system depends on the physical presence of the students, surgeons and tutors in the operating theatre for interaction to take place. OTIS makes physical presence unnecessary but does **not change the nature** of what is achieved. It therefore does not qualify as PI, to the extent that a distinction can be made.

Even the ability to interact between locations anywhere in the world is **not a new outcome**, since basic satellite TV and telephone technology made this possible decades ago. All that OTIS does is speed the process up.

To this extent, because OTIS improves the way things are currently done, rather than creating a completely new process, it should be seen as an example of **BPR rather than PI**.

Part (b)

Top tips. Note carefully the use of the question verb 'evaluate'; to evaluate means to 'appraise or assess the value of'. You must therefore make some value judgements to score well, and these should include limitations of the benefits as well as their upsides.

Note also the specific requirements of the question: you need to evaluate *five benefits in total*: three for 4 D, and two for society.

Benefits of OTIS to 4D

(i) Increased student throughput and enhanced training

Lack of operating theatre gallery space means that only a limited number of students can watch any operation and take part in question/coaching sessions. OTIS will overcome this constraint, potentially increasing the throughput of students in this phase of their training, and enhancing the level of surgeon/student and learning group interaction, *without* a significant commensurate increase in cost per student (principally in terms of surgeons' and lecturers' time). This would **enhance the quality of the training**, while increasing the hospital's **surplus of revenue over cost** and **generating funds for investment** elsewhere.

This could be of significant long-term benefit, depending on the cost/revenue balance currently experienced by the hospital. It will be limited in the short term, due to the high development and set-up costs likely to be incurred by OTIS, the cost of promoting the service to remote medical/teaching institutions, and the cost of training in use of the system.

There may be additional issues to be resolved before OTIS becomes fully operational and accepted: for example, the privacy concerns of patients, technological risks (audio-visual failure in the middle of a remote student-conducted operation cannot be countenanced) and liability issues (will the hospital be liable for surgical errors committed under its supervision?)

(ii) Potential to develop new educational and medical services

4D might be able to develop new educational services using OTIS, perhaps in the field of post-graduate training in new surgical techniques: this would represent a **new revenue stream**, if it can be harnessed (eg in the form of subscription– or licence-only access to the system for this purpose). Another development with similar potential might be the provision of on-demand consultation for purposes of remote diagnosis, with 4D's staff observing and commenting on patients' symptoms in 'virtual' teams with remote colleagues.

While interesting, these may not constitute significant benefits, depending on the level of demand for each option, and whether and how much 4D is practically able to charge for the service. It may be argued that 4D should not seek to **over-exploit its medical/teaching staff**, whose work load is already likely to be heavy.

(iii) Enhanced reputation for excellence

The raised profile of 4D through its unique **world-wide exposure** may be valuable in various ways: in attracting additional government and medical/educational **grant funding**; in **attracting and retaining surgical 'talent'** as teaching surgeons; in attracting **quality students**; and in attracting links (and associated **knowledge-sharing**) with other prestigious hospitals. This is likely to be a significant benefit, as 4D is effectively in competition with other medical and educational institutions for all these core 'resources'.

Benefits of OTIS to society

(i) Raised standards of surgical training

OTIS makes the clinical expertise of 4D available on a regional, national and international basis. This should raise the standard of surgical training in under-resourced hospitals, both through observing the 4D surgical team *and* the 'reverse' procedure of supervision by them.

This is potentially a major benefit, particularly in developing countries, but the extent to which it will be of value in any given country or region will depend on the current standard of surgical training, and the availability of other teaching hospitals and clinical supervision. It may also be limited by lack of ICT infrastructure: countries most in need of the expertise may lack the broadband internet service required for streaming of video footage and interactive guidance/support. They may also be unable to invest in the technology at their 'end' of the system.

(ii) Reduced costs of surgical services

The reduced cost of training surgeons (with less resources, space and personnel required) may enable hospitals to reduce the cost of surgery to patients and medical funds, and to have more resources left for other areas of their budgets.

Again, this is potentially a major benefit, particularly in developing countries, but the extent to which it will realistically be of value in any given country or region will depend on whether the demand for surgeons currently outstrips supply; whether surgeons, once trained, remain in the country or region; whether trained surgeons remain in the public sector – and whether cost savings are therefore available to fund-holders, and passed on to patients, or not. (Highly trained surgeons in areas where such skills are in short supply may choose to work in the private sector, or lucrative specialisms such as cosmetic surgery, in which the longer term benefit to society will be significantly reduced).

36 Transfer prices

Text reference. Transfer prices are covered in Chapter 12 of your BPP Study Text.

Top tips. Questions on transfer pricing in E3 are more likely to focus on the purpose and role of transfer prices in controlling a business, rather than the numerical perspective. This question considers transfer pricing from a behavioural point of view – by mentioning that divisional managers are not consulted – but also from an ethical point of view. Be clear about the ethical issues. These include the legality of the policy, tax considerations and the advisability of a policy where subordinates' evaluated performance is affected by actions of superiors over which they have no control.

Easy marks. There are number of frameworks you can use, including the stakeholder view and the profit-maximisation view. Whatever approach you take, your argument should be consistent and logical, setting out the advantages and disadvantages. On the issue of tax avoidance/evasion, some countries have catch-all provisions outlawing schemes whose sole purpose is to avoid paying tax. Do not ignore the international aspect of the question.

Part (a)

<u>Reasoning behind the transfer pricing policy</u>

Although P plc is a multi-national, it is incorporated in the UK, and investors using stock markets in the UK are the ultimate destination of its dividend stream. **P plc's performance is measured** by profits and earnings per share figures which are reported **in sterling**. As P plc is a business it is **profit-maximising** and its directors have an obligation to **minimise costs**.

Transfer pricing regimes can be very complex. P plc not only faces the business problems of operating in different countries, but also **currency risk** and **varying rates of taxation**.

P plc's transfer prices have to be designed on the understanding that **unit variable costs** and **sales prices** from the point of view of P as a whole are not constant, if only because of the currency risk.

(a) **Output optimisation**. The firm will seek to gain a profit-maximising level of output. Transfer pricing decisions will be made from the point of view of the organisation as a whole.

(b) **Tax avoidance**

    (i) Calculating a profit-maximising level of output will involve for the firm as a whole consideration of **tax liabilities**. Doubtless, P plc has **tax accountants** who are able to deal with the complexities of international tax law. This needs to be **centralised** to take into account how the tax regimes of different countries interact with each other.

    (ii) **Excise duties** can be minimised with low prices.

(c) **It is very hard in practice to identify a level of output** which will enable each part of a multi-national business to maximise its own profits. Currency risk make it very hard to determine such a price on a mechanical basis.

(d) Most countries in the industrialised world enable free **cash flow** between countries, but some developing economies place **limits on currency transactions**. Transfer prices can minimise this problem.

(e) It is often **hard to determine where in the value chain 'value' is added**. The only use for **part processed products** is further processing. P plc can probably justify its transfer prices to the authorities if there is no external market as a reference point.

<u>Problems with the system</u>

(a) **Governments and multinational bodies are increasingly vigilant** about the use of transfer prices to minimise tax/excise payments or to hinder competition.

(b) **Divisional performance assessment is made a lot harder**. If transfer prices are distorted, it becomes difficult to get a genuine picture of how efficiently a manufacturing plant is working. Some plants might have an unrealistically high reported 'profit'.

Part (b)

<u>Organisational purpose</u>

Designing appropriate transfer prices to maximise the profits of the business is in **accordance with its fundamental purpose**, which is to maximise owner-wealth in the **long term**. While P is not breaking the law, governments might put restrictions on its activities.

<u>Focus of decision making</u>

Furthermore, **letting tax considerations dominate commercial decisions puts emphasis in the wrong place**. Tax rates change easily, and so good tax planning one year can be rendered invalid the next. The same is true of transfer pricing. If tax considerations dominate decision-making, adverse consequences might include a harsher tax regime.

<u>Distributive justice</u>

P has invested in certain countries due to a favourable tax climate. It could be argued that manipulation of transfer prices goes against **distributive justice** for the reason that the firm benefits from public expenditure on infrastructure, education, law enforcement and so forth, and so avoiding the tax means that other people are paying unduly. Arguably this could be construed as violation of distributive justice. P's ethical consultants could argue that P brings employment and prosperity, which are **social benefits**.

P's subsidiaries prepare tax returns and if these are **honestly** prepared, the transfer pricing system is clear and open to government officials. P plc is deceiving no-one, nor is it guilty of any coercion and distortion. Tax evasion is **unethical and illegal**, but there is no evidence that P is doing this.

Corporate citizenship

Nonetheless, P still needs to consider its reputation and its position as a **good corporate citizen**. Although there is no evidence P is actually evading tax, if there is a public perception that it is behaving anti-socially this could generate negative publicity, which in turn could damage P's business prospects.

Impact on managers' rewards

P's transfer pricing policy could also have ethical implications for its pay and rewards system.

Although there is no information in the scenario about this, it is possible that managers and staff in the overseas divisions could receive performance related pay based on the performance of their divisions.

However, if P plc determines the transfer price without any reference to the divisions, this could unfairly disadvantage some divisions.

For example, if a transfer price is set in order to lower profit in a country with a relatively high tax rate, this restriction of profit could jeopardise the performance related pay of staff and managers in that country.

37 Royal Botanical

> **Text reference**. The balanced scorecard is dealt with in Chapter 13 of your BPP Study Text.
>
> **Top tips**. Of the marks available for part (a), a good proportion is likely to be allocated to a sensible explanation of the balanced scorecard idea, but the second requirement, to analyse its usefulness for the organisation in question, is equally important: don't overlook it.
>
> We have looked at the usefulness of a balanced scorecard approach to the Royal Botanical Gardens from the perspective of long-term strategic considerations. Note that your audience is 'eminent scientists': if they are unfamiliar with the balanced scorecard concept, they are also likely to be unfamiliar with unexplained management accounting terms!
>
> **Easy marks**. You are unlikely to score five marks for explaining the balanced scorecard, but a good summary might be worth four marks. You could expect to score some marks if you simply explained how the four perspectives would be applied, identifying, for example, universities and research establishments as relevant to the customer perspective.

Part (a)

To: The Management Board, The Royal Botanical Gardens
From: Your Name, Senior Management Accountant
Date: [Today]

BRIEFING NOTES: THE BALANCED SCORECARD

The balanced scorecard concept

The balanced scorecard model was developed in 1990 by *Kaplan and Norton*. They argued that financial objectives and measures are, by themselves, insufficient to direct and control organisations effectively. There needs to be a broader set of performance measures and perspectives, in order to avoid the problems of 'short-termism', which arises when managers are judged against short-term performance targets which do not take into account the long-term, complex effects of their decisions.

Kaplan and Norton proposed **four key perspectives for a balanced 'scorecard'** on managerial performance, for each of which the organisation will describe its long-term goals, the success factors established to achieve those goals, the key activities which must be carried out to achieve the success factors, and the key performance indicators which can be used to monitor progress.

(i) Financial perspective
How do we create value, and manage the financial resources entrusted to us? While profitability is not a primary goal for the Gardens, we are nevertheless accountable for our use of our financial resources to the

government (as main grant provider and representative of our 'owners', the Nation). We also need to maximise our effective use of the revenue streams available to us (through admission fees, grants and academic sponsorship) to develop the Gardens and related services.

(ii) Customer perspective

What do our customers value and how do they rate our performance? In the case of the Gardens, we may identify our customers in terms of various stakeholder 'publics': public visitors (botanical enthusiasts and tourists), the academic and corporate communities to whom we provide research and information, and the Nation whose horticultural heritage we conserve and manage.

(iii) Internal business perspective

What business processes must we excel at (our internal 'critical success factors')? The internal business perspective identifies and reports on the business processes that have the greatest impact on customer satisfaction, such as plant conservation (our core 'product'), research, servicing enquiries and handling visitors.

(iv) Innovation and learning perspective

What new services do our customers (including research customers) need? How can we continue to improve and add value? While the customer and internal process perspectives identify the current parameters for success, the Gardens need to foster learning and innovation, in order to continue to satisfy our stakeholders and to 'compete' successfully for grant funding, visitors and academic standing. This perspective relates particularly to the development of new services, and the development of staff.

Usefulness of the balanced scorecard approach for the Royal Botanical Gardens

The above briefing is specifically tailored to the situation of the Gardens. The model as originally devised was applied to commercial organisations, and uses the terminology of 'shareholder value', 'product quality' and so on. From our tailored description, however, it should be clear that the concept is also relevant to organisations such as the Gardens.

Balance financial and non-financial goals – It may be argued that we start from a less single-minded financial perspective than commercial organisations, and do not need to be reminded of our non-financial aims. However, the pressure to justify the annual Central Government grant on a five-yearly basis may cause a bias towards financial – and short-term goals. The balanced scorecard can thus help us to avoid the problems identified by Kaplan and Norton, and to **align our various strategic objectives across the organisation**.

Effective resource management – At the same time, lacking the discipline of the profit imperative, systematic performance measures for financial control may be all the more important, to **help us manage our available resources effectively** (and to support the business case for renewal of grants and sponsorships).

Support grant applications – The Management Board should find its hand strengthened in grant submissions and sponsorship-seeking, if it can show that it is controlling performance across a **range of specific, measurable and relevant indicators** – which balance the needs of various internal and external stakeholders.

Motivate managers – The balanced scorecard approach can also help **empower and motivate managers**, by involving them in the analysis of the organisation and its environment, and the formulation of meaningful success factors and performance indicators that reflect their contribution, and to which they can commit themselves.

Time and effort to implement – It must be recognised that a balanced scorecard **requires sustained effort to implement and maintain**, and represents a very significant organisational change (which may cause concern and uncertainty). It may be resisted because it 'moves the goalposts' for managers, and raises both visibility and accountability for performance. Performance measurement is not a substitute for strategic management: so implementing the scorecard should not be seen as a universal recipe for success.

Part (b)

> **Top tips.** To score well in this question you need to recognise that there are two parts to the requirement: (i) discuss the process to develop the balanced scorecard; and (ii) give examples of measures that could be used in the scorecard.
>
> Again, though, make sure you answer relates specifically to the Royal Botanical Gardens. For example, are the measures you suggest suitable for them?

The process of developing a balanced scorecard for the Gardens

Kaplan and Norton proposed that the introduction of the balanced scorecard could be undertaken in a way that would lead naturally to an awareness by managers at all levels of how overall strategy was to be implemented. This method is essentially one of **participative change management**.

(i) Translating the vision

The first stage is to build a consensus among managers around the organisation's vision and strategy.

The Gardens already has a mission statement, from which it can identify key strategic themes: for example, conservation and the development of knowledge and understanding. and formulate desired outcomes for each of the four perspectives. This is probably best done by a group of senior managers and scientists, with appropriate input from the Management Board.

(ii) Communicating and linking

The vision articulated by senior management must now be communicated downwards, and this should be done by delegating the development of key performance indicators to a cross-functional project team. This team should represent all functional groups within the Gardens organisation, with a clear reporting structure and programme of communication back to key stakeholders.

One possible methodology would be to:

- Map and define the four perspectives in relation to each of the strategic themes
- Identify desired outcomes for each perspective
- Identify critical success factors and key tasks in achieving the desired outcomes
- Develop performance measures and targets for each
- Establish timescales and methods for measurement (eg using visitor surveys, post-completion review of research projects, financial ratios, process benchmarking and so on).

As an example, the Gardens' strategic theme of developing knowledge and understanding might be seen from each of the four perspectives: financial (securing and efficiently using research grants); customer (maximising service to universities and pharma companies); internal (supporting staff botanists in study and research); and innovation/learning (maximising knowledge sharing with other facilities). The processes required to pursue these aims could be mapped and analysed too identify the key tasks of each, and KPIs/targets developed to measure progress and attainment: in other words, 'What do we need to do well?' and 'How will we know if/when this is being achieved?'

(iii) Business planning

The detailed performance indicators (KPIs) resulting from this second stage in the process can be used as direct inputs into the process of strategic implementation.

Examples of performance measures (KPIs)

From the **financial perspective**, sample KPIs may include: cost per visitor (or per enquiry filled, or per species conserved or per area of the Garden); or revenue earned per university/corporate client (or per visitor, or per period); or target growth in revenues generated by all or each means.

From the **customer perspective**, sample KPIs may include: number and value of visitor tickets sold; number of visitors expressing satisfaction (or visiting again, or taking out 'season tickets') and/or visitor complaints; number of queries responded to the enquirer's surveyed satisfaction; number of queries answered within a target response time; awards and commendations won (for conservation or tourism or research).

From the **internal perspective**, sample KPIs (depending on the processes being measured) may include: frequency and status of publish researched; number of safety/security incidents within the Gardens; average time for set-up of new displays and educational experiences; number of press mentions secured by publicity and PR; researcher satisfaction with the speed and fairness of internal grant allocations; percentage of procurement orders fulfilled on time and in full; and so on.

From the **innovation and learning** perspective, sample KPIs may include: reduction in number of unsatisfied research queries; number of staff improvement suggestions submitted/adopted; and hours/numbers of staff involved in training and development activities.

38 Management styles

Text reference. Chapter 12 includes Goold and Campbell's approaches to running divisionalised conglomerates. Chapters 9 & 10 discuss change management.

Marking scheme

			Marks
(a)	Definition of strategic control; definition of strategic planning; 1 mark each	2	
	Highlighting the differences between the two	2	
		Total	4
(b)	For each valid point made and embedded in the case (ie specifically about the impact the change in planning culture will have on the CEOs.)	Up to 2	
		Total up to	11
(c)	For each sensible stage / approach to change management, embedded in the case	Up to 2	
		Total up to	10
		Total	25

Part (a)

Top Tips. The scenario again provides you some useful information, and the explicit reference to Goold and Campbell's strategic management styles gives a clear indication of the issues you should be looking for.

Although (a) is only worth four marks it, the discussion of the different approaches to 'corporate parenting' it prompts should alert you to some of the issues that will be relevant in (b). Your answer to (a) should contain a brief definition of the two styles and then a comparison between the two.

Examiner's comments. Parts (a) and (b) were not well answered. This appeared to be due to a lack of syllabus knowledge, with candidates being unsure of the differences between the two styles.

The styles described by Goold and Campbell refer to the way a corporate parent seeks to influence the behaviour and returns from its business divisions. The **strategic planning** style involves a flexible strategic type of control influence and a fairly **high degree of central planning influence**. The corporate centre establishes extensive planning processes through which it works with business unit managers so that they make substantial contributions to strategic thinking. An emphasis is plan on longer-term strategic objectives, and performance targets are set in broad terms.

The **strategic control** style involves a fairly **low degree of planning influence from the centre**, but a tighter strategic control. The centre leaves the planning initiative to business unit managers, but it will then review plans for acceptability. Firm targets are set for a range of financial an non-financial performance indicators and performance is judged against them.

The strategic planning style establishes the framework in which business unit managers can work, and then encourages them to contribute to strategic thinking within that framework, whereas the **strategic control style allows managers more freedom about how they work**, with the corporate centre being a resource they can use if they wish to, but they are not bound to do so.

The amount of **senior management time given to each business unit** is greater under a strategic planning style than a strategic control style. Under a strategic control style, senior management attention is focused on the core strategic issues.

Part (b)

> **Top tips.** The key to doing well in (b) is to relate the impact of the changes directly to the CEOs of the former divisions. You should identify what the changes are, and then discuss the impact they will have on the CEOs. The question does not ask for a general discussion about changes in planning cultures, and you will score very few marks if your answer is not relevant to the scenario.

C used to operate a system of 'strategic control' so the CEOs of the former divisions in C will be used to operating under that system when dealing with their board of directors.

Business objectives. The CEOs were used to having a framework of objectives, both financial and non-financial, established for them by the corporate centre.

However, under the new structure, the overall framework will evolve from the planning process and each division, , will be expected to **develop its business plan in conjunction with the corporate centre** and through this contribute to the achievement of corporate goals This will represent a significant change for the divisional CEOs who are used to being given the framework, rather than having to go through a discursive process to set the framework itself. They may also find their proposals rejected.

Pursue own business strategies. The CEOs were used to planning and pursuing their own business strategies, within the overall business objectives guidelines set by the corporate centre.

However, under the new system, the CEOs will have to **develop strategies within a more closely defined framework** prescribed by the corporate centre. The strategies will be geared towards an overall corporate objective rather being driven by divisional objectives alone, as the old ones were.

The CEOs will find the new system **much more formal** than they are previously used to, with the centre having a far greater involvement in the decision making process.

Although the divisional CEOs will still have some degree of **autonomy**, it will be far less than they are used to and they may find this restrictive.

The need for formal planning and achieving central approval means management is likely to find the new process is **much more time-consuming** than the old process they were used to.

Group financial control. The divisional CEOs are also likely to find that the corporate centre now **controls expenditure and funding at a group level**, so they will now be competing with other divisions for scarce resources. They will not be used to doing this.

The centre will allocate resources according to which projects will deliver the best value for the group – rather than funds being allocating autonomously by division. The CEOs may find this frustrating, because it will mean they are not able to pursue projects they want to.

Discussions with the corporate centre. The CEOs will have been used to using the corporate centre as a sounding board to check that their plans and decisions are acceptable. In C the corporate centre would react to decisions and requests made by the divisional CEOs; it is unlikely to have imposed unilateral corporate decisions in its own right.

However, under the strategic planning system employed by B, the **centre will be much more proactive**, so the CEOs will now find themselves receiving directives initiated by the centre.

It is likely that the divisional CEOs may **resent the greater involvement of the centre**, perceiving it to be head office interference in their business. This will be particularly true if the involvement of the centre causes **delays in the decision-making process**.

Part (c)

> **Top tips.** Part (c) requires you to show the process of change should be managed. There a number of models which are relevant to change management, and there is no single right way of managing change.
>
> The model answer shown below is based on Kotter and Schlesinger's 'Six approaches' to dealing with change and resistance to change. However, provided you have described a logical model for implementing change, and applied it to the scenario, you will get credit for this. Once again, application to the scenario is important here to score well: remember the staff in question are senior staff, and B is keen to retain them after the acquisition.

Change can have a significant impact on people's circumstances, and the extent of the changes the CEOs are facing will mean that they are likely to be concerned about them. Some are likely to oppose them.

Therefore the changes will have to be **handled carefully so that B does not alienate the CEOs**, because it will want to retain them in the new business. The board of directors of C were removed but not the CEOs, suggesting that B sees them as valuable to the new business.

Nature and types of change

The scale of the re-organisation means that B is undertaking a **transformational change**, rather than an incremental change. Therefore it is likely that the board of directors will want to **implement the change programme quickly**, rather than introducing it gradually. However, they will still need to allow time for the CEOs to ask questions, provide comment and for them to be as reassured as possible about the changes ahead. Not doing so will delay change and may lead to a loss of divisional managers.

There is no single way to implement change successfully, but the manner in which a change is introduced is very important in it being implemented successfully. However, it will be useful to consider the following approaches to introducing the change.

Ways of implementing change

Communication and education. The structures and processes used at B need to be explained fully to the CEOs. This explanation should include a review of the benefits of the system which B operates, both for the CEOs as individuals, and for the company as a whole.

The **board of directors of B should be involved** in this communication process to demonstrate that the CEOs are important to the new business, but also that the changes themselves are important.

However, it would also be useful for some of the **CEOs from B's existing business to be involved**, so that they can explain the structure to their peer groups, and explain its benefits.

Throughout the communication process, it will be important to **encourage the new CEOs to ask any questions** they may have, so that the communication process is a two-way process. This should minimise the risk of any confusion.

Moving from a strategic control system to a strategic planning system will involve a large cultural change for the new CEOs. They will need clear guidance on how the **strategic planning process operates** at B; **what their involvement in it is;** and how their **behaviours will need to change** to fit into the new structure.

It will be useful for them to be given some **documentation about the strategic planning process**, and about their role in it.

Participation and involvement. It will be useful for some of the existing CEOs from B to discuss this with the new CEOs; and it would be useful to use the last strategic planning cycle as a case study to work through. This would demonstrate to the new joiners not only that the process actually works, but also what is required from them in the process. By working through the cycle, the new CEOs may even be able to identify areas where improvements can be made and included in the next planning cycle. If they feel that they are valued in the process, the new CEOs are less likely to resist the change.

In addition, allowing the two sets of CEOs to spend time together should help the new joiners feel more integrated into the business.

Facilitation and support. The new CEOs should have an **appraisal meeting** with the director they report to, to discuss the opportunities for them in the new company and to set their objectives going forward. The CEOs may initially feel that the changes will have a detrimental effect on them. However, the counselling managers can overcome the CEOs' negative perceptions by getting them to focus on the opportunities available going forward instead.

Negotiation. The appraisal system can be used to offer **rewards and incentives** for adapting to the new culture and performing successfully under it. The divisional CEOs will be relatively important employees in the new company, which may make B decide to offer them an initial incentive to stay with the company and embrace the new culture.

Co-optation. If there are some CEOs who continue to resist the changes, they could be co-opted into a change management team to **explain then changes to the other employees from C**. This will make it harder for them to resist the changes.

Coercion. Ultimately, if the CEOs remain unwilling to adapt, they should be removed from the business as quickly as possible. This will prevent any discontent from spreading amongst their staff.

39 Performance measurement

Text reference. Performance measurement and Neely's '4 CPs of measurement' are discussed in Chapter 13 of the Study Test.

Marking scheme

			Marks
(a)	For each appropriate *function* identified and described in general terms	1	
	For each function, if it is embedded in the case study material and described in terms of how it can help D, up to a further 1 ½ marks available	1 ½	
		Total up to	10
(b)	For each appropriate step or stage described in *developing* a performance measurement system in general terms	1	
	For each step or stage related to the case study to recommend how the performance measurement system should be developed at D, up to a further 1 mark available	1	
		Total up to	15
		Total	25

Part (a)

Top tips. The way to approach this question is to use specific issues highlighted in the scenario to guide your answer rather than answering too generally. Students who presented answers which were too general and did not relate to the specific issues highlighted in the scenario scored poorly.

The requirement did *not* ask you to describe a performance management system, or the benefits of a performance management system, but asked you specifically to apply them to D. Nonetheless, the examiner has still commented that many answers to this question were very general and did not address the problems D was facing.

Equally, you should not have spent time describing the current problems at D. You need to identify the problems from the scenario, because they can help indicate some of the areas where a performance measurement system could help D, but remember the question is asking about the performance measurement system, not the current problems at D.

A sensible way to approach this requirement was to select a suitable model of the functions of performance measurement systems, and then use that as a framework to explain how such a system could benefit D. In the model answer we have used Neely's 4 CPs, but you could have used PRIME equally well (Planning, Responsibility, Integration, Motivation, Evaluation).

However, students who tried to answer this requirement without using one of these frameworks scored poorly, because their answers lacked any clear structure.

The functions that an effective PMS will perform for D are shown below, and can be summarised as the 'Four CPs of Measurement'.

1. Check position – Effective performance measures will allow the partners to understand how well D is performing at present.

    The performance measures can be both financial (revenues, profitability) and non-financial (client satisfaction), and they should look to benchmark actual performance against target figures for each measure chosen.

    Performance can be measured for both the partnership as a whole and also for individual teams within the partnership.

Given the current problems with inter-term rivalry, the partners may wish to include a measure looking at the degree to which teams work together to secure business rather than the current practice of competing against one another.

The partners should also use PMS to benchmark D's overall performance in key measures against their competitors to gauge how well the partnership is performing.

2   Communicate position – Once the current performance levels have been measured, they should be communicated to the partnership's key stakeholders.

The key internal stakeholders here will be the partners (as both the owners of the business and the team leaders), and the consultants themselves. The consultants need to be aware of both the performance of their individual teams but also the partnership as a whole.

By communicating performance in the key measures chosen, D will be able to demonstrate how the current practices of teams competing against each other for business are damaging the firm. This in turn will help them justify the need for a new performance measurement system.

3   Confirm priorities – The performance measures chosen to be included in the PMS should be those which are important for the success of the business. By extension, their inclusion in the PMS communicates this importance to the stakeholders of the business.

Therefore the inclusion of measures around client satisfaction and knowledge sharing alongside the existing targets for new client acquisition will reinforce the importance of changing the organisational culture of the partnership.

Perhaps equally importantly, the new PMS will formalise this change, and communicate the new priorities to the consultants.

4   Compel progress – The consultants currently get paid large bonuses on the basis of their performance against a single performance measure – acquiring new clients.

We expect that the consultants will still be able to earn large bonuses, but in the future bonus payments will be linked to their performance across the range of multi-dimensional measures.

This should again help change the behavioural culture in the business, not least because the consultants' pay and career development prospects will now be linked directly to the new PMS. This will force the consultants to realise that it is no longer sufficient simply to bring new business to the practice at any cost, and that working together with colleagues and sharing knowledge with them instead of competing against them is equally important.

However, the new PMS will compel progress not only in individual consultants, but also across the partnership as a whole. If the partnership overall is failing to reach its performance targets this will be highlighted through the PMS, and so the partners will need to introduce remedial measures to improve performance.

Part (b)

> **Top tips.** As with part (a), the way to approach this question is to think specifically about the context – the performance measurement system being developed is specifically for use in D.
>
> However, note also that the question relates to the process that should be used in *developing* the performance measurement system, not in *operating* it.
>
> **Examiner's comments.** This question was not well answered. In particular, in (b) candidates tended to focus on how a performance measurement system *operates* rather than how it should be *developed*.

D should go through the following stages when developing their performance measurement system:

1   Obtain senior management commitment and support for the project, and achieve buy in from the key stakeholders

It is important that the rationale for the new performance measurement system is communicated to all stakeholders in order to overcome potential barriers to its implementation. This will be particularly important in D, because although the partners are committed to the new multi-dimensional performance measurement system (PMS) the consultants who have earned high bonuses under the existing structure will need to be convinced of its merits.

The partners' support for the project could be demonstrated through a briefing to the consultants explaining the rational for the new PMS, and showing how it will benefit the partnership as a whole. They could also demonstrate that the new system is not designed to prevent the consultants from earning bonuses. By contrast, they will still be able to earn their bonuses, but in order to do so they must buy in to the new culture being promoted by the PMS.

2   Identify the key outputs required from the PMS

The key outputs should relate back to the stakeholders requirements. In D's case this will be providing cutting edge computer simulations for its clients (client requirement) in a manner which promotes the profit and reputation of the partnership (partner requirement).

3   Identify the key processes in providing the outputs

An effective control system needs to consider the inputs and processes in a system as well as the outputs from it. In D's case this should be done by documenting the business cycle from winning new business to delivering a finished model to a client. The documentation should involve a walkthrough of the current process, plus discussions with management and staff about the issues they face with the current process.

4   Identify the interfaces between the various parts of the firm and with other key service providers

D will need a number of people to all work together to provide a high quality service to their clients. For example, sharing knowledge between teams, and sharing best practice in customer relationship management will help teams improve the service they provide to their clients, alongside the current technical expertise they use in developing their models.

5   Develop performance indicators for the key processes

Performance indicators are critical for D to be able to measure how well it is managing the key areas of its business. Whilst there are obviously financial indicators around new business earned, chargeable hours billed and profits generated, the new multi-dimensional performance system should also look at non-financial indicators such as client satisfaction and levels of knowledge sharing between teams.

6   Identify data sources for performance indicators chosen

The data required will ultimately depend on the performance indicators which D chooses to measure (stage 5 above). As far as possible they should all be quantifiable, although it is likely that some measures may have to be qualitative.

The following are some possible measures D may consider using alongside the core financial indicators: chargeable time to non-chargeable time ratios; customer satisfaction surveys; percentage of key deadlines achieved; staff satisfaction surveys (particularly around aspects of training and development).

7   Develop reporting system

Again, the precise nature of how this is developed will depend on how D's management want to communicate information, but we suggest one suitable method will be through an electronic report circulated to the teams or posted on an intranet.

8   Implement the system

Note that the implementation of the new system should be accompanied by staff training to ensure that the consultants (and the partners) know how to interpret the data, and can identify which areas of performance need to be improved.

9   Review effectiveness of the system

There are three aspects to consider here:

– When the system is introduced initially it may have some bugs or faults in it. So the partners would be advised to pilot it on one team before rolling it out across the whole partnership.
– Once the system has been introduced it will be important to assess whether it does actually lead to any change in the culture and performance of the partnership.
– It will be important to regularly review the processes and indicators measured to ensure that they remain relevant if the nature and scope of D's work changes over time.

Answers

40 International acquisition

> **Text Reference.** Performance measurement is covered in chapter 13 of the Study Text.

Marking scheme

			Marks
(a)		For each element of information identified	½
		For embedding the elements of information in the scenario and relating them to the target company, up to a further 1½ marks each	1½
		Total up to	15
(b)	(i)	For each difficulty well explained in the context of the scenario	Up to 2
		Total up to	6
	(ii)	For each disadvantage of ROI, well explained and related to the scenario	Up to 2
		Total up to	4
		Total	25

Part (a)

> **Top tips.** The way to approach (a) is to think about the context of the acquisition. EEE has historically produced high quality products. It is now looking to respond to competition by reducing the cost base of its production. So is it trying to move from a **differentiation** to a **cost leadership** strategy? What are the implications of this for its business model? What characteristics must an acquisition target have to help EEE achieve its aims?
>
> Note the primary motivation for the acquisition is to reduce production costs, so the most important characteristics should relate to production capabilities, not the potential for market growth in the target's country.
>
> However, note the wording of requirement (a) carefully – it does not ask you about the *characteristics* of a possible target, but rather the *information* EEE needs to assess the suitability of a potential target. A sensible approach would be to identify the factors EEE should consider in appraising the suitability of a target, and then the information it needs in order to assess those factors.
>
> **Marks available.** The marking guide for this question indicates that up to two marks were available for each well-justified requirement relating to the target company, up to a total of 15 marks.
>
> In the answer below we have identified eleven areas where EEE could seek information about the suitability of an acquisition target: production capabilities; production capacity; equipment; labour supply; supply chain; infrastructure; management and control; stakeholder interests; corporate image; market share; and financial analysis.
>
> However, the marking guide suggests that you would not have needed to include all of them to score well in this question. 7 or 8 well justified, relevant areas should have been sufficient to secure a good mark.
>
> **Examiner's comments.** This question was generally not well answered. Many candidates failed to read requirement (a) carefully enough and so failed to answer the question set. They were required to assess the suitability of the acquisition target (company) not the country which it is in. Detailed analysis of Porter's diamond was largely irrelevant here.

The reason for the decline in EEE's sales is that it has faced increasing competition from companies in neighbouring countries who have **lower production costs** than it. EEE is now looking to acquire one of these competitors to relocate its production to the acquisition in order to take advantage of its lower cost base.

However, before making the acquisition EEE needs to undertake some extensive intelligence to find out the strengths and weaknesses of potential targets.

Production capabilities

Quality standards – One of the key differences between EEE and its competitors is that EEE produces much higher quality goods than its competitors. By transferring production to the newly acquired division, EEE would have to accept a trade-off between lower costs and lower quality.

However, EEE will need to ensure that the products produced by the new manufacturer will still be sufficiently good quality to meet its **customers' requirements**.

Cost vs quality – In this context, EEE would be advised to undertake some market research to assess the relative importance of cost and quality in customers' purchasing decision. If low cost is the most important factor, then the suitability of potential targets will be affected by **how low (and possibly also how well controlled) their production costs are**. In effect, EEE would now be looking to adopt a cost leadership strategy instead of using quality as a differentiating factor compared to its competitors.

Product range and specification – Although the companies in the neighbouring countries are competitors to EEE, they may not be producing exactly the same products to EEE. Therefore EEE needs to be sure that the production lines can produce goods to the specifications and designs it requires.

Production capacity

EEE is looking to transfer its own production to the manufacturing division it acquires, alongside the division's existing production. Therefore, it should be looking for a company which has **sufficient capacity to take on EEE's production** while still maintaining its own existing production requirements. Alternatively, EEE should be looking to acquire a company which has **scope to expand its factory size** to meet the additional capacity requirements.

Equipment

EEE should look at the **age** and **condition** of target companies' production equipment. If a company has old equipment, there is a higher risk of failure or breakdown, potentially disrupting production. Equally, it may mean that EEE has to replace the equipment in the near future. (If this is the case, EEE should look for a reduction in the purchase price of the acquisition at allow for this. EEE may feel that if it can acquire the company cheaply, and then install new machinery to its own specification – or even use some of the machinery from the plant it is closing in F – this is an option which is worth considering).

Labour supply

In the same way that EEE needs to review the production equipment's capacity and its ability to deliver goods of sufficient quality, so it also needs to consider the **size and competencies of the labour pool** in potential target companies. For example, what are there skill levels if EEE needs them to take on additional tasks?

EEE should also look at the **external labour market** in the geographical area around the production plants, in case it needs to recruit additional staff to support additional demand. If any of the equipment production requires skilled labour, EEE should assess the availability of suitably skilled staff in the area.

Supply chain

The increased production levels post-acquisition are likely to increase the volume of materials bought in from suppliers. EEE will need to investigate that the target companies have secure contracts with their suppliers, and that the suppliers will be able to fulfil larger orders reliably.

Infrastructure

EEE should consider the geographic location of any potential acquisitions and the **infrastructure networks** around it. For example, if it hopes to use the new division to export products to a range of neighbouring countries, the location will need to be well served by road or rail links.

Management and control

EEE will also need to consider the **skills of the current management team** in the acquisition. Will the existing team be competent to manage the enlarged operation, or will EEE need to second some its own staff to manage the new division? Equally, EEE should assess the quality of **management and financial information** produced by the target companies, again with a view to assessing whether it will be able to provide sufficient information to allow it to **monitor the performance of the division** post-acquisition.

Stakeholder analysis

EEE needs to identify the key stakeholders in the target companies, and consider their response to a potential takeover.

Owners – As the companies are private companies, the owners' intentions are particularly important. Are they prepared to sell the company, or do they wish to retain control of an independent company, possibly growing it through acquisitions of their own? Would the current owners want to (or be prepared to) stay on and manage the division post-acquisition?

Employees – If EEE acquires the company will the current managers and staff be prepared to work for foreign owners? How well will the existing working culture fit with the organisational culture of EEE?

Suppliers – EEE will need to be confident that the target company's existing suppliers will be prepared to continue to supply the division once it has a parent in a foreign country.

Corporate image

Although EEE is looking to use the acquisition to reduce its production costs, it still needs to consider its corporate image. If the company it acquires has a **reputation** for producing very cheap, low quality goods, this could damage EEE's reputation for producing high quality products. Therefore, EEE should consider the reputation of potential target companies in their host countries, and in the industry more generally.

As part of its research into possible target companies, EEE should also assess what the competitor believes it **position in the industry** to be (in terms of cost and product quality).

Market share

One of the benefits of the acquisition for EEE will be to strengthen its (export) sales to neighbouring countries. Therefore the size of the potential company will be important; it needs to be sufficiently large so that by acquiring it, **EEE gains a significant share of the market** in its country.

EEE should also look at the size of the overall market in the target's country, to assess the **scope for future expansion**.

Market segments – As well as looking at overall sales, EEE should also assess the size and type of customers which the potential acquisitions serve. It will only be beneficial for EEE to acquire new customers if they can be **served profitably**.

Financial analysis

Finally EEE should examine the financial position of the targets very closely – including its financial statements for the last 3 –5 years, and its current budgets and forecasts. EEE should consider both the **profitability** and the liquidity of the operation.

Also, EEE should consider any **long-term contracts** from suppliers or leases which the target has already signed up to, and any **liabilities** which it may inherit as a result of the acquisition. In connection with this, EEE should also assess the pay and conditions for which the current employees work. (This could be important to make sure that there are no issues in respect of working time directives or minimum wage rates, for example, and also that EEE will not face any strike action if the workers are unhappy with their terms and conditions).

Conclusion

Ultimately, EEE's choice of which company to acquire should be decided by a combination of its potential to **revitalise EEE's sales**, the ease with which EEE can **incorporate and manage the division**, and the **price** which the vendors will be seeking for it.

As far as possible, in all of its investigations about the capabilities of potential acquisitions, EEE would be advised to substantiate its research through **direct observation** of the production line, rather than relying solely on discussions with management and looking at reports. In this way it can establish how the company *actually* operates rather than how its managers think/claim it operates.

Part (b)

> **Top tips.** Although the scenario mentions ROI and RI as two possible approaches to performance measurement, you should not have limited your answer to (b) (i) too narrowly to the difficulties of applying these measures. You should also have considered the more general problems associated with performance measurement in a multinational organisation.
>
> By contrast, requirement (b) (ii) focuses specifically on the disadvantages of EEE choosing ROI as its primary performance measure. So you should have kept your comments about ROI for (ii) and discussed the more general difficulties of performance measurement in a foreign subsidiary in part (i).

> **Examiner's comments.** In (b), many candidates only focused on the difficulties of using ROI and RI as performance measures, rather than on the difficulties of measuring the performance of different divisions in different countries.
>
> **Marks available.** The marking guide indicates that each difficulty well explained and relevant to the context of the scenario is worth up to 2 marks each, up to a maximum of 6 marks. Again, it would be possible to identify more difficulties than you need to score 6 marks. We have listed what we think are the most important difficulties in the answer below, but have included two additional ones in the box at the end of the answer. These are equally valid, and you would have earned marks for them if you included them in your answer.

(i) **Impact of becoming multinational** – Currently EEE is based entirely in F, and so the acquisition of the new division will mean it becomes a multinational company for the first time. Performance management in a multinational company brings different challenges to managing a company based in a single country.

When assessing the performance of the foreign division, EEE will need to allow for any differences in the economic conditions between F and the foreign country; for example, for example, **the potential impact of different inflation rates** on reported revenue and costs figures.

Impact of price differences on profits – Also, because F is more developed than its neighbouring countries, it is likely that products are likely to sell at a higher price in F than the neighbouring countries. Consequently, profitability could be affected by where products are sold to rather than the numbers of products sold.

Comparability of figures – The division may have different accounting policies than EEE, which would mean that its results are not necessarily comparable with other divisions. For example, if the foreign division **values assets differently**, this could lead to difficulties in comparing its performance to the other divisions using ROI or RI as the performance measures. Similarly if the age of the non-current assets is different across the various divisions, this could also distort comparisons.

Issues with **foreign currency translation** may also affect the comparability of divisions in different countries.

Furthermore, if EEE introduces a **transfer pricing** policy post-acquisition this could affect the profit the division reports. Therefore EEE must ensure the transfer prices applied are equitable and encourage the acquired decision to take decisions which are **in the best interests of the group** as a whole.

Division's expectations – We do not know what level of **performance measurement the division is used to**, or what level of management/financial information is available as a basis for performance measurement. If EEE wants to introduce more complex performance measurement processes, it will need to educate the division about them – explaining the benefits of them, and what information it needs for them.

Accordingly, EEE is likely to favour using some fairly simple performance measures initially.

Goal congruence – EEE needs to ensure that the performance measures it employs encourages the divisional managers to make decisions which are in the **best interests of the group as well as the division**. For example, the two approaches EEE is considering (ROI or RI) may **discourage the division from investing in new capital equipment**. This may mean the division may show a better performance in the short term than it would have done if it had made the investment, but its longer term performance (and therefore the longer term interests of the group) will be weakened by the lack of investment.

> <u>Other valid points</u>
>
> **Selecting reference measures** – One of the issues which EEE will face is deciding **what the most important performance factors of the division are**: for example, overall profitability, revenue growth, productivity levels, or returns on investment are all aspects of performance it could look to monitor, but they may require different behaviours from the division.
>
> **Financial and non-financial measures** – There is a danger that EEE will concentrate primarily on financial performance. These measures are suitable for measuring the business's current and past performance, but are not necessarily helpful in shaping future strategies. EEE should also consider looking at **customer-based measures**, **business process**-based measures, and **innovation and learning** based measures as suggested by the **balanced scorecard**.

(ii) If EEE chooses ROI as its primary performance measure, it could face some problems surrounding the **application of non-current asset values** in the performance measurement calculation.

Encourages short-termism – One potential disadvantage of using ROI is that it may **cause EEE to reject some profitable opportunities**. If a return on investment is measured year by year, it may be below the target return in the first year, but then above it in subsequent years, as the net book value of the non-current assets decreases. However, it is possible EEE may reject the project because it needs to show a satisfactory profit and ROI to its shareholders in year one.

In this respect, **ROI encourages short-termist decision making**. By contrast, if EEE chooses RI as its primary performance measure it would not have this problem, because RI deducts an imputed interest charge for the use of assets, rather than using net book value in the calculation.

Discourages asset replacement – If profit remains constant year on year, **ROI increases as assets get older**. If ROI is calculated as a return on net assets, then net asset value reduces each year due to depreciation. If ROI is calculated as a return on gross assets, the costs of older assets is likely to be less than the cost of buying the equivalent asset now.

Consequently, using ROI **could discourage EEE from replacing older assets** with new assets. However, this could damage EEE's productivity and performance in the longer term. Again, ROI encourages short-termism.

Lack of flexibility – Another disadvantage of ROI is the **lack of flexibility applied to the discount factor**. EEE would need to apply the same discount factor to all projects or divisions, even if they have different levels of risk attached to them. Having identical target returns may be unsuitable for EEE now it is a multinational business.

Overall, RI is a more flexible performance measure than ROI. ROI may lead to EEE rejecting some investments which it would have accepted under RI. Therefore if it adopts ROI as its primary performance measure, its longer term performance may suffer.

41 Computer company

Text reference. The balanced scorecard is discussed in Chapter 13 of the BPP Study Text for E3.

Marking scheme

			Marks
(a)	For identifying and correctly explaining each of the four components of the Balanced Scorecard	1 mark each	
		Total	4
(b)	For each appropriate and relevant measure, well justified and linked back to the question scenario.	Up to 2	
	Up to a maximum of 4 marks for each of the four perspectives	Total	16
(c)	For each relevant change management process discussed	Up to 2	
		Total	5
			25

> **Top tips.** Requirement (a) is a test of pure knowledge. However, be careful not to spend too long on this part. There are four marks available for an explanation of the four components of the Balanced Scorecard model – one mark per component. This means you only need to give a brief explanation for each component before moving on.
>
> It is crucial that you read requirement (b) very carefully and notice that it asks for *measures*, not *targets*. So, for example, if you suggested that 'DD should ensure that all patents are registered' you would have scored no marks for this: it is a target, not a measure. However, you would have scored marks for including the measure 'Number of patented innovations.' This distinction may appear subtle, but once again it reinforces the importance of reading the question carefully, and answering the exact question that the examiner sets. A measure is a proposal for how performance should be measured in order to record and control it. A target is a statement of the level of performance which should be attained.
>
> Note also that the question asks specifically for two measures for each of the components. If you gave more than two measures for any component you would only get marks for the first two you include.
>
> Part (c) asks you to discuss the issues associated with introducing the balanced scorecard in the context of change management. Kaplan and Norton (who devised the balanced scorecard) produced a four stage approach for dealing with the practical problems of introducing the balanced scorecard for the first time. The answer below is based on their four stage approach. However, if you did not know this model, you could have still made some relevant points by applying more general principles of change management, such as the importance of keeping people informed about the changes, and the importance of explaining the need for the changes. Change management models such as Lewin's 'Unfreeze, move, refreeze' approach might also have been some help here.
>
> **Easy marks.** Part (a) is a pure test of knowledge. If you had a good understanding of the Balanced Scorecard model, this should have given you some very easy marks.

Part (a)

The balanced scorecard aims to highlight the **financial and non-financial elements** of corporate performance, through measuring **four perspectives of performance**: financial, customer satisfaction, internal efficiency and innovation.

Financial perspective – This addresses the question, 'How can we succeed financially and create value for our shareholders?' and it covers measures such as growth, profitability, return on capital employed and shareholder value.

Customer perspective – This considers how an organisation must appear to its customers in order to achieve its vision. It asks the question 'What do new and existing customers expect of the organisation?' – aspects which could be measured in terms of quality, speed, reliability and value for money of the organisation's products.

Internal business perspective – This considers what business processes an organisation needs to excel at in order to achieve financial and customer objectives. For example, it could be measured in relation to the efficiency of the product development process.

Innovation and learning perspective – This considers how an organisation can continue to create value and maintain its competitive position through improvement and change. It could be measured, for example, in relation to the acquisition of new skills, or the development of new products.

Part (b)

> **Tutorial note.** The question only asks you to provide **two** measures for each of the components of the balanced scorecard model. For tutorial purposes we have included a wider range of measures which would all have been relevant here in text boxes below, but you should only have included two measures for each component of the model. You would **not** have scored any additional marks if you included more than two measures for any of the components.
>
> Some of the ideas may fit into more than one perspective; for example, the number of patents filed could be relevant to the internal business perspective or the innovation and learning perspective. However, you should not have simply repeated the same measure in more than one perspective, because you would not score any marks for the repeat.

Financial perspective

Cash flow – Currently, DD employs 30 scientists and engineers who are working on various research projects, but none of these projects have been made commercially available. Consequently, DD is not generating any sales revenue, and so has a negative cash flow. However, monitoring cash flow once it starts selling its products commercially will allow DD to measure how successful its sales are. DD cannot afford to continue with a negative cash flow if it is to become a successful commercial organisation.

Return on capital employed – DD does not have any shareholders, and is currently entirely dependent on the funding it receives from Mr X. However, as an entrepreneur Mr X will want to see a return on his investment. If DD does not start delivering an acceptable return on the capital Mr X has invested, he could withdraw his funding in favour of another investment opportunity.

NPV of R&D expenditure – Once DD's strategy changes to being a commercial organisation, it needs to focus more on projects whose financial benefits outweigh their costs. Measuring the NPV of projects will indicate how successfully they are achieving this.

Measuring NPV will also give an indication of how accurately DD forecasts the costs of developing a new product, and the level of sales it can generate from it. If DD's forecasts are over-optimistic, then it could be committing to project which will not generate value in the longer term.

Sales growth – Once DD starts marketing and selling its products commercially, looking at sales growth will provide a measure of how successful the products are in the marketplace.

Customer perspective

Customer feedback – DD has only been established for three years, and does not currently sell any of its processors. Therefore when DD starts selling commercially, it will be essential to develop a good reputation among customers and potential customers. Feedback from customers will provide a good measure of how well DD is delivering what its customers want.

Growth of market share – DD believes its innovative processor is significantly faster than any currently available. Therefore, once it introduces the processor commercially, DD should be able to gain market share from existing players in the market. Measuring the growth in their market share will enable DD to see how successfully it is doing this.

Percentage of sales from new products – A key factor in DD's growth over the longer term will be continuing to develop new products which meet customer needs better than any competitors' existing products can, so that DD builds up a balanced portfolio of products. One way DD can measure the success of new product development is by measuring sales from products developed in the last year as a percentage of total sales. Such a measure will indicate not only how successful DD is in its research and development of new products, but also how good it is at marketing them.

New customers acquired – As it is a new entrant into the market, a key factor in DD's commercial success will be its ability to attract new customers. Measuring the number of new customers acquired will enable DD to see how successfully it is doing this.

Internal business perspective

Actual introduction schedule compared to plan – One of the key changes which Mr X is looking to introduce at DD is moving the staff away from pure research projects onto the development of commercially viable products. One way he could introduce more discipline and structure over the development process is to develop a timetable for when new products become commercially available. Alongside this it would then be important to measure when the new products actually become commercially available compared to the original timetable.

Development vs research time – Another way of assessing how successfully the shift in focus from 'research' to 'research and development' is being adopted by the scientists will be to measure how much of their time is spent on pure research projects compared to how much is spent on their commercial development.

Time to develop new products – DD's cash flow will be affected by how quickly it can make new developments commercially available. One way of measuring the efficiency of the development process will be measuring the time between a new research idea being registered and it being developed into a commercially available product.

> **Level of defect rates** – It is likely that DD will emphasise the speed of its processor when marketing it, as a source of differentiation from competitors' products. However, given that DD is aiming to supply superior products it needs to ensure that they all work as intended. A measure looking at the level of defects would help ensure that this desired level of quality is maintained.

Innovation and learning perspective

Number of patents filed – Although DD's engineers have published a number of academic papers, they have not filed any patents. However, patenting new ideas could help DD develop a competitive advantage over its rivals. Therefore, measuring the number of patents filed will indicate the scientist's success in developing commercially viable new products.

Number of modifications required in product development – Initially, it is likely that the pure research ideas will have to go through a number of modifications and prototypes as the scientists develop them into a commercially viable product. However, as the scientists become used to developing their ideas they should need less modifications to develop their initial idea into a product. Therefore measuring the number of modifications required will indicate how successfully the scientists are adapting to the new commercial process.

> **Cost per patent filed** – Measuring the cost per patentable discovery would indicate the effectiveness of DD's researchers in developing new products.

Part (c)

As DD becomes more commercial it will need more **quantitative measures** of performance, and it can use the balanced scorecard to provide these. DD will also need to look at **external measures** alongside internal ones, and again it can use the balanced scorecard to introduce this balance.

However, the proposed change in strategy and culture will have a major impact on DD's staff and so it will have to be managed carefully because Mr X is keen to avoid losing any of the current research staff.

To this end, the balanced scorecard should be introduced via a four-stage approach.

Translating the vision – Mr X will need to explain what DD's new, more commercial, focus will mean to the research scientists in terms of their everyday work. Mr X will also need to explain the relevance of the four perspectives of the scorecard to the scientists' work, and in particular he will need to emphasise the impact of customer requirements compared to the previous scenario where the scientists work was governed purely by academic interest.

Communicating and linking – Once the overall approach has been explained, DD's strategy needs to be linked to departmental and individual objectives. Mr X should discuss and agree objectives with the researchers and the marketers based on the four perspectives of the balanced scorecard.

It is important to include the marketers as well as the researchers so that some of the new research going forward is market-led rather than being determined by academic interest.

Business planning – The scorecard can be used to help prioritise objectives and allocate resources in order to allow DD to make the best progress towards its strategic goals. At the moment, DD does not have a business plan and the scientists appear largely autonomous in their work. However, Mr X should develop a business plan and support that plan by ensuring that the scientists' efforts are concentrated on those projects which look like they will be the most successful commercially.

Feedback and learning – It will take time for the changes in culture and strategy to become embedded at DD. However, Mr X and all the staff will need to use feedback on performance issues constructively to promote progress against four perspectives of the balanced scorecard.

One area which may need to be revisited in the light of feedback is the balance of time the research staff spend on pure research projects compared to commercial development projects. Allowing the scientists sufficient time to pursue their own interests will help sustain their motivation, and should encourage them to remain with the company; but this needs to be balanced with the need for them to spend enough time on commercial developments to sustain the company's financial performance.

42 Global environmental charity

Text reference. The balanced scorecard is discussed in Chapter 13 of your BPP Study Text. Resistance to change, and overcoming resistance to change are discussed in Chapter 9.

Top tips. When answering **Part (a)**, it is very important that you recognise the context of the scenario. E is a charity, it is global, and it has 45 autonomous divisions – one for each country in which it operates. E has also been criticised for the lack of control and accountability within it, because each independent division does pretty much want it wants to.

So, the balanced scorecard can help E by establishing clearer goals for the organisation as a whole, and improving goal congruence. Importantly also, the scorecard doesn't just focus on profit measures, which could be useful since E is a charity rather than a company seeking to maximise profits.

However, given the apparent lack of control within E at the moment, will the Board and the CEOs have the skills to introduce the balanced scorecard successfully? How much will the culture of the organisation need to change? Will the CEOs resent it as a challenge to their autonomy / authority?

This last question provides a link between parts (a) and (b) of the question. If the divisional CEOs see the introduction of the balanced scorecard as a threat to their autonomy this is a reason why they might resist it.

Note that for **part (b)** you are specifically asked to discuss **four** reasons why the CEOs might resist the changes; so make sure your answer clearly discussed four separate reasons. Also, remember that you were asked to 'discuss' the reasons, so simply presenting a list of reasons would not have scored well. Similarly, make sure your answer focuses specifically on reasons why the CEOs in E would resist the change, rather than simply discussing general reasons why people might resist change.

Although you should still relate your answer for **part (c)** to the scenario, Kotter & Schlesinger's five ways of managing resistance to change should provide a good framework here. However, remember it is the CEOs who are resisting the change, so make sure your suggestions are appropriate to their position in the organisation.

Part (a)

Advantages

Help set goals – Currently the CEOs' meetings usually finish with no clear decisions about a unified direction of the charity to take. Using the scorecard will provide a framework to establish goals and objectives for the CEOs to work towards.

At the moment, the divisions all seem to act independently, largely because no clear decisions about strategy are agreed. Having the scorecard in place should help E focus on its key strategic goals, and should therefore make it harder for divisions to justify acting independently.

Goal congruence – The balanced scorecard will force the divisional CEOs to look at all aspects of the charity's objectives, and make them employ success measures for their particular division that support the corporate goals of the organisation as a whole.

Range of perspectives – The balanced scorecard looks at a range of perspectives rather than only financial, profit-driven ones. This is likely to be appropriate for E, since it is a charity and therefore its objectives are not primarily driven by shareholder value or profitability.

Value for money – Although E does not have shareholders, it still needs to show its donors that it is using the money they have donated effectively and efficiently and for the benefit of the causes it supports. If E adopts the balanced scorecard, it could set targets for how efficiently it uses its funds, and could then report to its donors about how well it has used the money that has been raised.

Internal and external factors – The balanced scorecard will encourage the CEOs to look at both internal and external factors. The environment is becomingly increasingly competitive, so E will need to find innovative ways of attracting funds, but it will also need to make sure its own internal processes are as efficient as possible so that as much of its money as possible can be allocated to its main goal – protecting endangered species and habitats.

Disadvantages

Too much information – The scorecard will lead to the CEOs having a wide range of performance measures to aim for, and being provided with a large amount of information about how their divisions have performed against those measures.

There is a danger that the CEOs (with no experience of any similar controls) will **not know how to interpret this information** or what to do with it. In which case, there is a danger they might simply ignore the information from the scorecard.

Equally, there is a danger that some of the measures could give **conflicting signals** to the CEOs, and so they may interpret the results incorrectly. The CEOs are likely to need quite a lot of training and guidance to use the scorecard.

Poorly constructed measures – E has not had a performance measurement system anything like the balanced scorecard before. There is a danger that if it introduces the scorecard, but the scorecard measures are poorly selected, they could generate responses which hadn't been foreseen and could actually damage performance rather than improving it. For example, although E needs to improve control and accountability, if the measures focus too much on these aspects of performance, then E could lose sight of the overall need to maintain its donations.

Applicability of measures – One of the four perspectives of the scorecard is 'Customers', but E doesn't have 'customers' in the sense, for example, that a retail organisation does. The Supervisory Board will have to clarify what each of the four perspectives means for E (for example, 'customers' could be 'beneficiaries') otherwise there is a danger that the divisional CEOs will view the scorecard as being irrelevant and will ignore it.

Concerns about poorly constructed measures or inapplicable measures mean that E will have to **validate the measures it proposes to use** very carefully before it actually begins to use the scorecard.

Culture change – Currently, the CEOs enjoy a lot of autonomy and have largely ignored any direction given to them by the Supervisory Board. For the balanced scorecard to be implemented, there will need to be a significant change in this corporate culture so that the CEOs follow the corporate plan rather than acting autonomously. The CEOs are likely to resist such a change.

Time to implement – The need to select appropriate measures to use and the potential cultural change involved, mean that the scorecard will not be a quick solution to E's problems. It seems that the Board view the introduction of a new performance measurement and control system as a matter of urgency. However, it is likely to take a considerable amount of time to develop, and implement, an appropriate scorecard.

Part (b)

> **Note:** Make sure you clearly identify the **four** reasons you are discussing in turn.

1. **Fear of unknown** – Although the Supervisory Board have decided to introduce the new performance measurement system, there is no evidence that they have explained to the CEOs **what changes are going to be introduced** and **how the changes will affect them**. Even if the CEOs have been told a balanced scorecard system is going to be introduced, they may not know what this is. Consequently, the CEOs may be resisting the changes because they are an unknown quantity to them.

2. **Don't appreciate need for change** – The Supervisory Board have not explained to the CEOs why the changes are necessary. The CEOs may not be aware of the criticisms of E for its lack of direction. If they think E is performing better than it actually is, they may not appreciate the need for more formalised performance measurement and control. In which case, they might resist the changes as simply being bureaucracy being imposed on them, rather than appreciating that they are designed to help improve E's performance.

3. **Potential loss of power** – At the moment, the CEOs have a high degree of autonomy. However, they may be concerned that the introduction of a more rigorous performance measurement system will reduce this autonomy, and make them subject to more control.

   In particular, specific CEOs may resist the changes if they are worried about the performance of their divisions which might not be performing as well as others. By having a more effective performance measurement system, E will be able to identify those divisions which are not performing very well, but this is something it might not have been able to do previously.

4   **Lack of consultation** – It appears that the Supervisory Body have decided to implement the changes without any consultation with the CEOs. Given that the CEOs are relatively senior members of E, it is likely that some of them will be upset that they have not been consulted about the changes. Consequently, as a reaction to the lack of consultation, they will resist the changes.

Part (c)

Communication is crucial in overcoming resistance to change.

As a first step in overcoming the resistance to change, the Supervisory Board needs to communicate the reasons **why** the change is needed, and **how** the change will be introduced to the CEOs.

After this initial communication, the following steps could also be taken:

Education – The CEOs also need to be educated about the balanced scorecard: what it is intended to do, and how it should be used.

Participation – The CEOs should be consulted about the scorecard and encouraged to participate in designing the measures. If the CEOs feel they have contributed to the new performance measurement system they are less likely to resist it.

Negotiation – Some of the CEOs may still resist parts of the change, despite communication and education. The Supervisory Board may need to negotiate with the CEOs and may have to make some concessions to get the CEOs to agree the changes.

Manipulation – If some of the CEOs continue to resist the changes, the Board could try to make these CEOs feel guilty for doing so; for example, by explaining that the changes are proposed for the good of the organisation as a whole, and that their resistance threatens this greater good.

Coercion – If the CEOs continue to resist all 'voluntary' attempts to make them accept the changes, the Board could force them to do so. This might even involve threatening them with redundancy if they do not accept the changes and endorse the new performance measurement system.

43 Pipeco

Part (a)

> **Top tips.** This part of the question includes lots of calculations. Nonetheless, do not be frightened by it. If you work through the figures and information methodically you will find that the calculations are actually quite simple. In particular, do not become confused by the Examiner's talk of countries and options: there are effectively three possible courses of action available and each should be assessed in much the same way.
>
> The information given to you is clearly set up for evaluation using discounting. Calculating the three NPVs (including the use of probability weighting) would be worth half the sixteen marks available for computations. Each of the three possibilities requires a different level of investment, so to make them comparable, the use of **profitability index** is a good idea, particularly given that capital rationing is implied in the scenario, and would be worth another three marks or so. Another constraint is the Board's desire for increasing profits which may not be met by a project that incurs greater costs that revenues in its early years. A profit forecast for each option could gain extra marks.
>
> In addition to the number crunching, the marking scheme indicates a clear requirement for qualitative analysis and there is an explicit instruction to make recommendations. So don't spend all your time on the numbers. (a) is worth 29 marks in total: the calculations are worth up to 16, meaning 13 are available for your recommendations.
>
> **Easy marks.** The only difficult thing about this requirement is deciding how to set about using the numerical information available. There is actually half a mark available for saying why the option of doing nothing is not acceptable. Thirteen marks are available for the non-financial evaluation. This emphasises the need for good time management, since these marks are easy to get if you allow enough time for this aspect of your report. Also, this distribution of marks indicates that the Examiner is looking for a balanced answer; do not get bogged down in the numbers.

Answers

> **Examiner's comments.** Unfortunately, too many candidates became engrossed in the computations and did not attempt to go beyond the numbers they had calculated.
>
> Common errors included incorrect NPV calculations and failure to provide profitability indices, non-financial analysis or recommendations.

The current decline in Pipeco's revenue and profits is likely to continue unless significant action is taken to develop the business. Doing nothing is, therefore, not an option. There are three possibilities for further investment within the available funds of $2 million.

Option 1 Country A

Investment in Country A would require an outlay of $1.5 million. The project has a NPV of $195,490 and a PI of .1303. Profit would be $60k for the important initial five year period, though this would rise to $170k for years six to ten before falling back to $100k in years eleven to fifteen.

Option 1 Country B

The cost of investing in Country B would be $2 million; the project NPV is $198,685 and the PI 1.0993. Profit in years one to five would be $115k; this level of profit would be maintained until the end of year eight, when it would fall to $55k in years nine and ten. However, it would rise to $255k in year eleven and this level would be maintained until the end of year fourteen.

Option 2

Option 2 would require an initial investment of $1.45 million followed by a further investment of $425k after one year had passed. Using an expected value of contribution for purposes of comparison, this option produces a NPV of $213,033 and a PI of 1.1160.

Financial assessment

Option 1A has the highest PI and may therefore be regarded as the best investment. However, Option 1B, is a larger scale project and produces a **higher absolute profit**. This option may therefore be of interest to the parent group in its drive for cash to pay dividends. However, equally, the parent group may have other investment opportunities that could use the extra $500k more efficiently than Option 1B.

The use of an expected value for cash inflows to assess Option 2 makes it comparable with the other two options and on this basis it would seem to fall somewhere between Option 1A and Option 1B in attractiveness, since its PI falls between theirs. However, the expected value itself conceals the **enhanced risk inherent in Option 2**. Both cases of Option 1 involve operations that are essentially similar to those undertaken at present. Option 2, on the other hand is acknowledged to involve a **different business model**, with completely **unfamiliar production methods** and **market conditions**. It is therefore **inherently much riskier**.

In fact, there is a 50% probability of a very marginal NPV of $7175 and a 20% probability of a negative NPV of $207,900. The attractive NPV of $836,750 and PI of 1.4557 have only a 20% probability of coming to pass.

Other factors

> **Top tips.** Make sure you do not say things under this sort of heading that would be better kept for parts (b) and (c).

Both versions of Option 1 would involve setting up large-scale manufacture for the first time in a foreign country. This is an **inherently risky strategy**. Pipeco has exported extensively within Western Europe but has no experience of manufacture outside its home country. The company would have to overcome **problems in all areas of management**, including the acquisition of premises; the recruitment and training of staff; the creation of both upstream and downstream supply chains; the management of finance and taxation; and the marketing of its products. None of these problems is insurmountable, but they are likely to have an adverse, but unquantifiable, effect on the forecast financial data. Since Option 2 involves taking over an existing operation, it does not suffer from any of these disadvantages. It does, however, raise another problem, which is discussed below.

The advantage of Option 1 is that it would allow Pipeco to continue to **exploit its core competences** in low-cost manufacturing.

Option 2 also represents a **major new venture**. Pipeco would continue to operate in its home country but would enter completely new markets with products that were not only new but also manufactured by processes with which it has no experience. In addition, Pipeco would be moving out of a business to business commodity market, where sales depend on holding costs down, and into one where success depends on product differentiation and design and sales are made to retailers and specifiers such as architects. It seems unlikely that any core competences Pipeco has attained would be **easily transferable** to these new products and markets.

A further consideration is that Option 2 would require Pipeco to take over and reinvigorate an existing but **underfunded** business. The directors of Pipeco have no experience of such a venture, which must be regarded as an extra risk factor. Assistance from the parent group may be available and may ameliorate this disadvantage.

The advantage of Option 2 is that it offers the potential for **higher margins** than Pipeco currently enjoys. Also, the market is expanding strongly; it may be that the Option 1 infrastructure market does not have the same **long-term potential** and may reach maturity in the same way that the Western European infrastructure market has done.

Recommendations

Option 1 in country A is the least attractive prospect. The choice lies between Option 1 in country B and Option 2. A decision will depend largely on the decision-maker's degree of risk aversion: Option 2 offers the potential for higher returns but is much riskier than Option 1 in country B.

Part (b)

> **Top tips**. There are lots of things Pipeco would be interested in when it came to deciding between country A and country B. However, you are only offered six marks for dealing with this requirement: the implication here is that the Examiner will be happy with half a dozen brief but well-made points. However, note the examiner's comment below – and do not make your answers too brief.
>
> **Easy marks**. Very simple PEST topics such as political stability, transport infrastructure, educated workforce and regulatory requirements are valid here, and should occur to you with barely a moment's thought.
>
> **Examiner's comments**. Some candidates were *too* brief in their answers, failing to provide enough depth. Other problems were the perennial lack of application to the scenario and, in particular, lack of consideration of the competitive environment in the two target countries.

Pipeco would need a great deal more information before committing to Option 1 in either target country. Here are some examples.

Political and legal. Is the host country **politically stable**? For EU countries, there is little threat of expropriation or other draconian measures, but consideration must be given to the likelihood of sharp increases in **taxation** or substantial cost-enhancing changes in **business regulation** if there were to be a change of government.

What is the government policy and degree of influence on the kind of infrastructure development that Pipeco hopes to be involved in? Are there **favoured suppliers**?

Economic. Economic management depends on government policy: what are the current fiscal and monetary policies? Is the Euro in use? What are the prospects for growth, inflation and employment? Is the government interventionist or laissez-faire?

Social. Is society **stable**? What are the main **demographic features**? Is the labour force generally **well-educated**? What is the position, influence and attitude of the relevant **trades unions**?

Technological. What is the current state of the **transport and communications infrastructure**? To what extent is broadband available?

Competitive environment. What is the current state of the **five competitive forces** both generally and in relation to the large extruded pipe industry? Who is the market leader? How many direct competitors are there and what is their size? Ditto for suppliers and customers? What barriers to entry exist?

Part (c) (i)

> **Text reference**. Relationship marketing is dealt with in Chapter 8 of your BPP Study Text.
>
> **Top tips**. Relationship marketing is a large and complex topic and only the most basic aspects can be dealt with in an answer worth only six marks.

> If you know what relationship marketing is, the easy way to approach this question is to start off with a definition: this would be worth two marks. You could then go on to discuss its advantages in the context of Pipeco's business. The classic justification for working at relationship marketing is the very large cost associated with acquiring a new customer, as compared to the moderate expense of remaining on good terms with an existing one.

(i) Relationship marketing is a complex topic, but in its simplest sense is the process of **managing a company's relationships with its customers** in order to make repeated sales to them. There has been a **decline in loyalty on the part of customers**: they show an increasing willingness to shop around for the best deal. They are also unlikely to complain about poor service: instead, they will simply take their business elsewhere. Relationship marketing is a response to these trends.

Costs of new customer acquisition

The basic rationale of relationship marketing is to **avoid the heavy expense involved in acquiring new customers**: it is far cheaper to keep existing ones. This requires a company-wide commitment to high levels of **customer service** and a continuing process of two-way communication with customers, to find out what they want and to make sure that they are satisfied with what they get.

Switching costs

Relationship marketing is not as applicable to Pipeco's present operations as it is to some other businesses. The effort and cost involved in relationship marketing are most appropriate in markets where **switching costs are high** and a lost customer is therefore probably lost for a long time. Pipeco operates in what is effectively a commodity market, where **switching costs are low**. In such markets, where customers make buying decisions mostly on price, it can be fairly cheap to acquire new business. On the other hand, quality of service can be the only real way for a supplier to **differentiate** its market offering, so a commitment to good customer service, if not to the full spectrum of relationship marketing practices would be advantageous to Pipeco.

Were Pipeco to undertake Option 2 for its future development, relationship marketing would become much more relevant, particularly where important specifiers were concerned. In their case, **cultivating a habit of using Pipeco products** would be most advantageous to the company.

In general, relationship marketing, if effective, offers several advantages besides lower promotional costs.

(a) **Turnover from each customer may expand**; customers can develop habits; they will buy new items from trusted suppliers rather than research new ones; new products can be developed in response to customer interests and requests; and over time, they will tend to expand the scale of their operations.

(b) **A satisfied customer is the best possible form of promotion**: new business may be introduced by informal recommendation.

(c) Habitual customers are more likely to complain that to go elsewhere. This gives the company an opportunity not just to **correct the immediate problem** but also to **learn from** it for the future.

(d) The long-term relationship can benefit **staff motivation and morale**: it is pleasanter to deal with satisfied customers than to spend much of the working day dealing with irate ones.

Part (c) (ii)

> **Easy marks**. There was a mark available for recognising the magnitude of the changes involved and another for recognising the importance of the staff in both companies.
>
> **Examiner's comments**. There was a degree of confusion about what the wording of this question required you to do.
>
> The Examiner's approved approach is that the question has two distinct, though similar, elements that should be dealt with separately. One element is about relationship marketing and the other about the Option 2 acquisition. Although both elements deal with change management, the Examiner felt that they should be considered separately. Very few candidates realised that they should not be run together and answered accordingly.

(ii) We have already remarked that Option 2 represents a **major change of strategy for Pipeco**. It will be necessary to integrate the target company's operations, techniques and people into the expanded company while continuing to run the existing Pipeco business. There is the possibility of significant redundancies and there will certainly be a need for extensive training, adjustment of practice and careful project management.

HRM and staff issues following the acquisition

Mergers and acquisitions frequently fail to produce their intended benefits, often because of **cultural incompatibilities, power struggles and jealousies**. A successful takeover will depend on effective leadership. This must start with a **clear vision** of where the merged business is going and how it is to get there. This vision must be communicated effectively and the change process driven from the top. The staff of both Pipeco and the target company will inevitably be apprehensive about the possibility of **Job losses**: the way to deal with such fears is to act quickly to determine whether they are necessary and, if so, implement them rapidly and fairly. There is then the best chance of the remaining staff putting the trauma behind them and contributing to the change process. Pipeco seems to have an enlightened attitude to such matters and should be able to navigate any HRM problems that eventuate without too much difficulty.

Introduction of relationship marketing

Improving customer service

The introduction of relationship marketing will have implications for all parts of the merged company, since all activities make their contribution to the **high standard of customer service** involved. Pipeco should aim to build on the target company's existing sales and marketing skills and experience since its own staff are unlikely to possess them to any great degree. At the same time, there will be scope for **extensive training** for suitable staff in most functions.

Relationship marketing is based on the simple principle of enhancing satisfaction by precision in meeting the needs of individual customers. This depends on extensive two-way **communication** to establish and record the customer's characteristics and preferences and to build a long-term relationship. *Adcock* mentions three important practical methods that Pipeco will be well advised to adopt.

(a) A **customer database** should be built using an IT system for the rapid acquisition and retrieval of the individual, customer's details, needs and preferences.

(b) **Customer oriented service systems** that go further than ordinary customer care should be developed: this involves structure, technology and processes and has particularly important implications for culture and HRM practices such as recruitment and training.

(c) **Extra customer contacts** should aimed for, with all staff appreciating their importance to the relationship.

44 Island transport

> **Text references.** Environmental analysis such as Porter's Five forces and PEST analysis is assumed knowledge for E3 (because it is covered in the E2 syllabus).
>
> Performance and control measures are covered in Chapters 12 and 13 of the BPP Study Text for E3.
>
> Methods of expansion are covered in Chapter 5.

Part (a)

> **Top tips.** This question offers you ten marks for an analysis of threats from changing market conditions. *Porter's* five forces would make a good framework for an answer at two marks per force providing PEST was also added. The Examiner was also prepared to accept a free form answer that would deal with threats of all kinds: this emphasises the importance of planning your answer with a little thought and not rushing after the first idea that occurs to you. The five forces and PEST both provide frameworks for brainstorming, but would not gain marks in themselves as pieces of theoretical knowledge.

> **Easy marks.** S Company's poor bottom line, despite its monopoly position, and its reliance on the rather unreliable tourist industry are obvious matters for discussion.

Reliance on tourist industry. S Company is **heavily reliant** on the tourist industry. Even its freight and provisions business must be derived in significant part from the tourist element of the islands population. Much of its business is therefore seasonal and subject to the variability of the islands holiday market. If it lost the contract to service the new development it may find its other business being undermined by the successful applicant.

Cost increases reducing margins. S Company is the only operator of ships to the islands: it is a monopolist and ought to be able to make **excess profit** as a result. However, the company made profit of only £120,00 on a turnover of £4.8 million. This is just 2.5%, which is very poor, particularly as sea fares have increased steeply in recent years. In fact, the company has not been able to increase its charges sufficiently to cover cost increases. A vigorous programme of **cost reduction** is needed, but the company is owned by its directors and staff, which may limit its vulnerability to the pressure of potential takeover and inhibit its ability to make painful cuts in labour costs.

Price regulation. As S Company has a **monopoly** of an essential service, National and local government will inevitably be very interested in the fares on the Company's ships. It seems highly likely that there is at least some informal **control over the fares** that S can charge, based in part on the islanders' ability to pay. This may be self-imposed by S in order to avoid the imposition of a formal regime.

(**Assumption**: since a mooring in the conventional sense of a kind of permanent anchor in open water would not be very useful for embarking freight and passengers, we assume that the reference to mooring rights means the right to use dock facilities)

Renewal of docking rights. We only know of one specific supply that S Company receives, but it is an essential one: **docking rights** on the island and the mainland. These rights are due for renewal in one year's time. The **suppliers' bargaining power** will depend on the availability of alternative docking facilities, but it is unlikely that there are many of those, especially on the islands. The dock operators may be in a very strong position, particularly as the construction of the proposed holiday complex is likely to attract competitors into S Company's market.

Market cannibalisation. Sea transport and air transport are different industries and their services are to some extent **substitutes** for each other. The downside of S Company's business model, therefore, is that it competes with itself; the upside is that it is well placed to take advantage of any longer term trend by passengers to move from one means of travel to the other.

Increased competition from airlines. S is the only ship operator but there are other airlines serving the island and air fares are increasingly subject to competition. The air operators have not been able to maintain their previous considerable premium over the surface fare but it does still exist to some extent. Should the surface fare increase to be roughly comparable with the air fare, the **substitution effect is likely to increase**. Some passengers might be unwilling to travel by air, but an increased number are likely to fly. In these circumstances, S Company will effectively find the substitution effect working against it, since it does not have a monopoly of air transport to the islands.

The **intensity of competitive rivalry** is increased by two features that will probably affect S Company's markets.

(a) Suppliers will compete where buyers can **switch easily**: this is likely to apply to S Company's air operations, if current trends to the low fares model apply in this market.

(b) High fixed costs will tempt suppliers to **compete on price in lean times**, since any contribution is better than none. We are not told anything about S Company's cost structure or those of its competitors, but aircraft are expensive capital items and we might expect fairly high fixed costs to be present.

Low barriers to entry. The barriers to entry into S Company's markets appear to be fairly low for companies already involved in shipping and aviation. The general growth of tourism on the islands and the new project in particular may well draw in new competitors. Ships and aircraft are inherently mobile and could easily be moved to the islands routes; there are probably few scale economies available in such a relatively small market; and customers would incur no switching costs. The only barrier that might be of significance is **regulation**, which may take effect through direct control of operations or through restrictions on the availability of slots at ports and airfields.

Part (b)

Top tips. This is a sensible numerical exercise for this paper, linking the calculations to a genuinely strategic issue. However, the data are scattered about the scenario: you must go through the setting carefully to make sure that you have noted all the relevant points.

In the Enterprise Strategy paper, you should expect to find computations set in a context of strategic decision-making, and you should be prepared to use the computations you perform to inform the strategic decisions you suggest.

We differ slightly from the Examiner in our computation: he calculated the income from fares on a 26 fortnight basis and assumed that the cost of the dock works would occur at time 1 rather than time 2.

Easy marks. Even if you have forgotten about the equivalent annuity method, you should be able to do the rest of the computation.

Examiner's comments. Almost all candidates appeared unable to calculate an equivalent annual value. Also, few were able to provide a clear and relevant net present value calculation.

S Company should quote an annual price of £116,896.

Contract pricing

We assume that the cost of the port works will be incurred during year 2.

	Year	Cashflow £	20% discount factor	Present value
Purchase of new ship	2	(7,000,000)	0.694	(4,858,000)
Scrap value of existing ship	2	250,000	0.694	173,500
Scrap value of new ship	7	4,000,000	0.279	1,116,000
Port works	2	(1,000,000)	0.694	(694,000)
Freight contribution	2	2,000,000	0.694	1,388,000
Passenger contribution	3–7	1,267,071	2.077	2,631,707
Net present value				(242,793)
Divide by 20% factor years 3–7 to give equivalent annual cash flow				(116,896)

Workings

(1) 20% discount factors

  Years 1–2   1.528
  Years 1–7   3.605
  Therefore, years 3–7   2.077

(2) Passenger contribution

  Assume maximum number of passengers to be carried

  Average annual return journeys by sea = 500 × 0.9/14 × 365
  = 11732.14286

  Net revenue per journey (£120 – 12) = £108

  Annual total net contribution: 1,267,071

Part (c)

Top tips. The requirement employs the interesting phrase 'control measures'. By this, the Examiner does not seem to mean *performance measures* but something like *matters the company will have to take particular care over*. His own suggested solution uses the phrase 'control issues'.

Our solution follows the Examiner's lead and looks at measures that will be taken to achieve control. However, if you adopted the alternative interpretation of the requirement – performance measures – and used the balanced scorecard approach to guide your answer you would still have earned credit for this.

Easy marks. Careful attention to the timing and value of costs and cash flows is obviously going to be vital to this new venture.

> **Examiner's comments.** Most candidates suggested a number of measures, but these were often very general rather than being applied to the specifics of the situation. Also few candidates distinguished clearly between the control measures relevant to the bid process and those that should be used during the operation of the contract.
>
> **Tutorial note.** For the purposes of this answer, 'control measures' are not taken to refer to performance measures (measurable performance criteria such as KPIs) used for control, but measures (or actions) taken to *achieve* control: that is, control mechanisms and the issues on which they focus.

Control measures during the bid process

(i) Financial control measures

From the point of view of the supplier, S, the ideal bid is one that is priced high enough to earn at least the desired **rate of return** while being lower than the next lowest **competing** bid in order to obtain the business. (In the absence of industrial espionage, bidders cannot know the level of their competitors' bids and are thus motivated to bid as low as they feel they can in order to secure the business.) It is therefore essential for bidders to **prepare their estimates of cost and revenue very carefully**, in order to avoid contracts that lead to losses. This is particularly important in the case of contracts that extend several years into the future, such as the one S Company is considering.

(Assumption: there is a single contract, for both the building materials and the subsequent movement of passengers.)

Both **capital costs and potential operating costs and revenues** must be estimated in detail and with care. S Company must be sure of its cost of capital and the risk premium it requires. The element of risk involved will make CVP and **sensitivity analysis** an essential part of the company's preparation of its bid, so that it is aware of the variations in costs and revenues that would result in an overall loss. This will require significant input of information from M and it may be appropriate to make the bid subject to guarantees from M of minimum revenues.

Cash flow forecasts should be prepared, as the timing of cash flows may affect the magnitude of capital charges.

A large part of the company's operating cost is likely to consist of **fuel purchases**. The current uncertainty over future fuel prices will make it appropriate for the contract to permit increases in fares to cover higher fuel costs.

The success of the overall project will depend on the timeliness of the construction of the holiday resort, the dock improvements and the new ship. It is likely that both sides will wish to incorporate **penalty clauses** in the contract to allow for losses incurred as a result of delays that are the other party's responsibility.

(ii) Non-financial control measures

S will have to take care over the **security and confidentiality** of its bid information, and associated analyses, so that competitors do not have access to comparative information, and so that (unless cost transparency is in operation) it does not make itself vulnerable to the customer on post-contract negotiation on price.

In general terms, it will have to examine the **feasibility** of the service levels expected of it: not just in financial terms (can it provide the service at the agreed cost?) but in terms of availability of vehicles (including maintenance schedules, peak periods); the availability and skills of staff (and the ability to maintain staffing levels year round) and planners/co-ordinators; the company's ability to guarantee the safety of passengers in transit; and so on.

S will also need to put controls in place to ensure that the process is fully **documented**, adding to the company's 'competence/knowledge base' for review and learning for future bids. There should be a clear trail for all bid decisions, analyses and management processes: this will be particularly valuable for 'debriefing' in the event that the bid is unsuccessful – or if the bid is successful, but the contract subsequently runs into problems.

Control measures during contract operation

(i) Financial control measures

It will be essential for S Company to operate its services in line with the **budgets** prepared for its bid if it is to be financially healthy. The contract duration is for five years, which is a long time to run at even a small loss, so rigorous budgetary control procedures should be in place, in which managers are called upon to justify variances to budget and tasked with finding solution to prevent them from recurring.

The company should also monitor **market developments** so as to be able to forecast and make adjustments for future changes in costs and revenues. These may, for example, arise as a result of an increase in the price of oil or a shift in holiday fashion and availability.

Internal controls should already be in place as part of S's compliance obligations and internal policies. Assets should be safeguarded from inappropriate use or loss/fraud (eg security during the building works, segregation of duties in procurement, vetting of staff in high-risk positions); the risks of financial loss/liability should be identified and managed (eg taking out liability insurances); and the quality of internal and external financial reporting should be supported (eg by proper maintenance of records, accounting checks).

(ii) Non-financial control measures

S Company would be entering into a kind of **joint venture** with M for the life of the contract. While a degree of trust between the parties would be desirable, it will be necessary for S Company to monitor M's behaviour to ensure that all is as it should be. Ideally, the contract should allow for the negotiation of variations to account for changed circumstances. It should also clearly set out the **procedure for handling any contract disputes**: escalation procedures, alternative dispute resolution procedures, provision for arbitration and so on.

Processes and relationships for **contract management** should be put in place. This will partly be driven by M, but reciprocal engagement will be required by representatives of S: eg for ensuring that contract terms are adhered to, communication is maintained, working together on performance monitoring and improvement and so on.

S Company must develop and appropriate process for **performance measurement**, perhaps based on a balanced scorecard, so that its development continues. The contract will eventually come to an end, and the directors of S Company must ensure that it is in a fit state to continue to compete.

Meanwhile, S should continue to operate its **non-financial control procedures** eg monitoring and reporting in regard to health and safety, pilot/master accreditation and skill maintenance, equipment/vehicle age and maintenance, legal compliance and so on, that were already in place before the contract started.

Part (d)

Top tips. The requirement to 'identify' is at the fairly low level of *comprehension*, so very brief descriptions of what you propose will be satisfactory.

Ansoff's product market vector model provides a useful framework for brainstorming possible routes that S Company could follow.

It is important in questions like this not to indulge in fantasy. The Examiner is asking you to combine imagination with realism, so suggestions such as building a suspension bridge to the islands or digging a tunnel are not appropriate.

Easy marks. Suggestions built around product and market development, such as new air routes, are probably the easiest to generate.

S Company is involved in air and sea transport to the islands and has a monopoly of the latter. Using the *Ansoff* matrix as a framework we might suggest developments along the lines below.

Market penetration

- Build market share in the air ferry market, perhaps by increasing promotion, including joint schemes such as air miles and deals on rail fares.
- Increase overall market size, perhaps by joint promotions with the islands hotel operators, including cultural and sporting events

Market development

- Enter similar markets, including winter holiday transport: this would increase off-season utilisation of aircraft in particular.
- Provide air transport from a larger number of airfields, perhaps including those close to major centres of population (assuming this is not done already)

Product development

- Create holiday package products on the islands, providing accommodation of various kinds and an accommodation agency service
- Offer premium and economy services where possible
- Provide improved services on the mainland such as hotels for overnight accommodation and car parking facilities with shuttle buses to the docks and airports used.

Diversification

- Offer aircraft maintenance services to other operators.
- Integrate forward along the agricultural products and flowers value system
- Enter the cruise market.

45 Specialist cars

Part (a)

> **Text reference.** The five forces are assumed knowledge in E3, brought forward from E2.
>
> **Top tips.** This is a fairly straightforward question dealing with the application of one of the more important theoretical models. The Examiners have given you lots of information about CCC's industry in the scenario, providing you with something sensible to say about each of the five forces. It is not necessary to give a detailed explanation of the theory, but a very brief summary of the nature of each force is a good idea: there was one mark available for 'correct identification of all five forces'. There were also five marks available for reaching conclusions about the **influence** of each force. (Note that you were required to *evaluate* CCC's competitive environment.)
>
> A very important point about any question on the five forces is that you must make it clear at the outset that you understand just what the industry in question is. Here, for example, CCC is not competing in the mass-produced sports car market, nor in the prestige limousine market.
>
> **Easy marks.** You should have been able to recognise the final sentence of paragraph five of the setting as a pretty clear statement of the position of substitutes.
>
> **Examiners' comments.** This part of Question 1 was generally answered well. Common errors were failure to explain **why** identified factors were relevant and failure to assess their overall impact. (Emphasis added by BPP.)

According to *Porter*, a firm's **ability to make high profits** depends on the effect of **five competitive forces** that affect the industry it operates in. CCC competes in the luxury sports car market in Europe. The industry is characterised by very high quality, a large element of individual design specification by customers, very skilled labour and correspondingly high prices. There are six companies operating in this market, including CCC.

Threat of new entrants

Porter tells us that the threat from new entrants is limited by the existence of **barriers to entry** and the **expected reaction** from existing competitors. Barriers to entry to CCC's market seem to come in three forms.

(a) The incumbent firms have made **significant investment** in the development of their **products** and in building their **brands** through sales and marketing effort. An entrant would almost certainly have to match this investment.

(b) The incumbent firms employ highly skilled, specialised and experienced **labour forces** and reward them appropriately. An entrant would find it difficult and expensive to assemble a comparable workforce.

(c) The incumbent firms have a great deal of **human and intellectual capital** based on years of experience. An entrant without the equivalent qualities would have to invest in a long period of unprofitable operations in order to acquire it.

These barriers seem to be sufficiently high to safeguard the positions of the six existing market suppliers, except, perhaps against an entry via a takeover of one of them.

The **reaction** of the incumbent firms to the entry of a newcomer would probably be based on sales and marketing effort emphasising points (b) and (c) above.

Rivalry among existing firms

We are told that historically there has been little price competition between CCC and its peers; this is unsurprising, given that the market displays some of the characteristics of an oligopoly and that the suppliers have, presumably, achieved significant **differentiation of their products** using the same means as CCC. This market structure will have minimised direct competition. Rivalry is therefore unlikely to have a great effect on CCC's profit potential.

Threat of substitute products

A substitute product is one that competes for the same spending. Cars like those produced by CCC are just one category of very expensive, exclusive, luxury objects. We are specifically informed that substitutes for CCC cars include yachts and round the world cruises: there are many more and their suppliers are all competing for the same discretionary spending. Such products are a **significant threat** to CCC's profits.

Bargaining power of suppliers

Each firm in a value system attempts to extract for itself as much of the value created in the system as it can. There thus tends to be bargaining about price and credit terms in any supplier-customer relationship. Like most firms, CCC buys a range of components and assemblies, most of which seem to be of a more or less generic type. Such items would be available from more than one supplier and competition should keep the prices at a reasonable level. There is, however, the matter of the work carried out by SSS, which represents the single most significant cost item in each car. SSS is in an enviable position, since CCC's customers demand that their engines are prepared by this supplier. CCC therefore has **no bargaining power** at all. SSS Ltd is thus able to seize a great deal of value and reduce CCC's profits.

Bargaining power of customers

Just as CCC bargains with its suppliers when it can, so its customers are now bargaining over the price of their cars. This represents a change in behaviour apparently driven by recession and a consequent unwillingness to spend freely. The recent reduction in CCC's profitability indicates that the firm's customers now have **significant bargaining power.**

Conclusion

The directors of CCC feel that the fall in their profits is traceable to customer price sensitivity. It may be that the availability of substitutes and the bargaining power of SSS are also having an effect.

Part (b)

> **Top tips**. This question combines a numerical exercise with a strategic issue, and it is important to recognise this combination is popular with the Examiner.
>
> The question is only partly about computation. There are 'up to 12 marks available for calculations', but that is less than half of the total marks available. You could not pass this question on calculations alone, even supposing you made no errors at all.
>
> To score a reasonable mark in this question, you must make **appropriate interpretative comment** on the numbers. You are asked to '**Evaluate** the financial position so to score well you must apply some critical judgement. A few marks would be available for valid basic comparisons with the industry averages, but the bulk of the discussion marks would only be awarded for more detailed analysis and evaluation.
>
> **Easy marks**. The easiest marks here are for the calculation for SSS Ltd of the simple indices given in the table of industry data and for comparing the one with the other.

Examiners' comments. The Examiners were scathing about candidates' apparent inability to provide any but the most basic comment on the results of their computations. This reinforces our comment earlier about achieving a balance in your answer between calculation and analysis.

SSS Ltd – performance analysis

Measure	Industry	SSS Ltd
Gross ROCE (W1)		99.7%
Pre-tax ROCE (W2)	11.2%	17.9%
Gross profit rate (W3)		43.1%
Pre-tax profit rate (W4)	4.3%	7.7%
Non-current assets turnover (W5)		2.75
Receivables days (W6)	65	22
Payables days (W7)	28	64
Inventory days (W8)		61
Revenue per employee (€) (W9)	128,500	306,875
Pre-tax profit per employee (€) (W10)	5,526	23,750
Dividend cover (W11)		2.05
Current ratio (W12)		1.68
Quick ratio (W13)		0.73

Workings

(1) $\dfrac{(1{,}455 - 1{,}398)}{(100 + 960)}$

(2) $\dfrac{190}{(100 + 960)}$

(3) $\dfrac{2{,}455 - 1{,}398}{2{,}455}$

(4) $\dfrac{190}{2{,}455}$

(5) $\dfrac{2{,}455}{894}$

(6) $365 \times \left(\dfrac{146}{2{,}455}\right)$

(7) $365 \times \left(\dfrac{244}{1{,}398}\right)$

(8) $365 \times \left(\dfrac{232}{1{,}398}\right)$

(9) $\dfrac{2{,}455{,}000}{8}$

(10) $128{,}500 \times 0.043$ and $\dfrac{190{,}000}{8}$

(11) $\dfrac{190}{65}$

(12) $\left(\dfrac{232 + 146 + 32}{244}\right)$

(13) $\left(\dfrac{146 + 32}{244}\right)$

Comments

Most of the value offered by numerical analysis comes from **making comparisons**, either with similar companies or with preceding periods. Unfortunately, here we have no preceding period information, so it is **impossible to discern trends**. Also we have only a few comparable figures for the industry as a whole. Comment on SSS Ltd must therefore be to some extent tentative.

In those performance figures for which we have industry comparators, it is clear that SSS Ltd is **outperforming the industry average** by a comfortable margin. Pre-tax ROCE is over 50 percent higher, while pre-tax profit margin is almost 80 percent higher. Also, revenue per employee and profit per employee are 2.4 times and 4.3 times the industry average respectively.

These figures fit well with CCC's view that SSS Ltd makes as much profit from an engine as CCC does from a complete car. SSS Ltd is not only creating a high level of value through the skills of its employees: its strong bargaining position (explained earlier) allows it to extract even more value from its downstream link to the customer, CCC.

Traditional accountants' ratios are interesting. **Dividend cover**, at just over 2 times is not, perhaps, as high as one would hope to see in a public company, but seems perfectly adequate in a small owner-managed business. The owners of such companies will take the income they require in a variety of ways, including salary, fees, benefits in kind and dividends, as seems most convenient and tax-efficient from time to time.

Receivables and payables days, at 22 and 64 respectively, stand the industry averages, 65 and 28, on their heads. Largely as a result of this, the current and quick ratios, at 1.68 and 0.73, are significantly lower than is traditionally recommended. However, SSS Ltd does not appear to be a company that is likely to have difficulty in paying its bills as they fall due. Rather, it seems likely that its bargaining power both as a supplier and as a purchaser enables it to follow a very aggressive cash management policy, using cash from its purchasers and credit from its suppliers as significant contributions to its working capital.

The current ratio would be even lower were it not for a moderately high figure of 61 for **inventory days**. At first glance, this may seem high for a company that manages its working capital carefully, but it is probably quite reasonable given the nature of the company's specialist activities.

SSS Ltd receives engines from CCC for modification and performance upgrades. This may well involve the installation of **very expensive components and sub-assemblies**. Whether bought-in or made in-house, these are likely to be produced in small batches: the batch sizes will be the result of a reasonable compromise between production and inventory costs. Delivery of bought-in items is also likely to be subject to long lead times. Both of these factors will lead to rather higher inventory than might be achieved in more routine manufacturing.

Further comment

SSS Ltd's overall high performance is further indicated by its relationship with CCC. SSS Ltd dominates this relationship, refusing to enter into an exclusive contract to supply CCC or even to negotiate over price. It can do this because of the esteem in which it is held by CCC's customers. This esteem is indicative of highly effective marketing of the kind that is based on personal recommendation and a reputation for consistently high quality. The SSS Ltd brand is a very valuable asset and very solidly based.

Part (c)

> **Top tips**. The Examiners anticipated that you would be able to identify and discuss a number of possible courses of action for CCC, rather than concentrating on one, as the wording of the question might have led you to do. Always bear in mind the number of marks available and ask yourself if you have covered enough points to justify a good proportion of them.
>
> Also, where there is more than one possibility to discuss, a conclusion and recommendation will normally be expected. In the case you were asked to 'advise the directors' so this should have prompted you to discuss a range of possible options before recommending a preferred option, and explain why you have chosen it.
>
> **Examiners' comments**. There was little discussion in depth of the possible options.

The directors of CCC might consider four possible courses of action to overcome the problem presented by the bargaining strength of SSS Ltd.

218 Answers

1   A new supplier

SSS Ltd's strength lies largely in its reputation with CCC's customers. If CCC could find another supplier capable of the same quality of work and could succeed in shaping its customers' perceptions of that work by means of careful marketing communication, it might be possible to play one off against the other. The potential for achieving this would depend to a great extent on the nature of the work to be done. Expensive plant and equipment, complex technology, skilled hand work and intellectual property rights are all factors that might limit a supplier's ability to achieve the necessary competences. Poaching staff from SSS Ltd might be worth attempting.

2   In-house engine preparation

CCC might be able to bring its engine preparation work in-house. Its ability to do this would be subject to the same caveats as the new supplier option outlined above. The staff poaching tactic would also be relevant here.

3   Aggressive bargaining

So far, CCC has had no success in price negotiations with SSS Ltd. However, it may be that the threat of CCC's undertaking either of the two options outlined above might induce the owner of SSS Ltd to be more flexible. There is a simple cost-benefit calculus: by reducing his prices he would also reduce the threat that CCC may take drastic action to undermine his business.

4   Acquisition of SSS Ltd

Top tips. The Examiner stated that it was not necessary to attempt a valuation of SSS Ltd in order to obtain full marks.

SSS Ltd is an **attractive takeover target** for CCC. Acquisition would enable CCC to both **capture the value** created by SSS Ltd through its own products and prevent competitors from making use of its services. The problem would be the negotiation of a **suitable price** and form of consideration. The owner of SSS Ltd might welcome such a proposal as an exit route from his business and might be willing to accept shares in CCC, perhaps in combination with a cash sum, as consideration. A directorship contract might also be considered. Valuing SSS Ltd would be difficult and might require extensive negotiation and professional advice.

Conclusion

CCC should approach the owner of SSS Ltd on an amicable basis to discuss future options. The bargaining stance outlined above under option 3 might be the opening gambit, with the possibility of an agreed acquisition being held in reserve. If neither of these options meets with success, options 1 and 2 might then be reconsidered.

46 AAA

Text reference. Chapter 13 of the BPP Study Text for E3 covers the balanced scorecard; Chapter 4 deals with benchmarking; and Chapter 7 looks at knowledge management.

Part (a)

Top Tips. Read the requirements of this question very carefully, because this should highlight the relationship between (a) and (b). Notice the instruction in (b) that 'you should refer to your answer to part (a) in making your comparison.' However, notice the difference in instruction between the two parts – (a) requires an appraisal of performance; (b) requires a Board level report.

Requirement (a) alone is worth 25 marks – one quarter of the whole examination. Of these, 10 of the marks are available for calculations, meaning that there are 15 marks available for the analysis of the figures. The key to doing well in (a) is to use the calculations alongside the information provided in the scenario to present sufficient **insight** and **analysis** to earn yourself a good number of those 15 marks. Simple statements such as 'Gross profit is lower than budget' score very poorly because they make no attempt to explain **why** the variance may have occurred. Use the data provided on BBB to help you decide what calculations to conduct for the balanced scorecard of AAA.

> Similarly, merely demonstrating your knowledge of the balanced scorecard model is not sufficient to pass this question. You need to demonstrate to the examiner that you can **apply** the model, **interpret** its results, and then **appraise** the results.
>
> **Easy marks.** Section (a) offers some easy marks for the calculations of comparisons, differences and ratios. Every correct, relevant calculation is worth ½ each.
>
> **Examiner's comments.** The first part of this question (worth 25 marks) was very poorly answered. Candidates cannot expect to pass a strategic level examination by preparing answers with little or no strategic analysis in them. Simply stating that a figure is higher or lower than budget is not sufficient – candidates need to go on and explain why the variance may have occurred.

AAA Balanced scorecard report 200X

The Balanced Scorecard looks at a company's performance from four different perspectives: Innovation and learning; internal business processes; customer; and financial.

We shall consider AAA's performance in each of these areas below.

Innovation and learning perspective

We budgeted for the launch of ten new product lines; we actually launched twelve, but of these only one was successful compared to a budget of four. This requires further investigation, since these figures may indicate a **degree of over-optimism** both about the volume of R&D we are able to undertake and about the overall competence of our R&D organisation. There is a risk that AAA is developing new product lines for which there is no demand. Alternatively, the marketing aspects of new product development may require attention if new line are not being promoted effectively.

Internal business perspective

The closing **cash balance** of J$179 million is much lower than the J$485 budgeted. We note that pre-tax profit at J$652 million is J$138 million lower than budget, which may account for some of the J$306 million shortfall. We have no figures that would indicate any specific cash shortfall, though we note that average inventories are J$20.6 million shortfall above budget. It is not really appropriate to use these average figures to discuss the year-end cash position, but their magnitude compared with the budget variance seems to suggest that significant demands have been made on cash during the year, and may suggest that there are **weakness in the business's working capital management**.

Inventories themselves deserve comment because they have run significantly above budget in all categories, and total almost 30 days cost of sales.

Finished goods inventory is particularly noticeable, having averaged J$38.2 million against a budget of J$20 million, an adverse variance of 91%. This represents 22.6 days rather than the 11.8 days budgeted. There could well be a line here to the significant overall sales variance, but it also looks like controls over the level of finished goods held could be improved.

WIP, at 0.47 days, is significantly higher than the 0.18 days budgeted, which should raise concerns over the efficiency of the production process – especially if AAA are operating a JIT manufacturing system.

Raw material inventories, at 6.75 days, also seem significantly high for a routine mass production operation; the budget, at 5.58 days seems to indicate an acceptance that this is normal. Greater attention to delivery scheduling may be fruitful.

Headcount averaged 2,259, against 2,128 budgeted, an increase of 6.16%. Unfortunately, there does not seem to have been a corresponding increase in worthwhile activity. **Sales** were significantly down on budget (2.35 million units against 2.40, an adverse variance of 2.1%; J$m1,793 value against J$1,941, an adverse variance of 7.6%; sales per employee J$793,714 against J$912,124, an adverse variance of 13%). The increased headcount alongside lower than budgeted sales means that sales per employee have fallen from 1,128 (budget) to 1,040 (actual). This indicates that efficiency is falling, although this could be in part due to AAA's products becoming less desirable in the market place.

The adverse variance in unit production cost of sales (J$262 against J$259) is also likely to reflect this increase in headcount. There may also be a link between the employment of new, inexperienced staff and the clear indications of **deteriorating quality**.

Output quality seems to have been much worse than expected, with rework, customer returns and warranty claims all much higher than budget.

The actual number of units rejected and sent for **rework** was 54,000 against a flexed budget of 29,375; this represents an adverse variance of 84%.

Warranty claims and other returns amount to 8.4% of all units sold. This is a very high figure, especially when we consider the number of units which also had to be reworked. This suggested there are serious problems in AAA's quality control procedures.

Recommendation: the company should give urgent attention to rethinking its quality management procedures. The level of failures is much too high and the existence of a separate output inspection function is symptomatic of an out-dated approach.

Customer perspective

The quality issue has already been highlighted. 84 warranty claims and returns per '000 units equates to 197,400 dissatisfied customers in the year. We must not overlook the effect of the high rate of returns on our reputation and brand values.

The average selling price is almost 6% below budget; which in the light of quality issues suggests AAA may be having to discount prices to generate sales. This, combined with the returns problem and the 50,000 unit shortfall on the sales budget indicates a degree of customer dissatisfaction that should be of concern.

Financial perspective

AAA is a listed company and **EPS** is a key market indicator; its shortfall on budget of 8% is reflected in its **share price**, which, at J$334.5, is over 16% lower than planned. Not surprisingly, the company's poor performance is translating into a loss of value for its shareholders.

The main reasons for the shortfall in EPS are clear: **turnover** shows 7.6% adverse variance and **gross margin** of 65.6% is lower than the planned 68%: together these effects produce a gross profit shortfall on budget of 10.8%. These figures should be a serious cause for concern. Sales are below budget (probably due to quality issues damaging the company's brand) yet at the same time direct costs (%) are over budget. Some of the overspend may reflect the high labour costs associated with the level of re-working currently being required, but there should be wider concerns that costs are not being controlled tightly enough.

Net margin, at 36.4%, is similarly disappointing when compared with the 40.7% budgeted and indicates that indirect costs are also higher than expected. It has already been remarked that headcount is significantly above budget; and this will have an impact on the level of direct costs. However, AAA needs to review its level of overheads critically in the light of below budgeted sales.

Average capital employed was J$2,835 million, which is 11.2% higher than expected. Taken together with this, the fall in turnover and the evident increase in costs of all types produce a **return on capital employed** of 23%, against a budget of 31%. Again, this is an indicator that the company is not currently generating the level of value that it should be.

Summary

AAA's performance is disappointing compared to budget expectations. Important features are significant quality problems and failure to control costs of all kinds.

Workings

Cost of sales

Actual = J$m1,793 – 1,177 = 616
Budget = J$m1,941 – 1,320 = 621

Production volume

Sales revenue – factory profit = factory cost of sales

J$m1,793 – 1,177 = 616

Unit production cost of sales = J$262

$$\text{Production volume} = \frac{616,000}{262} = 2,351,145$$

Since revenue and cost totals are given to the nearest J$million, the accuracy of this figure is spurious, but it does indicate that production and sales volumes were of similar magnitude.

Sales per employee

Budget $\dfrac{J\$1,941m}{2,128}$ = J$912,124

Actual $\dfrac{J\$1,793m}{2,259}$ = J$793,714

Variance $\dfrac{(912,124 - 793,714)}{912,124} \times 100\% = 12.98\%$

Number of rework units flexed budget

$30,000 \times \dfrac{2.35}{2.40} = 29,375$

Rework budget percentage

$\left(\dfrac{54,000}{2,350,000}\right) \times \dfrac{29,375}{54,000} = 1.25\%$

Selling price per unit

Budget: $\dfrac{J\$1,941m}{2.4m}$ = J$808.75

Actual: $\dfrac{J\$1,793m}{2.35m}$ = J$762.98

This is $\dfrac{808.75 - 762.98}{808.75} \times 100 = 5.66\%$ less than budget, ie adverse.

EPS variance

$\dfrac{(50 - 46)}{50} \times 100\% = 8\%$ adverse

Share price variance

$\dfrac{(400 - 334.5)}{400} \times 100\% = 16.4\%$ adverse

Turnover variance

$\dfrac{(1,941 - 1,793)}{1,941} \times 100\% = 7.6\%$ adverse

Gross margin

Budget: $\dfrac{1,320}{1,941} = 68.0\%$

Actual: $\dfrac{1,177}{1,793} = 65.6\%$

Gross profit variance

$\dfrac{(1,320 - 1,177)}{1,320} \times 100\% = 10.8\%$ adverse

Net margin

Budget: $\dfrac{790}{1,941} \times 100\% = 40.7\%$

Actual: $\dfrac{652}{1,793} \times 100\% = 36.4\%$

Capital employed variance

$\dfrac{(2,835 - 2,550)}{2,550} \times 100\% = 11.2\%$ increase

Return on capital employed

Budget: $\dfrac{790}{2,550} \times 100\% = 30.98\%$

Actual: $\dfrac{652}{2,835} \times 100\% = 23.00\%$

Part (b)

> **Top tips.** Requirement (b) asks you to make some calculations and then use them to compare two companies' performance in the form of a report to the directors. You should realise that a report to the directors needs to contain strategic insights, and pitch your answer at that level. Directors are unlikely to want to sift through large amounts of mundane comparative analysis.
>
> **Easy marks.** The requirement for (b) asks you to prepare a report and tells you two marks are available for this. Do not throw easy marks like this away! Part (b) also offers some further easy marks for basic calculations – again worth ½ each.
>
> **Examiner's comments.** The first part of this question was also poorly answered. Candidates need to provide a strategic analysis of the scenario information to score the marks available.

From: Management Accountant
To: Board of Directors
Date: 21 November 200X

BENCHMARKING PERFORMANCE – AAA AND BBB

Terms of reference

This report benchmarks AAA's performance against that of BBB, using the limited information available. Computations to support the analysis appear in the Annex.

Analysis of performance

Turnover, units sold and headcount all indicate that AAA is about three times as large an enterprise as BBB. AAA achieves a higher revenue per employee than BBB, which may reflect both marketing scale efficiencies and the higher average selling price obtained. However, BBB does not appear to be buying turnover, since its return on capital employed is 35%, which compare very favourably with AAA's 23%.

A further implication of the data mentioned above, is that BBB's internal processes and its control of direct and indirect costs must more efficient than AAA's. This is borne out by **BBB's higher margins, both gross and net,** and its unit cost of sales, which, at J$223, is only 85% of AAA's. This deduction assumes that there is no significant difference in costs between operating in Jurania and Mesnar.

As a result of **BBB's greater efficiency** its profitability (gross and net) is actually greater than AAA's, despite AAA's turnover being three times that of BBB's.

The differences in efficiency are also highlighted by the ROCE figures of the two companies. BBB's ROCE is 1½ times AAA's suggesting it is **generally better value for its shareholders**.

It is also necessary to remark that **BBB derives a marketing advantage** from its lower selling price. BBB's products are **more competitively priced** than AAA's, which taken together with concerns over the quality of AAA's products, suggest AAA's market share may be under threat from its smaller rival.

A further customer-related point of comparison is **BBB's low level of warranty claims**: this is just over 25 per thousand units sold, which contrasts very favourably with AAA's figure of 56. This suggests BBB's quality management controls are better than AAA's, in which case this is an areas of its internal controls which AAA needs to improve.

A final indication of efficient processes is given by **BBB's low level of inventory**: 14 days, or less than half of AAA's 30 days. Given the nature of the business – mass production of similar products made to order for customers – we should be looking to hold very low levels of inventory. The internal benchmarking report has already commented on the high levels of inventory which AAA appears to hold.

Conclusions

The limited information we have indicates that BBB is significantly more efficient than AAA in its business operations and competes more effectively and profitably, in the market place. In order to compete with BBB, and maintain market share, AAA needs to improve its key business process and overall efficiency.

Annex

Supporting data

Item	AAA	BBB
Turnover (J$million)	1793	560
Units sold (millions)	2.35	0.78
Employees	2259	740
Sales per employee (J$'000) (BBB: 560/740)	794	757
Average selling price per unit (J$) (BBB: 560,000/780)	763	718
Return on capital employed (%) (BBB: 557/1,589)	23	35
Gross margin (%) (BBB: (1,400-435)/1,400 × 100%)	66	69
Net margin (%) (BBB: 557/1,400 × 100%)	36	40
Unit production cost of sales (J$) (BBB: (435,000/780)/2.5)	262	223
Inventory days (BBB: 17/435 × 365)	30	14
Warranty claims per 1000 units sold (BBB: 19,800/780)	56	25

Part (c)

> **Top tips.** The examiner has acknowledged that (c) was a difficult question. However, the key to answering it successfully is to identify the way knowledge management and competitive advantage link together. If you focus on knowledge management or competitive advantage alone you would score poorly. However, an accurate definition of each of the terms would earn you a couple of marks.
>
> **Examiner's comments.** In (c) most candidates failed to recognise the link between knowledge management and competitive advantage, and just provided a discussion of knowledge management.

A firm has **competitive advantage** when it is able to earn higher profits than its rivals. Competitive advantage is likely to be underpinned by the possession of either **unique resources** or **core competences** (which are the activities and processes through which resources are deployed) that competitors cannot easily imitate or obtain. Typically, competitive advantage will be developed by strategies based on price, differentiation, focus, or becoming the industry standard and thus achieving **lock-in**.

Knowledge management includes all the processes, technologies and interactions required to enable to organisation to create, share and exploit knowledge for business purposes. Its importance lies in the common experience of organisations that the possession of such abilities can form a major source of competitive advantage.

AAA could use knowledge management to address the weaknesses exposed by comparison with BBB, and create a competitive advantage over B.

Improvements in quality management. AAA has a significant problem with **quality**. Almost certainly, some quality failures can be traced to problems that could be solved by sharing knowledge about causes and cures. Such problems might include improper assembly or handling techniques, inadequacies of equipment and poor co-ordination of work. It might also be appropriate to investigate whether any problems arise from the split of responsibility for assembly and inspection.

Cost control. AAA seems to have a generally higher **cost base** than BBB, though perhaps enjoying some economies of scale. A system of sharing and spreading locally created improvements in efficiency might reduce costs significantly. There is a clear role for factory management here, in ensuring that **best production practice** is used, but there are probably also areas of indirect cost that could be improved by learning from other, similar organisations (including possibly BBB).

Understanding customer requirements. A common use of knowledge management technology is to record and share details of **interactions with customers**. No doubt AAA sells to intermediaries: knowledge of their attitudes and reactions is very important, but it would also be useful to have some awareness of the views of the ultimate consumer as well. An improved focus on **customer priorities** might result from systematic recording and analysis of feedback from sales staff and, in particular, from careful examination of comments linked to returns and warranties.

This focus may lead AAA to **re-design some of its products**, thereby giving it new opportunities to provide a tailored product which customers really want. This will lead to a competitive advantage based on AAA's focus on customer requirements.

47 AFR

Text reference. Product portfolio analysis and the Boston Consulting Group (BCG) matrix are covered in Chapter 4 of the BPP Study Text for E3. Competitive strategies are covered in Chapter 5.

Chapter 13 looks at performance measures and controls.

Part (a)

Top tips. This question requires you to apply your knowledge of product portfolio management.

The key to doing well in (a) is to consider the portfolio as a whole. Simply presenting the BCG matrix and showing where each product would fit within it is not adequate. You are asked to evaluate the portfolio – and this evaluation should include an assessment of each products value to AFR's portfolio such as its present financial returns (ie. its contribution margin and share of AFR's total earnings), its future potential and ability to raise AFR's present share price by holding-out the promise of good earnings in the future. The evaluation should also consider the overall strength of that portfolio in terms of the competitive strength of the products (ie. relative market share) and availability of successor products to replace earnings lost by decline of older products.

Easy marks. Section (a) offered some easy marks for the calculations and for factual application of the BCG matrix. The question advised you how many marks were available for the calculations, and you should have seen these as easy marks, because the calculations required were not difficult.

Examiner's comments. It was encouraging to see candidates' ability to apply their management accounting knowledge to prepare a product portfolio analysis and an NPV analysis. Many candidates correctly recognised the need to use the BCG model to answer part (a), but they then focused on each product separately without recognising the need to evaluate the three products as a portfolio or recognising the impact they have on each other.

AFR's Product portfolio

AFR has three strategic business units (SBUs) in its portfolio. Their relative market shares and the growth rates in their respective markets can be summarised as follows:

	Relative market share	Market growth rate
Office furniture	0.67	+15%
Bedroom furniture	1.12	-5%
Lounge furniture	0.42	+2%

We can also summarise the contribution which each of the SBUs makes to AFR's overall profitability.

	Contribution to profit	Contribution margin	%share of total contribution
Office furniture	0.81	19%	41%
Bedroom furniture	0.44	14%	22%
Lounge furniture	0.75	12%	38%
Total	2.00	15%	100%

The differing characteristics of the three SBUs mean that AFR has a reasonably balanced portfolio, and this can be expressed by showing the position of each of the SBUs on the Boston Consulting Group (BCG) matrix.

Relative Market Share

	High	Low
High (Market Growth Rate)	Stars	Question marks
Low	Cash cows	Dogs

The BCG

Office furniture

Using this BCG classification, office furniture would be classified as a '**Question mark**' (or 'Problem child'). Although AFR currently only has a relatively low share of the market, the overall market is an attractive one to be in, since it is experiencing high growth.

According to the BCG, Office Furniture would be expected to be a **net cash user** because of the costs of developing the product, building stocks and of its promotional launch. Its cash requirements will need to be cross-subsidised from other units in the portfolio.

We do not have any cash flow information for the business. However, we do know that office furniture generates the highest contribution margin (19 %) of the three divisions, and provides the largest contribution to total profit.

However, the main financial benefit from question marks will lie in their ability to generate strong earnings in the future. But for this to happen they need to gain a stronger competitive position than the office furniture of AFR has at present. Its low relative share is a weakness.

Bedroom furniture

The bedroom furniture SBU has the opposite characteristics from office furniture, namely a high relative market share in an unattractive market which is actually declining rather than growing. This division is a '**cash cow**' and, according to the BCG should be net cash positive, meaning that AFR could take some of the cash generated from the bedroom furniture SBU to cross-subsidise the cash requirements of the office furniture SBU.

However, it is a much smaller division, and provides the lowest contribution of the three divisions so the amount of cash generated may be limited.

Lounge furniture

The lounge furniture SBU has a relatively low market share of a market which is exhibiting slow growth. Therefore it is a '**dog**.' It may generate a modest net cash inflow or outflow, but it is likely to be essentially cash neutral despite accounting for 38% of AFR's total contribution.

The lounge furniture division earns the lowest contribution margin (12 %) of the three divisions. This is likely to be a result of AFR's small size in the market and its inability to grow its market share in the segment. It's factory capacity could be transferred to support the growth of the Office Furniture range. However it remains the second largest provider to total contribution (38%).

Outlook

Overall, because AFR's three SBUs fit into different quadrants of the BCG matrix we can say that it has a relatively balanced product portfolio.

Each of the SBUs generates a significant contribution to fixed costs, and this is consistent with the organisation being profitable throughout all of its history.

However, one area of strategic concern for the business should be that it doesn't have a 'star' product which it can look to maintain high returns and profitability in the future. If the bedroom or lounge furniture decline in the short-run, and before Office Furniture achieves a stronger position, this could damage AFR's earnings.

Working

> **Tutorial note.** In the exam, you would not score any marks for including elementary workings like these. However, they are included here to support the figures used in the answer.

Market share

Office furniture $\frac{4.23}{6.35} = 0.67$

Bedroom furniture $\frac{3.20}{2.85} = 1.12$

Lounge furniture $\frac{6.04}{14.25} = 0.42$

Margins

Office furniture $\frac{0.81}{4.23} = 19\%$

Bedroom furniture $\frac{0.44}{3.20} = 14\%$

Lounge furniture $\frac{0.75}{6.04} = 12\%$

Part (b)

> **Top tips.** Your answers to (b) should link to the evaluation you have done in part (a), rather than merely stating the possible strategies offered by the BCG matrix. For example, you should identify that the lounge furniture division is a 'dog' so the BCG would recommend it is either divested or held. In part (a) you should identify that this division accounts for 38% of AFR's contributions to profits, and so divesting of it would not be a sensible strategy. This reflects the importance of thinking critically about models rather than just learning them.
>
> **Examiner's comments.** In part (b) many candidates gave general strategic advice, as offered by the BCG model, rather than reviewing its suitability to AFR's particular product portfolio.

AFR's product strategies

Office furniture

The BCG matrix would suggest that an appropriate strategy for the office furniture SBU as a question mark would be one of '**building**' – investing large amounts of capital on it with the aim of increasing market share as a result.

However, the fact that the market leader (DS) is operating a cost leadership strategy means that AFR will need to adopt a different generic strategy in order to compete. In this case, the most appropriate strategy for AFR to choose would appear to be one of **differentiation**, distinguishing itself from DS's 'basic' furniture. AFR may choose to differentiate on the grounds of quality or design, but whatever basis it chooses it will still need to make a significant marketing investment to promote its brand image.

Bedroom furniture

The BCG matrix suggests that the appropriate strategy for bedroom furniture as a cash cow would be to **hold its current position**, and to use the surplus cash it generates to invest in other SBUs.

However, a potential problem with this strategy is that bedroom furniture appears to be AFR's smallest SBU, generating only 22% of the firm's total contribution. Therefore, it is possible the amount of cash it generates may not be sufficient to meet the needs of other areas of the business, particularly the office furniture division.

The fact that it has earned "a good reputation for style and quality", and levels of customer satisfaction are high, suggests that the bedroom furniture SBU, like the office furniture SBU, should pursue a strategy of **differentiation** focusing on the style and quality of the product. However, compared to the office furniture SBU, the amount of investment required for marketing and branding the bedroom furniture SBU should be relatively low because of the mature nature of the market. Nonetheless, AFR will need to be aware of any initiatives undertaken by NKO and/or MK aimed at increasing their market share, and be prepared to respond as necessary.

Note. You could also have used an Ansoff analysis here to suggest AFR could add additional features on to the range it provides to existing customers (product development) or look to move into new market segments (market development), for example supplying bedroom furniture for hotels.

Lounge furniture

The BCG matrix would suggest that lounge furniture, as a 'dog', should either be **held** or **divested**. Although AFR is only a relatively small player in the market, lounge furniture still accounts for 38% of its total contribution to profit, so divesting of this SBU would clearly not be an appropriate strategy for the business as the moment.

Similarly, AFR's unsuccessful attempts to increase its market share indicate that a growth strategy would not be appropriate. Therefore, management should adopt a similar strategy for lounge furniture as for bedroom furniture – that is, **hold their position** in the market and differentiate themselves from their competitors by virtue of the range of styles and fabrics they offer.

Because much of AFR's lounge furniture is made to order, they should promote this 'tailor made furniture' as a **unique selling point**, which should enable them to increase prices and thereby raise margins above the current 12%.

Alternatively the management of AFR could consolidate its position by rationalising the range to the best-selling items and possibly have some made in cheaper cost locations overseas. This would improve contribution in the dwindling market whilst also releasing capacity to keep up with the growth in demand for office furniture.

Part (c)

> **Top tips.** Part (c) is a standard question about project appraisal and investment decisions. However, unlike the papers at the Managerial level, E3 assesses 'strategic investment appraisal'. Therefore in addition to the NPV calculation candidates need to provide some insights around the competitive environment and the risks involved in the project, the uncertainties involved in forecasting sales of unknown projects before finally advising the Board whether or not to proceed with the investment.
>
> **Easy marks.** If you worked methodically through the NPV calculation and then considered the implications of the figures, you should have been able to score heavily. The question advised you how many marks were available for the calculations, and you should have seen these as easy marks.

Project appraisal

If AFR were to invest in the new range of dining furniture it would allow them to move into a market which is growing quickly, but which some of their main competitors have not yet moved into.

However, for the investment to be financially worthwhile it will need to generate a **positive net present value**, when its projected future cash flows are discounted for the 10% cost of capital.

Preliminary calculations suggest that AFR will need to sell 465 units per year to break even.

NPV calculation for Dining Furniture

	T_0 $	T_{1-5} $	T_{1-5} $
Investment in capital equipment	(120,000)		
Fixed costs		(80,000)	(80,000)
Contribution from 400 units (W1)		96,000	
Contribution from 500 units (W2)			120,000
Discount factor @ 10%	1	3.791	3.791
Net present value at 400 units	**(59,344)**	(120,000)	60,656
Net present value at 500 units	**31,640**	(120,000)	151,640

Breakeven point = 465 units sold per year (W3)

Workings

(1) Contribution per unit = 800 – 560 = 240

Contribution from 400 units = 240 × 400 = 96,000

(2) Contribution from 500 units = 240 × 500 = 120,000

(3) Breakeven = $500 - \dfrac{\left(\dfrac{31,640}{(31,460 + 59,344)}\right)}{100} = 465$

The R&D manager appears to have under-estimated the number of units which need to be sold in order to break even, claiming it is 'just over 400.'

The preliminary calculations suggesting that AFR will need to sell 465 units per year to break even, support the manager's uncertainty over this lower figure, and suggest that her estimate that sales need to be 'closer to 500 units each year' is more realistic.

Sales projections

At this stage, there does not appear to be a consensus on the level of sales which AFR could expect to achieve. The R&D manager is confident that sales will exceed 400 units per year, while the marketing thinks demand is likely to be less than 500.

Ultimately, any decision about whether to proceed with the investment should depend on whether the Board are confident of achieving the level of sales required to breakeven, so they should ask for some more detail on the projected sales numbers for making a final decision.

Levels of uncertainty

The R&D manager and the marketing manager also appear to disagree about the desirability of the new designs. The R&D manager is very confident that his 'stylish designs' will prove popular, but the marketing manager is more cautious because she considers the designs 'unusual'.

The marketing manager also feels that the selling price may be too high.

Again, the uncertainty over the number of sales and selling price means that any sales projections must also be uncertain, and this will reduce the amount of confidence could have in them.

Recommendation

Given that the dining furniture market is growing rapidly, with a number of small retailers, we suggest AFR should be able to penetrate this market pursuing a **differentiation strategy** if it chooses to do so.

However, we recommend that before making such a decision, AFR should conduct **market research** to identify the level of sales and the selling price which it can expect to achieve.

In addition, the research should also consider whether the current designs and the current unit product (one table and six chairs) are desirable to the market, or whether there are alternatives which would prove more attractive to the consumer.

Part (d)

> **Top tips.** Part (d) asks you to recommend appropriate control measures. You should be familiar with a wide range of control measures. The key to answering this question successfully was not merely to list (or discuss) control measures but to identify which measures were be most appropriate to the scenario and explaining why they were appropriate when making your recommendation. Note (d) part (ii) also draws on your knowledge of project management which you should have brought forward from Paper E2.
>
> When this exam was sat, some students interpreted control measures to mean 'controls metrics' in both (i) and (ii); some took it to mean 'steps to be taken to ensure control' in both (i) and (ii), and others interpreted it as control metrics in (i) and steps to be taken to ensure control in (ii). The model answer below treats control measures as metrics for monitoring the performance of the existing product ranges, and steps to be taken to ensure control when developing the proposed new range. The Examiner gave credit for any of the different interpretations provided the measures suggested were relevant to the scenario.
>
> **Examiner's comments.** Part (d)(i) saw the same failings as part (b). Students' answers were too generalised, and they chose to list standard controls rather than applying this knowledge and trying to recommend controls that were applicable to the scenario.

(i) Control measures for existing product ranges

> **Top tip.** Although this question was not about the balanced scorecard (and you didn't need to mention it in your answer) it would have been worth thinking about the different perspectives of the balance scorecard to help think of as many relevant measures in your answer as possible. In E3 it is often useful to try to 'think widely' to make sure you don't miss out on different aspects of a scenario.

AFR should introduce the following control measures for each of its existing product ranges:

- **Monthly budgets** should be prepared, and actual figures reported against those budgets. Any significant variances to budget should be highlighted and the reasons for them explained, thereby allowing management to see how contribution to profit is varying from expected levels.
- **Key performance indicators** (KPIs), including non-financial KPIs should be set for the key business processes, in particular sales and quality management. Actual performance achieved should be monitored against the targets set on a weekly basis, and any deviations from expected performance investigated as a matter of urgency.
- **Sales targets** should be established for the sales staff, possibly linked to commission or bonus payments to sales staff. A performance based remuneration scheme should help motivate the staff and boost sales, provided that the scheme sets realistic targets.
- Because AFR's differentiation strategy is based on the style and quality of its product, AFR should introduce **quality assurance procedures** to ensure quality standards are maintained across all the SBUs. Of particular importance will the number of customer complaints, and ensuring that these are minimised.
- AFR should introduce a **formal investment appraisal** and approval process for any large items of expenditure – for example, capital expenditure on new machinery or revenue expenditure on marketing campaigns. This will ensure that the company's funds are directed towards the projects which will best deliver value for it.

(ii) Control measures for the proposed new product range

AFR should introduce the following control measures for the project to develop its new range of dining furniture:

- Before time and resources are spent on the project, a **business case** for the project – showing projected costs and benefits – should be approved by the Board.
- A **project manager, project team and project steering committee** should be appointed, and project roles and responsibilities should be clearly defined.
- A **project initiation document** should be prepared, and it should set out the goals of the project, its deliverables, and estimates of the costs and time expected to be incurred. This should be supported by network analysis.
- AFR should use **project control tools** such as Gantt charts and project gates, so that the progress of the project can be managed against the expected timelines.

- The continuing **viability of the project** should be checked at regular intervals. If the actual design or prototype production costs prove to be more expensive than the budgets used in the business case or project initiation document, this should be highlighted as soon as possible in case they impact on the decision about whether or not to continue with the project.
- **Vendor selection procedures** should be put in place, and the suppliers of the new production machinery and other large capital items should be selected though a competitive tendering process. New production machinery is likely to account for a large part of the total investment costs and so it is important to ensure value for money on this expenditure.
- Once the project is complete, a **project completion report** should be prepared, identifying whether costs and timetables have been kept to, and highlighting any areas which could be improved in future projects

48 Food manufacturer

Text reference. Chapter 4 in the BPP Study Text covers Gap analysis. Ansoff's growth matrix and competition, products and markets are covered in Chapter 5.

Part (a)

Top tips. This question requires you to apply your knowledge of how companies develop strategy.

Requirement (a) offers a number of marks for pure knowledge; with (i) requiring a definition of gap analysis and then an explanation of how it is useful to a company. (ii) also offers some knowledge marks for explaining the Ansoff matrix. Because you are asked to explain a specific model, a diagram of Ansoff's model would have been useful here. However, to score well in (ii) you need to explain how the matrix can be used in strategic planning, rather than simply describing the matrix. Note the requirement to include examples relevant to AA.

Examiner's comments. Most candidates made a good start to this question, displaying sound knowledge of gap analysis and Ansoff's matrix. However, candidates still appear weaker at *applying* models to a scenario based question, rather than just discussing the relevant models.

(i) Gap Analysis

Gap analysis as a strategic analysis tool quantifies the difference between an **organisation's objective** for the period under review, and its **forecast based on an extrapolation of the current situation**, allowing for any new projects which are planned.

A gap is often calculated in terms of **sales, profits** or **ROCE**.

However, gap analysis should not just involve the quantification of the gap, but differences should be classified in a way which aids the understanding of performance and facilitates improvement. This should help an organisation to make informed **plans about how to improve future performance**.

Hence gap analysis can be used in strategic analysis as both an indicator of actual performance, and also a starting point for **new strategies to close the gap** between actual performance and desired objectives.

(ii) **Ansoff's model** provides a means of classifying the alternative options by which firms can achieve growth.

	Product Present	Product New
Market Present	Market penetration	Product development
Market New	Market development	Diversification

Ansoff's growth vector matrix

The four cells of the matrix illustrate that a strategy should be based on selling either new or existing products to either new or existing markets.

The four strategic options which result are:

- **Market penetration** – continuing to sell existing products to existing markets, but getting existing customers to buy more. This can be achieved through advertising, or sales promotions (including time delimited price reductions).
- **Market development** – continuing to sell the existing product range, but expanding into new markets. For AA this could mean securing contracts with wholesalers in new countries, or securing a new supermarket as a customer.
- **Product development** – launching new products, but selling them to existing markets. For AA this could mean launching new product lines – for example, new canned products or a new range of sauces.
- **Diversification** – launching new products, and selling to new markets. If AA decided to open its own retail outlets and sell all its products under the AA brand rather than as supermarket own brands, this would be a diversification strategy.

However, while Ansoff's matrix is useful in generating a range of strategic options, it does not in itself indicate the best strategy for a firm to pursue. Once the options have been generated, they will still need to be evaluated before they are implemented.

Part (b)

> **Top tips.** (b) (i) is an unusual requirement, and the calculation for initiative 1, in particular, needs some careful thought. Remember that the impact of the initiatives is already included in the latest forecast.
>
> By contrast (b) (ii) offers three easy marks for categorizing each of the initiatives to one the quadrants in the Ansoff matrix. You should not overlook this part even though it only offers three marks.
>
> **Examiner's comments.** The numerical elements of this question ((b)(i) and (c)) were poorly answered. Candidates are strongly advised to practise more quantitative analysis questions so that they can demonstrate the basic management accounting skills which may be required to support strategic decisions.

(i) Net sales revenue gap

	€m
Budgeted net sales revenue	480.00
Forecast net sales revenue	426.30
Net sales revenue gap	53.70
Advertising campaign (W1)	3.55
New product line (W2)	8.02
New wholesaler in Eastern Europe (see note)	12.00
Other unexplained differences	30.13

Workings

(1) Advertising campaign

Increase in gross revenue: (89.4 – 42.9) × 8% = 3.72

Less discount (assumed at average rate): $3.72 \times \left(\frac{20.1}{446.4}\right) = 0.17$

Increase in net sales revenue: 3.72 – 0.17 = 3.55.

(2) New product line

Gross sales 8.40

Less discount (assumed at average rate): $8.40 \times \left(\frac{20.1}{446.4}\right) = 0.38$

Increase in net sales revenue: 8.02

Note. The net revenue of €12 million from the new wholesaler in Eastern Europe is assumed to be net of discounts given, so no further adjustments are required to this figure.

(ii) The **advertising campaign** is a **market penetration strategy**, because it is designed to get existing customers to buy more of the existing products.

The **new product line** is a **product development strategy**.

The **acquisition of a new wholesale partner** in Eastern Europe is a **market development strategy**, because the wholesaler is a new customer for AA.

Part (c)

> **Top tips.** You are told that there are 18 marks available for calculations in (c), so this means you should allocate just over 30 minutes to the calculation. The mathematics involved is not complicated, but to score well you need to work through the information provided in the scenario carefully, and apply the figures in the right order. For example, the returns need to be taken off before discounts are applied, (because the customers will not get a discount for orders they return). Nonetheless there are some easy marks available; in particular with respect to the calculation of the costs.
>
> Importantly, though, you should notice that (c) is not purely a calculation question, with 7 marks being available for an analysis of the supermarkets' profitability. The issues should be clear to spot: S3's cost drivers are disproportionately higher than the other two supermarkets, prompting questions about their value chain management, and their ordering process.
>
> **Easy marks.** If you work methodically through the calculation in (c) and then consider the implications of the figures, you should be able to score heavily. The question specifically advises you how many marks were available for the calculations, and you should view a proportion of these as easy marks.
>
> **Examiner's comments.** The numerical elements of this question ((b)(i) and (c)) were poorly answered. A number of candidates confused 'Customer Account Profitability' with absolute 'Profit', which led to them drawing the wrong conclusion about the profitability of each supermarket.
>
> Candidates are strongly advised to practise more quantitative analysis questions so that they can demonstrate the basic management accounting skills which may be required to support strategic decisions.

Forecast customer account profitability for 2007/8

	S1 €	S2 €	S3 €
Gross Revenue	58,000,000	24,000,000	108,000,000
Less returns (2.1% of Gross Revenue)	1,218,000	480,000	3,672,000
Adjusted gross revenue	56,782,000	23,520,000	104,328,000
Less discount (3% of Adj gross revenue)	1,703,460	470,400	8,346,240
Net revenue	55,078,540	23,049,600	95,981,760
Cost of sales (80% of gross revenue)	46,400,000	19,200,000	86,400,000
Gross profit	8,678,540	3,849,600	9,581,760
Gross margin	15.8%	16.7%	10.0%
Sales visits €685 per visit	8,220	10,275	149,330
Purchase orders €148 per order	8,732	3,848	112,480
Standard deliveries €2,250 per delivery	234,000	715,500	1,354,500
Rush deliveries €6,475 per delivery	45,325	12,950	1,023,050
Total customer costs	296,277	742,573	2,639,360
Customer profit	8,382,263	3,107,027	6,942,400
Customer account profitability (on net revenue)	15.2%	13.5%	7.2%

> **Tutorial note.** The question tells you that prices are charged to generate a gross profit margin, before any *discount*, of 20%. Therefore cost of sales are 80% of gross revenue. You should use the gross revenue figure before discounts *and returns* to calculate the cost of sales. The returns are, in effect, an additional cost to the business.

Margin analysis

Although the cost of sales is the same (80% of gross revenue) for all three supermarkets, S3 generates a net margin (7.2%) of only approximately half that which S1 and S2 generate.

In part this reflects the **higher discounts offered to S3**, which S3 may have been able to negotiate as a result of the volume of business they give AA. However, the lower margins earned from S3 also reflect the **higher operating costs which are incurred in dealing with S3**.

Cost drivers for each supermarket

	S1	S2	S3
Number of sales visits per €m	0.20	0.60	2.00
Number of purchase orders per €m	1.00	1.10	7.00
Number of purchase orders per delivery	0.50	0.10	1.00
Average purchase order value (€m)	0.98	0.92	0.14
Number of standard deliveries per €m	1.80	13.30	5.60
Number of rush deliveries per €m	0.10	0.10	1.50

The **number of sales visits** made to S3 is significantly greater than those made to the other supermarkets, and works out at 4 per week. It may be that S3 has a number of different sites which need visiting separately, but even so this number of visits seems very high. It is possible that AA thinks it must have a lot of contact with S3 because of the volume of sales it generates; but the profitability analysis does not justify this level of attention.

S1 and S2 raise less frequent, and much larger, **purchase orders** than S3. The relationship between the number of purchase orders and the number of deliveries for S2 is unusual with one purchase order generating 12 deliveries. This may suggest that purchase orders are raised centrally, but deliveries are made to regional depots rather than to a central repository. However, the high number of deliveries made to S2 as a result damages the margins earned from it.

Nonetheless, S3's purchase ordering is still the least efficient of the three, and the fact S3 raises **one purchase order for every delivery** suggests that it does not plan its orders. Instead it orders on an ad hoc basis when it runs out of a good.

The **number of rush deliveries** ordered by S3 would again suggest that it has a very inefficient ordering system, or else that it is very poor at predicting customer demand. Either way, the high number of rush deliveries S3 requires is very costly for AA.

S3's margin is reduced still further because their **level of returned goods** is higher than those of the other two supermarkets. This may again be due to the disproportionately higher number of batches being delivered to S3.

Despite S3 generating the largest sales revenue for AA, the net margin earned from its business is very low, and AA should seek to address this.

Part (d)

> **Top tips.** Your answer to (d) must to link to the calculation you have done in (c), because (d) asks you to evaluate the strategy in relation to the 'least profitable' of AA's major supermarket customers. To this end, if you fail to complete the calculation in (c) you should make an assumption as to which supermarket was least profitable, and state this at the start of your answer to (d).
>
> The model answer is based on S3 being the least profitable, because it returns the lowest net margin %. However, in absolute terms, S2 is the least profitable, so it is possible you could have selected this. Provided your evaluation in (d) is relevant to the supermarket you identify as being least profitable you will still get credit for this.
>
> The key to answering this question successfully is to consider the suitability and acceptability of the three strategies in the context of the scenario. For example, S3 generates 24% of A's revenue, so refusing to sell to it is clearly not a sensible strategy.
>
> Notice that the question also requires you to recommend your preferred strategy, so you must form a conclusion at the end of your evaluation.

Our analysis in (c) indicated that S3 generate the poorest margin returns, so we will evaluate the three proposed strategies with respect of S3.

Refusing to sell to S3 is unlikely to be a feasible option. S3 is forecast to generate €108 million (24%) of sales revenue for 2007/08, and just under €7 million of customer profit. It is unlikely that AA could afford to lose a customer of this size, and if it did there could be negative publicity around the industry.

Furthermore, although S3 generates the lowest % margin, it is still **contributing €7 million towards covering fixed costs**. If AA stopped selling to S3 it would either have to down-size its operations, or else reallocated these fixed costs over a smaller revenue base. Neither of these options suggests that refusing to sell to S3 is a viable strategy.

Reducing the number of cost generating activities would be a suitable and feasible strategy, particularly if it involved introducing a more effective inventory management and ordering system so that S3 was able to reduce the number of purchase orders placed.

However, this strategy may not be acceptable because **S3 may not want AA telling it how to run its business**. Even more so, given the relative sizes of the two companies. If S3 generates 24% of AA's sales revenue, it is likely that S3 is a larger company that AA, in which case it may resent AA interfering in its business.

Introducing new technologies to reduce the level of cost-generating activities is therefore likely to be the best of the three strategies for AA to adopt.

If AA developed an **extranet system** which linked to the inventory and sales systems at the major supermarkets, it could manage deliveries and orders on behalf of its customers. AA would be able to monitor inventory levels and customer demand, and thereby take responsibility for re-ordering for goods as required.

We do not know how what systems AA has in place for **receiving orders, invoicing and collecting payment** from its customers, but it is likely that technology could reduce costs here too. For example, customers could use an electronic data interchange (EDI) to raise paperless orders, and payments could be collected through electronic funds transfers.

Consequently we **recommend that using technology** to reduce the level of cost-generating activities is the strategy which AA should pursue. It will reduce costs for both AA and also its customers, so it will be mutually beneficial for both parties.

49 Machine components

> **Text Reference.** E-commerce and IS strategy are covered in chapter 7 of the Study Text.
>
> **Top tips**. Requirements (a) and (b) are general requirements about e-commerce and IS. They do not relate specifically to AAA or the scenario.
>
> Note that in (b) you need to consider the potential impact of IS on three different levels of strategy – corporate, business and functional.
>
> **Easy marks**. Requirements (a) and (b) offer some relatively easy marks for factual knowledge, so should give you confidence at the star of the paper.
>
> **Examiner's comments** (on the question as a whole). The main focus of this question was the impact that IS strategies have on an organisation's business strategy. This is a key theme in contemporary business strategy. However, it was disappointing that a number of candidates answered this question poorly, failing to read the question requirement carefully and discussing how IT in general, rather than e-commerce, has impacted on business. Candidates must answer the question set by the examiner, rather than using a question to demonstrate knowledge which is irrelevant to the question set.

Part (a)

E-commerce consists of the buying and selling of products and services over electronic systems like the Internet. E-commerce has challenged traditional business models and has changed the way businesses and their customers inter-relate, both in terms of the way goods are bought and sold, and also the way information is communicated.

New business model – E-commerce enables the suppliers of products and services to interact directly with their customers instead of using **intermediaries** (for example, hotels can now sell rooms directly to overseas holiday makers rather than going through a tour operator or a travel agent). In this way, e-commerce has enabled business to improve the effectiveness of their downstream **supply chain management**.

Opening up global markets – The Internet is global in its operation; and so e-commerce allows small companies to access the global market place, whereas previously they would have been restricted by their physical infrastructure.

New online marketplaces – The emergence of online marketplaces (such as Amazon.com) means that small enterprises can now gain access to customers on far greater scale than the previously could.

Increases speed and scope of communication – The internet allows online transactions to be completed very quickly. It also allows new networks of communication – between businesses and their customers (most notably through e-mail); and between customers themselves (for example, discussing product features or quality through chat rooms, and forums).

Increased price transparency – Potential customers can readily compare prices from a range of suppliers before making a purchase, thereby increasing the level of price competition in the market.

Part (b)

An organisation's Information Systems (IS) strategy is its long-term plan for systems to use information in order to **support the overall business strategies** or create new ones.

So, IS strategy will have an impact on corporate and business objectives through the way which it contributes to an organisation's **ability to achieve those objectives**. To this extent, IS strategy can be seen as a **functional (operational) strategy**, in that the relative success of its **implementation** will help determine the success of business and corporate strategies.

In most cases, functional strategies are designed in the light of the more strategic corporate or business strategies. However, IS strategy is unusual in this respect because it can act as a **change trigger** which requires an organisation to change its corporate strategy, business strategy and its other functional strategies.

Impact on corporate strategy. An IS strategy of implementing e-commerce in an organisation based in a single country could lead to a corporate strategy of market development, to take advantage of the global range of the internet.

Impact on business strategy. The increased availability of performance information should highlight which products and markets are performing well for an SBU, and which are performing poorly. Therefore the IS system may lead to a change in the products and/or markets served with by a business unit.

Impact on other functional strategies. The production systems, logistics, and accounting systems may all need to be changed to meet the demands of e-commerce. Marketing and customer services strategies may also need adapting to reflect the business's changing marketplace. In turn, this may affect staffing levels, the skill sets staff need, and may also change the locations where staff are employed (for example if operations are outsourced or off-shored).

Part (c)

Top tips. Requirement (c) is asking you to prepare a discounted cash flow statement. Perhaps the most important thing to note here is the timing of when cash is paid or received. The question states that all cashflows arise at the end of the period to which they relate. Also, you are told the new systems are expected to be implemented 12 months after the contract is agreed. This means that the benefits from the additional gross margins will not be received until years 2 – 6. Note, the scenario tells you that any benefits after 5 years from implementation should be ignored, so this means your discounted cash flow should only extend to year 6.

Easy marks. The calculation in (c) is not mathematically complex, so if you work methodically through the figures given in the question, and note the timings carefully, you should be able to score heavily. Together, requirements (a), (b) and (c) account for half the marks available for this question. So you should be able to accumulate a number of easy marks before you even start your evaluation of the system's proposed benefits (in part (d)).

Financial evaluation of Project E

	T0 $'000	T0.5 $'000	T1 $'000	T2 $'000	T3 $'000	T4 $'000	T5 $'000	T6 $'000	$'000
Inflows									
Additional gross margin (W)				33	37	40	44	49	
Outflows									
Accounting package	(14)								
Tailoring		(20)							
E-commerce package	(11)								
Populating database		(5)							
Training			(10)						
Support				(5)	(5)	(5)	(5)	(5)	
Hardware and networking			(40)						
Broadband				(4)	(4)	(4)	(4)	(4)	
Total outflows	(25)	(33)	(50)	(9)	(9)	(9)	(9)	(9)	
Total net cashflows	(25)	(33)	(50)	24	28	31	35	40	
Discount factor @ 15%	1	0.933	0.87	0.756	0.658	0.572	0.497	0.432	
Present value	(25)	(31)	(44)	18	18	18	17	17	
Net present value									(12)

Part (d)

> **Top tips**. Requirement (d) has the highest mark allocation in the question, so make sure that you allow sufficient time to answer it thoroughly.
>
> Note that you are asked to evaluate both 'strategic' and 'competitive' benefits. This distinction in the question should help you structure your answer: look at strategic benefits first, and then move on to look at competitive benefits. Also, note the verb requirement – to evaluate – so you need to present a balanced answer, including any limitations to the system's benefits as well as the benefits themselves.

Strategic benefits

International marketplace – Possibly the most significant strategic benefit of the e-commerce system is that if will enable AAA to reach an international, potentially global, audience. This offers AAA significant opportunities in terms of market development.

Mining and oil exploration are global businesses, and so being able to sell to new customers outside its own country should allow AAA to achieve the **sales growth** which it has been unable to do over the last two years. The sales manager expects the introduction of e-commerce to generate turnover growth of 10% each year for the foreseeable future.

However, in order to realise this benefit, AAA will need to ensure that it has the **operational resources** (production capacity, distribution networks etc) to **cope with any increase in demand**. This will include making sure that AAA's upstream supply chain can cope with any increase in demand.

One of AAA's strengths at the moment is the level of service it offers customers. If the drive for expansion means it is unable to fulfil customer orders or to **meet customer expectations**, then its reputation (and then potentially also its sales) will suffer.

Equally, if the development of the international business means that prices all become quoted in US dollars with **no option for local currency**, this may mean that African customers who used to pay in local currency may move their custom elsewhere (especially if the local currency weakens against the dollar).

Commercial image – If AAA wants to expand and serve an international marketplace, it needs to present an image which supports that ambition. Potential customers will want to be able find out about the company, its capabilities and credentials, and the website will allow them to do so.

The interactivity of the website should also help improve the levels of customer service AAA can offer its customers, so is a competitive benefit as well as a strategic one.

Competitive benefits

Improved customer service and customer information – The sales manager has noted that customers are increasingly mentioning that they would like to be able to order online. Therefore, if the new system showed a list of all previously supplied components, and a price, they would be able to do this without having to phone or fax their order in. Moreover, the customer would be able to **get the information immediately** without waiting to design a price as they do at the moment. This will support AAA's aim to provide the highest levels of customer service.

The online ordering would also **support the international growth**, because the website could take orders 24 hours a day.

We are not told anything about AAA's competitors in the scenario, but to a degree the extent to which the online ordering facility is a competitive benefit will depend on the **comparative levels of service** offered by AAA's competitors. It may be that some of them already offer a similar service, which is why customers have mentioned it to the sales manager.

Also, AAA will need to review its **customer service arrangements** to ensure that it has enough staff on hand to deal with any queries. It is likely that queries will now be more complex. Simple orders will be processed on the e-commerce system, so the ones which require assistance are likely to be more complex. As AAA prides itself on the personal service is provides, it will need to ensure that the e-commerce remains properly supported by customer service staff.

Moreover, online ordering would only be available for previously ordered products. Unique products, reverse engineering would still need to be ordered in person, and will continue to take longer to price up due to the complexity of the design process involved.

Internal information management – AAA should be able to **reduce the costs** currently incurred by the 'estimator' in creating paper-based drawings of the components, and in the **time taken** for these drawings to be passed to the costing clerk and then priced up.

As noted from the customer's perspective in the previous point, if the new e-commerce system contains a database of previous orders, component specifications, and technical drawings this would allow AAA to standardise, and therefore speed up, its order preparation process.

However, this standardised process would not benefit the reverse engineering services, because there each job is unique so there wouldn't be any information in the database to help with such jobs.

Improved cash collection times – At the moment customers pay by cash or cheque usually within 30 days of an order being fulfilled. AAA could investigate the possibility that customers who order online pay, (either in part or in full) at the **moment they make the order**. This will be beneficial to AAA's cash flow management.

However, as AAA is a relatively small company it may find that trade customers do not want to change their credit terms, especially as they will still have to wait for AAA to produce the goods after the order is made. In which case, the e-commerce system will not generate any significant benefits in this area.

Moreover, AAA does not currently have a problem with bad debts, which again reduces the upside potential from improving cash collection processes.

Improved inventory management – One of the theoretical benefits of e-commerce is that is allows a business to reduce its inventory levels; instead of producing goods and then trying to sell them, the business responds to demand 'pull' and produces on demand. However, this appears to already be the way AAA operates, and it only hold very low levels of finished goods inventory. Therefore, there are unlikely to be any significant benefits from the e-commerce system in this respect.

Part (e)

> **Top tips.**
>
> Part (e) of the question asks you to advise AAA whether or not to invest in the proposed project, therefore your answer needs to make a firm recommendation. Although the question asks you to use parts (a) and (d) in your answer, you should also ensure your advice is consistent with your financial evaluation from part (c).
>
> We cannot overstate the importance of this – make sure your advice is consistent with your answers to the earlier requirements.

Answers

For

Strategic benefits – AAA would gain significant strategic benefits by adopting the e-commerce project, particularly in a global industry (such as the mining and oil exploration industry).

Corporate growth – The e-commerce project would offer new opportunities for growth, overcoming static sales for the last two years.

Customer expectations – AAA prides itself on the level of customer service it offers its customers, and the e-commerce project would both respond to customer wishes and enhance customer service. Increasingly, business-to-business suppliers are offering e-commerce facilities, and so AAA needs to keep pace with this trend.

Against

Business process changes – It is likely that if AAA adopted the e-commerce model, it would also have to change other aspects of its business processes to adapt to the higher volumes of business and shorter timescales involved.

Negative net present value – Based on the cost and benefit forecasts, the project shows a small negative net present value. However, there are a number of assumptions in this forecast (for example, indirect costs stay the same despite the increased volumes; underlying sales would stay the same without e-commerce project) so the marginal nature of the net present value calculation means it should not be considered as conclusive evidence against the project.

Advice

AAA should invest in the project. Although the NPV is marginally negative, and there may additional investment required in supporting projects, the longer strategic benefits to the company are likely to outweigh these costs.

Part (f)

> **Top tips.** When tackling requirement (f) it is important that you appreciate the difference between AAA's reverse engineering projects and its standard products. The reverse engineering projects are unique, and so it is unlikely they can be sold via the website using a standard price list in the way that standard products can. Therefore, the benefits will accrue from marketing and making existing customers aware of the reverse engineering side of the business, rather than direct online sales.

The e-commerce project is aimed at directly increasing the volume of business AAA generates from 'standard' product sales. The complex, one-off nature of the 'reverse engineering' projects means AAA will not be able to sell them directly on line in the same way, but instead AAA could use the e-commerce platform to generate extra demand for its reverse engineering projects.

Cross-selling – At the moment, AAA does not advertise its services. However, it could use the e-commerce platform to advertise and promote the full range of services it offers. Therefore, customers who are looking initially to purchase standard components without realising AAA also offered reverse engineering services may subsequently also purchase reverse engineering services.

Direct marketing – AAA could also email customers who have purchased standard components, informing them about the additional range of services it offers. The e-commerce system should have a database which gathers all the email addresses of customers, and AAA can use this to send subsequent marketing messages.

Some customers may not wish to receive these e-mails, viewing them as junk mail, and so customers need to be offered the option of not receiving any subsequent marketing mail from AAA when they make a purchase.

Online questions – AAA could offer a facility for potential customers to contact an estimator to discuss potential work, and may also show some of the more frequently asked questions pre-answered. Equally, AAA could host a forum for customers to discuss issues among themselves. Either of these options should help create 'noise' about AAA's products and services which in turn should help promote demand.

50 Training College

Study Reference. The BCG matrix is covered in chapter 4 of the BPP Study text for E3. SWOT analysis is assumed knowledge for E3 because it is covered under the syllabus for E2.

Part (a)

Top tips. Part (a) requires a relatively simply application of product portfolio management; but do not spend time discussing the matrix; rather apply it specifically to AAA's portfolio. Note that you are asked to evaluate the portfolio, so you need to consider it as a whole. How strong is AAA's portfolio overall? For example, does it suggest good earnings in the future? Are there successor products to replace declining, older products? Are the cash cows strong enough to support other divisions which need cash to support their growth? However, note you were not asked to draw the matrix so you did not need to do so.

Easy marks. Requirement (a) is a relatively simply question, based on a core area of the syllabus (BCG matrix).

AAA's Product portfolio

AAA has four strategic business units (SBUs) in its portfolio. Their relative market shares and the growth rates in their respective markets can be summarised as follows:

	AAA's market share %	Largest rival's market share %	Relative market share	Market growth rate
F&A courses	40	30	1.33	Slow/Medium
Marketing courses	15	40	0.38	Decline
Law courses	35	30	1.17	Rapid
HRM courses	20	40	0.50	Rapid

Balanced portfolio – The BCG matrix indicates that AAA has a relatively **well balanced product portfolio**, with one SBU in each quadrant of the matrix.

F & A is a '**cash cow**' – it should generate cash which AAA can use to develop other divisions, in particular HRM.

Marketing is a '**dog**' – this appears to be a declining market, so AAA should consider whether it wants to continue offering these courses in their current format, particularly if the Marketing faculty is a drain on the College's resources overall.

Law is a '**star**' – the law faculty helps AAA's competitive strength, because it has a high market share in a growing market. However, AAA may still need to **use some of the cash generated by F&A** to invest in the Law faculty; to help sustain its market share as competitors try to erode its market share.

HRM is a '**question mark**' – the high market growth rate suggests the opportunity for AAA's HRM courses to grow; and it should be able to **use some of the cash generated by F&A** to support this growth.

However, although AAA's portfolio appears reasonably well balanced, one possible concern is whether the F&A faculty can generate enough cash to support the requirements of both Law and HRM.

Equally AAA needs to consider the interrelationships between the SBUs. For example, some employers may use AAA because it offers marketing courses as well as F & A, Law or HRM courses so the employer can deal with a single college for all their training requirements. Therefore, if AAA is considering divesting the marketing faculty, before it does so, it needs to assess the knock-on effect such a decision could have on other faculties.

Part (b)

Top tips. For your quantitative analysis in (b) (i) you should have prepared a variance analysis looking at actual performance compared to budget.

However, note that (b) (i) and (b) (ii) need to be used in conjunction with each other. Requirement (b) (i) asks you to produce the quantitative analysis, and (b) (ii) then asks you to use this analysis to identify and evaluate the financial strengths and weaknesses of AAA's performance. From reading the initial case study scenario, and from the portfolio analysis in (a), you may have thought that AAA was a successful college, but this cannot hide the fact it has some weaknesses.

> Your answer for (b) (i) should have only contained a numerical analysis. The requirement tells you that all the marks were available for the calculations, so you should not have made any comments on the figures in (b) (i). You should have saved these for (b) (ii). However, you should have tried to select calculations for (b) (i) which allow you to comment on them in (b) (ii).
>
> For tutorial purposes, the answer below contains a comprehensive set of the calculations you could have produced from the information provided in the scenario. You would not have been expected to produce all of these calculations to earn the 14 marks available. 5 or 6 relevant sets of variances should have been sufficient to score well in this requirement. We have included 6 in the main body of our answer, and then a further 2 in the text box below. You would have earned marks if you calculated any of these variances, or any other valid calculations.
>
> However, note that the comments you make in (b) (ii) should be based on the calculations you presented in (b) (i), so you need to plan your answer to ensure consistency between the two parts to the requirement. Also, note that the requirement is to analyse AAA's performance *as a whole*, not the performance of individual faculties. You should have identified that AAA's overall performance was poor, and identified which faculties were the main causes of this, but you should not have analysed the performance of individual faculties in great detail. There are few, if any, marks available for detailed analysis of the individual faculties.
>
> **Easy marks**. Question (b) (i) only requires some relatively simple calculations. Requirements (b) (i) and (a) together offer 22 marks before you have to start evaluating and analysing the scenario.
>
> However, the scenario also provides you with a number of clues about the issues AAA is facing so you should have been able to use these to score marks in (b) (ii).

(i) Sales Revenue (A)

	Actual A$m	Budget A$m	Variance A$m	Variance %
F&A	4.2	4.5	(0.3)	(6.7)
Marketing	0.8	1.0	(0.2)	(20.0)
Law	4.0	4.0	0.0	–
HRM	3.1	3.5	(0.4)	(11.4)
Total	12.1	13.0	(0.9)	(6.9)

Profit (before interest and tax) (B)

	Actual A$m	Budget A$m	Variance A$m	Variance %
F&A	0.6	1.0	(0.4)	(40.0)
Marketing	(0.1)	0.5	(0.6)	(120.0)
Law	0.6	1.0	(0.4)	(40.0)
HRM	0.4	1.0	(0.6)	(60.0)
Central costs	(1.4)	(1.2)	(0.2)	(16.7)
Total	0.1	2.3	(2.2)	(95.7)

Profit margin (B)/(A)

	Actual %	Budget %	Variance	Variance %
F&A	14.3	22.2	(7.9)	(35.6)
Marketing	(12.5)	50.0	(62.5)	(125.0)
Law	15.0	25.0	(10.0)	(40.0)
HRM	12.9	28.6	(15.7)	(54.9)
Total	0.8	17.7	(16.9)	(95.5)

Student Days (C)

	Actual A$m	Budget A$m	Variance A$m	Variance %
F&A	2,030	2,000	30	1.5
Marketing	410	450	(40)	(8.9)
Law	2,100	2,000	100	5.0
HRM	1,150	1,500	(350)	(23.3)
Total	5,690	5,950	(260)	(4.4)

Revenue per Student Day

	(C)/(A)	Actual A$m	Budget A$m	Variance A$m	Variance %
F&A		2,069	2,250	(181)	(8.0)
Marketing		1,951	2,222	(271)	(2.2)
Law		1,905	2,000	(95)	(4.8)
HRM		2,696	2,333	363	15.6
Total		2,127	2,185	(58)	(2.7)

Revenue Variances

	Actual A$m	Budget A$m	Variance A$m	Variance %
F&A	0.1	(0.4)	(0.3)	
Marketing	(0.1)	(0.1)	(0.2)	
Law	0.2	(0.2)	0.0	
HRM	(0.8)	0.4	(0.4)	
	(0.6)	(0.3)	(0.9)	

Volume variance = (actual – budgeted student days) x budgeted revenue per student day
Margin variance = (actual – budgeted revenue per day) x actual number of student days

---

Alternative quantitative analysis you could have calculated

Revenue per member of staff (FTE)

	Actual A$m	Staff numbers	Revenue per FTE A$'000
F&A	4.2	23	182,609
Marketing	0.8	6	133,333
Law	4.0	26	153,846
HRM	3.1	18	172,222
Total	12.1	73	165,753

Profit per member of staff

	Actual A$m	Staff numbers	Profit/(loss) per FTE A$
F&A	0.6	23	26,087
Marketing	(0.1)	6	(16,667)
Law	0.6	26	23,077
HRM	0.4	18	22,222
Central and corporate	(1.4)	14	100,000
Total	0.1	87	1,149

Student days per FTE

	Student days	Staff numbers	Student days per FTE
F&A	2,030	23	88
Marketing	410	6	68
Law	2,100	26	81
HRM	1,150	18	64
Total	5,690	73	78

Revenue comparison – AAA, BBB and CCC

	AAA Revenue A$m	AAA Market share $'000	Total market $m	Market share $'000	BBB Revenue A$m	BBB Market share $'000	CCC Revenue A$m
F&A	4.2	40	10.5	15	1.6	30	3
Marketing	0.8	15	5.3	40	2.1	15	0
Law	4.0	35	11.4	30	3.4	25	2
HRM	3.1	20	15.5	25	3.9	40	6
Total (excl 'other')	12.1				11.0		13

(ii) Strengths

Student numbers in F&A and Law higher than budgeted – Actual student numbers in F&A and Law were better than budgeted. However, this 'strength' is tempered by the fact that the faculties' revenue per student day was less than budgeted, suggesting that the discounts offered have been greater than budgeted in order to secure student numbers. Consequently, the positive variance in student days has not translated into a positive revenue variance.

Revenue per student day in HRM higher than budgeted – The HRM faculty has achieved a significantly (16%) higher revenue per student day than was budgeted. However, this 'strength' is tempered by the fact that student days were 23% below budget, so overall revenue was still below budget.

Weaknesses

Low profit before interest and tax (PBIT) – AAA only earned A$0.1 million profit before interest and tax, which was 96% ($A2.2 million) below budget.

The budget assumed AAA would generate PBIT of nearly 18%, but the actual figure was less than 1%. This low level of profit suggests AAA needs to look at its business model very critically, because a **1% margin is not sustainable**, and is clearly below expectations.

Furthermore, because AAA runs all its courses as face-to-face rather than online it is possible that it has taken out loans to buy new premises as the business expanded. If this is the case, then once the profit figures are adjusted to **take account of interest costs** AAA could well be loss-making.

In this respect, AAA's financial performance doesn't support the idea of it having a well balanced product portfolio.

Revenue shortfalls – The Law department was the only department which achieved its revenue budget, the other three fell short of budget due to a combination of **adverse volume and margin variances**. This illustrates that even though AAA attracting fewer students than it budgeted to, it is still having to offer greater discounts that it budgeted for. This suggests market conditions are significantly less favourable than the budget anticipated.

Price elasticity – The variance figures also illustrate that, with the exception of the law faculty, demand was more price elastic than the budget had assumed. In particular, although the HRM faculty earned a A$0.4 million favourable margin variance from maintaining high prices, the corresponding shortfall in student numbers caused a A$0.8 million adverse volume variance.

Poor cost control – Although sales revenue was A$0.9 million below budget, PBIT was A$2.2 million below budget. This suggests there is an adverse cost variance of A$1.3 million. This would be a weakness in any circumstances, but is a particular concern for a business whose sales revenues are under pressure.

Poor performance of marketing faculty – The problem of poor cost control is most important in the marketing faculty, which made a **loss before interest and tax of A$0.1 million**. The budget assumed that the faculty would have costs of A$0.5 million on revenue of A$1.0 million, generating a departmental PBIT of A$0.5 million. The actual results show that the faculty incurred **costs of A$0.9 million (80% higher than budget)** on revenue of A$0.8 million, resulting in the department being loss-making.

However, management do not appear to have done anything to address this issue, suggesting that they **do not deal with problems** very quickly.

Overspent corporate and central costs – AAA should be able to budget is central costs quite accurately, as a number of these will be fixed or semi-fixed. Therefore the 17% overspend on corporate and central costs is a cause for concern; particularly in the context of revenues being below budget.

Weak financial control – Overall, the combination of costs running over budget, and revenues falling below budget suggest that AAA's financial controls are weak, such that it has not been able to take any corrective actions to reduce the variances during the year.

Poor budgeting compounds variances – Although AAA's actual results for the year are poor, it appears likely that the variances between actual and budgeted profitability have been exacerbated by unrealistic budgeting. For example, the marketing faculty was budgeted to have a **PBIT margin of 50%**, whereas all the other faculties' budgeted margins between 20%-30%.

Part (c)

> **Top tips.** Make sure you appreciate the distinction between requirement (b) (ii) and requirement (c). (b) (ii) asked you to look specifically at the strengths and weaknesses of AAA's financial performance; (c) asks you for a more general, qualitative analysis of the strengths and weaknesses of AAA's overall strategic position. Therefore, be careful not to let (c) become a repetition of points you have already made in (b) (ii).
>
> In the same way, that you must appreciate the distinction between the requirements for (b)(ii) and (c), so you must also make sure you understand exactly what requirements (c) and (d) are asking: (c) asks for strengths and weaknesses, while (d) asks for opportunities and threats. Requirements (c) and (d) together, in effect, ask you for a SWOT analysis of AAA, but your answer to (c) should focus on the *internal* factors, while (d) should focus on the *external* factors.
>
> The scenario provides you with a number of points which you could use in your SWOT analysis. To this end, you should have used these as the basis for your strengths, weaknesses, opportunities and threats. You should not have introduced additional factors of your own. The Examiner wants you to pick up on the points he highlights in the scenario, and identifying these will earn you the marks available here.

Strengths

Well-established business – AAA is now a well-established college, and it has grown to become one of the **largest and most reputable colleges in A**. Its good reputation for the quality of its courses is a strength it can look to build on to help differentiate itself from other training providers.

Barriers to entry – AAA's **reputation** may also act as a barrier to entry deterring potential new training providers from joining the market. AAA's **size** may also act as strength against potential new competitors. AAA should be able to obtain **economies of scale** in its costs compared to a smaller competitor, meaning it should be able to offer its courses more cheaply than a smaller competitor. However, AAA's current cost overspends suggest it may not be exploiting its economies of scale as well as it could.

Weaknesses

Narrow product range – AAA does not offer the same range of 'Other' courses that BBB or CCC do. Therefore, companies which wish to use a single tuition provider for all of their professional training are likely to choose BBB or CCC in preference to AAA.

Bargaining power of large employers – AAA offers 'bulk purchase' discounts to large employers who send their students for tuition with them. Because the employers make up a large part of AAA's business they are in a strong bargaining position when negotiating with AAA. The fact that these employers are beginning to **demand larger discounts** (in excess of 20%) will increase the pressure on AAA's margins.

Low switching costs – The pressure on AAA's margins is increased by the relative ease with which employers can transfer their training contracts from AAA to another college.

Inflexible pricing structure – AAA charges a single price for its courses whether they are for employer-funded students and self-funded students. If AAA's competitors have a more **flexible pricing structure**, this may make them more attractive to potential customers. The fact that AAA's larger customers are now looking for significant discounts indicates the **price is an important factor** for companies when they are deciding which training provider to use.

No online courses – AAA has no plans to develop online courses, preferring to concentrate on 'face-to-face' courses instead. As some of the competitors are developing online courses, this will give them a competitive advantage over AAA.

By developing their e-learning capabilities, AAA's competitors can offer a **wider range of course options to students**, and they can also market themselves as being more **innovative and dynamic** in their approaches to learning than AAA. Moreover, as more students choose to study online rather than in the classroom, the colleges' **overheads could be reduced** – for example, because they would need less classroom space.

Composition of management team – AAA's management team consists of four senior tutors alongside the Chief Executive. The tutors are primarily focused on their prescribed faculties, rather than on corporate functions such as marketing and public relations, IT, HRM and finance. Therefore, the Chief Executive has to be responsible for all the central functions, even though he may not have much experience in any of these areas.

Lack of financial leadership – AAA does not appear to have a finance director, which is why the Chief Executive (a lawyer) has to oversee the finance department. Given the concerns over the reliability of the budget figures, and given AAA's financial performance, the absence of a finance director to impose financial control is a concern.

Part (d)

> **Top tips.** As we noted in connection with part (c), your answer to (d) needs to focus on external factors – opportunities and threats.
>
> However, note that the questions asks you to identify 'opportunities' not 'strategic options'. To score the marks available you must explain how the factors are opportunities for AAA, rather than simply presenting them as strategic options. For example, saying 'AAA could introduce e-learning' would score few marks because you are identifying the *option* rather than the *opportunity*. To score the full marks available for that point you need to say 'The market for e-learning is growing and AAA could take advantage of this to offer e-learning courses.'

> **Tutorial note.** For tutorial purposes, the answer below tries to include a wide range of relevant points, but you would not need to make all of these points to score the 8 marks available.

Opportunities

Economic growth in AAA – A has been growing rapidly and the business and financial community has become well established. This has led to the **business training industry being buoyant in most sectors**, with demand for law and HRM courses rising quite rapidly. This means there should be opportunities for AAA to **increase sales** further without having to capture market share from its rivals.

If demand continues to rise, AAA may become less reliant on its existing big customers for revenue, in which case their bargaining power to secure discounts will be reduced.

Social factors – Government policy in A has led to an **increase in literacy and education levels** among younger people in the country. In conjunction with the rise of secondary and tertiary industries in A, this is likely to lead to an increase in the number of **people seeking professional qualifications**, increasing the potential demand for AAA's courses.

Increased range of courses – At the moment, AAA does not offer the range of 'Other courses' offered by BBB and CCC. Therefore, AAA could also increase revenues by extending its range of courses to offer some of these 'Other courses.'

Technology and e-learning – Although AAA currently has no plans to develop online courses, the market for e-learning and online tuition is growing and so is a potential source of additional revenue.

Perhaps equally importantly, if AAA persists with its strategy of not offering them while its rivals do, the e-learning capabilities AAA's rivals develop are likely to become a threat to AAA's revenues in future. So, if AAA does not take advantage of the opportunity, it will become a threat.

Threats

Intense rivalry between colleges threats margins – AAA, BBB and CCC currently control the majority of the training industry between them. However, the rivalry in the market appears to be quite intense, enabling large employers to play one college off against another to secure **discounts**. Such rivalry could pose a threat to AAA profitability, and indeed the **industry's ability to sustain its profitability**.

This rivalry could also extend to trying to **capture the best teaching staff** from rival colleges. The quality of its staff could be a source of competitive advantage for AAA, but 2 tutors have left AAA's law faculty to join BBB. At the moment this should not be a major problem (AAA has 26 law tutors) but there is a threat that more could leave if rival colleges offer them better terms and conditions than they currently receive at AAA.

Answers 245

Threats to market position – CCC is the largest college, and, depending on the size of the market for other courses, AAA and BBB are vying for second place. However, whereas AAA has tried to grow organically, the other two have been more acquisitive. If CCC and BBB continue to acquire smaller colleges they could become significantly larger than AAA; in effect, creating a 'Big Two' in the market, rather than the existing 'Big Three.' If that becomes the case, AAA may find it increasingly difficult to compete for business against the 'Big Two,' particularly from larger employers.

Possible merger between BBB and CCC – Although it is only a rumour at the moment, if the merger between BBB and CCC were to happen it would dramatically alter the balance of power in the industry, to AAA's disadvantage.

e-learning as a substitute for taught courses – A number of colleges and institutes are considering providing online courses. These online courses are a substitute for AAA's face-to-face taught courses, and an increase in their popularity could lead to a decline in the demand for face-to-face courses. Demand for marketing courses already appears to have been affected as a result of the growth of e-learning courses.

New entrants – The growth of e-learning will reduce the capital requirements for a potential new training provider wanting to enter the market. At the moment, the Marketing Institute is the only Institute which offers its own courses. However, other Institutes are considering providing their own courses, and if they did so this would reduce the demand for independent colleges like AAA to teach the material.

Change of government – There is likely to be a general election within two years, which could lead to a change of government. The existing government's policies have supported economic growth, and with it the demand for business training courses. However, there is no guarantee that the opposition party will follow similar policies.

51 European Bank

Text reference. Customer relationship marketing is dealt with in Chapter 8 of your BPP Study Text.

Top tips. Did you notice you were asked to produce a report? Therefore the whole of your answer to this question should have been presented in a report format.

Part (a) is a test of knowledge only, so you do not need to relate it specifically to the scenario. But note, even though there are only 4 marks available there are still effectively two parts to the question: (i) explain what customer relationship marketing is; (ii) explain how it differs from transactions marketing.

Whereas Part (a) didn't require any application to the scenario, **Part (b)** must be specifically related to the scenario. Don't simply discuss the advantages and disadvantages of customer relationship marketing; but look directly at how they are affecting AAA. For example, what impact could customer relationship marketing have on customer defection rates, and how is it affecting staff morale within the bank?

If you weren't sure exactly what 'customer lifecycle value' was (**Part (c)**), Part (d) might have given you a clue. This highlights the importance of reading **all** the requirements of the question before you begin answering it! Remember also to apply the concept of customer lifecycle value to the student account campaign.

The majority of marks in **Part (d)** are available for calculating the lifecycle value, but there are still 4 marks available for analysing the figures. The calculations themselves are not particularly complex, although you need to remember that the probability that customers remain loyal is 80% on a 'reducing balance' method (that is, it is 80% of what it was the year before; not simply 0.8 each year).

For **Part (e)**, did you discuss **five** changes? The question clearly asks for five, so this is how many you should have given. And you need to suggest changes which will stop (or at least significantly reduce) the bonus scheme penalising branches who recruit (and retain) lots of student account holders.

Part (f) is, in effect, a summary at the end of your report. Based on your analysis in parts (b)-(e), should the Bank continue with the student account campaign? If it does, how should it revise the bonus scheme to prevent a repeat of the problems which have affected Branch 32?

Examiner's comments. The Examiner noted that the requirement to calculate the lifetime value of a student account was poorly answered. A number of students ignored the information about the 20% defection rate completely, while others failed to note that the 20% defection rate happened each year, rather than their being a single 20% defection over the 10 year life cycle. In addition, many students provided only a very weak analysis of the results of their calculations.

REPORT – CUSTOMER RELATIONSHIP MARKETING IN AAA

To: Senior Managers, Personal Banking Division
From: Management Accountant
Date: Today

Terms of reference

This report examines the concept of customer relationship marketing and looks at its potential benefits for AAA. In particular it discusses the value of the student account campaign, and how the campaign affects the branch managers' bonus scheme.

(a) Customer relationship marketing

Customer relationship marketing involves using marketing resources to **retain**, rather than simply attract, customers. It focuses on establishing loyalty among existing customers, and establishing a **long-term relationship** between an organisation and its customers.

This long-term approach contrasts with **transactions marketing** which takes a short-term approach and focuses on making one-off sales to new customers, rather than retaining existing customers.

However, it is often more expensive to attract new customers than to retain existing ones, so customer relationship marketing could be a more cost effective approach than transactions marketing.

(b) Customer relationship marketing and student account holders

There are number of advantages and disadvantages for AAA in using customer relationship marketing to deal with student account holders.

Advantages

Establishing customer loyalty – Offering the students free banking for three years should help establish customer loyalty, and reduce the defection rate. Although it is very easy for personal customers to switch banks, by keeping the students as customers for three years (during their free banking period) AAA may be able to develop some customer loyalty which will deter the students switching away from it in future.

Longer term benefits – Although students may not be profitable customers in the short-term, they could be high value customers in the longer term. This could come about in two different ways.

First, if the students are happy with the banking service they are being offered by AAA, they may then consider AAA as a provider of lucrative additional services, such as loans, insurance and credit cards in the future. This could allow AAA to generate additional revenues with very little additional marketing cost in the future.

Second, if the students subsequently start up their own businesses then they could use AAA for business banking. Experience has shown that business customers tend to be more loyal than personal customers.

Pay back period – After the end of their free banking period, student account holders contribute €140 revenue each year. This means that the costs of the free banking period of €230 (3 x €60 operating costs, plus the initial recruitment cost €50) would be paid back in less than two years (excluding discounting).

Maintaining competitive position – AAA's competitors all offer a range of incentives to attract and keep personal customers. At the moment, AAA's offer of three years free banking is the joint market leader of any of the deals offered by the major banks. This should help allow AAA to gain a competitive advantage over its rivals.

Disadvantages

High defection rates – It is very easy for customers to change banks, and experience has shown that personal customers have a high defection rate. Therefore there is a risk that students could defect away from AAA, either during their free banking period or shortly afterwards. In such cases, AAA would not recover the costs of the free banking period for those students.

Low return on marketing investment – All the new student accounts run at a loss for the first three years, and this will reduce the bank's profitability in the short term. It will be important for AAA to monitor the level of defection rates on its student accounts, because if they are too high the return on the marketing investment (free banking for three years) may not justify the cost being spent on it.

Impact on staff motivation – It appears that having a large number of student accounts adversely affects a branch manager's performance bonus. Therefore, unless the bonus scheme is amended to reflect this, staff may be reluctant to sign up student account holders.

Equally, AAA is likely to find that branch managers in branches with a high number of student accounts, and who therefore earn lower bonuses than their colleagues, will suffer a drop in morale and might leave the company. There is a danger that **customer service levels could fall** in those branches as a result, and if customer service standards fall this could again increase the risk that the **students will defect** to another bank.

(c) Customer lifecycle value

The idea of customer lifecycle value is to try to estimate the present value of the net cash flows a customer will generate over their lifetime as a customer.

These 'net' cash flows reflect the **revenues** generated by a customer, less the **initial costs** of acquiring that customer, and the **on-going costs** of subsequently providing goods or services to them.

AAA could apply these ideas to each of its student account customers to indicate whether the students are likely to generate a positive return over the length of time they hold their accounts with the bank.

However, in order to do this, AAA will have to estimate **how long** it thinks each **customer will remain with the bank**, whether they will **purchase any additional services** such as credit cards and insurance, and whether they will **generate any additional revenue** for the bank, for example by referring friends or family as customers.

These estimates highlight one of the key issues for AAA using customer lifecycle value to justify the student account campaign. It relies on AAA making assumptions about students' future behaviour at a relatively early stage in their lifecycle, but there is no guarantee about how accurate those assumptions will be.

(d) Customer lifecycle value of a student account

Time	Event	Amount (€)	Probability still loyal	Expected value (€)	Discount factor (10%)	NPV (€)
0	Recruitment cost	−30	1.00	−30.0	1.000	−30.0
0	Administration cost	−20	1.00	−20.0	1.000	−20.0
1	Account costs	−60	0.80	−48.0	0.909	−43.6
2	Account costs	−60	0.64	−38.4	0.826	−31.7
3	Account costs	−60	0.51	−30.7	0.751	−23.1
4	Bank charges less costs	140	0.41	57.3	0.683	39.2
5	Bank charges less costs	140	0.33	45.9	0.621	28.5
6	Bank charges less costs	140	0.26	36.7	0.564	20.7
7	Bank charges less costs	140	0.21	29.4	0.513	15.1
8	Bank charges less costs	140	0.17	23.5	0.467	11.0
9	Bank charges less costs	140	0.13	18.8	0.424	8.0
10	Bank charges less costs	140	0.11	15.0	0.386	5.8
	Lifetime value					−20.3

This initial analysis suggests that the lifecycle value of the student accounts is likely to be negative.

Cross-selling. However, this analysis ignores the potential benefits from AAA selling any additional products, such as loans, insurance or credit cards. The net present value from these could well be greater than €20 in which case the 'adjusted' lifecycle value would be positive.

Equally, these calculations do not allow for any additional revenues which would be generated if the student encourages their family or friends to bank with AAA.

Defection rates. Also, the validity of the lifetime value figure depends very much on **the rate at which customers defect**. The current model uses a constant defection rate of 20% per year, and AAA should try to build up a database of real student account behaviours to see whether this is reasonable.

In particular, it will be important to establish whether the defection rate remains constant between years 3 and 4, when students start being charged for their accounts. If the defection rate rises, then it could mean that the 'adjusted' lifecycle value becomes negative again.

(e) Possible changes to branch managers' bonus scheme

Currently, the bonus scheme rewards managers for the profitability of their branch, which, in effect, penalises branches with a high number of new student accounts (in their initial three year free period).

If AAA chooses to continue with its customer relationship marketing approach to student accounts, the bonus scheme needs to be changed to reflect this.

Five possible changes AAA could make are:

1. Measure customer satisfaction – The personal banking division could revise the bonus scheme so that it includes non-financial measures, such as customer satisfaction, as well as purely profit-based measures. For example, if students feel they get excellent service from their local branch of AAA, they may be less likely to defect to another bank. So if managers and their staff strive to provide their customers with excellent service, this will benefit both them and the bank. Managers should be rewarded for this, even if their branch does not achieve the 'base level' of profitability currently required to trigger a bonus payment.

2. Add back recruitment costs – When a branch opens a new account, it incurs a recharge cost of €30 for central marketing costs. However, where this is a central cost which individual managers cannot control, the Personal Banking Division could agree to exclude this charge from the profitability figures on which managers bonuses are calculated. This will significantly mean that the manager's profitability is only reduced by €20 when an account is opened, instead of the current figure of €50.

3. Treat initial costs as a central cost – This option builds on the previous idea. The Personal Banking Division could agree to account for all the costs up to the end of the third year of a student account as central costs. In this way, theses costs will not reduce the profitability of any individual branches.

The calculation of lifecycle value shows that the cumulative present value at the end of year 3 is – €148, so adding this back to branches' profits will significantly improve their profitability. If the subsequent profits (after more than three years) are still allocated to the branches, then those branches who recruit and retain student account holders will be rewarded for doing so.

However, there is a danger that this might be seen as skewing the reward scheme too far in favour of those branches with a high number of student account holders, which will make it unpopular with those managers who do not have a university nearby.

4. Exclude student accounts altogether. Rather than looking to exclude only costs, the bonus scheme could be revised to exclude all revenues and costs from student accounts altogether. This might be a fairer approach than just removing costs. However, there could be a lot of work involved in stripping out all the revenues and costs relating to all the student accounts held with the bank.

5. Set 'base level' profitability for personal banking division as a whole. Under the current scheme, a branch manager can only get a bonus if the profit from their individual branch achieves a certain 'base level' of profitability. However, rather than setting this 'base level' for individual branches, the Group could set a 'base level' for the personal banking division as a whole.

In addition, a percentage of the manager's bonus could be determined by divisional results, and the remainder by their own branch's performance. This approach will help to reduce the discrepancy in bonuses between branches, and would also be relatively easy to administer.

However, it may be resented by managers whose branches currently generate high profits, and so who currently earn high bonus levels.

(f) Conclusion – future proposals for the student account campaign

This report has highlighted various advantages and disadvantages of the student account campaign and customer relationship marketing for AAA.

Offering the three year free banking deal gives AAA a strong competitive position against the other major banks in securing a potentially valuable segment of the market.

However, the high defection rate among personal banking customers might threaten the value of customer relationship marketing approach.

Establishing accurate defection figures for AAA student accounts will be critical in deciding whether or not to continue with the student account campaign. The campaign has now been running for three years, so AAA should be able to track real defection rates over those years, and will soon be able to start gathering the information for years 3–4 where students come to the end of their free banking period.

The current implied 20% defection rate suggests that the campaign in itself is loss-making. However, the present calculations for lifetime value ignore the value of potential added services which customers might bring. When these are included the campaign is likely to generate a positive net value.

On this basis, it is recommended that the Personal Banking Division continues with the student account campaign.

Moreover, the positive net value of the campaign could be increased further if AAA offers its customer a very high standard of service such that their defection rate is reduced.

The branch managers' bonus scheme should therefore be amended to include a measure of customer service as suggested in option 1 of section (e) of this report.

52 ReuseR

Study Reference. Acquisitions and growth are discussed in Chapter 5 of the BPP Study Text for E3. Benchmarking is covered in Chapter 4.

Part (a)

Top tips. A good way to approach part (a) is to think about the context of the acquisition. ReuseR wants to expand its business further and gain access to new markets where it does not currently operate. Therefore the extent to which a target will allow ReuseR to achieve these goals will be a very important factor in the acquisition decision. It seems likely that ReuseR is primarily looking to move into new geographical markets, but it is possible some of the target companies could also provide it with the opportunity to move into new product markets.

However, the scenario also identified that ReuseR has historically found it difficult to manage the merger of operations after an acquisition. Therefore the culture and management style of the target company could also be important – how well it will 'fit' with ReuseR's own internal context.

Market access – ReuseR is looking to grow its business and gain access to new markets where it does not currently operate. Therefore one of the key criteria for judging potential acquisitions will be the markets in which they operate, and whether they will provide ReuseR with the new growth opportunities which it wants.

In this respect, the overall size of the recycling market in the targets' countries is important, because it will illustrate the **scope for future expansion** in that country.

Market share – Although ReuseR is looking at acquiring relative small companies (sales revenue of €10 – €30 million per year), it will still want to be confident that the companies have sufficient presence in their domestic markets so that acquiring them provides ReuseR either with a strong base for future growth.

In this respect, ReuseR will also need to assess how **scalable** the business is – whether it has a **growth focus**, or whether it is a **niche business**. If the target is a niche business, ReuseR will need to know whether its business processes could cope with a significant increase in the scale of its operations.

Product portfolio – At the moment, ReuseR is heavily dependent on glass recycling, which earns over 40% of ReuseR's contribution to profit. However, sales growth from glass recycling seems quite low, so ReuseR could benefit from making acquisitions which allow it to diversify its product portfolio. A useful aspect to consider will be the materials the potential targets recycle, and more importantly the expected growth rates in demand for recycling those materials.

A present issue in recycling is the lack of facilities for recycling plastics and end of life electrical products. If a target could enable ReuseR to offer these services, then it could be a lucrative addition to the company's product portfolio.

Capacity and scope for growth – Given the focus on growth an expansion, ReuseR should assess whether the target companies have sufficient capacity to recycle more material at their existing plants, or alternatively whether they have scope to expand their plant sizes to meet any additional capacity requirements.

However, ReuseR should also consider the degree of overlap between its existing operations and the target companies' operations, and therefore whether there is any scope for **savings on common costs** or economies of scale.

Recycling equipment – ReuseR should also look at the **age** and **condition** of target companies' recycling machinery and equipment. If a company has old equipment there is a higher risk of failure or breakdown, potentially disrupting operations. Equally, it may mean that ReuseR has to replace the equipment in the near future. (If this is the case, ReuseR should look for a reduction in the purchase price of the acquisition at allow for this.)

CSR and pollution – ReuseR should also look at how environmentally friendly the recycling processes the companies use are. This also links to the previous point. If the plants are using old machinery, it could be energy inefficient, and also create more pollution than more modern machinery.

Technology and skills – ReuseR has introduced several innovative ways of collecting and recycling waste, and it is likely that ReuseR will continue to look at process improvements in order to try to reduce costs. Therefore, if the target companies have already introduced new technologies, these could be useful for ReuseR to acquire.

Infrastructure – Distribution costs are an important area of concern at ReuseR, so the Board are likely to be keen that these costs in any companies acquired are as low as possible. One way distribution costs could be reduced is by the target company being conveniently located to its main customers, or with good communication links to potential new customers.

Management and control – ReuseR has identified that it wants to acquire companies outright, rather than acquiring a division of a company. In this context, it will need to consider whether the existing management teams of the target company will want to remain in place after the acquisition or whether ReuseR will need to second some of its own staff to manage the new subsidiaries. If the existing teams remain in place, ReuseR will need to consider their skills, both at managing the business and in producing the management and financial information which ReuseR will require. The **quality of financial information** which ReuseR's existing subsidiaries provide to the head office has already been identified as an area which needs improving.

Cultural fit – As well as considering how well it can incorporate the subsidiary into the Group and manage it, ReuseR will also need to consider how well the acquisition's culture and business strategy fits with ReuseR's own. This is likely to be an important issue because ReuseR is looking at **acquiring companies in foreign countries**. Language differences may also be an impediment to successful integration.

However, the importance of this issue may be reduced because of the relatively small size of the company being acquired. ReuseR may decide that rather than trying to match the acquired company's strategy and structure to its own, the company is small enough simply to fit into ReuseR's existing structure.

Key employees – Nonetheless, if there are certain **key employees** that ReuseR will want to stay with the company after it is acquired, then it will need to assess whether those employees will be prepared to work for new owners – and possibly new managers.

Price and financial due diligence – Alongside these operational and managerial consideration, ReuseR also needs to consider whether the price the vendors are asking for the company appears reasonable. For example, ReuseR should assess the returns it is making on its assets, and how well established its relationships are will its main customers. If it currently has a number of large contracts which may not be renewed, then the current revenue figures may not actually reflect its future prospects.

Part (b)

> **Top tips.** Note that there are two parts to this requirement:
>
> (i) Calculate the forecast contribution to profit for each product
> (ii) Evaluate the Operations Director's proposal (in the light of the figures you have calculated).
>
> It is crucial that you address both parts of the requirement, and you do not simply do the calculation: not least because you are that there are only 8 marks available for the calculations, out of a total of 15.
>
> At strategic level, you need to use the calculations you do to help inform strategic issues.

Answers 251

> The Operations Director has proposed that ReuseR should only continue recycling materials which generate a contribution to profit in excess of 45%. But, for example, what would this do to ReuseR's product portfolio? Which products would ReuseR stop recycling if it adopted this approach? The calculations can help you answer these questions.

Forecast product profitability for 20X9

	Revenue €m	Collection costs €m	Recycling costs €m	Distribution costs €m	Contribution to profit €m	Contribution %
Glass						
2008 actuals	79.8	(7.1)	(21.5)	(7.3)		
% change	3%	2%	4%	5%		
2009 forecast	82.2	(7.2)	(22.4)	(7.7)	44.9	55
Wood						
2008 actuals	42.3	(4.7)	(14.0)	(5.1)		
% change	(2%)	2%	0%	5%		
2009 forecast	41.5	(4.8)	(14.0)	(5.4)	17.3	42
Paper						
2008 actuals	46.5	(3.7)	(13.0)	(4.2)		
% change	(5%)	2%	0%	5%		
2009 forecast	44.2	(3.8)	(13.0	(4.4)	23.0	52
Metal						
2008 actuals	14.1	(1.4)	(5.4)	(2.0)		
% change	13%	2%	4%	5%		
2009 forecast	15.9	(1.4)	(5.6)	(2.1)	6.8	43
Tyres						
2008 actuals	12.4	(0.9)	(3.5)	(1.2)		
% change	1%	2%	0%	5%		
2009 forecast	12.5	(0.9)	(3.5)	(1.3)	6.8	55
Others						
2008 actuals	19.1	(1.5)	(5.5)	(2.1)		
% change	4%	2%	0%	5%		
2009 forecast	19.9	(1.5)	(5.5)	(2.2)	10.6	54
2009 Forecast total	216.1	(19.7)	(64.0)	(23.0)	109.5	51

Focus on profitability – By looking at a measure of profitability, the proposal will encourage a focus on costs as well as revenue. This should be useful in helping ReuseR manage its costs more efficiently.

Product portfolio – However, the proposal does not appear to take account of the ReuseR's product portfolio as a whole.

The operations director has suggested that ReuseR should stop recycling any materials which generate a contribution to profit of less than 45%. Based on the forecast figures for 20X9, this would mean that ReuseR stops recycling wood and metal.

Metal is the fastest growing product, and market demand looks set to continue to grow. Therefore, although metal is forecast to only make a 43% contribution in 20X9 this figure could be expected to rise as the volume of metal business increases and ResueR can benefit from economies of scale in its metal recycling business. ReuseR should also be wary of discontinuing its fastest growing product, considering that revenue growth appears limited in its other products.

Wood – Equally, although wood generates a 42% contribution, it currently accounts for just under 20% of ReuseR's revenue [20x9: 41.5 / 216.1 = 19.2%] and still makes a contribution to profit of over €17 million. If

ReuseR stopped recycling wood it may not be able to find alternative new business from other materials to make good the shortfall in contribution to profit.

One-off or incremental change – However, given that the volume of wood recycling business is declining it would be sensible for ReuseR to look to gradually reduce the amount of wood recycling business it does, and look for replacement sources of revenue. However, the operations director's proposal suggests that the ReuseR should immediately stop recycling any materials which generate less than 45% contribution, rather than gradually phasing them out.

Reliability of figures – Another risk in the proposal is that it would be based on a single year's worth of figures rather than a longer term average. Although the contribution for a material may be below 45% in one year, it may have been above it the year before, and could return to being above 45% the following year. However, it will be impractical to keep changing the materials which ReuseR does or doesn't accept.

Customer convenience – Another very important issue which the Operations Director appears to have overlooked is what ReuseR's customers might want. It is likely that its customers would prefer to deal with a single supplier to deal with all their recycling needs. Therefore if ReuseR stops recycling wood or metal, customers who recycled wood and metal in conjunction with other products (including glass) may stop using ReuseR for all their recycling needs. This is likely to have a significant adverse affect on the business' profitability.

Part (c)

> **Top tips.** A change which curtails business units' autonomy is unlikely to be popular with the managers of those units.
>
> ReuseR is faced with the dilemma of how to implement the change (which it believes is necessary to improve business performance) in a way which minimises the ill-feeling among the managers. The manner in which the change is implemented will be crucial, so Kotter & Schlesinger's ideas about the different possible styles for managing change and resistance to change could be a useful framework to use here.

Nature of the change

If the change goes ahead, it is likely that ReuseR will want all the restructuring to take place at one time rather than allowing it to be phased in gradually over a longer period. Given the scale of the re-organisation, the change is therefore best considered as a **transformational change**, rather than an **incremental change**.

Dealing with resistance – However, it is likely that the managers of a number of the business units will oppose such a change because it will reduce their authority, and will **therefore feel like a demotion to them**. Therefore, a crucial aspect of managing the change will be **overcoming the managers' resistance to change.**

In this respect, the HR director's point is very important. The changes will have to be managed carefully so that they do not damage the managers' morale. In particular, the managers need to realise that the changes are not a personal attack on them, but a means of improving the business' performance as a whole.

In this respect, although the change will be transformational rather than incremental, ReuseR will still need to allow time for the managers to ask questions and to obtain reassurances about the impact of the changes. Not allowing this is likely to create a strong feeling of discontent among the business units.

Ways of implementing change

Although there is no single way to implement change successfully, the manner in which a change is introduced is very important in it being implemented successfully. ReuseR should consider the following issues when dealing with this change.

Communication and education. The reasons for the change need to be **explained fully to the managers**. This explanation should emphasise that by centralising control over the business units ReuseR can get better for value for money from its contracts, and will therefore be **more profitable as a whole**.

The explanation should also include a review of how the managers role will change, and should illustrate that the managers will still have an important role in managing the operations of their business units. It is likely that the managers may view the changes as **making some of their current skills obsolete**.

This could well be the case, so the communications need to be **open and honest**, and explain that there will be changes in the nature of the role. However, while some of the current aspects of the role will no longer be required, there will be new aspects which the managers will need to do instead.

In order to demonstrate its support to the managers, ReuseR needs to ensure they are given **training** for any new roles they will be required to take on.

Board involvement. ReuseR's directors should be involved in this communication process and should visit the business units to explain the changes. This will demonstrate that the business units are still considered important to the new business, and also that the changes themselves are important.

Throughout the communication process, it will be important to **encourage the business unit managers to ask any questions** they may have, so that the communication process is a two-way process. This should minimise the risk of any confusion, but will also help reassure the local managers that they are still listened to.

Collaboration and participation. This will bring the managers directly into the change management process. Although some decisions will be centralised, the business unit managers will still have valuable knowledge about what routines and processes work well and what works less well.

The knowledge they possess means that the local managers should be involved in identifying issues which need to be addressed in the new strategy. As well as benefiting ReuseR as a whole, this **inclusive approach** will again help make the business unit managers feel they are still valuable to the business.

Negotiation. The reward system can be used to incentivise managers to adapt to the new culture and performing successfully under it. ReuseR seems to be prioritising cost control and efficiency so managers could be given targets for key performance measures in these areas. If they feel these targets are realistic and achievable, they could act as an important incentive in persuading them to stay with ReuseR and support the changes.

Imposed change. Ultimately, however, it is likely that some of the managers will remain unhappy with the changes, and those who are not prepared to accept the changes, will have to be removed from the business. This will prevent any discontent from spreading amongst their staff, which is important given the already high levels of staff turnover.

Part (d)

> **Top tips.** The question asks you to *evaluate* the contribution which benchmarking could make to ReuseR, so you need to consider the advantages of benchmarking but also the limitations to its benefits. However, make sure you also consider these advantages and drawbacks in the specific context of ReuseR. Do not simply give a generic evaluation of benchmarking as a process.
>
> Note, in particular, that the ReuseR proposal is for an internal benchmarking exercise only – it is not comparing ReuseR's performance against any external best practices or competitors, and so this is likely to limit its value to some degree.
>
> The answer below tries to give a wide range of valid points you could have made. However, a well-explained point is likely to have scored 1 ½ – 2 marks, so you would not have needed to make all the points we do to score a good pass on this question.

Benchmarking allows an organisation to learn from best practice. A number of organisations use benchmarking exercises to compare their processes against competitors or best-in-class performers, but the one ReuseR has proposed only compares its own business units with each other.

<u>Benefits of benchmarking for ReuseR</u>

Improved performance – By comparing the performance of business units against each other, ReuseR will be able to identify which appear to be the best performers. If it can then bring the performance of the other units up to the same level, it will deliver improved performance across the group – particularly in cost control.

Benchmarking should lead to **performance targets being set**, which although they are challenging should be achievable.

Challenge existing processes – However, as well as setting targets, the benchmarking exercise might also encourage the business unit managers to challenge why things are done in a particular way. These challenges could lead to process improvements across the group.

Accepting responsibility for change – The benchmarking comparisons should be carried out by the managers who are responsible for each key area of performance. Consequently, benchmarking should also **encourage the managers to take responsibility for any changes necessary** to improve the performance in that area.

Problems with ReuseR's benchmarking proposal

Internal only – Often one of the key benefits of a benchmarking exercise is being able to compare performance against external best practice. However, ReuseR's proposal only looks to measure the performance of its divisions against each other. Although this may lead to some improvements, it may still mean that ReuseR's performance efficiency lags behind its competitors or the leading practice for any given functions. There is a danger the exercise could create a false sense of security.

Identifies effects rather than causes. Benchmarking focuses on performance, but does not, in itself, identify the reasons why performance is at a particular level; be it good or bad. Therefore, while benchmarking may identify that some business units are not performing as well as others, ReuseR's senior management will still need to identify the reasons for the performance and then, if necessary, make changes to the processes underlying them.

Problems of comparability – ReuseR has subsidiaries in a number of different countries. Depending on cultural and infrastructural differences between the country it may prove very difficult to make like-for-like comparisons between the subsidiaries. The differences identified between the units may reflect the context of the units rather than the relative internal performance of the units.

Potentially demotivating – Poor results from a benchmarking exercise can be disproportionately discouraging and **demotivating**, particularly to the managers of the business units which perform poorly.

Quality of information – Benchmarking will lead to an **increased flow of information** that must be monitored, summarised and assessed. There are already problems with the quality of management information being received by ReuseR's head office and the business units having to take time to benchmark performance could exacerbate this problem.

Efficiency versus effectiveness – There is a danger that benchmarking may encourage ReuseR's managers to try improve the efficiency with which they do the things, whereas actually they need to be looking to see whether there are better ways of doing things overall. In effect, the two proposals (benchmarking versus centralisation) highlight the difference here: benchmarking is trying to get the business units to reduce costs by being more efficient, but centralised procurement is a more radical solution and challenges the way ReuseR deals with its suppliers overall.

Historical exercise – Benchmarking is essentially an historical exercise. It looks back at past performance, and will encourage business units to improve their performance to match the performance of the best performing divisions. However, it does not, in itself, do anything to develop new competences or opportunities which could give ReuseR any competitive advantage in the future.

53 Domusco

Text reference. Financial performance measures are covered in Chapter 12 of the BPP Study Text for E3. The balanced scorecard is covered in Chapter 13.

Corporate Social Responsibility is discussed in Chapter 2.

Part (a)

Top Tips. Note there are in effect two parts to the requirement here. Firstly you need to evaluate the use of ROCE as a performance measure and secondly you need to advise what alternative measures the directors could use. In your evaluation, you should weigh up the advantages and disadvantages of ROCE as a performance measure, but try to apply these in the context of a construction company rather than simply presenting general comments.

One of the MD's complaints – that there is too much focus on internal, financial measures – should have highlighted the importance of finding alternative measures which focus on both financial and non-financial indicators. The balanced scorecard could be very useful in this respect. Another advantage is that it has a customer focus: again, dealing with the MD's complaint about the excessive focus on internal measures.

Advantages of ROCE as a performance measure

Driven by profitability – ROCE measures profitability in relation to the capital resources used. In this respect, it measures both profitability and efficiency (how well Domusco employs its capital). Domusco is a listed company, and measuring profitability and capital utilisation could be important measures for shareholders.

Domusco has a considerable amount of assets on its statement of financial position (including its land bank and work-in-progress) and generating a return on these assets is the essence of how it makes its profits.

The MD's own story indicates that some types of housing generate higher ROCE returns than others. This would suggest that it is in Domusco's interest to concentrate on building larger developments than smaller ones.

Figures easily identified and understood – The figures can be easily agreed to the accounts. Moreover, because ROCE is expressed as a percentage rate of return, it is in a format which management are easily familiar with.

Allows comparisons between sites and projects of different sizes. ROCE is a percentage measure and therefore does not favour larger investments against smaller ones, as some absolute measures might do.

Disadvantages of ROCE as a performance measure

Discourages investment in the future and encourages short-termism – This is the point that the MD is making. If the profitability (PBIT) of the division remains constant from one year to the next, the division's ROCE will decrease over the two years if it makes a significant investment in assets (such as land bank) in the second year.

The desire to keep ROCE as high as possible may discourage the division from buying the land, although that land could deliver significant benefits to the division in the future, once houses have been built on it ready to sell.

It is possible that a long-term project like a new housing development might not generate any profits in its first year, even though capital will need to be invested in that project. However, the project is likely to generate profits in subsequent years, once the houses can be sold.

Lack of goal congruence. Measuring performance based on divisional ROCE will encourage the divisions to look at potential developments in isolation, rather than considering their benefit to the Domusco group as a whole. For example, the MD has noted that larger developments generate higher returns that smaller developments. However, Domusco has traditionally focused on building higher quality housing aimed at the higher end of the market, so it may prefer to build smaller developments, rather than large mass produced developments.

In part, this also links to another issue the MD raised. Because ROCE is an internal financial measure, it could underplay the importance of looking at what customers want, and how satisfied they are with Domusco's work. Producing a poor quality development may not affect the current year's ROCE, but it may damage Domusco's reputation in the longer term, and will affect its ability to sell other developments in future.

Distorted by currency changes. The profits and assets of Domusco are spread across several countries with different currencies. If the currency of the host country falls in comparison to Zee (Domusco's home country) then the profits will translate back at a lower value against the assets. This will make ROCE appear to have fallen. To compensate for this, Domusco will need to index the value of the assets in each country to the level of the exchange rates, which in turn will make ROCE a more complicated measure to use. (One of the advantages of using ROCE we identified above is that the figures are easily identified and understood).

Alternative measures

Non-financial measures – One of the MD's main concerns is that Domusco focuses too much on financial measures. However, it is also important that Domusco looks at the efficiency of its **internal processes**, and making sure it keeps up to date with new **technologies and construction techniques**.

External factors – The MD highlighted that ROCE has an internal focus and doesn't take account of market conditions as a whole. In this respect, measuring **market share** and **growth** would be very useful.

However, external factors should also take account of **customer satisfaction**. For example, for the house building division, a useful measure would be the number of customer complaints received which require Domusco to return to newly finished properties and undertake repair work.

Balanced Scorecard – The Balanced Scorecard would allow Domusco to combine **financial perspectives** with **non-financial** and **external perspectives**.

Financial perspective – The financial perspective would ensure Domusco maintains a focus on profitability, but could also include measures on working capital management.

Answers

Customer perspective – This would measure, for example, customer satisfaction or the number of complaints with Domusco's work. Trends in market share could also be measured here.

Internal processes – Health and safety is an important issue at Domusco, and so it will be important to have targets to reduce the number of incidents or accidents.

Managing the efficiency of the business's processes will also be important for keeping any **delays in construction** as low as possible.

Innovation and learning – Measures here could look for example, at new construction techniques introduced, or the number of environmentally friendly materials used in the construction process.

Part (b)

> **Top tip.** Note the requirement here is to 'analyse the profitability' of the possible development. At strategic level, such a requirement (to analyse) doesn't simply mean 'calculate the profitability' of the development, but that you should also use the findings from the calculations to analyse the possible issues they highlight.
>
> In particular, in this case, how should Domusco react to the levels of uncertainty which currently seem to be attached to the project? Do the possible levels of profit justify the potential risks involved? And ultimately, therefore, should Domusco accept the government's invitation to undertake the development?

High cost, high revenue scenario

	Year 0 Z$m	Year 1 Z$m	Year 2 Z$m	Year 3 Z$m	Year 4 Z$m	Total Z$m
Project costs	0	(275)	(350)	(375)	(350)	(1,350)
Loan (at start– Year 0)	(600)					(600)
Cash inflows	0	110	560	850	930	2,450
Net cash (outflow)/inflow	(600)	(165)	210	475	580	500
Discount factor 12%	1	0.893	0.797	0.712	0.636	
NPV	(600)	(147)	167	338	369	127

Low cost, high revenue scenario

	Year 0 Z$m	Year 1 Z$m	Year 2 Z$m	Year 3 Z$m	Year 4 Z$m	Total Z$m
Project costs	0	(130)	(160)	(340)	(380)	(1,010)
Loan (at start – Year 0)	(600)					(600)
Cash inflows	0	110	560	850	930	2,450
Net cash (outflow)/inflow	(600)	(20)	400	510	550	840
Discount factor 12%	1	0.893	0.797	0.712	0.636	
NPV	(600)	(18)	319	363	350	414

High cost, low revenue scenario

	Year 0 Z$m	Year 1 Z$m	Year 2 Z$m	Year 3 Z$m	Year 4 Z$m	Total Z$m
Project costs	0	(275)	(350)	(375)	(350)	(1,350)
Loan (at start – Year 0)	(600)					(600)
Cash inflows	0	102	509	771	842	2,224
Net cash (outflow)/inflow	(600)	(173)	159	396	492	274
Discount factor 12%	1	0.893	0.797	0.712	0.636	
NPV	(600)	(154)	127	282	313	(33)

Low cost, low revenue scenario

	Year 0 Z$m	Year 1 Z$m	Year 2 Z$m	Year 3 Z$m	Year 4 Z$m	Total Z$m
Project costs	0	(130)	(160)	(340)	(380)	(1,010)
Loan (at start – Year 0)	(600)					(600)
Cash inflows	0	102	509	771	842	2,224
Net cash (outflow)/inflow	(600)	(28)	349	431	462	614
Discount factor 12%	1	0.893	0.797	0.712	0.636	
NPV	(600)	(25)	278	307	294	254

Levels of uncertainty involved – It is quite hard for Domusco to assess the likely profitability of the development due to the levels of uncertainly in the figures, particularly in the cost figures.

The extent of this uncertainty means that the worst case scenario sees the project generating a negative net present value of (Z$33) million, but the best case scenario sees it generate a positive Z$414 million.

The rugged nature of the terrain may suggest that it would be prudent for Domusco to base their cost estimates on the project manager's higher cost figures.

However, it is possible that even these higher cost figures may not be high enough, depending on what problems are encountered during the construction process.

Potential significance of contract – Despite the obvious concerns about the uncertainty surrounding the cost figures, if this project delivered the best case scenario results, this would make it more profitable than any of the other five main contracts which Domusco has under construction.

The fact this is also a government contract in Domusco's home country of Zee adds a further potential issue.

If Domusco decides not to accept this contract, and another company delivers it successfully for the government, the government may give that company first refusal on any subsequent contracts.

Given the levels of economic growth and development Zee is currently enjoying, Domusco may decide that it needs to look at this project as part of a wider portfolio than as a stand-alone project.

Part (c) (i)

> **Text reference.** Corporate Social Responsibility is discussed in chapter 2 of the Study Text.
>
> **Top tip.** The requirement in (c) (i) was simply for a brief explanation of the concept of CSR. You were not asked to relate it the scenario. Also note that there were only 4 marks available here so you should not have spent too long on this part of the requirement.

(i) Corporate social responsibility (CSR) is a business's responsibility to be accountable to all its stakeholders (including investors, employees, communities and suppliers) and to society as a whole.

CSR demands that businesses manage the economic, social and environmental impacts of their operations to **maximise the benefits** and **minimise the downsides**. Key CSR issues include governance, environmental management, responsible sourcing of materials, labour standards, human rights, and community relations.

Although a number of CSR issues contain an ethical dimension, CSR is a broader concept that simply acting ethically. CSR also compels businesses to act in a way that provides benefits to society – either through economic development or through environmental improvements, community projects, and any other measures that improve people's quality of life.

CSR recognises that a business has **economic** and **legal duties** in addition to its **ethical duties**. However, the major value of corporate social responsibility is that it encourages businesses to take account of **social costs and benefits** when they are fulfilling their economic duties.

Part c (ii)

> **Top tip.** In effect, in this part of the requirement you need to apply the issues you have identified in (c) (i) to the specific circumstances of the Mesta project.
>
> How will Domusco's various responsibilities to its shareholders, employees and the environment influence the decision whether or not to accept the Mesta project?
>
> The scenario identified the environmental issues with the site and there are obviously CSR issues relating to these. However, you shouldn't have restricted your answer to these issues alone.

(ii) **Minimising environmental damage** – Environmental campaigners have highlighted that the proposed site for the development is home to several rare plant species and also contains a number of sites of archaeological interest.

This puts Domusco in a bit of a dilemma. There is a high profile campaign against the development, and so Domusco could suffer some negative publicity if it carries out the work.

However, the work can only go ahead if the development is officially approved, and permission is granted by the authorities for the land to be built on.

Economic interests – If the land is going to be built on (whether or not Domusco is the builder) Domusco has to consider its economic obligations to its investors as well as the environmental interests.

Domusco is a listed company, and so it has a duty to its owners to maximise their wealth. In which case, if further analysis indicates that the project will be profitable and economically viable, then this is a valid argument for accepting the project.

In which case, Domusco's management need to try to balance the aims of continuing profitability with those of environmental sustainability and preservation.

This might involve trying to **work with the environmental groups** to minimise the impact of the development. Although the environmental groups oppose the development, Domusco may be able to work with them to look at ways in which the development could be modified to reduce its negative environmental impact. For example, it might be possible to showcase some of the archaeological sites as features within the new development.

Acting in best interests of society as a whole – CSR requires businesses to act in a way that provides benefits to society as a whole. The Zee government has stated that the Mesta development is required to help Zee sustain its economic growth. This economic growth is a benefit to society. So again, there is a conflict between the economic benefits and the environmental costs of the project.

Domusco might also consider the extent to which the development will provide a **sustainable community**, for example one which combines houses, office and work spaces and leisure facilities for residents, such that residents' travel requirements are reduced. Domusco should also consider the extent to which the development includes some low cost **social housing**.

Economic risks – However, the level of uncertainty in the figures which are available at the moment, means that Domusco should not accept the contract without carrying out a more detailed assessment of potential costs and revenues. This again highlights Domusco's responsibilities to its owners (shareholders).

Ensure safety and working conditions of employees – There are already concerns about contractors taking on inexperienced staff and breaching health and safety guidelines.

Taking on this new project will add further to the demand for labour, and so could mean that additional, inexperienced staff will be used. If there was an accident at the site, this could generate significant adverse publicity for Domusco.

Part (d)

> **Text reference.** Outsourcing is discussed in chapter 5 of the BPP Study Text.
>
> **Top tips.** The scenario highlighted a number of key points: health and safety issues, a shortage of experienced / skilled staff, and issues with wage levels.

> However, your answer shouldn't simply restate these points as problems with using subcontractors. You should also think more critically about the situation. In effect, the dilemma facing Domusco is whether to outsource the work to contractors or to retain all the work in-house. If the work is retained in-house, Domusco can control quality more easily, but its cost structure will change. In effect, full time employees will be a fixed cost for Domusco, but contractors are a variable cost.

Quality of work – Domusco has established a good reputation as a high quality builder, but if the sub-contractors are using inexperienced staff, there is a danger that the quality of the work they produce will not meet these standards.

There are two possible consequences of this:

If defects in the work are not spotted by Domusco's project management inspectors, then the number of **customer complaints** is likely to increase, and Domusco's reputation could be adversely affected.

If the defects are spotted by the inspectors, the increase in the number of defects could lead to **delays** in completing the project while the defects are made good. Again, if a number of projects are delayed this could again damage Domusco's reputation.

Impact on staff motivation – Domusco's own staff are clearly unhappy about the perceived lack of experience in the staff which subcontractors are using, and also the fact that they know some sub-contractors are paid more than them. There is a danger that if this situation is allowed to continue, the motivation of the in-house staff (and the quality of their work) may fall. In the worst case scenario, there is even a risk that the in-house staff will refuse to work alongside the sub-contracted workers.

Setting standards – If the directors do decide to continue using sub-contractors they will need to impose some minimum experience standards (that is, to require that sub-contracted workers must have a certain level of experience before they can work on a job).

As well as dealing with staff motivational issues, this is also important to address **safety issues**. Now the employee survey has highlighted the lack of safety awareness in the workplace, the directors have an obligation to improve safety levels so that their own workers are put at risk of an accident in the work place.

Basis of pay – The sub-contractors are currently paid a fixed fee for a contract, so the quicker they finish it, the quicker they can move on to the next one. In this way, the structure of the reward scheme may be contributing to the decline in quality.

If Domusco employed in-house staff they would be less likely to rush jobs simply to move on to the next one. However, this issue could also be addressed with contract staff if the terms of the contracts were re-negotiated, for example, such that there is a retention clause in the contract giving Domusco the right to withhold some of the payment if the work does not meet agreed quality standards.

Availability of staff – The boom in the construction industry has led to a number of inexperienced people seeking work in the construction industry. We do not know if the contractors are using these inexperienced staff because they are cheaper than more experienced staff or because the high levels of demand mean that there are no more experienced staff available.

If the problem is being caused by the high levels of demand, then Domusco will have a similar problem as the contractors if they try to recruit more staff. They will either have to recruit inexperienced staff and train them up themselves, or try to attract experienced workers away from their existing jobs.

The idea of recruiting relatively inexperienced staff and training them up may prove more attractive. These staff will be cheaper to recruit, and if Domusco administers the training then the staff will follow the practices and procedures that Domusco want them to.

Core versus peripheral skills – Another issue which Domusco should consider is whether it brings some jobs back in house, and leaves others to be done by contractors.

Domusco's management have previously identified that they do not wish to employ large numbers of staff who may be located in the wrong area or have the wrong skills for the jobs that need doing at any particular time. In-house labour is, in effect, a fixed cost whereas contract costs are variable. Domusco will only need to use a contractor when there are projects which need doing.

In this respect, Domusco may want to continue to use contract labour for very specialist skills, (which may only be needed intermittently), but increase the number of less specialist skilled workers in house. There is likely to be a more regular demand for labourers with less specialist skills.

Project management or construction – One final issue which Domusco needs to consider is where it sees or its core competences and skills. Historically Domusco has seen itself a construction company. However, it is possible it could decide its core competences are now in project management and building quality management (because it always uses its own staff for these roles) rather than construction itself.

If Domusco sees these more managerial functions as its core competences, then it is more likely to keep construction workers as contractors rather than increasing the numbers of them employed in house.

54 Zubinos

> **Text reference.** Mission statements are discussed in Chapter 2 of the Study Text. Franchising is discussed in Chapter 5, and Web 2.0 technologies are covered in Chapter 7.

Part (a)

> **Top tips.** The directors' suggestion indicates that Zubinos currently does not have a mission statement, yet the company has still grown quite successfully.
>
> This should lead you to question what practical value a mission statement would be for the company.
>
> Nonetheless, because the question asks you to discuss both the advantages and disadvantages of a mission statement, you do need to consider both sides of the argument.
>
> However, make sure your answer does not become a general discussion of the advantages and disadvantages of mission statements: you need to relate your points to the specific circumstances of Zubinos' business.

> **Tutorial note:** There are a number of valid advantages and disadvantages you could discuss in this part of the question. For tutorial purposes we have tried to include as comprehensive a range of advantages and disadvantages as we can, but you would not need to include all of the points we make to score well in this question (which is only worth 8 marks).
>
> We have included some additional points in text boxes at the end of the answer because you would get credit for them if you included them.

Zubinos business has grown rapidly in recent years and Luis Zubino is keen for this expansion to continue – including overseas growth.

As the business grows, it will be important that the staff understand the goals and objectives of the business, and their role in the business. The directors may look to use a mission statement to summarise the purpose of the business going forward.

Advantages of developing a mission statement

Basis of competition – The mission statement will determine the basis on which Zubinos competes in the industry, for example whether it wants to remain a trendy, high quality coffee shop chain which creates a strong brand and a reputation for customer service or whether it is prepared to lower production costs in order to increase margins.

Consistency of offering – A mission statement will help Zubinos ensure that all aspects of its business are consistent with the basis on which it is competing in the market. For example, assuming it remains focused on the high end market, then all its processes, from sourcing raw ingredients through to customer service must be of sufficiently high quality to support this strategic position.

Determine behaviours – A mission statement will help promote the desired values and behaviours in Zubinos staff. This will be important as the company expands, so that all new staff understand the culture of the company: for example, the mission statement could identify that using good quality ingredients and offering good customer service are key factors which differentiate Zubinos from its competitors.

Maintaining these high standards could be a particularly important issue if Zubinos does decide to adopt the franchise model.

Ethical framework – Mission statements often encompass an ethical framework. Luis Zubino is a strong advocate of using Fair Trade products, and the mission statement could highlight the commitment to only using products which deliver sustainable livelihoods to farmers and their communities.

Satisfy key stakeholders – Businesses need to ensure they meet the needs of their key stakeholders, and a mission statement can help a business achieve this purpose. (Producing a mission statement should also help ensure a business identifies who its key shareholders are).

For Zubinos, the Board, the private equity company (KPE), employees, supplier and customers are all key stakeholders. Zubinos' mission statement should demonstrate how it will give its suppliers a fair deal, serve its customers and reward its employees, recognising that customer loyalty and employee loyalty will be very important to maintaining its success.

Fits with rational planning model – Mission statements can play an important role in the strategic planning process, but they are most suitable for companies which have a formal planning model. In such companies, a mission statement can influence the way a company implements its planned strategy and it can act as a reference document against which future business plans can be judged. Zubinos seems to have a relatively formal planning process, as it produces five year plans which are approved by the Board and its investors (KPE).

Disadvantages of developing a formal mission statement

Time consuming – Creating a mission statement will be time consuming, especially as Zubinos has never had one before and so it will need to be developed from nothing. If the mission statement does not generate any positive results in terms of corporate values and profitability, then the time spent developing it will have been wasted.

Confusing priorities – Zubinos has ambitious plans to open new shops in the UK and across Europe. The senior management team will have a number of practical issues to consider in terms of the locations of these shops, and how the expansion will be managed – for example, whether to expand by organic growth or through the franchise option. Whilst developing a mission statement could be useful in guiding the strategic planning process, it is debatable whether it is a top priority at the moment. Spending too much time developing a mission statement could deflect attention from these more pressing issues.

May be ignored – Mission statements usually contain high level, general principles. If the principles in Zubino's mission statement are not specific enough to tie down to practical objectives they will have little impact on individuals' behaviours and so could be ignored. Again, if a lot of time and effort has been spent in developing the mission statement, this will be wasted.

May be too restrictive – At the moment, the majority of Zubinos revenue comes from its UK coffee shops. However, revenues from its merchandise and from its overseas sales are likely to increase in the future. Moreover, as Zubinos grows and develops, its strategy may need to emerge and adapt, depending on changes in its environment.

Consequently, if the mission statement is too restrictive it may actually prevent the company taking advantage of new opportunities which arise.

Part (b)

Top tip. Part (b) only requires you to calculate the forecast net income to Zubinos from the franchise operations. You should not include any analysis about whether or not Zubinos should accept the proposal here; save this analysis for part (c).

(i) Zubinos profit forecast from franchises

	20X7 £m	20X8 £m	20X9 £m	20Y0 £m	20Y1 £m
Share of total sales (6% of total sales)	0.6	2.4	5.4	11.1	18.9
Mark up on supplies (W)	0.2	0.8	1.7	3.5	6.0
Total income	0.8	3.2	7.1	14.6	24.9
Initial fees to GF (£25,000 per new shop)	(0.5)	(0.8)	(1.3)	(2.0)	(3.0)
Annual fees payable to GF (3.5% of total sales)	(0.4)	(1.4)	(3.2)	(6.5)	(11.0)
Fees payable	(0.9)	(2.2)	(4.4)	(8.5)	(14.0)
Net income from franchise	(0.1)	1.0	2.7	6.1	10.9

Working

	20X7 £m	20X8 £m	20X9 £m	20Y0 £m	20Y1 £m
Total franchise sales	10.0	40.0	90.0	185.0	315.0
Gross margin @ 60%	6.0	24.0	54.0	111.0	189.0
Cost of sales	4.0	16.0	36.0	74.0	126.0
Zubino's mark up (CoS × $5/105$)	0.2	0.8	1.7	3.5	6.0
Original cost to Zubinos	3.8	15.2	34.3	70.5	120.0

Part (c)

> **Top tips.** Although your answer to part (b) should not include any analysis of the calculations you have done, you should make use of them in part (c) when analysing GlobalFranch's proposal. For example, one of the issues Zubinos should consider is whether the franchise is likely to be the most profitable way for it to expand.
>
> Although you need to make sure your answer is related specifically to the context of Zubinos, c (i) is effectively asking you to analyse the advantages and disadvantages of franchising as a method of growth.
>
> Make sure you also appreciate how parts (c) (i) & (ii) fit together. In (c) (i), you need to analyse the issues, and then on the basis of this analysis you need to recommend whether or not Zubinos should accept GF's proposal. Make sure (c) (ii) doesn't simply become a repetition of (c) (i).
>
> The ideas of suitability, feasibility and acceptability should provide a useful framework for helping you make your recommendation in (c) (ii).

(i) <u>Methods of growth</u> – The franchise offer will allow the business to grow much more quickly than if Zubinos grows organically. However, Zubinos will need to decide whether it continues to open its own shops or whether it relies only on franchises for its growth.

Zubinos existing 5 year plan already shows it opening an additional 50 new shops by 20Y0, with pre-tax operating profit forecast to increase from £1.2 million (20X5) to £11.0 million (20Y0).

However, a number of these new shops are planned to be in Europe, so there is a danger that they may be in areas where franchises may also open new coffee shops, in which case Zubinos' own shops could be competing with the franchised shops.

<u>Profit maximising or satisficing</u> – The forecast figures for the franchise show that Zubinos receives a contribution to profit of approximately 3% of the total revenue earned from the franchisees.

	20X7 £m	20X8 £m	20X9 £m	20Y0 £m	20Y1 £m
Sales	10	40	90	185	315
Retained by Zubinos	(0.1)	1.0	2.7	6.1	10.9
Margin retained	(1.0)%	2.5%	3.0%	3.3%	3.5%

From this amount Zubinos will have to pay any **marketing** or **administration** costs associated with the franchise.

However, the business plan for Zubinos owned shops shows a pre-tax operating profit of approximately 9%. Therefore, before agreeing the franchise deal, Zubinos should assess whether it can actually increase its profits more by growing organically than through the franchise route, given the terms it has been offered by GF.

An alternative issue it should consider is whether it can renegotiate the terms of the deal with GF so that Zubinos retains a greater share of the overall sales.

Far Eastern markets – One of the main advantages of the franchise model may be the opportunity of opening shops in the rapidly growing Far Eastern market. It is likely to be harder for Zubinos to open its own shops in that market, due to the geographical distance to its UK base, and the cultural and language differences between the Far East and the UK.

Franchisees – who are local businesses, and therefore also have local market knowledge – will not face these **potential barriers to entry**.

Lower capital requirements – In the franchise model, the franchisee will incur the capital costs of opening the new shops (for example, the costs of the buildings and fitting out the kitchen equipment). Therefore, the franchise model will allow Zubinos to expand without having to raise the capital it would need to set up company-owned shops.

Risk and rewards – Moreover, if Zubinos were to open new shops itself, it would have the uncertainty of not knowing whether the shops will successful in new locations. The franchising arrangement will reduce the risk involved. Although Zubinos will have to pay an initial fee of £20,000 to GlobalFranch for each new shop opened, this is a much lower cost than if it was to open the shops itself. If a franchised shop fails, the franchisee will bear the majority of the costs.

However, the trade off from this lower risk is that Zubinos retains a lower share of the profit under the franchise deal.

Ability to support growth – We have already identified that the franchise option will allow the business to grow much more quickly than if Zubinos grows organically. Although the businesses will be run by the franchisees, Zubinos will still be responsible for supplying the coffee and branded product lines which the franchisees sell in the shops. Therefore, Zubinos will need to consider whether its current suppliers can meet the increased demand which will be needed.

If the current suppliers cannot meet the demand, Zubinos will have to find alternative suppliers who can provide them with products of similarly high quality.

Zubinos should also consider the **working capital requirements** associated with the expansion, assuming that it has to buy the coffee and branded products in advance.

Different competences – At the moment, Zubinos' skills lie in running its own shops. If it moves into franchising this will require it develop different skills – in particular, relationship management either with GlobalFranch or with individual franchisees.

Control and brand image – Equally, under the franchise model, Zubinos will have to ensure that all the franchisees are offering products and customer service which meet its required standards. GlobalFranch may monitor the franchisees on Zubinos' behalf, but ultimately Zubinos still needs to be aware that poor franchisee performance could harm its brand.

5 year deal – From a contractual perspective, Zubinos should consider whether it is happy being tied into a five year deal with GlobalFranch. A five year initial deal seems quite long, particularly as Zubinos has no guarantee that GF will deliver the sorts of figures it has promised.

Confidential information – Another risk from the franchise deal is that franchisees could use Zubinos experience and business support to get them established, but then set up their own coffee shops as competitors.

(ii) Suitability

The franchise option appears a suitable way of allowing Zubinos to expand, because it will allow Zubinos to expand more rapidly and with lower capital requirements, than if it grows organically.

However, the franchise option is perhaps more suitable as a means of entering the fast growing Far Eastern markets, than for expanding into Europe. Zubinos has no existing interests in the Far East, but may face some significant barriers to entry (for example, culture and language). By contrast, there are less barriers to entry in Europe, while there is a danger that franchised shops there will end up competing with Zubino's own company-owned shops.

Feasibility

There do not appear to be any issues with the feasibility of this option. There appear to be a number of potential franchisees who are keen to open franchised outlets and GF's core competences are in establishing and managing franchise business.

Expanding through the franchise arrangement will mean that Zubinos will have lower capital and financing requirements than if it grows by opening new company-owned shops.

Acceptability

Acceptability is likely to depend on whether speed of growth or profitability are valued more highly. It appears that it in terms of margin %'s, it will be more profitable for Zubinos to open its own shops rather than using the franchise model.

In particular, the low margins which the franchise appears likely to generate are unlikely to be acceptable to KPE (which owns 40% of Zubinos shares).

Moreover, the terms of the deal (a minimum 5 year contract, with a fixed percentage of revenue being paid to GF) seem quite inflexible. As a commercial deal, it might be more acceptable to Zubinos if there was more flexibility in the percentages of sales revenue payable to GF: for example, having different % bands depending on the level of revenue generated from each shop.

Recommendation

Although GF's proposal will allow Zubinos to expand more rapidly than by opening new company-owned shops, particularly in the Far East market, the current terms of GF's proposal do not appear very favourable to Zubinos, Therefore, Zubinos should reject the current proposal, although it should not rule out using franchising as a means of growth in future with different commercial terms.

Part (d)

> **Top tip.** A good way to approach this question is to consider what marketing opportunities the internet and e-marketing would offer Zubinos which would not be available through traditional media. Although you do not need to use any framework to answer this question, the 6 Is framework could be helpful – with interactivity being a particularly important feature of e-marketing.
>
> Note also that your E3 syllabus makes specific reference to Web 2.0 technologies, and so you should have considered how they could be useful in this context. The scenario has already identified that Zubinos has an online chatroom, so could this be extended in any way to provide additional marketing materials?

Interactivity – Interactivity is a key feature of electronic media, creating a dialogue between supplier and customer. Often this dialogue is through e-mail exchanges, and for example, if Zubinos had a loyalty card scheme which required customers to provide an email address and a postcode, it could use e-mails to provide customers with information about new blends of coffee they are introducing, or any seasonal specialities they have in their shops.

In this way, the internet can be used to help retain and re-activate existing customers.

Advergames – Alternatively, Zubinos could run some online games in which webusers can register to be eligible for prizes provided they provide certain personal data. For example, prizes could include a month of free coffees at Zubinos shops.

Once users register their details, Zubinos marketing team will have contact details through which to contact potential customers, and they will also have some intelligence about their customers.

Intelligence – This ability to obtain customer intelligence is another way which distinguishes e-marketing from traditional marketing. Because advertisers using traditional media do not engage in any dialogue with potential customers, they cannot use their marketing to find out anything about customers' requirements, and also which products or services are meeting them most effectively.

Individualisation – Another important characteristic of electronic media is that they allow marketing messages to be **tailored to specific market segments**.

The interactivity noted above also promotes individualisation. Once customers have registered for the loyalty card, or the advergame, if Zubinos is having a special event or promotion at one of its shops near them, the customers could receive an email about the event, possibly also with a promotional discount voucher.

Interactivity and product design – The idea of interactivity could also be extended to allow customers to have an input into the range of coffees and foods Zubinos offers, or the layout and ambience of its shops.

Consumer generated content – Zubinos website already has an online communications area which allows users to 'chat' online. However, in additional to offering this general 'chatroom' facility, Zubinos could also use the website to encourage users to talk about their experiences in Zubinos: what they liked, what they didn't like so much, and what else they would like Zubinos to offer.

Blogs – In addition to the forum on Zubinos' own site, there are likely to be other blogs and discussions where people are talking about Zubinos. Again, these can provide useful information about what they like and dislike.

Viral advertising – Zubinos should consider ways in which it can use social networking sites to promote its shops. For example, it could run some video clips showing people enjoying their coffees in its shops, or showing how a trip to Zubinos can brighten up people's days. If these clips are popular, and are shared by a large number of webusers, they will help increase Zubino's **brand awareness**, and could help it **acquire new customers**.

Search engine optimisation – Potential customers now use the internet to search for information about possible products. Zubinos needs to ensure that if potential customers enter a web search for coffee shops or cafes then its details come near the top of the resulting listings.

The way Zubinos' website is constructed will affect the likelihood of it appearing on the first page of search engine listings. Zubinos will also need to ensure that a search for coffee makers or kitchen appliances brings up the link to its coffee machines.

Banners and click throughs – Zubinos should also investigate the possibility of building links to its website from other sites. For example, it could create some banner adverts or click through links from lifestyle magazines which target the same 20-to-25 year old age range Zubinos focus on.

Although it will have to pay a commission for the number of visitors who come to its site via the link, this should still prove a beneficial marketing tactic, because it will increase the number of visitors to Zubinos website as well as improving its search engine ranking.

MOCK EXAMS

CIMA – Pillar E
Paper E3
Enterprise strategy

Mock Exam 1

You are allowed **three hours** to answer this question paper.

You are allowed **20 minutes** reading time **before the examination begins** during which you should read the question paper and, if you wish, highlight and/or make notes on the question paper. However, you are **not** allowed, **under any circumstances**, to open the answer book and start writing or use your calculator during this reading time.

You are strongly advised to carefully read ALL the question requirements before attempting the question concerned (that is all parts and/or sub-questions).

Answer ALL compulsory questions in Section A.

Answer TWO of the three questions in Section B.

DO NOT OPEN THIS PAPER UNTIL YOU ARE READY TO START UNDER EXAMINATION CONDITIONS

SECTION A

Strategic level pre-seen case material

Question 1

Clothing manufacturing in Europe

Since the 1960s there has been a decline in the number of UK and European clothing manufacturers due to competition from cheaper, and sometimes higher quality, imported clothes. The clothing industry generally has become much more fashion conscious and price sensitive. This has led to a reduced number of companies that are still in business in Europe. Some companies have moved all or part of their manufacturing processes to other countries to achieve a cheaper operating base, and up until recently this has allowed them to continue to compete on price.

Many companies have had contracts to supply High Street retailers for over four decades and are highly dependent on retaining these key customers who wield immense buying power over the small manufacturers. A number of family owned manufacturing companies, that had been highly profitable once, have ceased trading, or are operating at very low margins, as a direct result of the High Street retailers being able to dictate terms of business and prices.

An additional factor that has put the main High Street retailers under more price pressure has been the appearance and market growth of new High Street retailers and their new brands, who have procured their goods mainly from overseas sources.

The result is that the few companies that are based in the UK and Europe which are left in the business of clothing manufacturing are having to look very hard at their strategic plans in order for them to manage to maintain their business over the next few years.

History of Kadgee Fashions (Kadgee)

Kadgee was formed in post-World War Two in a European country, and has remained as an unlisted company, although its shares are now held by others outside of the founding family. Kadgee quickly established itself as a high quality manufacturer of both men's and ladies clothes. By the 1960s Kadgee had a turnover equivalent to €25 million, and had nine factories operating in two European countries.

During the late 1960s Kadgee suffered its first major fall in sales, and found that it had large stocks of men's clothes that had been manufactured without specific sales contracts. Kadgee managed to sell off some of the stocks, albeit at below cost price. However, the management decided that it should not manufacture clothes without a firm contract from a retailer in future.

In the early 1970s the range and design of its men's clothing was changed several times, but it continued to make little profit. In 1973, Kadgee sold its men's clothing range and designs and some of its manufacturing equipment to a large listed company. Kadgee decided to concentrate on expanding its ranges of ladies' clothing to meet the growing demands of its main customers (see below).

During the next few years, Kadgee consolidated its position and its profitability increased again. In the early 1980s its then Chief Designer persuaded the Managing Director to expand its clothing range to include a range of girls' clothes. This new limited range was launched in 1982 and was immediately sold out. Kadgee has positioned itself at the upper price range of clothing, and has never tried to mass produced low cost clothing.

During the 1980s Kadgee continued to expand its ranges of ladies and girls' clothes. A further change that occurred was that many of Kadgee's customers were starting to dictate the styles and types of clothing required and Kadgee's designers had to manufacture to customers' specifications.

However, during the 1990s Kadgee suffered a number of setbacks. It also saw many of its competitors suffer losses and cease trading. Kadgee had been able to stay profitable only because of its particular customer base and because it sold high quality clothes that commanded a premium price. However, Kadgee saw its margins on many product lines reduced greatly and also it started to lose many of its smaller customers, who choose to import, at much lower prices, clothing produced in Asia.

Kadgee's shareholders

Kadgee has remained an unlisted company. At the end of 20X5 29% of its shares were held by the company's founder who is no longer on the board, 60% by current directors, 11% by employees. The company has 200,000 shares of €0·10 each in issue and has a total of 400,000 authorised shares. The shares are not traded but the last time the shares were exchanged was eight years ago, when shares were purchased at €8·00 each.

Kadgee's customer base

Kadgee manufactures clothing for a number of European and international clothing retailers, including many well known High Street retailers. It manufactures clothing in the medium to higher price ranges and its customers require top quality designs and finishing to maintain their brand reputation.

The majority of Kadgee's clothing is manufactured for its customers under the customers' own label, for example, clothing manufactured for one of its customers called Portrait is labelled as 'Portrait'.

In 20X5, Kadgee's customer base, analysed by sales value, was as follows:

	20X5 revenue €m	% of Kadgee's total sales %
Portrait	24.0	32.3
Forum	16.8	22.6
Diamond	13.5	18.1
Zeeb	5.1	6.9
JayJay	4.5	6.0
Other retailers of ladies' clothes	7.3	9.8
Haus (children's clothes only)	3.2	4.3
Total	74.4	100.0

Most of Kadgee's contracts are renewed at the start of each fashion season. Kadgee is currently negotiating for clothing sales for the summer season of 20X7.

Human Resources

In the clothing manufacturing business one of the most crucial aspects to achieve customer satisfaction is quality. Kadgee has been very fortunate in having a skilled, very dedicated workforce who have always adapted to new machinery and procedures and have been instrumental in suggesting ways in which quality could be improved. This has sometimes involved a very minor change in the design of a garment and the designers now work much more closely with the operational staff to ensure that the garments can be assembled as quickly and efficiently as possible.

Losses made by Kadgee

Kadgee has suffered from falling operating profit margins due to the pressure exerted by its customers over the last ten years. For the first time in Kadgee's history, it experienced losses for five years through to, and including, 20X2. During this time Kadgee increased its loans and its overdraft to finance operations.

In 20X0, Kadgee refinanced with a ten year loan, which was used to repay existing debt, and also to invest in the IT solutions discussed below, as well as to purchase some new machinery. Kadgee also invested in its design centre (see below), which was completed in 20X1.

During 20X1, the company invested in new IT solutions enabling its customers to be able to track all orders from the garment cutting process right through to completion of garments and through to the delivery to customers' premises.

The IT solutions also enabled Kadgee to monitor its production processes including machine usage, wastage at various stages of production and speed of production through the various stages. This has enabled Kadgee's management to reduce areas that did not add value to the finished garment. The use of TQM throughout the business has also increased Kadgee's efficiency and enabled it to eliminate some other areas which did not add value to the finished garments.

While margins are still low, Kadgee has been operating profitably again since 20X3, albeit at lower margins to those achieved in the past.

Changes in the supply chain

Many of Kadgee's customers have needed to speed up the process of supplying clothing to their shops, so as to meet the demands of the market and to remain competitive. Kadgee has worked closely with its customers in order to achieve shorter lead times from design to delivery of finished products.

In 20X1, Kadgee introduced a new design centre, centralised at its Head Office. The design centre uses computer aided design techniques, which has helped Kadgee's customers to appreciate the finished appearance of new designs. This seems to have helped Kadgee to win new business and to retain its current customers. It has also contributed to Kadgee's ability to speed up the process from design board to finished article. Kadgee has also benefited from working closer with its customers and this has resulted in additional orders, which Kadgee's customers' would otherwise have procured from overseas sources.

Growing competition from China

During the 1990s and into the 21st century China has had a massive impact on the textile industry. China's manufacturing base is forecast to grow further and this will have a negative impact on many companies operating at a higher cost base elsewhere.

Many European companies have spent millions of Euros establishing manufacturing bases outside their home countries in the last 15 years. Many have opened factories in countries which have much lower operating costs. These include countries such as Turkey, Sri Lanka and Pakistan, as well as Eastern European countries.

The companies which have set up operations in these low cost countries did so in an effort to cut costs by taking advantage of low overheads and lower labour rates, but still managed to maintain quality. However, even the companies that have moved some, or all, of their manufacturing bases and have taken steps to reduce their costs, now have to reconsider their cost base again. This is because of the very low cost of Chinese imports, which they are having difficulty competing against.

Following the relaxation of trade barriers, there has recently been a deluge of Chinese clothing imports into Europe, the UK and the USA.

The quality of Chinese manufactured clothing is improving rapidly and it is now globally recognised that the "Made in China" label represents clothing of a higher quality than many European manufactured garments. Furthermore, the Chinese manufactured garments are being produced at a substantially lower manufacturing cost.

Kadgee has so far been operating in a market that has not been significantly affected by imported goods, as it produces medium to higher priced clothing, rather than cheaper ranges of clothes. However, many of Kadgee's customers are now looking to reduce their costs by either buying more imported clothes or by negotiating substantial price cuts from their existing suppliers. The purchasing power of European retailers being exerted on its suppliers is immense and Kadgee is under much pressure to deliver high quality goods at reduced operating profit margins from all of its customers.

Date: It is now 1 November 20X6.

Appendix 1

Statement of financial position

	At 31 December			
	20X5		20X4	
	€'000	€'000	€'000	€'000
Non-current assets (net)		9,830		11,514
Current assets				
Inventory	8,220		6,334	
Trade receivables and rent prepayments	19,404		18,978	
Cash and short term investments	119		131	
		27,743		25,443
Total assets		37,573		36,957

Equity and liabilities

	At 31 December			
	20X5		20X4	
	€'000	€'000	€'000	€'000
Equity				
Paid in share capital	20		20	
Share premium reserve	450		450	
Retained profits	21,787		20,863	
		22,257		21,333
Non-current liabilities				
Loans: Bank loan at 8% interest per year (repayable in 2010)	4,500		4,500	
	21,787		20,863	
		22,257		21,333
Current liabilities				
Bank overdraft	1,520		940	
Trade payables and accruals	8,900		9,667	
Tax	396		517	
		10,816		11,124
Total equity and liabilities		37,573		36,957

Note. Paid in share capital represents 200,000 shares of €0·10 each at 31 December 20X5

Income Statement

	Year ended 31 December	
	20X5	20X4
	€'000	€'000
Revenue	74,420	75,553
Total operating costs	72,580	73,320
Operating profit	1,840	2,233
Finance costs	520	509
Tax expense (effective tax rate is 24%)	396	517
Profit for the period	924	1,207

Statement of changes in equity

	Share capital €'000	Share premium €'000	Retained earnings €'000	Total €'000
Balance at 31 December 20X4	20	450	20,863	21,333
Profit for the period	–	–	924	924
Dividends paid	–	–	–	–
Balance at 31 December 20X5	20	450	21,787	22,257

Appendix 2

Kadgee's Cash Flow Statement

	At 31 December			
	20X5		20X4	
	€'000	€'000	€'000	€'000
Net cash inflow from operations				
Operating profit		1,840		2,233
Add back depreciation	1,965		1,949	
(Increase)/Decrease in inventory	(1,886)		(535)	
(Increase)/Decrease in trade receivables	(426)		(1,526)	
Increase/(Decrease) in trade payables and accruals	(767)		(604)	
		(1,114)		(716)
Net cash flow from operations		726		1,517
Finance costs paid		(520)		(509)
Taxation paid		(517)		(390)
Purchase of tangible fixed assets		(281)		(350)
Dividends paid		–		–
Cash Inflow/(Outflow) before financing		(592)		268
Increase/(Decrease) in bank overdraft		580		(194)
Increase/(Decrease) in cash and short term investments		(12)		74

Section A

Question 1

Unseen Case Material (Exam day material for Paper E3 only)

Background

Increasing competition in the clothing supply industry has seen clothing retailers looking to renegotiate their supply contracts with their existing suppliers. Kadgee is concerned that it may lose some of its major customers if it is unable to give them the price reductions they want.

Possible relocation to China

At the latest Board meeting, the Directors discussed the possibility of moving some of Kadgee's manufacturing to China. This could enable Kadgee to operate more profitably and would allow the company to be more confident in its ability to retain its existing customer base. Such a move would also allow Kadgee to compete more effectively in order to win new business.

The MD stated that Kadgee has also been approached by a Chinese clothes manufacturing company called LIN. LIN has proposed a joint venture with Kadgee, although the respective shares of the venture partners have not yet been decided.

LIN proposes that Kadgee should concentrate on doing what it does best, which is designing and distributing to the European market. Kadgee should continue to work with its current customers to agree designs, which could then be electronically transferred to a factory in China to manufacture. Kadgee would continue to supply its existing customers, but with clothes manufactured in China. This proposal would necessitate closure of all of Kadgee's European factories.

The proposed joint venture would require the construction of a large purpose built factory with manufacturing capacity of over 20 million garments per year. However, the Kadgee's Marketing Director and Operations Director are both concerned about whether the proposed joint venture will work well for the longer term.

Investment in IT

At the same Board meeting, the IT director also highlighted the importance of investing in IT in order to win new business. He presented a proposal to enhance Kadgee's existing IT systems to provide a secure extranet system which would be totally interactive, allowing existing, as well as new customers to browse through all of the available designs that Kadgee is offering to manufacture. The proposed system would allow customers to order online.

The system would also allow customers to personalise their orders, as they would be able to choose the colours, the materials and the designs they wanted. The IT director is confident that this additional functionality will allow Kadgee to secure a lot of new business as well as safeguarding existing customers. He is also confident that a price premium could be charged for clothes that are 'custom made' to customers' requirements, therefore enhancing the margins that could be achieved.

The proposal is forecast to cost €0.8 million for IT hardware and software, and will require additional IT maintenance and support costs of €0.2 million per year. The marketing budget would also need to be increased by €0.4 million per year for the first two years.

The IT director and the marketing director have almost secured their first new customer, BBZ, provided that the system is implemented. BBZ is a medium sized retailer in Europe and has not previously bought any clothing from Kadgee. It is forecast that the contribution to profit from BBZ's first order could be worth €0.2 million in the first year, and subsequent orders could generate, in total, a contribution of €0.4 million per year. However, BBZ have said they do not want to place any orders with Kadgee until the system is operational.

Two other medium sized customers who do not previously buy clothing from Kadgee have also expressed an interest in the 'custom made' production.

The marketing director has summarised the possible contributions to profit from these two other potential customers as follows:

	Probability	\multicolumn{5}{c}{Contribution to profit (€m)}
		20X7	20X8	20X9	20Y0	20Y1
Both possible customers sign up	0.35	0.4	0.6	0.7	0.8	0.9
One of the two signs up	0.45	0.2	0.3	0.4	0.4	0.5
Neither of them signs up	0.2	–	–	–	–	–

The Operations Director is concerned about the whole logic behind the proposal, and argued that it is trying to shift Kadgee from having mass production systems into small scale batch production.

However, at the Board meeting, the Finance director said that he felt this proposal was well worth considering, but that he wanted to see an investment appraisal over five years before making any further decisions. He suggested that although the current bank loan has an interest rate of 8%, the risk-adjusted discount rate used for any new investments should be 10%.

Required

(a) Discuss the scope and nature of the changes which are likely to be required by Kadgee if it decides to adopt the proposal to:

    (i)   Relocate its own manufacturing operations to China

    (ii)   Enter into a joint venture with for manufacturing in China

    (iii)   Develop a new interactive ordering system   **(15 marks)**

(b) Produce the investment appraisal the Finance director has asked for.

(*Note.* You should assume that all cash flows apart from the initial capital investment occur at the end of the year to which they relate). **(10 marks)**

(c) In the light of the investment appraisal, and of the circumstances in which Kadgee operates, evaluate the strategic benefits of IT director's proposal for Kadgee. **(10 marks)**

(d) Analyse the potential advantages and disadvantages to Kadgee of the proposal for the joint venture in China. **(15 marks)**

(Total = 50 marks)

SECTION B – 50 marks

Answer TWO of the THREE questions

Question 2

S4W is a publishing company whose customers include both large chains of booksellers and independent outlets.

The company owns three warehouses, strategically sited to ensure short delivery times to customers. The company's agents take orders using notebook computers, entering details while paying visits to customers. These are then downloaded into the head office order processing system and consolidated printouts of accepted orders are faxed to the relevant warehouse. Some orders are received at head office in writing and by telephone from booksellers. These orders received direct from customers are input immediately they are received and individual printouts of accepted orders are also faxed to the relevant warehouse.

At the end of each month the company sends an information pack to every bookseller. This includes marketing information, a listing of all orders booked during the previous month and a customer statement. The statement shows all unpaid invoices.

Each warehouse has its own local despatch system. When faxed orders are received, they are entered onto the system and, each Thursday, despatch documentation is produced. Orders are packed up and sent out on Thursdays and Fridays. The despatch system also produces the invoices. Where faxes are marked 'urgent', they are not entered onto the despatch system, but manual documentation is filled out and the order sent out straight away. Copy invoices are sent to the accounts department on a weekly basis for posting to customer accounts.

The company has called in a consultant to review its existing systems. Although the current systems are operating much as intended, the consultant has identified a number of shortcomings.

(1) The company does not have a long-term IS strategy.

(2) The sales and despatch process is extremely paper-intensive, with multiple keying in to systems at various points.

(3) Although the three warehouses use the same system as each other, the operating system installed is a proprietary one which is not compatible with the graphical interface-based OS at head office.

As a result of the consultant's preliminary review the company has decided to adopt a formal IS strategy to identify future development priorities.

Required

(a) Explain the benefits to S4W of an IS strategy and list the major stages in the development of such a strategy. **(15 marks)**

(b) Compare briefly the characteristics of information which S4W would use in strategic planning with those of information required for operational control. **(10 marks)**

(Total = 25 marks)

Question 3

S is a company which has traded very successfully within its domestic market for many years. It has achieved high levels of profitability in providing ground and soil sampling and testing services for a large range of clients in both the public and private sectors. This sampling is mainly undertaken to assess the suitability of former industrial land for building and public use.

In recent years, S has experienced strong competition and its Managing Director (L) has recognised that it is becoming more difficult to obtain new business from within its domestic market. Increasingly, it has been found necessary to offer more than the original basic ground and soil sampling and testing services in order to retain the loyalty of existing clients. This has necessitated a whole range of other services being offered such as testing for the presence of polluted substances in buildings, chemical analysis of water sources, geological surveys and providing for unfit land to be cleaned prior to becoming available for public use.

While these other services have been relatively successful, L is increasingly concerned about the prospects for sustaining the company's profitability because of increasing competition and saturation of the domestic market. With this in mind, L has asked you, as Management Accountant, to advise on the rationale for an overseas expansion strategy and the issues to be considered in its implementation.

Required

Produce a report to L which:

(a) Explains the business case for expansion overseas. **(10 marks)**

(b) Discusses the strategic and operational issues which the directors of S should consider before making a decision on whether to implement an overseas expansion strategy. **(15 marks)**

(Total = 25 marks)

Question 4

E is a multinational organisation and is one of the largest global producers of chocolate, coffee and other foodstuffs. E categorises the countries in which it operates as follows:

1. Less developed countries, from which E sources raw materials, but where there is no established local market for the finished products.

2. Fully developed countries, into which E imports raw materials, manufactures, and serves the local and export markets.

In every country in which E operates, it follows the OECD (Organisation for Economic Cooperation and Development) guidelines for multinationals.

In the particular case of country F, a less developed country, E has helped the local farmers to organise themselves into cooperatives to produce their crops. E has also funded schooling for the children of both the farmers and their workers, built and staffed a hospital and has provided other welfare benefits. E considers itself to be a good 'corporate citizen' and is used as an example of good practice on the OECD website.

Although the farmers' cooperatives are free to sell to E's two main competitors, they tend not to do so because of the close and friendly working relationship that they have with E. Both of E's main competitors are multinationals, but both are smaller than E.

E has recently been receiving some bad publicity in country F. The management of E feels that this is being organised by the government and the national labour union of country F. The government of F is reasonably supportive of business, but won the last election with a narrow majority. The government is now under pressure to raise the standard of living of the population. An election is due within the next fifteen months. The national labour union, which is increasingly being supported by the main opposition party in country F, is extremely anti-business. It would like to see all foreign companies removed from country F and all foreign-owned assets, and co-operatives nationalised.

The government of country F has stated that the prices paid for cocoa beans are too low, and that country F is not gaining sufficient tax revenue from the exports. The government of country F has threatened to impose an export tariff on cocoa beans, unless prices are increased, and unless E opens a manufacturing facility in the country F. The management of E feels that it has been targeted by the government because it is the largest of the three multinationals operating in the country.

The national labour union of country F has argued that the farm workers are being victimised by the farmers, who have become too powerful because of the cooperatives. It states that the government of F should not allow the farmers to operate in this way.

The management of E does not want to build a factory because the transport costs from such a factory to the nearest market for finished products would force the company to operate the factory at a loss.

The Chief Executive of E is due to meet with government ministers from country F to discuss E's future operations and involvement in the country.

Required

(a) Explain the advantages to E of conducting a stakeholder analysis of its operations in country F. **(4 marks)**

(b) Produce a stakeholder analysis for E's operations in country F. **(14 marks)**

(c) Evaluate the options available to E in its approach to the government of country F and recommend the option that you consider to be the most appropriate. **(7 marks)**

(Total = 25 marks)

Answers

**DO NOT TURN THIS PAGE UNTIL YOU HAVE
COMPLETED THE MOCK EXAM**

A plan of attack

We discussed the problem of which question to start with earlier, in 'Passing the E3' exam. (See page x, in the front pages of this Kit.) Here we will merely reiterate our view that Question 1 is nearly always the best place to start but, if you do decide to start with a 25 mark Section B question, **make sure that you finish your answer in no more than 45 minutes**.

However, take a good look through the paper before diving in to answer questions.

First things first

In the first five minutes of reading time, look through the paper and work out which questions you are going to do, and the order in which you are going to attempt them.

We recommend you then spend the remaining fifteen minutes of reading time looking at the Section A scenario, identifying key information in the unseen material and highlighting the key requirements in the question.

The extra time spent on Section A will be helpful, regardless of the order in which you intend to answer the questions. If you decide to answer the Section A question first, the time spent will mean you are already immersed in the question when the writing time starts. If you intend to answer the question second or third, probably because you find it daunting, the question may look easier when you come back to it, because your initial analysis could generate further points whilst you're tackling the other questions.

If you are a bit **worried about the paper**, it is likely that you believe the Section A question will be daunting. In this case, you may prefer to do one or both of the optional questions before tackling it. Don't, however, fall into the trap of spending too long on the optional questions because they seem easier. You will still need to spend half of the three hours writing time available on the Section A Case Study, because it is worth 50% of the marks.

It's dangerous to be over-confident, but if you're **not too nervous** about the exam then you should turn straight to the compulsory Section A question, and tackle it first. You've got to answer it, so you might as well get it over and done with.

Make sure you answer every requirement and sub-requirement in the question, and also make sure you include plenty of examples from the scenario. Bear in mind that one thing you are being tested on is your ability to apply your knowledge to deal with the specific issues identified in the scenario.

Analysing the questions

Examiners are continually frustrated by candidates' apparent inability to dissect the requirements of a question correctly.

If you do not analyse the question requirements thoroughly, you are likely to produce answers which are largely irrelevant to the question. So, make sure you do the following:

- Dissect the question requirements: what are the issues the examiner want you to address?
- Identify all the requirements in the question: is there more than one requirement?
- Be aware of the verb used in the question: how much detail do you need to give in your answer?

The questions themselves

Question 1 looks at a clothing manufacturing which is facing increased competition from overseas competitors. The preseen and unseen material provide a large amount of information about the strategic context in which the company operates, and you should draw on this in your answer.

The first part of the question looks at the type of change required by the company if it adopts a range of different strategies to improve competitiveness.

The second part requires you to produce a relatively simple investment appraisal, based on figures provided in the unseen case study material, and then in part (c) you need to use these figures and your ability to evaluate strategic options to evaluate one of the specific strategies the company is considering.

The final part of the question requires you to analyse the advantages and disadvantages of a joint venture as a means of overseas expansion.

Question 2 combines IT strategy and strategic planning, and you should have only attempted it if you felt comfortable with both parts of the question. The scenario is largely illustrative and the requirements are not as closely linked to its details as is often the case. Nevertheless, sometimes the Examiners set a question of this type and you must be prepared to answer it. The preparation of a solution does require a **sound knowledge of**

basic IT strategy and this is a very popular topic with the Examiners. You would be well advised to ensure you are confident with your knowledge of IT strategy before you sit your exams.

Question 3 is only moderately difficult but many candidates would avoid it simply because it deals with **global strategy**. There is a high probability of a question on this area of the syllabus in any exam, so make sure you can deal with it. Notice how the first requirement, for ten marks, asks about general principles, while the second part asks for a discussion specifically relevant to the subject company. In this situation it is imperative you tailor your answer to the company/scenario in question otherwise you will be losing easy marks.

By contrast to the other optional questions, **Question 4**, has few purely knowledge-based requirements. Instead, the scenario provides the majority of the information you need to answer this question. However, although this question may seem easier than the other optional questions, do not fall into the trap of writing general answers about stakeholders. Make sure you read the scenario carefully to identify all the parties involved, and then consider the specific relationships they have (or could have) with company E.

No matter how many times we remind you...

Always, always **allocate your time** according to the marks for the question in total and for the parts of the questions. And always, always **follow the requirements exactly**.

You've got free time at the end of the exam...?

If you have allocated your time properly then you **shouldn't have time on your hands** at the end of the exam. If you find yourself with five or ten minutes spare, however, go back to **any parts of questions that you didn't finish** because you ran out of time.

Forget about it!

And don't worry if you found the paper difficult. It is more than likely other students did too. However, once you've finished the exam you cannot change your answers so don't spend time worrying about them. Instead, you should start thinking about your next exam and preparing for that.

Mock Exam 1: Answers | 285

SECTION A

Question 1

Marking scheme

		Marks
(a)	**Relocation of manufacturing operations**	
	Up to 3 marks for discussion of scope of changes and up to 3 marks for nature of changes required	Up to 5
	Joint venture	
	Up to 3 marks for discussion of scope of changes and up to 3 marks for nature of changes required	Up to 5
	New ordering system	
	Up to 3 marks for discussion of scope of changes and up to 3 marks for nature of changes required	Up to 5
		Total up to 15
(b)	Identify cash inflows from BBZ contract	1
	Identify cash outflows: hardware and software	½
	IT maintenance and support	½
	Marketing	½
	Calculate probable cash inflows if: both customers sign up	2½
	one customer signs up	2½
	Calculate NPV of proposal	2½
		Total 10
(c)	Each benefit evaluated and related specifically to the IT director's proposal	Up to 2
		Total up to 10
(d)	Each potential advantage identified and related to Kadgee: up to 2 marks, up to a maximum of 8 marks for advantages	Up to 8
	Each potential disadvantage identified and related to Kadgee: up to 2 marks, up to a maximum of 8 marks for disadvantages	Up to 8
		Total up to 15
		Total 50

Part (a)

> **Text reference.** Types of change are covered in Chapter 10 of the Study Text.
>
> **Top tips.** The reference to scope and nature of the changes being required could have given you a clue that Balogun & Hope Hailey's change matrix might be useful as framework here.
>
> However, if you used the matrix, you should not have spent time simply describing it. Instead you should have used it to help you analyse the types of change being described in the scenario.
>
> Make sure your answer deals with all three of the proposals in turn because the speed and extent of change may not be the same for each of them.
>
> There are 15 marks available, and there are three proposals to consider. So you should assume there are up to 5 marks available for discussing each requirement, and you should divide your time up between the three parts of the requirement accordingly.

286 Mock Exam 1: Answers

> Also, when reading through the requirements for this question as a whole, you should have recognised that parts (c) and (d) look at the appropriateness of the two proposals, so you do not need to comment on that aspect of them here.
>
> Finally, note that the question is asking you about the type of change required by Kadgee (scope and nature of change), so you should have looked specifically at internal changes rather than changes in the external environment more generally. And for (a) (i) make sure you focus only on the changes, not the factors which might influence Kadgee's location decisions (eg Porter's diamond). You are not asked to discuss the factors which would affect where Kadgee decides to relocate, and so you would not score any marks for discussing them.

(i) <u>Possible relocation of own manufacturing to China</u>

Kadgee currently manufactures its own clothing from its European factories. However, the pressure to cut costs has prompted the Directors to look at the possibility of moving some or all of its manufacturing to China.

<u>Scope of change</u>

The proposal to move some or all of Kadgee's own manufacturing operations to China will represent a significant change to the detailed logistics of Kadgee's operations, and it will also result in a large number of Kadgee's existing manufacturing staff being made redundant.

However, it will not fundamentally change Kadgee's overall methods and approaches to clothes production. **Kadgee will still design and manufacture garments in house**, and it will still be manufacturing for same customers. Although this is a major change geographically, it is not such a major change in the overall organisation of the company.

In this respect, the proposal should be seen as a **realignment rather than a transformation** of existing practices.

<u>Nature of change</u>

Moreover, the change is essentially **building on existing methods and approaches** rather than challenging them. So again, despite the major geographical change, the nature of the change could be seen as incremental rather than being a 'Big Bang' change.

However, the **trigger for the change** is the potential long-term decline in performance which Kadgee could suffer due to the threat of low-cost competition from China. This threat means that **significant and rapid change to Kadgee's operations is necessary**.

To this extent, the fact that the trigger for change is the response to the critical problems facing the company means the change is better seen as a **reconstruction rather than an adaptation**.

(ii) <u>Joint venture</u>

If Kadgee moves to a joint venture arrangement with LIN not only do the manufacturing operations move geographically from Europe to China, but they move outside Kadgee's direct control.

<u>Scope of change</u>

In this option, **Kadgee will cease to be a manufacturing company**, and will become a design and distribution network. Again, it will result in a large number of manufacturing staff in the European factories losing their jobs.

However, the change in the focus of Kadgee's own competences represents a major **transformational change** to the existing business model. Kadgee will lose it manufacturing competences, and will rely on the joint venture partner to do its manufacturing for it.

<u>Nature of change</u>

The change from Kadgee being a manufacturing company to essentially being a design company represents a major change to its methods, processes and cultures.

If Kadgee pursues this option, it is likely to indicate that the external pressures of the changing competitive environment have forced it to take **decisive and rapid action** to retain its competitive advantage.

Moreover, once Kadgee has entered the joint venture, and once the new factory in China is build and ready to use, the changes to shift production to China are likely to take place quickly.

Therefore, the changes will be 'Big Bang' change, rather than an incremental change.

Looking at the scope and nature of this proposal together suggest that it is best seen as a revolution: a rapid and wide-ranging response to pressure for change, which leads to a fundamental shift in Kadgee's business model, and the way the company operates.

(iii) IT proposal

Scope of change

Building on existing capabilities – Whereas the relocation proposals will lead to the closure of Kadgee's European manufacturing operations, the IT proposal is more likely to lead to additional systems and processes being added to the existing operations.

So, in effect, the IT proposal is reinforcing Kadgee's current position.

Kadgee has historically designed quality designs in the medium to higher price range, and the IT proposal is designed to allow Kadgee to be able to charge a price premium.

Incremental change – In this respect, the change could be approached as an incremental change because it builds on existing methods. Although the new interactive online design and ordering process offers customers a lot more functionality, it is still building on existing processes rather than radically altering them.

In this respect, the change can be seen as a **realignment** of Kadgee's existing strategy.

However, the Operations Director's comment that the proposal is trying to shift Kadgee from a mass production environment to smaller scale batch production, suggests that there could be more far-reaching aspects of the change. If it changes the underlying culture of production, and the production processes this is not an incremental change.

If the existing business model is being challenged – and changed – then the change is more of a **transformation** than a realignment.

Nature of change

Whereas the proposals to move manufacturing operations to China are extensive changes which will lead to the closure of Kadgee's European manufacturing operations, and will result in large numbers of redundancies, the IT-based proposal will have a smaller scale impact, certainly in the short term.

The IT director's proposal appears to **involve adding the new interactive functionality on top of Kadgee's existing production methods** and processes.

Therefore, it will involve a gradual change, rather than a sudden one-off change. In this respect, the change is best seen as **incremental**.

Part (b)

Top tips. Note that this part of the question only produce the investment appraisal. You did not need to comment on it here. However, you should have noted that you did need to use the figures you calculate to help advise your answer to part (c).

The mathematics in the calculations should not be difficult, and the figures are given in the scenario. So if you work logically through the figures, you should have been able to score some easy marks here.

… Mock Exam 1: Answers

	T_0 €m	Year 1 €m	Year 2 €m	Year 3 €m	Year 4 €m	Year 5 €m	Total €m
Cash inflows							
BBZ contract		0.20	0.40	0.40	0.40	0.40	1.8
Other potential customers (W)	—	0.23	0.35	0.43	0.46	0.54	2.0
	—	0.43	0.75	0.83	0.86	0.94	3.8
Cash outflows							
Hardware and software	(0.80)	–	–	–	–	–	
IT maintenance and support	–	(0.20)	(0.20)	(0.20)	(0.20)	(0.20)	
Marketing	–	(0.40)	(0.40)	–	–	–	
	(0.80)	(0.60)	(0.60)	(0.20)	(0.20)	(0.20)	(2.60)
Net cash flow	(0.80)	(0.17)	0.15	0.63	0.66	0.74	
Discount factor (10%)	1	0.909	0.826	0.751	0.683	0.621	
Net present value	(0.80)	(0.15)	0.12	0.47	0.45	0.46	**0.55**

Working

	Year 1 €m	Year 2 €m	Year 3 €m	Year 4 €m	Year 5 €m	
Weighted probabilities						
Both customers sign up	0.40	0.60	0.70	0.80	0.90	
× 0.35	0.14	0.21	0.25	0.28	0.32	(1)
One signs up	0.20	0.30	0.40	0.40	0.50	
× 0.45	0.09	0.14	0.18	0.18	0.22	(2)
(1) + (2)	0.23	0.35	0.43	0.46	0.54	

Part (c)

> **Top tips.** The question asks you to *evaluate* the strategic benefits of the IT director's proposals, so you should first consider the advantages of the proposals and then move on to consider the limitations of them.
>
> One of the key limitations seems to be that it is a niche strategy, and therefore whether it will provide sufficient income to be a valid alternative to Kadgee's existing customer base. The calculations from (b) should have helped you reach this conclusion, by highlighting not only the relatively low NPV of the project, but also the relative uncertainty about how many customers will actually sign up for the scheme.

Advantages

Increase margins – By offering customers flexibility, the IT director's proposal should allow Kadgee to charge a price premium. This will help increase margins. The reduction in margins through customers trying to force down prices is the key threat facing the business.

In effect, the IT director's proposal allows Kadgee to increase its margins through adopting a differentiation strategy.

Focus on quality manufacturing – Kadgee has traditionally been a high quality manufacturer. Adopting a differentiation type strategy continues this focus on quality.

Preserve jobs in Europe – This strategy will allow Kadgee to retain its manufacturing plants in Europe rather than having to relocate them in China. Therefore it will preserve jobs at the European factories.

Disadvantages

Price premium – The IT director's strategy is based on creating a situation in which Kadgee charges customers a premium price. However, the majority of customers are trying to reduce the price they pay, so the idea of wanting to charge a price premium seems rather contradictory in these market conditions.

This strategy does not make any reference to **reducing costs** which seems to be a critical issue for Kadgee.

Customer bargaining power – A key factor in the success of the strategy will be the relative bargaining power between Kadgee and its customers, and therefore Kadgee's ability to sustain its margins. However, as the trend for moving production to cheaper outlets in China illustrates, the larger customers have very strong bargaining power in the clothing manufacturing industry.

Niche market – The early indications are that ability to have 'custom made' clothing is attractive to smaller or medium sized customers, but there is no indication that Kadgee's large customers are interested in it.

These large customers are the ones wanting to reduce prices, so it seems unlikely that this proposal alone will safeguard Kadgee's existing customers.

Also, the value which the new proposal generates is likely to be quite small compared to the revenue Kadgee generates from its 'traditional' sales to its existing customers.

It appears that this proposal targets a niche segment of the market only, rather than being a strategy which Kadgee can use across its whole market. Even if the 'custom made' facility were to prove successful, there must be a **concern about how scalable it is**.

Uncertainty about demand – There is a 20% chance that only BBZ sign up for the new scheme. If this were the case, then the NPV of the project would be negative.

Even if all three potential customers sign up, the project only generates a net cash flow of a €0.54 million over 5 years. Compared to the revenue that Kadgee currently gets from Portrait or Forum, these are still very small figures. As it stands, this proposal certainly cannot replace Kadgee's existing business.

Organisation structure – As the operations directors commented this proposal is likely to require Kadgee to change is production techniques from large scale manufacturing into small scale batch production. This will not only lead to it losing economies of scale, but there is also a question mark about whether Kadgee's production machinery is suitable for batch production.

Problems for marketing mix – An alternative to replacing large scale production with the customised range would be to offer the additional functionality alongside Kadgee's existing production range.

However, this would lead to confusion in Kadgee's marketing mix. On the one hand, it would be looking to reduce cost, but on the other it would be looking to create a niche market which charges a price premium.

Part (d)

> **Top tips.** Do not let your answer to this question become a general discussion of the advantages of joint ventures as a means of entering a new overseas market. Make sure you relate it specifically to Kadgee's circumstances. For example, Kadgee could either relocate its own manufacturing operations to China or enter into this joint venture. So a useful approach to this question might be to consider the advantages and disadvantages of the joint venture compared to Kadgee relocating its own operations.
>
> Also, if there is any relevant 'real world' knowledge you can include, make sure you do so. Although the pre-seen material did not identify the possibility of a joint venture, it clearly identified the issues Kadgee was facing and raised the importance of China as a location, so you could usefully have considered some of the ways clothing manufacturers have sought to respond to the threat of competition from lower cost countries in the real world.

Advantages

Gets into China – The joint venture will provide Kadgee with a means of getting its clothes produced in China, at the lower cost which its major customers want. However, the joint venture provides Kadgee with an alternative to having to build a wholly owned manufacturing operation in China.

Speed – Because LIN is already an established clothing manufacturer this should mean the joint venture will allow Kadgee to source clothes from China more quickly than if it had to establish its own manufacturing operations.

Supply chain networks – An important factor in this will be that LIN will already have pre-existing supply chain networks (for example, suppliers for raw materials such as cotton) whereas if Kadgee were to set up its own plant it would either have to arrange for its existing suppliers to transfer supply from its European plants to China, or it would have to set up contracts with new suppliers.

Benefit from local knowledge – The alliance with LIN will provide Kadgee with local knowledge about business cultures and business practices which it would not otherwise have. It will also overcome any potential language problems associated with moving into China. In this way, it could significantly ease Kadgee's entry route into operating in China.

Share of capital costs – There is likely to be a significant capital investment involved in building a new manufacturing plant in China. The joint venture will mean that these capital costs are shared between Kadgee and LIN, rather than Kadgee having to fund them all itself.

Offers scope for growth – The Chinese joint venture will build a large, purpose built factory to make Kadgee's clothes. Because the factory will be modern it should allow Kadgee to benefit from up-to-technology production technologies and efficiencies, thereby allowing it to obtain low costs.

Low costs on their own are a benefit to Kadgee, but it the factory increases Kadgee's **production capacity** it will provide a second benefit by allowing the scope for growth and potentially acquiring new customers – which Kadgee could acquire by offering to manufacture customers' clothes more cheaply than its rivals.

Disadvantages

Conflicts of interest – Conflicts of interest between Kadgee and LIN could potentially be a major disadvantage of the joint venture. Disagreements may arise over profit shares, and the relative shares of the partners have not yet been agreed. There could also be issues with the management of the joint venture – particularly around the quality of the garments of the goods produced. Kadgee will ultimately be responsible to its customers for the quality of the clothes, but they will produced by LIN.

Unequal interests – One of the main risks with joint venture arrangements is that venture partners can gain **confidential information** about each other which could subsequently be used competitively by one partner against the other.

This could be a risk for Kadgee here because LIN potentially stands to gain more from the venture. The venture will see Kadgee design and market the clothes and LIN make them. However, in time if **LIN develops its own design and marketing competences** (through working with Kadgee) it could eventually bypass Kadgee and deal directly with customers itself.

Ultimately the ability to actually make the clothes is crucial. Once Kadgee has lost its manufacturing capability, there is a risk that LIN can take over the supplier contracts for itself.

Profits shared – Kadgee will have to share the profits it earns from its clothing contracts with LIN so this will reduce its underlying profit.

Time taken to build new factory – LIN does not have any existing production facilities which can be used to make Kadgee clothing. The proposed new factory still has to be built. This means it might not be much quicker for Kadgee to partner with LIN than to build its own factory in China, and will be slower than if Kadgee decided to simply use existing Chinese clothing manufacturers to produce its clothes for it as they were required.

SECTION B

Question 2

Marking scheme

			Marks
(a)	Each benefit to S4W of having an IS strategy: up to 2 marks each	Up to 10	
	Each stage of IS strategy development listed: 1 mark each	Up to 5	
		Total up to	15
(b)	Each relevant characteristic of strategic planning information identified and compared with operational information: up to 2 marks each	Up to 10	10
		Total	25

Part (a)

> **Text reference.** Information strategy is covered in Chapter 7 of your BPP Study Text.
>
> **Top tips.** This question is designed to cover the essential ideas relating information systems to strategy.
>
> It is, perhaps, somewhat unrepresentative of the kind of question you are likely to get in the exam, which are more likely to deal with slightly more specialised topics, but it offers a very good workout on this general topic area.
>
> **Easy marks.** The easiest marks are to be found in the basic theoretical models of principle relevant to part (a).

The value of information

Information is an organisational resource similar to human skills, fixed assets, goodwill and so forth. Planning in all these areas is desirable, so that the organisation can adapt to a changing environment.

An organisation's financial investment in information technology is substantial, especially with the proliferation of computing power around different departments. Moreover, information technology covers areas of management which previously would have been distinct: high volume data processing (a computer department); telecommunications (which may have been a general administrative function); office administration (PCs were bought to replace dedicated word processors, which were themselves purchased to replace typewriters). Many organisations report dissatisfaction with the outcomes of their investments. Some overall direction is therefore required. This is clearly the case at S4W where a variety of incompatible systems is in use.

What is an IS strategy?

A strategy is a long-term plan, concentrating on the overall performance of the system, stating long-term objectives and goals, and outlining the measures to achieve them. As information technology is so pervasive throughout the business, and can affect significantly the relationship an organisation has with its customers, the IS strategy should be developed with the overall corporate plan. This was not done at S4W.

Why should S4W have an IS strategy?

Not only does IS have to compete with other investments (eg other non-current assets) or expenditure programs for resources, but also implementing IS can be very disruptive. Moreover, with the growth of end-user computing, it is important that there is at least some central direction to ensure that the IS resources are used to the best advantage of the organisation. This will not be the case if the organisation is plagued with incompatible hardware and/or software.

Benefits to S4W of having an IS strategy

A strategy for information systems will therefore be part of the overall organisational strategy and will be geared to meeting organisational objectives. As significantly, it demonstrates the importance of IS to senior management and their commitment to it. Finally, it has the function of laying down the plan for managing IS in terms of technical standards and organisational responsibilities.

Developing an IS strategy

A strategy for information and information systems, therefore, need not be developed independently of other planning exercises. Arguably, each user department in specifying its commercial strategy should be able to state what information it is likely to need. Information will already be available about file sizes and so forth. If, however, an information strategy is a panic response to poorly controlled costs, and perceived poor value for money delivered by investments in information technology, the strategy exercise will be more tightly defined.

Stages in developing an IS strategy

Many strategy developments are likely to conform in some respects to the model outlined below.

(a) Personnel devising the strategy are given **terms of reference**. The brief may be very broad, or quite narrowly defined. The terms of reference may be developed from the overall organisational strategy.

(b) A **plan** is made for the strategy development exercise. This means defining in more detail what exactly is the subject of the study, from considerations of potential competitive advantage to purely technical decisions which need to be decided at strategic level. The plan would detail the timetable, required resources, and specify the outputs of the planning process.

(c) Strategy **definition**. Three types of document are written.

   (i) The information systems strategy details the long-term information plan to support business strategies or to create new strategic options.

   (ii) The information technology strategy seeks to provide a framework for the analysis and design of the organisation's technical infrastructure (eg communications, computing hardware open vs proprietary systems).

   (iii) The information management strategy details the management of information systems, in terms of necessary resources, authorisation procedures for systems development projects, cost control, and management of the technology (eg security policy).

(d) Strategy **implementation**. The strategy is then set to work. To be successful, the exercise should have a high profile within the organisation and there should be suitable commitment to it from senior management. This means that any demarcation problems should be sorted out.

(e) **Review**. The success of the strategy should be reviewed on a rolling basis.

Part (b)

Strategic planning, management control and operational control may be seen as **a hierarchy of planning and control** decisions. Management control is always in the middle of the range.

(a) Top level management make strategic plans, and low level managers make operational control decisions.

(b) Strategic planning tends to cover a longer time period than management control, whereas operational control is exercised day-to-day.

(c) The most important decisions are usually strategic, and the least important are operational.

Strategic planning is a process of deciding on objectives of the organisation, on changes in these objectives, on the resources used to attain these objectives and on the policies that are to govern the acquisition, use and disposition of these resources.

Operational control decisions ensure that specific tasks are carried out effectively and efficiently. It focuses on individual tasks, and is carried out within the strictly defined guidelines issued by strategic planning and management control systems.

Strategic information is used by the senior managers of S4W to plan the objectives of their organisation, and to assess whether the objectives are being met in practice. Such information includes overall profitability, the profitability of different segments of the business, future market prospects, the availability and cost of raising new funds, total cash needs, total manning levels and capital equipment needs.

Strategic information therefore:

- Is derived from both internal and external sources.
- Is summarised at high level.
- Is relevant to the long term.
- Deals with the whole organisation (although it might go into some detail).
- Is often prepared on an 'ad hoc' basis.
- Is both quantitative and qualitative;
- Is incapable of providing complete certainty, given that the future cannot be predicted.

Operational information is used by 'front-line' managers such as S4W's warehouse foremen to ensure that specific tasks are planned and carried out properly. Operational information relates to the level of decision making referred to above as operational control. S4W's despatch procedures depend on detailed operational information: which quantities of books are to be despatched by which warehouse to which customers? The company's accounting function is also a heavy use of detailed operational information, not least for the preparation of invoices and statements.

Operational information

- Is derived almost entirely from internal sources.
- Is highly detailed, being the processing of raw data.
- Relates to the immediate term.
- Is task-specific.
- Is prepared constantly, or very frequently.
- Is largely quantitative.
- Has a high degree of accuracy.

Question 3

Text reference. Global business expansion is considered in Chapter 5 of your BPP Study Text.

Top tips. It is easy with this question to get bogged down in theoretical discussion about international expansion. As always, make it specific and relevant to the circumstances of the question. The examiner always points this out as an area of weakness in many answers. Remember, too, that this is a service business, because this has special consequences when expanding overseas. Required customer service levels in one country may not be expected in others, or vice versa, for example.

Easy marks. The business case for expansion revolves around the fact that the home market has become saturated. This does not automatically mean that the market overseas will be favourable, but it makes sense to at least consider it. As the company operates in a highly specialised and technical field, it is likely that the product (or service) life cycle is going to be at a different stage overseas, which could work to S's advantage. Full and thorough research of the market will be vital.

Note. Did you notice you were asked to produce a report? If you didn't you lost a very easy mark.

Marking scheme

		Marks
(a)	Each reason why S should expand overseas identified and explained: up to 2 each	Up to 10 10
(b)	Each strategic issue discussed and related to S: up to 2	Up to 8
	Each operation issue discussed and related to S: up to 2	Up to 8
	Overall mark for presenting answer as a report	1
		Total up to 15
		Total 25

Part (a)

REPORT

To: Managing Director
From: Management Accountant
Date: November 20XX
Subject: International expansion plans

The company has been finding the domestic market for its services to be both highly competitive and increasingly saturated. This report sets out the **rationale** for overseas expansion and the **strategic and operational issues** that will be relevant when making the decision whether or not to market overseas.

The points made in this initial report are only an indication of the issues involved. Further **research** in the chosen overseas market will be essential.

1   Business case for expansion

1.1   A primary reason for overseas expansion that is encountered by many companies is that of **overcrowding of the domestic market**. S is finding it increasingly difficult to obtain new business at home, to the extent that we have had to offer an increasing range of services to retain customer loyalty. This new range of services has amounted to a **product development strategy** (per Ansoff's product-market matrix) that has been necessary in the domestic market. These additional services may or may not be attractive to the overseas market.

The **increased level of competition** has proved costly for the company as it has necessitated the development of additional services. There may be better returns available overseas if the level of local competition is less intense.

1.2   It is likely to be the case that S has **comparative advantage in service levels, skills and technology**, both through its traditional ground and soil sampling services and the development of its more highly specialist services. Lesser developed economies in particular may not have local companies with such highly developed skills, meaning that **entry barriers are low** and S should be able to establish a dominant position more quickly. The **economies of scale** likely to be enjoyed by S means that costs can be kept down and profitability higher.

1.3   A related point is that the **product life cycle** for the range of services that S provides may be at an earlier point in development overseas. This means that existing services will have a longer life, guaranteeing a longer period of profitability for services that have reached the mature stage in the domestic market.

1.4   Expansion overseas results in **geographic diversification** for the company, which means that it can focus on one service (ground and soil sampling) in a number of markets, not several different ones at home. This spreads the risk. In the long term, this may prove to be the most profitable strategy, and S may be able to scale down its additional services in the domestic market. It must be recognised however that the development of the overseas market could require significant investment before returns are achieved.

1.5   There may be **investment incentives** in overseas markets. The availability of venture capital or local government assistance in the form of grants can make overseas investment particularly attractive. S would need to investigate the possibilities here.

1.6   An overseas presence could help increase the **prestige** of S at home. This differentiating factor, in addition to a **reduced dependence** on the domestic market, could encourage S in the longer term to be even more innovative in the services it provides, as its risk is spread and it can afford to take some chances (that competitors cannot) and further enhance its competitive position.

Part (b)

2   Strategic and operational issues

Before getting involved overseas, S must consider both strategic and operational issues.

2.1   Strategic

(a)   Most importantly, does overseas expansion 'fit' with the overall **mission and objectives** of the company? As a service business, S needs to make sure that its strengths and competences in soil sampling and testing will be well used overseas and will not deflect resources from the position that has been built up at home.

(b)   The company needs to make sure that it has the internal **resources** to expand overseas. These will be chiefly financial, but it will also require a lot of time and staff effort. Marketing the services to an overseas country will be a significant project, and one which the company has not undertaken before.

(c) S needs to decide what overseas market to enter, and what its **level of involvement** will be. It is advisable to start off with only a few markets at the most, to limit not only the costs of entry and market communications, but also the likely number of competitors.

The choice of market is obviously very important. Not only must there be an **accessible demand** to make the market attractive, but S must assess its **comparative advantage** in that market. Prior experience in the provision of its range of services will be an advantage here. The **risk** associated with the market must also be assessed. This will include political stability, economic infrastructure and other external influences.

(d) The **longer term objectives** for the overseas venture need to be established. Is it merely a way of getting through what could be a temporary domestic slowdown, or is there going to be a full commitment to overseas expansion? This will necessitate some organisational changes for S, both in structure and management.

(e) The **form of involvement** needs to be considered. Will the services be provided by a dedicated overseas subsidiary, or will they be marketed via a licensing agreement with a local company? A joint venture with an existing company may provide quick, knowledgeable and less risky access to the chosen market. Unless the subsidiary route is chosen, S will have to relinquish some control, which it may not be prepared to do.

2.2 Operational

These are more short term needs than the strategic issues presented above. Sales levels, profitability, cash flows, market share and capital expenditure requirements need to be forecast and planned in detail. In order to be able to do this, the following issues need to be considered.

(a) The **needs and preferences** of the foreign target market need to be established. This can only be achieved via an extensive programme of **market research** to establish forecast likely demand and establish levels of competition. Dealing with likely foreign **competitor responses** to the presence of S (such as price cuts) must be planned in advance.

(b) The **cultural implications** of doing business in a foreign country must never be underestimated. S has no experience of conducting business overseas and this often requires sensitive handling and staffing. Market share will suffer if local preferences are not taken into account.

(c) This particular industry is heavily subject to, and driven by, **regulations**. S is familiar with the rules governing land quality, pollution and testing in its home market. The rules overseas are almost certain to be different in some respects, and it is imperative that local knowledge and expertise is employed to make sure that the rules are complied with.

(d) The **costs** of doing business overseas will be affected by factors such as foreign tax regimes, access to technology, and availability of physical resources.

(e) **Management skills** will be vital, both for staffing and the level of control over the operation. This will have implications for the organisation structure. For example, expatriate staff from the home country may need to be seconded to the overseas market to help local staff. As this is a service business, service levels are important and S will want to ensure that they are consistent wherever it is doing business.

As can be appreciated from the analysis above, any overseas expansion will need a significant amount of **research and analysis**, in order that what is a difficult decision can be made with some confidence. S needs to **plan** this proposed venture, **involve staff** at all levels, and examine all the factors involved.

Question 4

Study Reference. Stakeholder analysis discussed in Chapter 2 of the Study Text.

Marking scheme

			Marks
(a)	Helps to identify power and interest of each group	1	
	Identify need for support and agreement of most powerful stakeholders	1	
	Helps identify stakeholders who could cause most disruption	1	
	Helps identify how to deal with stakeholders	1	
	Total		4
(b)	Each relevant stakeholder identified, categorised (power/interest etc) and discussed	Up to 3	
	Total up to		14
(c)	Evaluation of each option given in the question scenario	Up to 2	
	For recommendation: well justified and consistent with evaluation	2	
	Total up to		7
	Total		25

Part (a)

Top tips. Requirement (a) is only worth 4 marks, so should be kept brief. Although Mendelow's matrix supplies the relevant theory here, you should not have spent time describing the matrix. Instead you need to explain specifically how it could be useful to E in the context of analysing its operations in F.

Stakeholder analysis will allow E to determine the level of **power** which stakeholders could have over their activities in F, and the likelihood that they will show an **interest** in E's activities there.

By establishing the power and interest of the various stakeholder groups, E can analyse the degree of influence they are likely to have on its operations, and therefore the **relationship E should seek to develop with its stakeholders**. This might mean working in conjunction with a key stakeholder to make sure a strategy is **acceptable** to them; or ensuring that other stakeholders are kept **satisfied by**, or kept **informed of**, E's proposed strategies.

Stakeholder analysis will be helpful to E as it considers its future operations in the F, and the possible opposition there might be to them.

For E to be able to implement its operations successfully in F, those operations will have to **be acceptable to the key stakeholders** who could otherwise disrupt E's plans. For example, if the political party in power after the election does not support multinational operations in F, it will be very difficult for E to continue its operations there at all.

Part (b)

Top tips. The scenario identifies a number of stakeholders, and you should have used these to produce your analysis in part (b). You should not have introduced additional generic stakeholders from outside the scenario, and you would not have scored any marks for doing so.

A useful way of structuring your answer to (b) would be to use the quadrants of Mendelow's matrix as the headings under which to group the different stakeholders. Another useful approach could be to identify groups whose support E needs, and to identify stakeholders who could cause disruption for E.

Easy marks. Requirements (b) and (c) do not require any detailed technical knowledge; rather they require you to analyse the information given in the question scenario. If you worked through the scenario carefully, highlighting all the relevant stakeholders and issues, you should have been able to score well here. There are sufficient stake-holders identified in the scenario to provide an answer without you needing to include additional, generic ones.

Mock Exam 1: Answers   297

Key players – High power; high interest

The government of F – The government of F has significant **power** to affect E's operating environment, for example through imposing duties or imposing wage legislation designed to **increase the standard of living in F**. The government has traditionally been reasonably supportive of business, but in the run up to the elections it is coming under increasing pressure to take a **tougher stance on multinational companies** in F. This will increase the level of **interest** it takes in E's activities, and will mean it views E in a less favourable light than it has traditionally done.

The opposition party in F – The government only has a narrow majority and therefore the **opposition party can exert considerable pressure** on the economic and social policies in F. Given that there will be an election in the next fifteen months, the opposition party could soon become the government, thereby increasing its power further.

The opposition party and the government appear to have different approaches to businesses and foreign investment, and so **business policy could be an important issue in the election**. This gives the opposition party a strong interest in E's activities.

The opposition party also has close links with the national labour union which is strongly anti-business and wants to see all foreign companies removed from F. This means that the opposition party's **interest is likely to be hostile** towards E.

The national labour union – While the national labour union has a degree of power in its own right, this **power is increased by its close links to the opposition party**, especially since the opposition party may soon become the government. The union's **interest in E is hostile**, because it would like to see all foreign companies removed from country F.

The other two multinationals operating in F – E is the largest of the three main producers operating in F. At the moment, the close working relationship between E and the farmers' cooperatives means that the cooperatives tend not sell to E's competitors. However, if this relationship weakens the **competitors will try to gain business** from the cooperatives at E's expense.

However, while the other multinationals are E's rivals, their **interest is not entirely hostile**. Although the government is targeting E as the largest multinational, if E's negotiations fail, all the multinationals could suffer if harsher conditions are imposed on them. Moreover, the three multinationals might need to present a united front in trying to soften the stance of the national labour union and the opposition party towards foreign companies remaining in F.

High power; low interest

E's shareholders – E shareholders can be powerful in approving E's overall direction and policy, but they are more likely to be concerned with E's overall financial performance than the specific issues it faces in a single country. However, if E's operations in F make a significant contribution to its overall profit, then the shareholders are likely to be more interested in the outcome of E's discussions with the government.

Some shareholders may also be concerned at the suggestion that E is damaging the standard of living in F. Again, this issue in its own right is not so significant as the possibility that it may damage E's reputation as a good 'corporate citizen', which in turn could adversely affect revenues and profitability.

Low power; high interest

Farmers in F – The farmers have a good working relationship with E, but are ultimately **dependent on E** (or another foodstuff producer) to buy their crops. In this respect, the farmers have little power.

However, their **close relationship with E** suggests they will have a high degree of interest in E's future. For example, E has **helped the farmers form the cooperatives**, which improves their bargaining power when dealing with companies, and E has also helped with various other **welfare projects**. Consequently, the farmers are likely to want E to continue working in F.

The national labour union wants the government to break up the cooperatives, which would weaken the farmers' economic position. E's relationship with the farmers could well be discussed during E's meetings with the government, not least due to the union's claims that workers are being victimised by the farmers which E has supported.

Farm workers in F – Like the farmers, the farm workers have limited power over E. It is possible that they could withdraw their labour, but this presumes that there are alternative farmers they could go and work for, and this may not be the case.

However, like the farmers, the farm workers also have a strong interest in the situation. The farm workers are **dependent on the farmers for their jobs**, and the **farmers in turn depend on E** (or other producers) for their contracts to supply crops. If E were to leave and the demand for the farmers' produce was to fall as a result, this would affect the demand for farm labour, meaning the farmer workers would be likely to suffer a reduction in their incomes and their standards of living.

The OECD – The OECD has recognised E as an example of a **good corporate citizen**. Therefore the OECD will be keen for the farmers and farm workers in F to continue to receive a fair deal from E. Since E is a large company, the OECD will have a strong interest in E's position, but it is unlikely to be able to affect E's operations directly. If E is forced to agree any concessions which adversely affect the farmers, the OECD is likely to **express concern** at the changes, but it is unlikely to be able to reverse the decision.

Part (c)

> Note that for part (c) you need to make a recommendation at the end of your answer. This should also have alerted you to the fact that you need to evaluate at least two different options, giving you scope to then select your preferred one to recommend. Note the question only asks you to 'Evaluate' the options rather than to 'Identify and evaluate...' This is because the options you need to consider are identified in the scenario, so you should have limited yourself to these rather than inventing your own options.
>
> Although you might expect to have to evaluate options by looking at 'suitability, acceptability and feasibility' there are only 7 marks available here, so in this case you do not need to go into this much detail.

Although economically E might be best served by trying to **preserve its business as it currently is**, such an approach will **not be acceptable to the government** and therefore there seems little point in E considering this as an option.

Moreover, **it may be in E's interests to make some concessions to the current government**, because the government is more supportive to multinational companies than the opposition is. However, E needs to balance the cost of any concessions with the benefits from continuing to buy cocoa beans from F. Ultimately, E needs to try to maximise the returns it can earn for its shareholders.

Build manufacturing facility – The government wants E to open a manufacturing facility in F, but such a facility would operate at a loss. Therefore, this option is unlikely to be acceptable for E because it does not maximise the **returns it can earn for its shareholders**.

Increase prices paid to farmers – The government has stated that prices paid for cocoa beans are currently too low, and E could address this by increasing the prices it pays to farmers. Although this will mean E's profits are reduced, the bigger problem with this option is that is could be **politically damaging for the government**, because the labour union and the opposition party could illustrate it as another example of the farmers and the cooperatives being given favourable treatment.

Accept export tariff – The government has threatened to impose export tariffs if E does not built a manufacturing facility or increase prices. However, if the tariff is too high it might no longer make economic sense for E to source its cocoa beans from F. The government, however, is likely to view tariffs as a politically attractive option, because they are a way of earning additional income for F as a whole.

Provide additional infrastructure projects – One of the union's grievances is the disparity in living standards between the farmers and the farm workers. Currently, E can be seen as partly responsible for this due to the support it has given the farmers. One way E could address this is by funding some wider infrastructure projects which benefit the whole community. Such an approach would maintain E's image as a good corporate citizen, and would allow the government to demonstrate it has won concessions which benefit everyone.

Recommendation

E should try to negotiate an agreement with the government whereby the government introduces **a small export tariff** thereby providing some additional tax revenue, but alongside this E makes some **additional investments in infrastructure projects** which benefit the whole country, such as schools and hospitals for the general population rather than just the farmers' families.

This option will allow the government to demonstrate it has won concessions which **benefit the whole country**, but it should also mean it remains economically profitable for E to source its cocoa beans from F.

CIMA – Pillar E

Paper E3

Enterprise strategy

Mock Exam 2

You are allowed **three hours** to answer this question paper.

You are allowed **20 minutes** reading time **before the examination begins** during which you should read the question paper and, if you wish, highlight and/or make notes on the question paper. However, you are **not** allowed, **under any circumstances**, to open the answer book and start writing or use your calculator during this reading time.

You are strongly advised to carefully read ALL the question requirements before attempting the question concerned (that is all parts and/or sub-questions).

Answer ALL compulsory questions in Section A.

Answer TWO of the three questions in Section B.

DO NOT OPEN THIS PAPER UNTIL YOU ARE READY TO START UNDER EXAMINATION CONDITIONS

SECTION A – 50 marks

Strategic level pre-seen case material

Question 1

Introduction

Flyqual Airlines (FQA) is a member of N, an aviation alliance which includes another seven airlines based in different regions of the world. The purpose of the alliance is to extend a large range of travel opportunities to passengers of each constituent airline and FQA is now able to provide travel to over 500 destinations throughout the world by using alliance partners' routes. The benefits include more choices of flights to suit the passengers' travel requirements, easier transfers between member airlines and access to their passenger lounges, priority check-in at airport terminals and enhancement of frequent flyer programmes. Greater frequency of flights is provided by the various codeshare agreements which FQA has entered into with various airlines which operate both within and outside the N alliance. A codeshare agreement is where flights to a particular destination are operated by an airline which accepts passengers who have purchased tickets from other airlines.

As its name implies, FQA prides itself on providing a first rate passenger service and enjoys a strong reputation for quality service to passengers. As a consequence, FQA does not need to apply a low pricing policy for airline travel in response to sensitivity of market demand and is able to charge premium prices. FQA itself now flies to over 100 destinations worldwide from its home base in Asia and employs over 20,000 people around the world as aircrew, cabin attendants, maintenance staff, airport check-in operatives and ground staff.

Two large listed companies together hold the majority of the shares of FQA and the company is listed on its home stock exchange. These two companies are not themselves engaged in the airline industry although one of them does have subsidiaries whose business is in the export of goods.

FQA holds a 45% shareholding in a smaller airline. This smaller airline is not a member of the N alliance and engages mainly in short-haul scheduled and cargo flights around the Asia-Pacific region. FQA does undertake some short-haul schedules in the Asia-Pacific region but its principal business is in long-haul intercontinental flights to the USA and Europe.

Future demand for passenger air travel

Some airlines offer services at both the high quality and the basic "with no extras", so called "low-priced" or "no frills" end of the market. FQA has chosen to offer services at the high quality end of the market only.

The largest consumer markets over the next two decades are likely to be China and India. This is expected to result in large growth in air travel to and from, and within these countries.

It is estimated that by the mid 2020's three-quarters of the entire world fleet of very large aircraft will be used on flights from the largest airports in the world and 60% of these airports are situated in the Asia-Pacific region.

Future demand for air cargo

Demand for international cargo services is also expected to increase in areas of high population and industrial growth.

Demand for air cargo is influenced by the nature of the goods being transported, for example the need to transport perishable foods quickly. However, high value goods which are demanded in very quick time, such as high technology equipment have also grown and represent about 75% of the financial value of exports from Asia but only 40% of exports in terms of weight. This has resulted in significant growth in demand for air cargo.

Aircraft replacement within the industry

Traditionally, replacement of aircraft has been a result of economic cycles and developments of aircraft technology. Fuel prices have also had a major influence on aircraft replacement. Aircraft retirements on a large scale began to take place in 20X2 following a slow-down in global demand. Many airlines replace passenger aircraft before the end of their economic life in order to take advantage of new technology. Market conditions, legislation on noise and exhaust emissions and strengthening competition have resulted in an increasing demand by airlines for more fuel efficient and quieter aircraft. Some forecasts state that in twenty years' time only about 15% of the fleet which currently exists will still be operated by airlines across the world.

FQA's fleet of aircraft

The aircraft which FQA operate are all manufactured by either F (based in the USA) or C (based in Europe). The fleet of 170 aircraft is as follows:

	Leased	Owned	Seating capacity per aircraft
F 858	27	36	500
F 888	9	22	270
C 440	14	30	320
C 450	10	22	450

Of the 27 leased F 858 aircraft, seven are employed entirely for carrying cargo. The F 888 can be converted to fly long-haul, although it is normally used on short-haul routes. For conversion to long-haul, the F 888 would reduce the passenger capacity by 100 seats. The C 440 is used exclusively on short-haul routes. There are a number of aircraft whose leases are due to expire over the next two years.

Managerial style of FQA

FQA always prides itself on having staff who are dedicated to providing a high quality service. The Director of HRM regularly reviews FQA's human resource and remuneration policy taking account of legislation, industry practice and market conditions. The Board has however been under increasing pressure to reduce costs. This has resulted in much more emphasis being placed by the Board on individual and company performance than previously in determining human resource and remuneration policy. This has caused considerable staff discomfort over the last two years.

FQA faced difficult employee relations issues through the summer period of the last financial year. It encountered demands for higher pay from ground staff, for improved working conditions and reduced working hours from both air crew (pilots and flight engineers) and cabin staff.

Negotiations resulted in some improvements in pay for the baggage handlers and reduced working hours for air crew and cabin staff. However, the demands made by the trade unions were not met in full. The agreement made between FQA and the trade unions was on condition that targets in productivity increases were achieved. This has resulted in some voluntary redundancies being made. The strong tactics employed by the directors of FQA have resulted in many cabin staff feeling that they have been mistreated by the company.

In addition, FQA has faced many difficulties with suppliers, particularly its outsourced catering service at its home based airport in the capital city. The issue has been that the main catering service supplier (CG) has complained that the hard bargaining stance by FQA management has reduced its margin to such an extent that it is barely making any profit.

At the same time, the Director of Quality Management has made serious complaints regarding the reduced level of quality in the catering service itself following an increasing level of complaints from passengers over recent months. CG's management has responded by threatening to withdraw the service altogether unless FQA agrees to re-negotiate the price for the service which is supplied. In reply, FQA has stated that it will only renegotiate on price when the quality of the service has shown improvement over a sustained period and has threatened legal action for breach of contract if the service is withdrawn.

Pressure from shareholders

The Chairmen of the two largest shareholders of FQA have held discussions with FQA's Chairman and Chief Executive in an attempt to find ways to increase shareholder value. They have made it clear that they believe the running costs of the airline are too high and must be reduced to enable the airline to become a leaner and fitter organisation. This, they argue, will enable FQA to be better able to increase market share in the increasingly competitive airline industry by being able to pass on cost reductions to passengers.

The Chairman and Chief Executive of FQA, advised by the Board, have replied to the two Chairmen of the largest shareholders that any significant impact on lowering costs can only be achieved by reducing the staffing levels which will in turn impact negatively on quality. The Chairman and Chief Executive have warned that further reductions in the staffing levels in the existing operations will erode staff morale even more and may be counter productive in terms of achieving greater market share. At the same time as making this point, the Chairman has instructed the Director of HRM to give serious thought to how further staff reductions could be achieved.

Financial results for the previous two years

Extracts from the financial results for the previous two financial years for FQA are presented at Appendix A.

Competition data

The following information provides a short statistical comparison between FQA and two competitors in the last financial year:

	FQA	Competitor 1	Competitor 2
Revenue (in $ million)	10,895	17,784	8,632
Profit attributable to shareholders ($ million)	371	546	286
Share price at year end ($)	9.0	6.0	4.5
Shares in issue at year end (million)	520	1,100	600
Long-term liabilities ($ million)	4,220	6,400	3,330
Fleet size (number of aircraft)	170	290	165
Kilometres flown (million)	560	920	480
Aircraft departures (thousand)	152	250	130
Passenger load factor (overall % of capacity used)	80	75	73
Passengers carried (million)	27	42	22
On time departures (within 15 minutes) %	93	76	75

Cost structures

The following table shows the proportions of FQA's total costs which are accounted for by particular expense types:

Expense type:	% of total Operating Costs in the financial year ended: 30 September 20X6	% of total Operating Costs in the financial year ended: 30 September 20X5
Staff and employment overheads	21	21
Fuel	30	29
Landing and parking	10	9
Other (including maintenance, engineering and equipment)	39	41

FQA managed to reduce its exposure to increased fuel costs by using hedging techniques in the year to 30 September 20X6 which was a year when fuel prices increased significantly.

Date: The current date is 1 May 20X7.

APPENDIX A: EXTRACTS FROM THE ACCOUNTS OF FQA

Statement of financial position	At 30 September 20X6		At 30 September 20X5	
	$m	$m	$m	$m
Non-current assets (net)		8,408		7,918
Intangible assets		246		224
Total non-current assets		8,654		8,142
Current assets		2,669		2,469
Total assets		11,323		10,611
Equity and reserves		3,948		3,759
Long-term liabilities				
Bank loans				
(repayable 20X8)	1,000		1,000	
(repayable 20X9)	1,000		1,000	
(repayable 20Y2)	720		420	
Other long-term liabilities				
(including leases)	1,500		1,450	
		4,220		3,870
Current liabilities		3,155		2,982
Total equity and liabilities		11,323		10,611

Note. Paid in share capital represents 520 million shares at $0·50 each at 30 September 20X6.

Income statement

	Year ended 30 September 20X6 $m	Year ended 30 September 20X5 $m
Revenue	10,895	10,190
Total operating costs	10,135	9,745
Operating profit	760	445
Financing costs	-265	-235
Tax expense	-124	-53
Profit for the period	371	157

Statement of changes in equity

	Share capital $m	Share premium $m	Retained earnings $m	Total $m
Balance at 30 September 20X5	260	1,714	1,785	3,759
Profit for the period			371	371
Dividends paid			-182	-182
Balance at 30 September 20X6	260	1,714	1,974	3,948

Note. It can be assumed that the accounts for the year ended 30 September 20X6 are final and have been audited.

SECTION A

Question 1

Unseen Case Material (Exam day material for Paper E3 only)

Background

Although Flyqual Airlines (FQA) has built its reputation on providing a first rate passenger service it is coming under increasing pressure from shareholders to reduce its running costs and to become a leaner and fitter organisation.

Increasing competition

In addition to the increasing levels of competition being felt by FQA from foreign airlines, there is an ever growing threat from the low-price (sometimes called 'no frills') airlines. Three such airlines have already been established in FQA's home country.

The no frills airlines operate mainly on short haul routes although one of them is planning to establish a long-haul route to the USA.

Although the fares the low-priced airlines charge are variable, they retail their tickets at substantially lower prices than those of FQA's economy fares on the short-haul routes. Seats on the low-priced airlines are not guaranteed and they some sometimes oversell their seating capacity. This means that passengers can be left stranded at airports waiting for the next available flight, which may not even be on the same day. However, as the tickets are low-priced the airlines only provide minimal compensation if this occurs.

Not surprisingly, the standard of service offered by the low-priced airlines is basic, with extra such as food and beverages in the cabin being on sales whereas these items are a standard part of FQA's service. The ratio of cabin staff to passengers of the low-priced airlines is set to provide the minimum levels of cover in accordance with safety legislation. The cabin staff only carry out the most essential services to satisfy basic passenger comfort.

Nevertheless, the market share of the low-priced airlines is increasing as many of passengers are willing to accept lower standards of service for a cheaper flight. Some corporate customers are sending staff on low-priced airlines, especially where it is not essential that the employee arrives at a destination on a particular day.

FQA's Director of Corporate Development has prepared a paper for the Board which proposes that FQA should now enter the low-priced market on short haul flights at a reduced price. This will be in addition to FQA's normal full-fare services.

Maintenance Issues

As a result of budget cuts at FQA, some maintenance procedures on the aircraft were not completed and this led to a number of aircraft not complying with safety checks. This, in turn, led to an adverse safety report following a series of incidents which called into question the maintenance procedures at FQA.

The Engineering Director produced a report which stated that the safety procedures were being improperly applied by three technicians whom he dismissed. The Director went on to say in his report that the maintenance procedures were now perfectly safe.

However, an independent engineering consultant appointed by the Chief Executive to carry out a review of maintenance procedures, found that there were serious faults in the procedures as a whole, and the Engineering Director should have know about these.

The independent report went on to state that the budget for maintenance needs to be reviewed because it is inadequate to carry out the maintenance procedures which FQA should be doing, and it was simply down to good luck that there had been no serious incidents with FQA's planes.

The trades unions argued that the three technicians who had been dismissed had been used by management as scapegoats to cover up failings at a more senior level.

These maintenance issues have further strained relationships between management and staff within FQA. The trade unions have entered into discussions with FQA not only to have the three technicians reinstated, but also to have the pay and working conditions for all the maintenance staff reviewed.

The trade unions did not rule out strike action if the discussions were unsuccessful. Strike action by the maintenance staff would mean that all of FQA's flights would have to be suspended.

Cost of strike action

The Finance Director has estimated the cost of strike action in terms of lost sales revenue at $30 million per day, if the whole airline were to be closed down.

The variable costs of running FQA are estimated at about 40% of sales revenue.

In addition to this, there will be the cost incurred by the loss of customer goodwill. The Director of Sales and Marketing has explained that the potential cost of recovering lost business after a strike is likely to be substantial. There could be a reduction in sales revenue of up to 2% in the first year following the strike, although sales revenue is expected to recover in subsequent years. The Director of Sales and Marketing also estimates that additional marketing expenditure of $35 million will be required immediately after a strike to restore customer confidence in FQA.

The Finance Director has also calculated the cost of agreeing all the terms and conditions which the trades unions want would be about $33 million per year. (Maintenance staff cost currently constitute about 15% of Flyqual's total staff and employment overheads). The Board decided that FQA should reject the union's demands. In their place, the Board proposed a one-off settlement of 4% but this in turn has been rejected by the unions.

Required

(a) Identify the key stakeholders who will be interested in the disputes over maintenance procedures, and discuss the nature of their interest. **(14 marks)**

(b) (i) Calculate the number of days which FlyQual could tolerate a strike before it becomes more cost effective to agree with the trade unions' demands.

(Note. Use a discount rate of 6%, but ignore any taxation issues) **(9 marks)**

(ii) In the light of the calculations above, evaluate the Board's decision to resist the union's demands and negotiate a lower settlement. **(10 marks)**

(c) Analyse why the current proposal to enter the low-price 'no frills' market would be inappropriate for FlyQual. **(17 marks)**

(Total = 50 marks)

SECTION B – 50 marks

Answer two questions from three

Question 2

B is a public company that operates 100 supermarkets in a European country. There are a number of other supermarkets operating in the country and the market is fiercely competitive. All of the supermarkets find it difficult to generate any customer loyalty and have found that customers are very price sensitive.

Like all other supermarkets in the country, B suffers a higher staff turnover than other retail outlets and this is recognised as one of the reasons for relatively low customer satisfaction and retention.

The marketing director has suggested that the company would benefit from introducing a credit card that its customers could use in its supermarkets and in other retail outlets within the country. At present, although all supermarkets in the country accept credit cards for payment for goods, no other supermarket offers its own credit card.

The marketing director claims that, in addition to the appeal to the customers, the credit card would allow B to gather large quantities of data about its customers. He feels this would offer advantages in terms of data mining, data warehousing and relationship marketing.

You are the management accountant for B. The finance director has said that she is unfamiliar with these techniques and has asked you to provide some explanations and advice in the context of B's business.

Required

(a) Distinguish between data mining and data warehousing. **(6 marks)**

(b) Describe relationship marketing in the context of B's business applying the "six markets" model. **(12 marks)**

(c) Recommend, with reasons, three strategies that B can use to develop relationship marketing and improve customer loyalty. **(7 marks)**

(Total = 25 marks)

Question 3

C is a manufacturer of test equipment for electronic circuits. In the past, C was a dominant player in the international market. However, over the past three years, the company has found that its profits have declined as it has lost market share to other companies in the market.

C's business model consists of the following stages:

1. C's highly skilled engineers first visit client sites and, after discussions with the client's engineers, identify and design the appropriate testing equipment to meet the client's requirements. C's engineers are still recognised as the best in the industry, and customers agree that they produce the most effective solutions to the increasingly complex problems presented by C's clients. This stage of the process is seen as a very collaborative process between the engineers employed by C and the engineers employed by its clients.

2. In the laboratories at C, the equipment design goes through a fairly complicated process. Prototypes are developed, based on the discussions in stage 1. These prototypes are then tested. Once a final design is agreed, the plans are passed to the manufacturing department for production.

3. The manufacturing department of C then produces the appropriate equipment to the desired specification and installs it at the client's site.

4. After the equipment has been installed, C conducts maintenance on an annual basis.

It is standard practice within the industry for clients to pay a total price for design, manufacture and initial installation of the equipment and an annual maintenance charge after that. Total prices are quoted before design work commences. It is unusual for companies in the industry to maintain other manufacturers' equipment.

Although clients recognise the high quality of the solutions provided, they are increasingly complaining that the overall prices are too high. Clients have said that although other suppliers do not solve their problems as well as C, they do charge less. As a result, C has reduced its prices to compete with other companies. There is a suspicion that the manufacturing and installation stages of the business are not contributing sufficiently to the business because the costs may be too high.

Some of the Board of Directors of C have recognised that this situation cannot continue and have recommended that a value chain analysis be conducted, to identify the way forward for C. The Board feels that it is important that it identifies which activities in the current business model actually add value and whether all of them should be continued. One of the directors has suggested that C should actually be a solutions provider and not a manufacturer.

Although most directors are in agreement with the proposed value chain analysis, the managing director has argued that value chain analysis is a bad idea. He says that he has heard a number of criticisms of the value chain model.

You are the management accountant for C. The finance director has asked you to do the following:

Required

(a) Explain the benefits that C might gain from conducting a value chain analysis. **(12 marks)**

(b) Explain the criticisms of Porter's value chain model that could be relevant to C. **(8 marks)**

(c) Describe an alternative form of value chain analysis which could be more appropriate for C. **(5 marks)**

(Total = 25 marks)

Question 4

Callcom is a major telecommunications provider, and is listed on the stock exchange in the European country where it is based.

Until the mid-1980s, Callcom was a state-owned company, which held a monopoly over telecommunication services in its country. However, in 1984 the government deregulated the market and began granting licences to new rival suppliers. In 1986, Callcom was privatised.

Since the privatisation, competition has developed strongly in the telecommunications industry, while the industry itself has grown significantly. It now contains a range of landline telephone (fixed voice) providers, mobile service providers, internet service and cable TV providers.

Callcom has attempted to diversify and offer mobile phone and broadband services in additional to its traditional landline services. However, it has been unable to achieve a profitable market share in the mobile phone market and recently sold this part of its business to a larger mobile phone operator.

Callcom has been more successful in attracting broadband customers and has secured a large number of broadband subscribers. However, the growth in broadband services across the market as a whole has led to a decline in fixed voice market revenues.

A number of broadband providers have also developed the voice over internet protocol (VOIP) technology which allows broadband customers to hold telephone conversations for no additional call costs. Although Callcom has developed its own VOIP technology, VOIP presents a major challenge to Callcom, which has traditionally relied on fixed voice services as its largest and most stable revenue stream.

VOIP technology also raises important staffing implications. It is not yet clear exactly what the new VOIP networks will mean for staffing levels and skill requirements at Callcom, although it is likely that telecommunications providers will need less telephone exchanges and network buildings, and lower levels of network staff.

A high proportion of Callcom's engineers belong to the telecommunications union, and when Callcom announced some job cuts last year, the trade union members voted for industrial action to support their colleagues. The Industrial action lasted for several weeks and had a significant effect on both Callcom's financial performance and its reputation in the industry.

Another legacy of Callcom's history as a state-owned monopoly is that it still has a relatively bureaucratic culture and structure, and so is slower to respond to market opportunities than some of its younger rivals.

There are several potential 'new wave' growth opportunities, using VOIP technology and wireless communication. However, to take advantage of these Callcom's engineers will need training additional training in how to install wireless access points in public venues. The engineers have argued they should receive a large pay increase to compensate them for using the new skills required for this job, and have threatened further strike action if a pay award is not forthcoming.

Required

(a) Analyse the external and internal triggers for change in Callcom's strategy and operations. **(7 marks)**

(b) Evaluate how successful Callcom has been at managing change prior to the wireless access point project, and explain how a stage model of change could help Callcom manage the wireless access point project.
(13 marks)

(c) Discuss the reasons why Callcom's engineers might resist the change programmes **(5 marks)**

(Total = 25 marks)

Answers

**DO NOT TURN THIS PAGE UNTIL YOU HAVE
COMPLETED THE MOCK EXAM**

A plan of attack

As we mentioned in our 'plan of attack' for mock exam 1, the problem of which question to start with is discussed earlier in this Kit, in 'Passing the E3 exam; (page x in the Front pages). Here we will once again reiterate our view that question 1 is nearly always the best place to start but, if you do decide to start with a 25 mark Section B question, **make sure that you finish your answer in no more than 45 minutes**.

However, once again, take a good look at the paper before diving in to answer questions, and make sure you use your 20 minutes of reading time efficiently and effectively.

The next step

You may be thinking that this paper looks more straightforward than the first mock exam; alternatively, you may be thinking this paper is actually more difficult.

Option 1 (this paper looks all right) – If you've read the requirements carefully, and you don't feel too daunted by this paper, then that's encouraging. You should feel even happier when you've got the compulsory question out of the way, so you should consider doing Question 1 first. However, remember the advice we have given you before: make sure your answer deals specifically with the question requirements, and relates directly to the organisation and issues described in the scenario.

Option 2 (don't like this paper) – If you think this paper looks challenging, you may want to get the optional questions done first before tackling the Section A case study. However, don't forget that you will need half of the three hours writing time to answer the case study.

The questions themselves

- **Question 1** covers some core areas of business strategy: including stakeholder analysis and strategic options, for an airline company. The preseen and unseen material provide lots of detail about the industry and the company, and so you should have identified that the problem facing FQA is how to provide a high quality service and yet also reduce costs.

    The first part of the question asks you for a stakeholder analysis, and you should have felt this was quite an approachable question at the start of your exam.

    The second part asks you for a calculation about the cost of strike action, and then asks you to use the figures you have calculated to evaluate the decision to resist strike action.

    The final part of the question requires you to analysis why moving to a low cost model would not be appropriate for FQA. The information given in the scenario (describing the way FQA uses a differentiation strategy) should help you here.

- **Question 2** is quite a tough question, because it tests some quite precise areas of knowledge. Part (b) focuses on a specific model of relationship marketing, and you should only attempt this question if you know what the 'Six Markets' model is, and what the 'Six Markets' are. If you did not, you should have discounted this question immediately and selected your two optional questions as questions 3 to 4.

- **Question 3** is another question which requires specific knowledge to answer well. Although the scenario presents a company which is notionally a manufacturing company, you should have realised that its work means it more closely resembles a service company than a manufacturing company. Consequently you need to be careful how you apply Porter's value chain analysis in (a). The company will get value from assessing how it adds value in general terms, rather than by analysing its value creation activities in terms of the specific primary activities in Porter's value chain. Parts (b) and (c) pick up on the ideas that Porter's model is not really appropriate for service companies; a point the Examiner made in an article in *Financial Management* shortly before the relevant exam was sat. If you had not read this article, and were not aware of the alternative representation of the value chain for professional service companies, this is another question which you would have been well advised to avoid.

- **Question 4** is all about change management, but shouldn't present too many difficulties if you are comfortable with this area of the syllabus. Change management represents 20% of the syllabus so it is important you are prepared to answer a question on it. Again though, note that all three parts of the question relate directly back to the scenario and so your answers should not have dealt with change management issues in general, but should have related directly back to the company described in the scenario.

Once again, let us remind you...

You must always **allocate your time** according to the marks for the question in total and for the parts of the questions within it. And you must always **follow the question requirements exactly**.

You've got free time at the end of the exam...?

If you have allocated your time properly then you **shouldn't have time on your hands** at the end of the exam. However, if you find yourself with five or ten minutes spare, go back to **any parts of questions that you didn't finish** because you ran out of time.

Forget about it!

As we've told you before, don't worry if you found the paper difficult. Once your three hours writing time is over, there is nothing more you can do with your answers, so forget about them. If this were your real exam, you'd need to forget about the exam once you'd finished and start thinking about the next one. Or, if it were your last exam, you could start celebrating!

Mock Exam 2: Answers   315

Question 1

Marking scheme

			Marks
(a)	Key stakeholders identified, and the nature of their interest discussed:		
	Trades unions	Up to 3	
	Maintenance staff	Up to 3	
	FQA Senior Management	Up to 5	
	Customers	Up to 3	
	Alliance partners	Up to 3	
		Total up to	14
(b)(i)	Cost of agreeing to union demands	1	
	Calculating cost of pay offer	3	
	Calculating loss of sales revenue after strike	2	
	Additional marketing costs	½	
	Calculating extra costs from agreeing to union demands	½	
	Calculation of loss of revenue during strike	1	
	Calculation of days a strike could be tolerated	1	
		Total	9
(b)(ii)	For each relevant advantage or disadvantage of the board's proposal, discussed	Up to 2	
	Not more than 6 marks to be given in total for either advantages or disadvantages – evaluation should include both.	Total up to	10
(c)	For each reason identified and analysed as to why it is inappropriate for FQA	Up to 2	
		Total up to	17
		Total	50

Part (a)

> **Text reference.** Stakeholders are discussed in Chapter 2 of the BPP Study Text.
>
> **Top Tips:** Make sure you read the question requirement carefully before starting. As is often the case with strategic level questions, there are two components to the question: first you need to identify the key stakeholders in the dispute, and then you need to discuss the nature of their interest. In effect, this second part of the question is asking you to discuss the different viewpoints of the different groups affected by the dispute.
>
> Note, that you are only required to identify stakeholders specifically in connection to the dispute over maintenance, not general stakeholders in FlyQual as a whole.
>
> Also, you should not waste time describing Mendelow's matrix, or how to deal with the different groups. Stick precisely to the requirements of the question.

Trades unions – The trade unions have two different objectives:

(i) **Get technicians reinstated** – The first is to get the three technicians who have been dismissed reinstated. The unions feel the three technicians have been made scapegoats for the Engineering Director's failings. They want FQA to accept that, as the independent engineering consultant's report identified, there were serious faults in FQA's maintenance procedures as a whole, not just in the work of these three technicians.

(ii) **Improve pay and working conditions** – The union's second objective is to negotiate improved pay and working conditions for all the technicians.

The unions have quite a strong bargaining position here. If a strike is called, it will not have any cost to the unions. Therefore they afford to adopt quite a strong line in pressing for the outcome they want.

<u>Maintenance staff</u>

Maintenance staff as a whole – The maintenance staff want to secure higher pay and better conditions. Because relationships have between management and staff have become strained, there is less goodwill towards management than there might previously have been. Therefore, where previously staff might have accepted whatever deal management offered, now the staff are less amenable to management's offers.

Technicians dismissed – Although the three technicians themselves do not have much power in any negotiations with FQA the backing they have received from the union increases their power. Their primary concern is to prove they should not have been dismissed, and so should get their jobs back.

<u>FQA Senior Management</u>

Corporate social responsibility – The directors have a corporate social responsibility to ensure the safety of their passengers. Therefore they need to ensure that the faults which have been identified in the maintenance procedures are corrected.

Of all the directors, the **Engineering Director** has the most direct responsibility for ensuring the quality of the maintenance procedures. The critical nature of the independent consultant's report means that the Engineering Director's position must be under threat.

The other directors may, however, feel his position is untenable, particularly after the sacking of the three technicians. So the other directors may feel one way to help ease the tensions with the maintenance staff is if the engineering director resigns.

Responsibility to investors – As well as ensuring the safety of the airlines' passengers, the Board and Directors also have a fiduciary responsibility to manage the profitability of FQA.

In this way, they have to be relatively robust in dealing with the unions to ensure that any pay deal which is agreed does not lead to FQA's **costs increasing** too much.

Bad publicity – The senior management also have a third interest here, which is to try to minimise the level of bad publicity which might be caused by the dispute. Strike action will not only lead to a direct loss of revenue on the days when FQA's planes cannot fly, but it may also damage FQA's reputation with its customers, and prompt them to fly with other carriers.

Equally, if the findings of the independent report become public then this will also damage FQA's reputation and could lead to a fall in passenger bookings. Management need to take actions to **correct the faults which were identified in the report.**

<u>Customers</u>

Although customers do not have as much direct power to influence the outcome of the dispute as the unions, the staff and FQA's management, they could still have a strong interest in the out.

Passenger safety – Passengers will want to know that FQA's planes are safe before they board them. If the concerns about the quality of the FQA's maintenance procedures become widely know, this is likely to prevent some potential customers from using FQA.

Disruption to timetable – Passengers who have already booked with FQA will also want to know that the maintenance checks on their planes have been carried out properly before they fly. But, perhaps more importantly, this stakeholder group has a strong interest in the strikes being averted. If the disputes cannot be resolved, and strike action goes ahead this will lead to the cancellation of a number of flights. This could cause severe disruption for passengers who were supposed to be on the flights.

<u>Alliance partners</u>

FQA is a member of the 'N' aviation alliance. Part of the purpose of the alliance is to offer passenger greater flexibility and ease of travel through transfers and codeshare agreements.

However, if strike action prevents FQA from operating its flight, it won't be able to generate any business for the alliance, or carry any transferred passengers.

Therefore, 'N' has an interest in FQA resolving the dispute without it leading to strike action.

However, 'N' also has an interest in the dispute being settled without creating too much bad publicity and damaging FQA's reputation. If FQA's reputation is damaged, then because it is a partner in the alliance, this could also damage the reputation of alliance.

Part (b)

(i)

	$m	$m
Cost of agreeing to union demands ($33 million per year – in perpetuity @6%)		550.0
Costs of sticking to FQAs proposal and not agreeing to union demands		
Pay offer (W)	212.8	
Loss of sales revenue after strike		
(2% of annual total of $10,895)	217.9	
Reduction in variable costs (40% of sales revenue)	(87.2)	
	130.7	
Additional marketing costs	35.0	
		378.6
Extra costs from agreeing to union demands ($550m - $378.6m)		171.4
Lost revenue per day		30.0
Less variable costs (40% of sales revenue)		(12.0)
Impact per day		18.0

Number of days after which it is more cost effective to accept wage demands rather than allowing strike: (171.4 / 18, rounded up) = **10**

Workings

Pay offer from FQA
Current salary bill is 21% of total overheads (21% × $10,135)	2,128.4
Maintenance costs are 15% of total (15% × $2,128)	319.3
Proposed increase (4%)	12.77
In perpetuity @ 6%	212.8

(ii)

> **Top tips.** Note the verb here was 'evaluate' so you need to look at the advantages and disadvantages of the proposed suggestion.
>
> Note also the importance of linking your answer to the calculations in (b) (i). Remember that in E3, you shouldn't just do calculations: you need to think what these calculations tell you about whether a strategy is sensible or not. Is the business likely to be better served by giving in to the Union's demands or resisting them?
>
> You could also have considered some game theory ideas, because this could help analyse the situation the Board faces.
>
> However, one thing you should not have done is criticise the Board's plan for not considering outsourcing the maintenance function. Maintenance is a core part of the business, and given the problems Flyqual is already having with its catering contractors, it would not be sensible to outsource such a key area of operations.

There are a number of cost issues with the settlement that the Unions want, so the Board's alternative looks to keep wage costs more in check.

Advantages of Board's proposal

Controls level of wage costs increases – The wage increase the trades unions are asking for represents a 10.3% increase for the maintenance staff.

> **Tutorial note.** The Cost structure information in the pre-seen material shows that staff and employment overheads are 21% of total operating costs.

21% x $10,135 = $2,128.

The unseen material tells us maintenance staff costs account for 15% of the total: $2,128 \times 15\% = \$319.2$.

Therefore a pay rise of $33m = 10.3\% \left(\dfrac{\$33}{\$319.2}\right)$ increase.

Recognises pressure to reduce costs – As the Board has been under increasing pressure to reduce costs, giving a 10.3% wage rise to one section of the workforce is unlikely to be acceptable.

Precedent from baggage handlers dispute – When the baggage handlers wanted a pay increase, their demands were not met in full. Moreover, on this occasion the pay agreement was reached on the condition that productivity increases were increased. However, the current proposal for the maintenance workers doesn't appear to include any productivity increases.

Problems with the Board's proposal

Doesn't include any performance conditions – Although the Board is proposing a lower % increase than the unions want, his proposal still does not tie the salary increase to any performance conditions. Given the concerns around the quality of maintenance work being carried out, the Board could have proposed a pay settlement which linked remuneration to the quality of work done.

Moreover, although the Board's proposal would cap the wage increases, it doesn't actually help in their attempts to reduce costs. If the wage increases were tied to some **efficiency measures**, it might be possible to **reduce the number of maintenance staff** Flyqual needs to employ.

Doesn't deal with working conditions. The Board's proposal only deals with the salary aspect of the dispute. However, it is possible that by addressing some of the aspects of working conditions that the technicians are unhappy they may be able to negotiate a settlement at a lower financial cost that is currently being asked for.

Relations between FQA and its staff have been deteriorating in recent months, and if FQA wants to maintain the service it offers its customers it needs to ensure that its staff are motivated and working efficiently. However, simply proposing an one-off financial settlement will do little to address any employee relations issues.

Financial risks of strike – The financial evaluation shows that if the workers do go on strike, if the strike lasts for more than 10 days then this outweighs any potential benefits from seeking a lower pay settlement.

There is a risk that if the maintenance workers go on strike, the strike will only be called off when an acceptable pay award is offered. In this case, Flyqual will **suffer not only the costs of the strike but also the additional salary costs** going forward.

Moreover, if the strike goes ahead, this will mean that Flyqual suffers a high **level of one-off costs** in the first year. The 2% loss of revenue in the aftermath of the strike, plus the additional marketing costs will mean a one-off cost to operating profit of about $165 million, in addition to the direct loss of revenue from the days when Flyqual cannot operate any services.

Bargaining position – Given the figures involved, and the business critical nature of the maintenance work, it appears that the Board is in a relatively weak bargaining position when dealing with the unions. However, it does not appear that the Board is trying to negotiate a compromise with the Unions. For example, Flyqual could have discussed a deal with the unions in which the **pay increases were phased in over a number of years**.

Instead Flyqual seem to have simply rejected the union's demands. However, the union ultimately has nothing to lose in these negotiations, so it can afford to be more aggressive than Flyqual in holding out for a deal. Ultimately, though, if strike action goes ahead and lasts for any extended period of time, it could jeopardise the survival of the airline. This again suggests that the Board may have been too bullish in resisting the union's demands.

Part (c)

> **Text reference.** Porter's generic strategies, and Bowman's strategy clock are both covered in Chapter 5 of the BPP Study Text for E3.
>
> **Top tips.** Note that the question asks you specifically to analyse why entering the no-frills market would be inappropriate for Flyqual. Consequently, your answer does not need to give a balanced analysis of reasons why it might be appropriate and reasons why it would not: you should concentrate solely on the reasons why it is not appropriate.
>
> SAF (suitability, acceptability, feasibility) is a useful framework to use when looking at the appropriateness of a strategic option. By looking at Flyqual's business model, you will hopefully be able to realise it is aiming to compete by differentiation and high quality, rather than on the basis of low cost and low prices. This suggests the proposal is not suitable for Flyqual.
>
> Although you do not need to refer to any models in your answer, Porter's generic strategies and the value chain were both frameworks you could have used to help analyse why the proposal is inappropriate.

In order for a no-frills strategy to be appropriate for FQA it must be suitable, acceptable and feasible.

Suitability of cost structure

FQA's structure is not suited to a no-frills strategy. Many of the airline companies which have used the 'no frills' strategy have been **new entrants to the market**. They have **very low overheads** and have used the 'no frills' low-cost approach to **gain market share** before moving on to alternative strategies to cement sustain their position in the industry.

A key element in their strategy is achieving a **low cost base to sustain their low cost strategy**.

Flyqual's competitive strategy

However, FQA's approach has been to provide value to its customers by providing a **high quality service**.

The Board's reaction to the two largest shareholders' suggestions for lowering costs illustrates this. The Board argued that costs can only be achieved by reducing staffing levels which will in turn have a negative impact on quality.

Flyqual clearly seeks to **differentiate** itself from its competitors and **create its competitive advantage by the quality of service** it offers its customers, rather than by being a low cost operator.

In this respect, a no frills strategy would not be suitable for Flyqual.

Changes to business model, culture and operations

Given the context of Flyqual's operations, it also seems unlikely that it can achieve the changes to its cost based which would be required for it to become a no frills low-cost budget airline without significant changes to its business model, culture and operations.

Part of the recent employee relations issues appear to have come from having to control wage costs more tightly. However, if Flyqual were to move to a no-frills approach, it would need to control costs even more tightly, and so it is likely there would be even more unrest among the staff.

Suitability of reducing customer service levels

Low-cost budget airlines do not usually offer customer services such as free in-flight meals and drinks.

However, Flyqual sees in-flight service and its meals as an important part of the service it offers its customers.

One of the problems FQA has had with its main catering contractor is that the **quality of the catering service** has been below the standard which FQA's customers – and therefore FQA – expect.

If Flyqual moved to a 'no frills' strategy, it would need to abandon its tradition of excellent customer service. This is unlikely to be a suitable strategy for FQA because it damages **one of its core competences**.

Impact on marketing mix

At the moment, FQA can market itself as a high quality brand. However, if it also enters the no frills market alongside its existing premium product, this is likely to lead to **inconsistencies in its marketing mix**: is FQA's target market passengers who want a first rate service and are prepared to pay a high price for that, or is it passengers who are prepared to accept basic 'no frills' service but want to travel cheaply?

In this respect, introducing to a no-frills strategy alongside FQA's existing business will **not be suitable**.

Feasibility

Fleet size required

The proposal is for FQA to offer low-priced short haul flights in addition to its normal full-fare services. This suggests that FQA will need more aircraft capable of flying short haul routes.

We do not know whether FQA has sufficient funding available to acquire the extra planes required, especially since it already has a number of planes whose leases are due to expire over the next two years. Consequently, the feasibility of this strategy would need to be investigated very carefully.

Staff requirements

Equally, the proposal to run the 'no frills' service in addition to the existing short haul flights suggests that FQA will need to recruit additional staff – particularly cabin crew and baggage handlers for the additional flights.

Moreover, it will not be feasible for FQA to use the cabin crews who currently work on the premium service on the new 'no frills' services. The experienced crew's salary costs will be too high for the low cost model FQA is looking to introduce.

Acceptability

Acceptable to shareholders

The two largest shareholders have been putting pressure on FQA to reduce running costs and to become a leaner and fitter organisation.

They want to see FQA increasing market share by passing on cost reductions to passengers.

However, the current proposal will mean FQA introduces the no frills model alongside the existing business. It is debatable whether this will **make the organisation become leaner and fitter**, or rather, whether it will just lead to confusion about the levels of service which are being offered to passengers.

Acceptable to 'N' alliance

Many no frills airlines fly into regional airports that offer cheaper taking off and landing fees than the main national airports. However, these regional airports are often **relatively remote from the cities** they serve. This remoteness may cause problems if FQA passengers using the no frills service want to transfer to alliance partners flying from a different airport.

It is possible that the no frills service will be excluded from the alliance. It is likely that the alliance partners may prefer this, because they are likely to be premium carriers rather than no frills carriers.

Conclusion

Introducing the no frills business would appear to be inappropriate for FQA because it would require major changes in the structure and culture of the company which do not appear suitable, acceptable or feasible.

The extent of the changes required would represent a **revolution** rather than an **evolution** of existing processes. However, a revolution is normally only required when a company is facing a crisis and needs to change direction quickly.

There is no evidence to support the need for such a radical transformation. Although the airline industry is increasingly competitive, Flyqual's **financial position still appears relatively healthy**, and revenue and profit increased between 20X5 and 20X6.

If FQA really wants to move into the no frills sector it would be better advised to **set up a completely new low cost brand** to do this – rather than trying to restructure its existing business model.

Question 2

Study Reference. Data warehouses and data mining are covered in Chapter 7 of the Study Text. Relationship marketing is covered in Chapter 8.

Top tips. Requirement (a) is a test of factual knowledge, and does not require you to link your answer back to the scenario. You could have helped illustrate the difference between data mining and data warehousing by using an example, and there was a mark available for a relevant example. We have linked our example back to the scenario, but you did not need to do this.

In order to attempt requirement (b) you needed to know the 'Six Markets' model – a specific way of looking at the range of relationships involved in relationship marketing. If you did not know the model, you should not have attempted this question.

The way to approach (b) was to identify each of the 'Six markets' in turn and then provide an illustration of them in the context of B's business.

For requirement (c), there are a number of possible strategies B could use to develop relationship marketing and improve customer loyalty, but you only need to recommend three. The strategies could relate to any of the six markets. Note, however, that to score the marks available you need to explain why B should use the strategies.

Easy marks. If you knew the 'Six Markets' model, part (b) offered some easy marks because it is a simple application of this model. However, if you didn't know the model, this question was one to avoid.

Marking scheme

			Marks
(a)	Definition and explanation of data mining	Up to 3	
	Definition and explanation of data warehousing	Up to 3	
		Total up to	6
(b)	Description of relationship marketing	1	
	Contrast relationship marketing with transactional marketing	1	
	Application of each of the six markets (customer markets; referral markets; supplier markets; recruitment markets; influence markets; internal markets). For each market	Up to 2	
		Total up to	12
(c)	For each strategy recommended and supported with reasoned arguments	Up to 3	
		Total up to	7
		Total	25

Part (a)

Data warehouse – A data warehouse is a large-scale data collection and storage area, containing data from various operational systems, plus **reporting** and **query tools** which allow the data to be analysed. The key feature of a data warehouse is that it provides a single point for **storing a coherent set of information** which can then be used across an organisation for **management analysis** and decision making. The data warehouse is not an operational system, so the data in it remains static until it is next updated. For example, if B did introduce a customer credit card, the history of customers' transactions on their cards could be stored in a data warehouse, so that management could analyse spending patterns.

However, although the reporting and query tools within the warehouse should facilitate management reporting and analysis, data warehouses are primarily used for storing data rather than analysing data.

Data mining – By contrast, data mining is primarily concerned with **analysing data**. Data mining uses statistical analysis tools to look for **hidden patterns and relationships** (such as trends and correlations) in large pools of data. The value of data mining lies in its ability to highlight previously unknown relationships.

In this respect, data mining can give organisations a **better insight into customer behaviours**, and can lead to **increased sales through predicting future behaviour**. For example, if B were able to identify patterns in items which were purchased together, it could target its promotions to take advantage of this.

So, by identifying patterns and relationships, data mining can **guide decision making**.

Part (b)

The 'six markets' model' suggests that relationship marketing is applicable to six different markets, rather than just the market between producer and final consumer.

Customer markets – The customer market comprises the final consumers of a product or service, who remain the final goal for marketing activity. For B, this market comprises the **customers who visit its supermarkets and do their shopping there**. Issues such as customer satisfaction will be key here; in a competitive market, if customers are not satisfied with the service they receive they are likely to switch to a rival supermarket.

Referral markets – The referral market comprises people or organisations who, through their recommendation of a product or service, **persuade potential customers to join the customer market**. For example, customers who are impressed with the quality and price of the goods they buy at B might recommend B to their friends and relatives. Equally, a lifestyle magazine or a newspaper might publish an article which reviews B more favourably than its competitors.

Influence markets – Influence markets are similar to referral markets in that they direct the choices of the customer market. However, whereas the referral market often includes personal recommendations, the influence market contains organisations and institutions which, by publishing their views, can **influence customer choices** en masse. For example, if a consumer association recommends that B has the most ethical relationships with its suppliers, this may encourage potential customers to shop at B.

Supplier markets – This aspect of the model highlights that organisations need to **establish and maintain good relationships with their suppliers**, in order to ensure that they can consistently meet the needs of the final consumers. This is a particularly relevant issue in the supermarket industry, because supermarkets are often criticised for trying to suppress the price they pay to their suppliers. However, as B tries to increase customer satisfaction its relationships with its suppliers will be important to ensure that it avoids any stock-outs, particularly among its most popular product lines.

Recruitment markets – This aspect of the model highlights the importance of **people in delivering service to an organisation's customers.** In order to provide good service to its customers a firm needs to recruit suitable staff, and its ability to do this can be enhanced by establishing good relationships with **recruitment agencies** (to source staff) or **local colleges** (to encourage students to consider working for it in due course). For example, a customer's experience of B could be affected by the quality of service they receive from the check-out operator when they pay for their shopping, so B will benefit by recruiting staff who are friendly and efficient.

Internal markets – In order to support the overall relationship between an organisation and its customers, the **internal departments** of the organisation need to **work efficiently and effectively together**. For example, if B's purchasing and internal logistics departments do not source sufficient produce to meet customer demand, customers are unlikely to be satisfied however good the level of face-to-face customer service they receive from shop staff. In this respect, if B does introduce data warehousing and data mining, the analysts looking at the data reports need to work closely with the purchasing departments to optimise the number and type of products being ordered.

Part (c)

> **Top tips.** Note you are only required to recommend three strategies B could use to develop relationship marketing, and you should have only included three in your answer. For tutorial purposes we have included additional strategies which you could have included in your answer.

Targeted promotions – If B introduces the credit card and its data warehousing and data mining systems, it will be able to capture lots of information about customers' purchases. It could then use this to **send customers specifically targeted promotions and offers**. If customers receive offers which closely match their shopping patterns they are more likely to take advantage of those offers, thereby returning to B as repeat customers.

Offer discounts for repeat promotions – The market is fiercely competitive, and customers are price sensitive. Therefore if, when they pay for their shopping, B's customers receive a 'money off' discount for repeat purchases, B could in effect, **use price as an incentive to encourage loyalty**. To maximise the effectiveness of the offer, it should only remain open for a **limited time**.

Staff incentive programmes – B could introduce a **staff bonus scheme** which takes account of **customer satisfaction levels**. It appears that the high staff turnover is currently leading to poor levels of customer satisfaction, and in turn to poor customer retention rates. A bonus scheme operated throughout B would not only provide an **incentive for all internal markets** to contribute to improved customer satisfaction, it could also have the added benefit of **reducing staff turnover**.

Staff training – The current low levels of customer satisfaction may reflect poor customer service standards in B's stores, which would be consistent with having a high staff turnover rate and therefore lots of relatively inexperienced staff. One of the ways B could address this is to improve the quality of training it gives staff when they join. This will not only mean they can offer a better service to customers, but also if staff feel time is being invested in their training they may be more likely to remain at B for longer.

Mystery shopper – As the industry is very competitive it is important B compares the shopping experience (quality, value for money, customer service etc) it offers it customers with that of its rivals. One way it could do this is by introducing mystery shoppers who visit its stores and those of its competitors as if they were customers. These mystery shoppers could then identify areas where B needs to improve its customer offering.

Customer suggestions – One of the features of relationship marketing is emphasising the product benefits which are relevant to the customers. B could introduce customer comments or suggestions boxes in its stores to allow customers to suggest the improvements which would be most valuable to them. This has an added benefit of making customers feel valued, which could, in itself, improve customer loyalty.

Introduce new product ranges – If B introduces a data warehousing and data mining system, the resulting information it cold gather on customer tastes and spending habits may enable it to identify gaps in its product ranges. In which case, it could develop new products or introduce new ranges to fill those gaps, thereby improving its ability to meet customers' needs.

Question 3

Study Reference. Porter's value chain and Stabell & Fjelstad's alternative are both discussed in Chapter 4 of the Study Text.

Top tips. The Examiner who set this question had written an article in the CIMA '*Financial Management*' magazine shortly before the relevant exam and in it he explained that Porter's value chain is more appropriate to traditional manufacturing activities rather than to service or consultancy activities. This idea is central to this question.

The whole point here is that the detail of C's activities does not fit with the traditional value chain model. Although there is a manufacturing element to C's work, the main focus is on designing the equipment rather than making it. In this respect, C's activities are better viewed as a 'value shop'.

Consequently in (a) you should have looked at how C can use value chain analysis to consider, in general terms, how its various activities add value to the business and contribute to its competitive advantage, rather than trying to analyse C's activities in terms of how they fit together in terms of Porter's value chain.

You should not have wasted time drawing and/or describing Porter's value chain, nor trying to map C's activities onto it. The question did not ask you to, and therefore there were no marks available for doing so.

Requirement (b) again picks up on the issue that Porter's value chain is more suitable for manufacturing activities than service activities. Another issue is that, in Porter's model, the value creation process is entirely internal to an organisation. But this is not the case with C, because the design process involves a lot of consultation between C's engineers and their clients' engineers.

Requirement (c) is best answered by using Stabell & Fjelstad's alternative representation of the value chain for professional services firms (which is the model the Examiner featured in his article). The stages of C's business model fit very neatly into this model.

However, if you weren't aware of this model, you would have struggled to score well in this part of the question. So, as a general point, when preparing for your exams, always make sure you read any Study Notes articles in 'Financial Management which are relevant for your exams.

> **Easy marks.** If you had read the Examiner's article, and therefore were aware of weaknesses of Porter's value chain model in a service context, and of Stabell & Fjelstad's alternative model, parts (b) and (c) should have offered some easy marks.
>
> **Examiner's comments.** Although this was a popular question it was poorly answered by many candidates, who failed to apply their answers to the questions set. The question asked about the benefits and limitations of value analysis to C, not about the benefits and limitations of value chain analysis in general. Very few marks were earned for simply described the value chain model.
>
> For part (c), most candidates had clearly read the article in 'Financial Management' magazine and displayed good knowledge of the alternative model. This part of the question was well answered by most candidates.

Marking scheme

			Marks
(a)	For each benefit explained specifically in relation to C	Up to 2 Total up to	12
(b)	For each criticism explained and related to C	Up to 2 Total up to	8
(c)	Recognition of value chain as alternative model	1	
	For each of the alternative primary activities described	Up to 2 Total up to	5
		Total	25

Part (a)

Identify sources of value – The value chain illustrates the way business activities **link together** to **add value** from the **end-user's perspective.** As customers are increasingly complaining that prices are too high, C could use the ideas of the value chain to identify whether there are some activities which are not adding value from the customer's perspective and should therefore either be discontinued or done more cheaply.

Alongside identifying sources of value, the value chain also illustrates **how costs are caused** in a business. One of the key benefits of the value chain is in forcing an organisation to look at the **relationship between the value being added and the costs being incurred** in its business activities.

See the business as a whole – The value chain could also be useful for C in that it will encourage it to look at the business as a whole, rather than considering individual functions or process stages in isolation. To this end, the idea of **linkages** in the value chain is very important.

Identify potential sources of competitive advantage – One of the main purposes of the value chain is to help firms secure competitive advantage; for example, either by combining activities in new and better ways, or by managing linkages to increase efficiency and therefore reduce cost.

In this respect, the value chain can used to complement Porter's **generic strategies.** At the moment, it appears that C is following a **differentiation strategy** because it solves clients' problems better than its competitors do. However, it appears that **clients' lower cost solutions** are becoming increasingly more attractive to clients.

Therefore, the value chain can help **support C's management in deciding their strategy** going forward – in particular, whether they want to maintain a differentiation strategy in the light of clients' comments about costs.

Identify process improvements – A firm can secure competitive advantage by inventing new or better ways to do activities. By forcing a firm to look at all its activities, value chain analysis may highlight processes which could be **re-designed** or **outsourced**. For example, it is possible that C could **outsource the manufacturing part** of its business and concentrate on design activities.

Benchmark against competitors – C's clients have remarked that their competitors might not solve their problems as well as C, but they charge less. C could use the value chain as a model for analysing their competitors' activities, to see what activities they are doing differently, and where they are making cost savings.

Implement performance measurement – At the moment, there is a suspicion that the manufacturing and installation activities are not contributing as much to profits as they could, due to their costs being too high. However, there **do not appear to be any performance measures** to confirm this.

C could use the value chain as the basis for analysing the **value added by each stage of the process**, and for introducing **key performance measures based on the costs and value added** at each stage of the process. Once such measures are introduced, the directors will have much more reliable information about the contribution each stage makes to the business profitability overall.

Part (b)

It is not designed for use with service businesses – The most notable criticism of the value chain model is that it cannot easily be applied to service organisations. One of C's key capabilities is the expertise of its engineers, and they use their expertise to design solutions in response to the complex problems presented by their clients. Although **solution design is a critical business process for C** it does not fit with neatly with the primary activities described in the value chain. They are more suitable to processes in manufacturing organisations which deal with tangible inputs and outputs.

Role of technology development – Technology development is a secondary activity in Porter's value chain, however most of C's work is technology development. Therefore, technology development is actually the main **primary activity** for C.

The idea of the value system is difficult to apply to network organisations – The focus of the value chain is on how value is created within the **internal structure** of an organisation's value network, but it is much harder to apply to the wider context of value networks. This is important for C, because the solution design stage is a **collaborative process between C's engineers and the client's engineers**; and therefore does not fit with the idea of an entirely internal process.

This idea of a collaborative network would become even more important if **C outsourced its manufacturing** stage.

Detailed costing required – To make best use of the value chain idea requires a degree of **activity based costing** to establish the costs of the value activities. Given that C has to rely on suspicions about how much each stage of its business model contributes to profit, it is unlikely that C currently uses any activity based costing. Therefore it would be time-consuming and expensive to introduce, particularly if new systems have to be introduced to capture the costing data required.

Viewed as unnecessary and overly complicated – In addition, the engineers at C may not see the value of analysing their business in the depth that is required for a full value chain analysis. It is unlikely the engineers will appreciate the benefit of investing time and energy in the value chain analysis, because it will not help them with their design work, at which they are already skilled experts. If they feel that management are introducing seemingly unnecessary **bureaucracy and administration** the engineers' motivation for producing good quality designs may suffer as a result.

The cost of the analysis may exceed the benefits – The time and effort involved in setting up the value chain analysis (particularly if new cost capture systems are required) will be considerable. However, there is no guarantee that the value chain model will lead to increased profitability. Although detailed analysis could identify the stages of C's business which clients value most, and areas where C's costs could be reduced, this in itself will not necessarily reduce the loss of market share which C has suffered at the hand of its competitors.

Part (c)

The **design element of C's business is becoming increasingly important** at the expense of the manufacturing aspect. Consequently, C could be more usefully analysed as a professional services consultancy firm, rather than a manufacturing firm.

Therefore, while the support activities in the original value chain model remain appropriate, it would be more appropriate to change the primary activities to reflect Stabell & Fjeldstad's alternative representation of a **value chain for professional services firms**.

Problem acquisition and diagnosis – This activity relies on a combination of marketing effort and professional excellence. In C's case, the professional excellence of the engineers is required for solving the client's complex problems, and marketing effort is required to promote C's reputation for solving problems with the best solutions, thereby acquiring new clients for the engineers to work with.

Finding solutions – Again, this activity requires the professional expertise of C's staff. Unlike the 'Operations' activity in the original value chain model, this activity does not involve any physical transformation; rather it will involve C's engineers working with client staff to design possible solutions to their problems. (This represents stage 1 of C's business model.)

Choice between solutions – This activity also involves close consultation with the client. At this stage, C's engineers, in conjunction with their clients' engineers, will test the possible solutions before deciding on their preferred solution. (This represents stage 2 of C's business model).

Solution implementation – The preferred solution is then manufactured according to the design specification agreed with the client. (This is stage 3 of C's current business model).

Control and feedback – Once the solution has been built, it will need to be tested to check it works as intended before being installed. The ongoing annual maintenance also acts as a control, and should identify any repair work or modifications which are required to the equipment.

Question 4

Text reference. Triggers for changes and resistance to change are covered in Chapter 9 of the BPP Study Text.

Marking scheme

			Marks
(a)	For each external trigger identified and discussed, up to 2 marks For each internal trigger identified and discussed, up to 2 marks	Up to 4 Up to 4 Total up to	7
(b)	For evaluation of each aspect of change management prior to wireless access project, up to 2 marks For explaining how each stage in a stage model could help Callcom manage the project, up to 3 marks	Up to 6 Up to 8 Total up to	13
(c)	For each relevant reason discussed	Up to 2 Total up to	5
		Total	25

Part (a)

Top tips. A useful way to approach this question is to separate 'external triggers' and 'internal triggers' and use them as separate headings to structure your answer. Using the headings of PEST analysis would be a useful way of thinking about external triggers.

Note that the question also asks you to consider changes in Callcom's operations as well as its strategy. Some of the internal triggers (job cuts, training requirements) have prompted operational changes rather than strategic changes.

External triggers

Industry deregulation - The government's decision to privatise Callcom and deregulate the telecommunication industry, has forced Callcom to have to adopt a more competitive strategy rather than being able to sustain a monopoly position.

Technological developments – Developments in telecommunications technology have led to new products being available. Mobile phones, broadband, and wireless technology all offered opportunities for new product development, even though Callcom's venture into the mobile market was unsuccessful.

The development of **VOIP** may lead to changes at both the strategic and operational levels. At the strategic level, it may offer **growth opportunities** through additional wireless services. However, at an operational level, there are fears that VOIP technologies may lead to a change in the number and type of **network staff** which Callcom require.

Consumer trends – Public **demand for mobile phones and broadband access** has increased significantly across the market as a whole, and this has led a decline in fixed voice telephone revenues. However, Callcom has relied on these fixed voice revenues as its largest source of revenue so it will have to **develop its product portfolio** to ensure it has other revenue streams to replace the income from fixed line telephone networks if it continues to fall.

Internal triggers

Product decisions – Callcom's **senior managers** are responsible for directing its product and market strategies. So they will have developed Callcom's strategies for **entering the mobile phone and broadband markets**. Equally, the senior managers will have monitored the performance of Callcom's business units, and they will have identified that the **mobile phone business should be sold**.

Staffing levels – Callcom recently made some job cuts, which suggests that Callcom's managers have identified that staffing levels where higher than they needed to be, and so Callcom could make some efficiency savings by reducing its staff numbers. This is an operational change rather than a strategic change though.

Reaction to job cuts – When the job cuts were announced, the workers took strike action in attempt to prevent the cuts and to allow their colleagues to keep their jobs. The trade unions supported their members in this action. In effect, the unions and workers were trying to reverse the operational change proposed by the management.

Ownership and cultural change – As Callcom has developed from a state-owned monopoly to a listed company in a competitive industry, its organisation and culture needs to change to reflect its changed market position. However, Callcom is still more bureaucratic than many of its competitors, and slower to respond to market opportunities, so it would appear that this 'trigger' for change has only been partially activated.

Part (b)

> **Top tips.** The requirement here is quite complex so you need to read it carefully to ensure you understand exactly what you need to do.
>
> The question effectively has two parts: first you have to evaluate Callcom's success at managing change in the past; then second, you need to explain how a stage model could help it manage the current project.
>
> Note also the verbs used. You are asked to evaluate the success at managing change in the past, so you need to consider where it has been successful and where it hasn't. What has it tried to change? Products? Staffing levels? How successful has it been in changing them?
>
> You should have identified that a key problem Callcom has faced is resistance to the changes it has tried to implement.
>
> This is the link between the two parts of the question. Historically, the changes Callcom has tried to introduce have been blighted by resistance, but if wireless project is to be a success this resistance needs to be overcome.
>
> Can a stage model help it in this respect?
>
> Note you are not asked to describe or explain stage models of change, and you should not have spent time doing so. Instead, you need to consider specifically how a stage model of change (Lewin's three stage model?) could be useful for Callcom. For example, could it get people to be more positive about change?

Managing change to date

Product diversification – Callcom has successfully managed to extend its product range so that it can offer broadband services and VOIP as well as its traditional fixed voice telephone services.

However, fixed voice telephone services remain Callcom's largest source of revenue. And given that fixed voice telephone market is now a **declining market**, it appears that Callcom still needs to make some more changes to its product portfolio to ensure its longer-term profitability.

Slow response – Although Callcom has managed to attract a significant number of broadband customers it was unable to achieve a profitable market share of the mobile phone market. Callcom's relatively bureaucratic culture means that it is slower to respond to opportunities than its rivals. If Callcom entered the mobile phone market after its rivals this is likely to have contributed to its failure to win market share.

Cultural change – Callcom's relatively bureaucratic culture and structure are a legacy of its history as a state-owned monopoly. Although Callcom has seen a number of young, dynamic companies successfully enter the telecommunications market, it **does not appear that Callcom has been able to change its style** (or has wanted to change its style) to become more dynamic and responsive. This is despite being a privatised company for over 20 years (since 1986).

Staff management – One of Callcom's biggest problems in managing change appears to be its **unionised workforce**. Even if a proposed change is in the best interests of Callcom as a whole, if it poses a threat to some of the workforce then they resist it – most notably through industrial action.

It would appear that when Callcom announced job cuts earlier this year (prompting a strike) it did not explain why the cuts were needed. Better **communication** and dialogue with the staff could have prevented the damaging industrial action.

Managing the wireless access project

Lewin suggested that organisations could use a three stage process for managing a change process, and the concepts behind the three stages could help Callcom in their wireless action project.

The project has already been met with some resistance by the engineers who are threatening industrial action if they do not receive a large pay increase.

Unfreeze – The unfreezing process involves reducing the forces that are resisting change. At Callcom this will involve management explaining to the staff (and the unions) why the changes are required, and in particular highlighting the dangers if Callcom does not take advantage of new opportunities as they arise.

If Callcom's competitors take advantage of the new technology and Callcom doesn't, it will not be able to compete effectively. This could ultimately jeopardise the survival of the company as a whole, and therefore the jobs everyone who works for it. Faced with this choice, the staff and unions are more likely to support the change.

Change – The change aspect will require Callcom's engineers adopting new behaviours and attitudes required to make the wireless project successful.

Communication will be critical here, because the staff will need to understand **what** needs to be done, and **why** it needs to be done.

The strong union representation at Callcom means that this communication should not be just with the staff but with their union representatives as well.

However, for the changes at Callcom to be successful, it is important that managers do not simply try to force them through regardless of any resistance from the staff. There may be good reasons why the staff might be objecting to the changes. For example, they may have identified practical issues and problems with the proposals which the managers have not foreseen.

Refreezing - Refreezing means introducing the necessary mechanisms, such as reward systems, to ensure that the new behaviours and attitudes are maintained.

For example, although Callcom's engineers have demanded a large pay rise for learning the new skills required to install wireless access points, this may not act as an incentive for ongoing improvement and productivity. Instead, Callcom could consider some kind of bonus scheme whereby engineers are rewarded for identifying improvements in the process for installing the wireless access points.

Ultimately, though, following the three stage model cannot guarantee the success of the wireless access project as a whole. The three stage model only focuses on the internal aspects of the change, but the overall success of the project will depend on external factors as well as internal factors. For example, Callcom will need to monitor technological developments to see if there are any changes to the technologies, and it will have to see how its competitors are responding to the opportunity. Callcom's pricing and marketing strategies could be crucial to the success of the project.

Part (c)

> **Top tips.** A sensible approach to this question would be to take a practical approach. If you are facing change in your own life or work, what sorts of things might make you resist it?
>
> You may be able to use your answer for the first part of (b) to help generate some ideas here. Callcom has had problems with its staff when introducing changes in the past, and in part these have been due to poor communication. If the reasons for change or the benefits it could bring are not clearly communicated, people are unlikely to support the change.
>
> However, make sure that you answer to (c) does not duplicate points you have already made in (b).

Benefits not communicated – If Callcom's managers haven't explained the reasons for the change, and the benefits which will result from it, there is little motivation to change. In such circumstances the engineers might just view the change as 'change for change's sake', and reject it as unnecessary.

Fear of job losses – Callcom has already announced one round of job cuts earlier this year, and there is uncertainty about the impact VOIP will have on staff numbers. Therefore the engineers may associate change programmes with job losses, rather than as ways of improving the organisation's performance.

Fears about new technology – We do not know from the scenario how long the engineers have been working for Callcom, or experienced they are, but given the culture of the company it is likely that some have been working there for a long time. For them, changes which may also mean the introduction of new technologies, may be perceived as a threat. What if they do not understand the new technology or cannot cope with it? Again, do they risk losing their jobs?

Unwillingness to learn new skills – Alongside these concerns about being able to learn new skills, there may be some of the engineers who do not want to learn new skills. They may be quite content doing what they are doing, and so see no reason to change. To them, instead of being an opportunity to learn new skills, change might seen as forcing them to throw away existing skills.

Quality of new work – There may be concerns that new work will be more increasingly specialised and less interesting than their current work. For example, if the engineers currently carry out a wide variety of work, but then have to focus only on wireless installations, this may not be a very appealing change.

MATHEMATICAL TABLES

MATHEMATICAL TABLES

Present value table

Present value of 1.00 unit of currency, that is $(1+r)^{-n}$ where r = interest rate, n = number of periods until payment or receipt.

Periods (n)	1%	2%	3%	4%	5%	6%	7%	8%	9%	10%
1	0.990	0.980	0.971	0.962	0.952	0.943	0.935	0.926	0.917	0.909
2	0.980	0.961	0.943	0.925	0.907	0.890	0.873	0.857	0.842	0.826
3	0.971	0.942	0.915	0.889	0.864	0.840	0.816	0.794	0.772	0.751
4	0.961	0.924	0.888	0.855	0.823	0.792	0.763	0.735	0.708	0.683
5	0.951	0.906	0.863	0.822	0.784	0.747	0.713	0.681	0.650	0.621
6	0.942	0.888	0.837	0.790	0.746	0.705	0.666	0.630	0.596	0.564
7	0.933	0.871	0.813	0.760	0.711	0.665	0.623	0.583	0.547	0.513
8	0.923	0.853	0.789	0.731	0.677	0.627	0.582	0.540	0.502	0.467
9	0.914	0.837	0.766	0.703	0.645	0.592	0.544	0.500	0.460	0.424
10	0.905	0.820	0.744	0.676	0.614	0.558	0.508	0.463	0.422	0.386
11	0.896	0.804	0.722	0.650	0.585	0.527	0.475	0.429	0.388	0.350
12	0.887	0.788	0.701	0.625	0.557	0.497	0.444	0.397	0.356	0.319
13	0.879	0.773	0.681	0.601	0.530	0.469	0.415	0.368	0.326	0.290
14	0.870	0.758	0.661	0.577	0.505	0.442	0.388	0.340	0.299	0.263
15	0.861	0.743	0.642	0.555	0.481	0.417	0.362	0.315	0.275	0.239
16	0.853	0.728	0.623	0.534	0.458	0.394	0.339	0.292	0.252	0.218
17	0.844	0.714	0.605	0.513	0.436	0.371	0.317	0.270	0.231	0.198
18	0.836	0.700	0.587	0.494	0.416	0.350	0.296	0.250	0.212	0.180
19	0.828	0.686	0.570	0.475	0.396	0.331	0.277	0.232	0.194	0.164
20	0.820	0.673	0.554	0.456	0.377	0.312	0.258	0.215	0.178	0.149

Periods (n)	11%	12%	13%	14%	15%	16%	17%	18%	19%	20%
1	0.901	0.893	0.885	0.877	0.870	0.862	0.855	0.847	0.840	0.833
2	0.812	0.797	0.783	0.769	0.756	0.743	0.731	0.718	0.706	0.694
3	0.731	0.712	0.693	0.675	0.658	0.641	0.624	0.609	0.593	0.579
4	0.659	0.636	0.613	0.592	0.572	0.552	0.534	0.516	0.499	0.482
5	0.593	0.567	0.543	0.519	0.497	0.476	0.456	0.437	0.419	0.402
6	0.535	0.507	0.480	0.456	0.432	0.410	0.390	0.370	0.352	0.335
7	0.482	0.452	0.425	0.400	0.376	0.354	0.333	0.314	0.296	0.279
8	0.434	0.404	0.376	0.351	0.327	0.305	0.285	0.266	0.249	0.233
9	0.391	0.361	0.333	0.308	0.284	0.263	0.243	0.225	0.209	0.194
10	0.352	0.322	0.295	0.270	0.247	0.227	0.208	0.191	0.176	0.162
11	0.317	0.287	0.261	0.237	0.215	0.195	0.178	0.162	0.148	0.135
12	0.286	0.257	0.231	0.208	0.187	0.168	0.152	0.137	0.124	0.112
13	0.258	0.229	0.204	0.182	0.163	0.145	0.130	0.116	0.104	0.093
14	0.232	0.205	0.181	0.160	0.141	0.125	0.111	0.099	0.088	0.078
15	0.209	0.183	0.160	0.140	0.123	0.108	0.095	0.084	0.074	0.065
16	0.188	0.163	0.141	0.123	0.107	0.093	0.081	0.071	0.062	0.054
17	0.170	0.146	0.125	0.108	0.093	0.080	0.069	0.060	0.052	0.045
18	0.153	0.130	0.111	0.095	0.081	0.069	0.059	0.051	0.044	0.038
19	0.138	0.116	0.098	0.083	0.070	0.060	0.051	0.043	0.037	0.031
20	0.124	0.104	0.087	0.073	0.061	0.051	0.043	0.037	0.031	0.026

Cumulative present value table

This table shows the present value of 1.00 unit of currency per annum, receivable or payable at the end of each year for n years $\frac{1-(1+r)^{-n}}{r}$.

Periods (n)	1%	2%	3%	4%	5%	6%	7%	8%	9%	10%
1	0.990	0.980	0.971	0.962	0.952	0.943	0.935	0.926	0.917	0.909
2	1.970	1.942	1.913	1.886	1.859	1.833	1.808	1.783	1.759	1.736
3	2.941	2.884	2.829	2.775	2.723	2.673	2.624	2.577	2.531	2.487
4	3.902	3.808	3.717	3.630	3.546	3.465	3.387	3.312	3.240	3.170
5	4.853	4.713	4.580	4.452	4.329	4.212	4.100	3.993	3.890	3.791
6	5.795	5.601	5.417	5.242	5.076	4.917	4.767	4.623	4.486	4.355
7	6.728	6.472	6.230	6.002	5.786	5.582	5.389	5.206	5.033	4.868
8	7.652	7.325	7.020	6.733	6.463	6.210	5.971	5.747	5.535	5.335
9	8.566	8.162	7.786	7.435	7.108	6.802	6.515	6.247	5.995	5.759
10	9.471	8.983	8.530	8.111	7.722	7.360	7.024	6.710	6.418	6.145
11	10.368	9.787	9.253	8.760	8.306	7.887	7.499	7.139	6.805	6.495
12	11.255	10.575	9.954	9.385	8.863	8.384	7.943	7.536	7.161	6.814
13	12.134	11.348	10.635	9.986	9.394	8.853	8.358	7.904	7.487	7.103
14	13.004	12.106	11.296	10.563	9.899	9.295	8.745	8.244	7.786	7.367
15	13.865	12.849	11.938	11.118	10.380	9.712	9.108	8.559	8.061	7.606
16	14.718	13.578	12.561	11.652	10.838	10.106	9.447	8.851	8.313	7.824
17	15.562	14.292	13.166	12.166	11.274	10.477	9.763	9.122	8.544	8.022
18	16.398	14.992	13.754	12.659	11.690	10.828	10.059	9.372	8.756	8.201
19	17.226	15.679	14.324	13.134	12.085	11.158	10.336	9.604	8.950	8.365
20	18.046	16.351	14.878	13.590	12.462	11.470	10.594	9.818	9.129	8.514

Periods (n)	11%	12%	13%	14%	15%	16%	17%	18%	19%	20%
1	0.901	0.893	0.885	0.877	0.870	0.862	0.855	0.847	0.840	0.833
2	1.713	1.690	1.668	1.647	1.626	1.605	1.585	1.566	1.547	1.528
3	2.444	2.402	2.361	2.322	2.283	2.246	2.210	2.174	2.140	2.106
4	3.102	3.037	2.974	2.914	2.855	2.798	2.743	2.690	2.639	2.589
5	3.696	3.605	3.517	3.433	3.352	3.274	3.199	3.127	3.058	2.991
6	4.231	4.111	3.998	3.889	3.784	3.685	3.589	3.498	3.410	3.326
7	4.712	4.564	4.423	4.288	4.160	4.039	3.922	3.812	3.706	3.605
8	5.146	4.968	4.799	4.639	4.487	4.344	4.207	4.078	3.954	3.837
9	5.537	5.328	5.132	4.946	4.772	4.607	4.451	4.303	4.163	4.031
10	5.889	5.650	5.426	5.216	5.019	4.833	4.659	4.494	4.339	4.192
11	6.207	5.938	5.687	5.453	5.234	5.029	4.836	4.656	4.486	4.327
12	6.492	6.194	5.918	5.660	5.421	5.197	4.988	4.793	4.611	4.439
13	6.750	6.424	6.122	5.842	5.583	5.342	5.118	4.910	4.715	4.533
14	6.982	6.628	6.302	6.002	5.724	5.468	5.229	5.008	4.802	4.611
15	7.191	6.811	6.462	6.142	5.847	5.575	5.324	5.092	4.876	4.675
16	7.379	6.974	6.604	6.265	5.954	5.668	5.405	5.162	4.938	4.730
17	7.549	7.120	6.729	6.373	6.047	5.749	5.475	5.222	4.990	4.775
18	7.702	7.250	6.840	6.467	6.128	5.818	5.534	5.273	5.033	4.812
19	7.839	7.366	6.938	6.550	6.198	5.877	5.584	5.316	5.070	4.843
20	7.963	7.469	7.025	6.623	6.259	5.929	5.628	5.353	5.101	4.870

Notes

Notes

Notes

Notes

Review Form & Free Prize Draw – Paper E3 Enterprise Strategy (1/10)

All original review forms from the entire BPP range, completed with genuine comments, will be entered into one of two draws on 31 July 2010 and 31 January 2011. The names on the first four forms picked out on each occasion will be sent a cheque for £50.

Name: _____   Address: _____

How have you used this Kit?
(Tick one box only)

☐ Home study (book only)
☐ On a course: college _____
☐ With 'correspondence' package
☐ Other _____

Why did you decide to purchase this Kit?
(Tick one box only)

☐ Have used the complementary Study text
☐ Have used other BPP products in the past
☐ Recommendation by friend/colleague
☐ Recommendation by a lecturer at college
☐ Saw advertising
☐ Other _____

During the past six months do you recall seeing/receiving any of the following?
(Tick as many boxes as are relevant)

☐ Our advertisement in *Financial Management*
☐ Our advertisement in *Pass*
☐ Our advertisement in *PQ*
☐ Our brochure with a letter through the post
☐ Our website www.bpp.com

Which (if any) aspects of our advertising do you find useful?
(Tick as many boxes as are relevant)

☐ Prices and publication dates of new editions
☐ Information on product content
☐ Facility to order books off-the-page
☐ None of the above

Which BPP products have you used?

Text	☐	Success CD	☐
Kit	☑	Interactive	☐
Passcard	☐	i-Pass	☐

Your ratings, comments and suggestions would be appreciated on the following areas.

	Very useful	Useful	Not useful
Passing F3	☐	☐	☐
Planning your question practice	☐	☐	☐
Questions	☐	☐	☐
Top Tips etc in answers	☐	☐	☐
Content and structure of answers	☐	☐	☐
'Plan of attack' in mock exams	☐	☐	☐
Mock exam answers	☐	☐	☐

Overall opinion of this Kit   Excellent ☐   Good ☐   Adequate ☐   Poor ☐

Do you intend to continue using BPP products?   Yes ☐   No ☐

The BPP author of this edition can be e-mailed at: adrianthomas@bpp.com

Please return this form to: Nick Weller, CIMA Publishing Manager, BPP Learning Media Ltd, FREEPOST, London, W12 8BR

Review Form & Free Prize Draw (continued)

TELL US WHAT YOU THINK

Please note any further comments and suggestions/errors below.

Free Prize Draw Rules

1 Closing date for 31 July 2010 draw is 30 June 2010. Closing date for 31 January 2011 draw is 31 December 2010.

2 Restricted to entries with UK and Eire addresses only. BPP employees, their families and business associates are excluded.

3 No purchase necessary. Entry forms are available upon request from BPP Learning Media Ltd. No more than one entry per title, per person. Draw restricted to persons aged 16 and over.

4 Winners will be notified by post and receive their cheques not later than 6 weeks after the relevant draw date.

5 The decision of the promoter in all matters is final and binding. No correspondence will be entered into.